Islamic Jihadism and the Laws of War

Islamic Jihadism and the Laws of War

A Conversation in International and Islamic Law Languages

OMAR MEKKY

Regional Legal Coordinator for the Middle East and North Africa at the International Committee of the Red Cross (ICRC)

OXFORD
UNIVERSITY PRESS

OXFORD
UNIVERSITY PRESS

Great Clarendon Street, Oxford, OX2 6DP,
United Kingdom

Oxford University Press is a department of the University of Oxford.
It furthers the University's objective of excellence in research, scholarship,
and education by publishing worldwide. Oxford is a registered trade mark of
Oxford University Press in the UK and in certain other countries

First Edition published in 2023

Published in the United States of America by Oxford University Press
198 Madison Avenue, New York, NY 10016, United States of America

British Library Cataloguing in Publication Data

Data available

Library of Congress Control Number is on file at the Library of Congress

ISBN 978–0–19–888836–9

DOI: 10.1093/oso/9780198888369.001.0001

Printed and bound in the UK by
TJ Books Limited

Acknowledgements

Writing a book is a quite overwhelming journey marked with a multiplicity of mixed feelings and emotions that range from satisfaction, happiness, and euphoria to frustration, stress, and anxiety. In this journey, writing the book is merely one output of many personal and professional developments that this process helped me to endeavour. I would not have been able to undergo this process without the generous support of many great hearts and minds that I was fortunate enough to meet throughout my journey. First and foremost, I was extremely fortunate to have Professor Andrea Bianchi as my PhD supervisor and mentor, providing me with incredible support and advise, not only by reading lengthy chapters and writing comprehensive feedback and comments, but also for his conversation and the articles and books to which he referred me. This book could not have been finalized without his wise guidance, support, and open-mindedness.

At the very early stages of this journey, I was also privileged to be a student of Professor Andrew Clapham for one semester at the Laws of War class. Being a student in such an engaging course, at the very beginning of my journey, helped me to build a solid base on the subject and, as a result, strengthened my arguments in this regard. It was certainly a very rewarding and foundational experience that brought this book to where it is today. I am also grateful for my friend, colleague, and professor Ahmed Al-Dawoody who introduced me to Islamic law, almost twelve years ago, at the International Institute of Higher Studies in Criminal Sciences in Siracusa, Italy. Since then, his generous support and guidance with regard to this subject has never stopped. Thanks to him, I had access to an extraordinary library of Islamic law and jurisprudence books across the Middle East and beyond that assisted in nourishing this project.

In thinking of the themes of this book, I have benefited a great deal from the intellectual companionship of a number of individuals. My very good friends Jelena Plamenac and Ginevra le Moli, who have afforded me the luxury of engagement in first-rate conversations about the laws of war and much else. At the ICRC, the extensive conversations with my colleagues in the International Humanitarian Law and legal departments—Aly Elbadrawy, Ingy Abouloyoun, Basant Abdelmeguid, Tristan Ferraro, Tilman Rodenhauser, Jelena Pejic, and many more—who have further enriched this engagement. I am particularly indebted to my field-based ICRC colleagues and interlocutors who shared knowledge, opened doors for me, and with whom I had rich exchanges during my field missions to many conflict zones across the Middle East, where most of the chapters of this book have been written and contemplated. Their intelligent and refreshing insight has certainly resulted in sharpening the text in the most realistic way possible.

It is also worth mentioning that my professional journey from the judiciary to the humanitarian field would not have been possible without the guidance and support of Judge Cherif Atlam, who introduced me to the discipline seventeen years ago and continued to be remarkably supportive as our paths continued to cross until today. Also, finishing this journey would not have been possible without the generous investment and support of the Kathryn and Shelby Cullom Davis Scholarship, to whom I am extremely grateful.

As many authors know, one who undertakes this journey on many occasions can be quite bored, lonely, hopeless, and frustrated. For this, I have a lot of people to thank for boosting my morale and motivation at these difficult times in order to keep undergoing this challenging journey. My best friends from home: Mira, Saad, and Attar, who throughout my journey provided a tremendous kind support that only close friends can grant. I cannot be more thankful for having them in my life.

Finally, the last words of thanks and gratitude must go for my parents, Ahmed and Karima, and siblings: Judges Mahmoud, Mohamed, and Mona, whose unwavering, continuous, and unconditional love and support afforded me to find my own path in life and pursue it without fear. I dedicate this work to them and to all those who helplessly suffered and continue to suffer the legacies of the self-proclaimed 'Islamic Jihadism; and the war(s) against it.

…ents

Contents

Introduction

Religiously motivated violence has been the subject of intense debate within juristic circles for the past 100 years of Islamic history. The phenomenon entered the political landscape with the emergence of sociopolitical Islamist movements, such as the Muslim Brotherhood (*Al-Ikhwan Al-Muslimin*), *Hamas*, *Hezbollah*, the *Houthis*, the Islamic Court Union (*Ethad Al-Mhakem Al-Aslamya*), and the *Taliban*. Over time, some of these movements branched to form a more radicalized type of militant group, commonly referred to as Jihadist movements. The most prominent Jihadist movements operating today (2021) are *ISIS*, *Al-Qaeda*, *Hay'at Tahrir Al-Sham*, *Boko Haram*, *Al-Shabab*, *Ansar Al-Din*, and *Ansar Biet Al-Maqdis*. The notion of Jihad, as defined and evolved in Islamic law, has allegedly become the doctrinal and instrumental foundation for legitimizing Jihadists' resorts to violence as a mean of achieving either the ultimate goal of establishing the ideal Islamic state—'Islamic Caliphate'—or for fighting the enemies of Islam, be they internal or external.

In recent decades, the violent confrontation between the Islamic Jihadist movements and Western countries or Western-backed governments in the Middle East makes one wonder whether Samuel Huntington's 'clash of civilizations' has become an accurate description of today's geopolitical reality. In the same vein, when discussing the tensions between the Islamic world and the West, Bernard Lewis stated in the last page of his essay *The Roots of Muslim Rage*:

> It should now be clear that we are facing a mood and a movement in Islam far transcending the level of issues and policies and the governments that pursue them. This is no less than a clash of civilization. The perhaps irrational, but surely historic receptions of an ancient rival against our Judeo-Christian heritage, our secular present and the world-wide expansion of both.[1]

[1] Bernard Lewis, 'The Roots of Muslim Rage', *The Atlantic Monthly* (1990) 266, 47–60, 60. Available at: <http://pages.pomona.edu/~vis04747/h124/readings/Lewis_roots_of_muslim_rage.pdf> (last accessed 25 May 2019).

Islamic Jihadism and the Laws of War. Omar Mekky, Oxford University Press. © Omar Mekky 2023.
DOI: 10.1093/oso/9780198888369.003.0001

This is a narrative on which at the very least, the majority of the early and contemporary Jihadists' ideologues agree. Sayyid Qutb, one of the most prominent Islamic ideologues for the Jihadists' movements, stated in his revolutionary controversial manuscript *Milestones* that:

> [t]he *jahili* (barbaric ignorant) society is any society other than the Muslim society; and if we want a more specific definition we may say that any society is a *jahili* society as long as it does not dedicate itself to submission to Allah alone, in its beliefs and ideas, in its observances of worship, and in its legal regulations.[2]

In this statement, Qutb promoted the 'we and they' discourse that rejects any discrepancies between or coexistence of Islamic law and any other modern man-made laws. It essentially deepened the division of Good versus Evil between Islamic societies and Western societies. Qutb's statement of *Jahilya* was coupled with another piece of his aforementioned manuscript, which clearly states that the rationale for Jihad is:

> to establish Allah's authority on earth; to arrange human affairs according to the true guidance provided by Allah; to abolish all the Satanic forces and Satanic systems of life; to end the lordship of one man over others since all men are creatures of Allah and no one has the authority to make them his servants or to make arbitrary laws for them. These reasons are sufficient for proclaiming Jihad.[3]

Qutb's ideas were interpreted by virtually every Jihadists group around the globe as a scholarly legitimatization for Muslims to target Western countries and other secularized societies as well as secular Muslim states, as they are perceived to be '*Jahili* societies' and thus enemies of Islam.[4] This doctrine led Ayman al-Zawahiri, *Al-Qaeda*'s current leader, to publicly announce in a

[2] Sayyid Qutb, *Ma'alem Ala al-tariq* (Milestones) (Cairo: Dar Al-Shrouk, 1973) 80–2. In short, Qutb states that according to Islam, there are two societies: the Islamic and the *jahili*. This *jahiliyya* (the Pre-Islamic barbaric ignorant Arabia) was vicious in the past and is vicious today. Its viciousness varies in appearance and form but is one in its origin and roots. *Jahiliyya* is not a fixed period of time; it is a condition which recurs whenever society deviates from the way of Islam. This was so in the past, it is so in the present, and will remain so in the future. Sujata Ashwarya Cheema, 'Sayyid Qutb's Concept of Jahilyya as a Metaphor for Modern Society', *Islam and Muslim Societies* (2006) 2(2), 1–32. Available at: <http://www.academia.edu/3222569/Sayyid_Qutbs_Concept_of_Jahiliyya_as_Metaphor_for_Modern_Society> (last accessed 25 May 2019).

[3] Ibid., 70.

[4] Devin R. Springer, James L. Regens, and David N. Edger, *Islamic Radicalism and Global Jihad* (Washington, DC: Georgetown University Press, 2009) 34.

2007 video that: 'the near-term plan consists of targeting Crusaders-Jewish, as everyone who attacks the Muslim *Ummah* (community) must pay the price in our countries (Islamic Countries) and theirs (Western Countries)'.[5]

Reza Aslan argues that it is rather a 'clash of monotheism'.[6] Since the political agendas on all sides, whether on the Western side or the Islamic side, are couched in theological languages, it has become very difficult to ignore the staggering similarities between the 'antagonistic and ununiformed rhetoric' that fuelled the destructive religious wars of the past from that which drives the current conflicts in the Middle East.[7]

The re-emergence of Jihad in the parlance of international relations since the early 1970s has brought to the fore the question of this concept's relevance to the contemporary doctrine of international law. Given the origin and historical background of the concept of Jihad in Islamic history, there seems to be a considerable change in the way it is now being used. One benefit of studying the notion of Jihad from a historical perspective is learning that it was not always the way it is today. The change appears to be largely in the justifications, means, and methods of warfare compared with the way they were envisaged and practised in early Islam. Many Islamic Jurists argue that even the objectives of the contemporary Jihadists are relatively different. Nowadays, the call for Jihad is more frequently used by the leaders of Islamic resistance or insurgent groups than by state officials. Perhaps the most illustrative case in this regard is the statement that the leader of ISIS, Abu Bakr al-Baghdadi, issued on 1 July 2014 where he appealed to his followers (*Mujahdien*/Fighters) to 'go forth in the path of Allah, terrify the enemies of Allah and seek death in the places where you expect to find them'. He also enumerated instances of alleged oppression of Muslims around the world, promising his followers that 'every amount of harm against the Muslim *Ummah* will be responded to with multitudes more against the perpetrators'.[8] Needless to say, ISIS is not alone in this

[5] 'Advice of One Concerned', video by Al-Sahab Media. Posted to jihadists' websites on 5 July 2007, Available at: <https://archive.org/details/The-all-Interviewes-with-Dr-Ayman-al-Zawahiri> (last accessed 25 May 2019).

[6] Reza Aslan, *No God But God: The Origins, Evolution and Future of Islam* (New York, NY: Random House Trade, 2011) xxi. He argues that 'clash of monotheisms' mentality could be heard in the religiously polarizing 'good versus evil' rhetoric with which the United States launched the wars in Afghanistan and Iraq. It could be seen in the rising anti-Muslim vehemence that has become so much a part of the mainstream media's discourse about the Middle East. It should be read in the opinion columns of right-wing ideologues who insist that Islam represents a backward and violent religion and culture totally at odd with 'Western' values.

[7] Ibid.

[8] 'Islamic State Leader Abu Bakr al-Baghdadi Encourages Emigration', Worldwide Action, 2014. Available at: <https://news.siteintelgroup.com/Jihadist-News/islamic-state-leader-abu-bakr-al-baghdadi-encourages-emigration-worldwide-action.html> (last accessed 25 May 2019).

business. Today, the world is witnessing a wide array of Islamic Jihadist movements across the globe.

Although the twenty-year-long campaign the United States has waged against *Al-Qaeda* and the global Jihadist movements—commonly referred to as the 'war on terror'—relatively succeeded in destroying *Al-Qaeda*'s structure in Afghanistan and eliminating many of the groups' leaders, and despite the growing determination of many countries to take action against *Al-Qaeda* and its associates, no informed observers believe that these movements will be eliminated anytime soon.[9] A similar destiny is expected for the US-led international anti-terror campaign against ISIS and its affiliates across the world.[10] In fact, the political tensions and military confrontations that erupted across the Arab World in the aftermath of the so-called Arab Spring—whether in Syria, Libya, Yemen, Iraq, or Egypt—have contributed a great deal to the fuelling and strengthening of those movements.

This rapid rise of global Jihadism in the past few decades and the limited success of the anti-terror campaign in halting their expansion has left the international community with hard-hitting questions about the potential role that the different political actors can play in order to preserve and restore the world's peace and security. International law, since the end of the Second World War, has often been the chief instrument to address global conundrums of this kind. Nevertheless, in relation to this particular phenomenon, this research argues that international law, at worst, has very little to offer to solve the problem and, at best, cannot solve it alone. Simply put, international law is predominantly perceived by Jihadists—among other mainstream Muslims in the Islamic world—as a Western tool that is being used by Western-dominated bodies to enforce an absolute Western imperial agenda. Professor Mohamed Bedjaoui, Algerian diplomat and once the President of the International Court of Justice (ICJ), is one of the very few jurists in the Islamic world who speaks the language of the Third World Approach of International Law (TWAIL). He summarized the perception of the majority of the Islamic world regarding international law as follows: 'This classic international law thus consisted of a set of rules with a geographical basis (it was a European law), a religious ethical inspiration (it

[9] 'Beyond *Al-Qaeda*: The Global Jihadist Movement', RAND Project Air Force Report (2006), 17. Available at: <http://www.rand.org/content/dam/rand/pubs/monographs/2006/RAND_MG429.pdf> (last accessed 25 May 2019).

[10] Anthony H. Cordesman, 'Losing on All Fronts: The Mattis Resignation and Trump's Failed Strategies for America's Wars', Center for Strategic and International Studies (CSIS) (September 2018). Available at: <https://www.csis.org/analysis/losing-all-fronts-mattis-resignation-and-trumps-failed-strategies-americas-wars?fbclid=IwAR1d1N7K6v8xCyUqaEfQrF3cIizOTQUtknVlydad2gFgvreWs73ceVYkcJU> (last accessed 25 May 2019).

was Christian law), an economic motivation (it was a mercantilist) and political aims (it was an imperialist law).'[11] Bedjaoui further criticized the exclusion of the Islamic countries from the international law-making process.[12] Along the same lines, Antony Anghie argued that by the end of the nineteenth century, 'European expansion had ensured that European international law had been established globally as the one single system that applied to all societies. It was in this way that European international law became universal.'[13]

In the same vein, Professor Abdullahi An-Na'im, one of the most prominent modernist Islamic scholars, stated: 'the issue cannot be the West being the primary author of international law and fully conforming to its principles and underlying values versus the rest of the world struggling to subscribe to and comply with them.'[14] He further added: 'for international law to play a role in realizing shared ideals of justice and equality under the rule of law for all human beings, it must be both truly international and legitimately law.'[15] An-Na'im argued that no enforcement regime can cope with massive and persistent violations with only coercive mechanisms.[16] Instead, any legal system must assume a high level of voluntary compliance if it is to have the will and ability to enforce its rules in the exceptional cases where that is necessary.[17] He also added that coercive enforcement may ensure short-term compliance with the rules of international law, but it is not sustainable over time. Hence, the creation of voluntary compliance among the Jihadists movements is crucial for a better implementation of international law values and principles. Yet this process can only start if a genuine interaction between international law and the internal law of the Jihadists movements, that is, *Sharia* (Islamic) law, takes place. This is due to the evident role that Islamic law has played and continue to play in the cultural, political, and legal affairs of those movements.

For centuries, Islam and Islamic law have been a source of terror, distrust, and misunderstanding for Western countries.[18] As Reuven Firestone puts

[11] Mohamed Bedjaoui, 'Toward a New International Economic Order' (Paris: United Nations Educational, Scientific and Cultural Organization, 1979), 50.

[12] Ibid.

[13] Antony Anghie, 'The Evolution of International Law', 746 cited in: Andrea Bianchi, *International Law Theories* (Oxford: Oxford University Press, 2016) 219.

[14] Abdullahi A. An-Na'im, 'Islam and International Law: Toward a Positive Mutual Engagement to Realize Shared Ideals', cited in Mashood Baderin (ed.), *International Law and Islamic Law* (London: Ashgate, 2008) 71–9, 72.

[15] Ibid.

[16] Ibid.

[17] Ibid., 162.

[18] The terms 'the West' and 'Western countries' used in this study are referring to the United States and the Western European countries, specifically, the United Kingdom and France for reasons of their dominant positions in the global governance system and their influence and centrality to the ongoing policy decisions in the Middle East.

it: 'Islam is perhaps the most misunderstood religion to the West, and many stereotypes still hinder clarity about its tenets and practices. Western prejudice toward Islam is as old as Islam itself.'[19] This misunderstanding has created a cavernous gap in addition to contradictory readings between Islamic and Western scholarship in many fields of the study of Islam and Islamic law. Among the many areas of misunderstanding is the notion of Jihad, as James Turner Johnson clearly states, 'between Western and Islamic culture there is possibly no other single issue at the same time as divisive or as poorly understood as that of Jihad'.[20] This perception is supported by the fact that Jihad, in the most recent decades of Islamic history, was predominantly invoked as an instrument for the legitimization of political actions.[21]

The current state of scholarship on Jihad in the West is a 'practical problem' that suffers from a lack of 'preliminary work on a vast subject'.[22] Consequently, this lack of 'preliminary work' coupled with the legal and moral complexity of the subject left several unexplored questions in Western scholarship. Jihad has commonly been portrayed in Western literature as a holy war to force non-Muslims to convert to Islam.[23] There has also been a tendency in the West to conceive Islam as an inherently violent religion.[24] Richard C. Martin, for example, confirms that the modern Western media typically characterize Islam and Muslims as having a consciously 'discernible ethos of violence'.[25] Likewise,

[19] Reuven Firestone, *Jihād: The Origin of Holy War in Islam* (Oxford: Oxford University Press, 1999) 13; Ahmed Al-Dawoody, *The Islamic Law of War: Justifications and Regulations* (New York, NY: Palgrave Macmillan, 2011) 2.

[20] James T. Johnson, *The Holy War Idea in Western and Islamic Traditions* (Philadelphia, PA: Pennsylvania State University Press, 1997) 19; Al-Dawoody, *The Islamic Law of War* (n 19) 2. The word jihad stems from the Arabic root word J-H-D, which means 'struggle' and 'strive'. Jihad is an effort to struggle against evil thoughts, actions and aggression against a person, family, society, or country). Cherif Bassiouni, 'Evolving Approaches to Jihad: From Self Defense to Revolutionary and Regime Change—Change Political Violence', *Chicago Journal of International Law* (2007) 8, 119–46.

[21] On many occasions jihad was used for the purpose of armed resistance against foreign occupation, the struggle for self-determination, or retaliatory attacks against the West. M. Cherif Bassiouni, *Jihad—Challenges to International and Domestic Law—Hague Colloquium on Fundamental Principles of Law Series* (The Hague: Hague Academic Press, 2010).

[22] Fred McGraw Donner, 'The Sources of Islamic Conceptions of War' in John Kelsay and James Turner Johnson (eds), *Just War and Jihad: Historical and Theoretical Perspectives on War and Peace in Western and Islamic Traditions* (New York, NY: Greenwood Press, 1991) 31–69, 57; Al-Dawoody, *The Islamic Law of War* (n 19) 3.

[23] For centuries, Europe's perception of Islam has been linked with its magnificent spread and the broad expansion of its territories. Christian Europe was very much alarmed by this phenomenon, especially after the Muslim conquest of Spain. Firestone, *Jihād* (n 19) 13.

[24] For an Introduction to the conflict between the Islamic society and the West, see generally Bernard Lewis, *What Went Wrong? The Clash Between Islam and Modernity in the Middle East* (New York, NY: Harper Perennial, 2002).

[25] Richards C. Martin, 'The Religious Foundations of War, Peace, and Statecraft in Islam' in Kelsay and Johnson (eds), *Just War and Jihad* (n 22) 108; Al-Dawoody, *The Islamic Law of War* (n 19) 2; Fred Halliday, *Islam and the Myth of Confrontation: Religion and Politics in the Middle East* (London: I.B. Tauris, 2003) 35.

Margaret Pettygrove indicates, 'the demonization and reduction of Islam in popular American culture, particularly with respect to suicide bombings and political Islam, suggests that Islam is an inherently violent or extremist religion'.[26]

In addition, the series of terrorist attacks that were allegedly committed by Muslims recently have brought new perceptual dimensions and further associated Islam with violence in Western literature.[27] Accordingly, in most of the post-9/11 literature, the term 'Jihad' is used as a synonym of terrorism. Hence, on the one hand, a line of thought in the West has correlated the causes of these terrorist acts to Islamic religious extremism, and particularly to Jihad, while on the other hand, the alleged 'terrorists' themselves proclaimed that particular regional conflicts, the blind support of the West to authoritarian regimes in the Middle East, and the occupation of specific Muslim countries were the causes for which Jihad was declared.[28]

This research is therefore motivated by the following three observations. First, contemporary comparative and international law suffers from misconceptions about the notion of Jihad. This misconception will continue so long as there are different interpretations and aspects of Jihad which need further investigation and examination. The areas related to the legal theory of Jihad in Islamic law have in particular led to the centralization of the current debate on its implications rather than understanding its genuine meaning. Even Western literature affirms that the scholarship on this topic is 'considerably less well developed'.[29] Second, there is a widespread assumption that the Islamic legal tradition of international law (*Siyar*), also called the Islamic Law of Nations, is incompatible with contemporary international law and that it is the main cause of terrorism. Third, international events generally, and those related to the

[26] Margaret Pettygrove, 'Conceptions of War in Islamic Legal Theory and Practice', *Macalester Islam Journal* (2007) 2(3), 34–42, 35; Muhammed Abu-Nimer, 'A Framework for Nonviolence and Peace Building in Islam', *Journal of Law and Religion* (2000–2001) 15(1/2), 217–65, 221.

[27] For example, 12 October 2000, attack on the USS Cole in the Yemeni port of Aden; 11 September 2001, four planes hijacked and crashed into the World Trade Center and The Pentagon by 19 hijackers, 2,977 killed and over 5,000 injured; 27 March 2002, suicide bomb attack on a Passover Seder in a hotel in Netanya, Israel, 30 dead, 133 injured; 11 March 2004, multiple bombings on trains near Madrid, Spain. 191 killed, 1460 injured; 7 July 2005, multiple bombings on the London Underground, 53 killed by four suicide bombers, nearly 700 injured; 1 May 2010, New York, Faisal Shahzad, an Islamic Pakistani-American who received US citizenship in December 2009, attempted to detonate a car bomb in Times Square. All these criminal attacks were allegedly committed by Muslims and under the name of Islamic Jihad. See The Religion of Peace, 'Terror attacks—About the List of Attacks, 2001–2008'. Available at <http://www.thereligionofpeace.com> (last accessed 25 May 2019).

[28] Al-Dawoody, *The Islamic Law of War* (n 19) 3.

[29] Johnson, *The Holy War Idea in Western and Islamic Traditions* (n 20) 19. Johnson also states: 'There exist no general histories treating the understanding of normative tradition on religion, statecraft, and war in Islamic societies or in Islamic religious thought. Many significant subjects remain unexplored for lack of researchers with the necessary training and language skills.' Ibid., 22.

Muslim world specifically, corroborate the need for a better understanding of the relationship between contemporary international law and Islamic law and how their interaction can be explored and improved to enhance international relations and law. These three features of the current state of the field raise enormous practical legal problems that require in-depth scholarly inquiry if they are to be resolved.

Chapter 1 examines the particularity of Islamic law as an independent and unique legal system with a special focus on its definition, rationale, sources, and interpretation. It will also discuss the notion of *Siyar* or 'Islamic International Law'. Finally, it will tackle the evolution of the notion of 'Jihad' from Muhammad's first Islamic State to ISIS. Military and political achievements that marked the early history of Islam placed the Islamic society at the time in the position of receiving revelation, instructions, and guidance from Muhammad and his companions on warfare matters that led to the establishment of an extensive set of rules and legal precedents that laid down the boundaries of the notion of Jihad. In other words, the dictates of the Islamic law provide clear and binding precedents that not only contain *jus ad bellum* (rules regulating the reasons/justifications for the use of force) but also *jus in bello* (the rules regulating the conduct of hostilities).

Chapter 2 specifically examines *jus ad bellum* under Islamic law in both international and non-international armed conflicts. The purpose of this research is to evaluate the compatibility of these rules under Islamic law with Article 2 of the United Nations (UN) Charter, which prohibits states from the 'threat or use of force' against the 'territorial integrity or political independence' of any other state.[30] Moreover, it explores the definition of the right of self-defence in Islamic law and its compatibility with Article 51 of the UN Charter.[31] The research will further investigate the conformity of this definition with international law principles, such as those derived from the *Caroline* incident and the *Nicaragua* case before the International Court of Justice.[32] It will also tackle the use of force in its different forms, whether launched by state

[30] *Charter of the United Nations*, 26 June 1945, 59 Stat. 1031, T.S. 993, 3 Bevans 1153, 26 June 1945 (entered into force 24 October 1945) at art. 2 para 4.

[31] Ibid., at art. 51.

[32] ICJ, *Military and Paramilitary Activities Case* (*Nicar. v. U.S.*), Judgment, 27 June 1986. See generally Olaoluwa Olusanya, *Identifying the Aggressor Under International Law: A Principle Approach* (Oxford: Peter Lang Verlag, 2006) 105. The Caroline doctrine arises from an incident in the 1840s where British soldiers crossed into the United States to destroy a ship ferrying arms to insurgents in Canada. Both the United Kingdom and the United States agreed that anticipatory action was allowed only when the '[n]ecessity of that self-defense is instant, overwhelming, and leaving no choice of means, and no moment for deliberation'. After the Second World War, the Nuremberg Tribunal reaffirmed the Caroline doctrine. The case will be reviewed in detail in Chapter 2, Section 2.

or non-state actors, as treated under Islamic law. A rigorous study of the regulation of the use of force by non-state actors under Islamic law is significant for two major reasons. First, such study will allow international legal scholars to assess claims to which Jihad equates and justifies terrorism. Second, this study will allow an assessment of the degree of tolerance or intolerance that Islamic law provides for rebels or internal opponents of an Islamic government. The research will also discuss the legality of humanitarian intervention under Islamic law. In fact, a number of Islamic jurists argue that the principle of humanitarian intervention has stronger basis in Islamic law than in international law.[33]

Chapter 3 examines *jus in bello* under Islamic law. Studying the regulations of the conduct of Jihadists in hostilities in both international and non-international armed conflicts under Islamic law can provide hints for promising measures for humanizing armed conflicts in which Muslims, as followers of a religion that comprises one-fifth of the world's population, may be involved. Perhaps the best way to clarify the Islamic concept of international humanitarian law (IHL) and make it more readily comprehensible to those not familiar with Islamic doctrine is to explain it in the contemporary context of the Hague Conventions of 1899 and 1907, the four Geneva Conventions of 1949 and their Additional Protocols of 1977, the various weapons conventions, and customary international law.[34]

Chapter 4 will examine the counterterrorism legal framework as enshrined in multiple treaties, Security Council Resolutions, and domestic laws. It will focus on the legal instruments issued to combat the Islamic Jihadist movements,

[33] Sohail H. Hashmi, 'Is there an Islamic Ethic of Humanitarian Intervention?' in Anthony F. Lang. Jr (ed.), *Just Intervention* (Washington, DC: Georgetown University Press, 2003) 62–83. Hashmi argues that the ethics of humanitarian intervention in Islamic law must be seen as a subset of the general theory of Jihad and he cites the Quranic verse (4:75) that dictates: 'Why should you not fight in God's cause and for those oppressed men, women, and children who cry out, "Lord, rescue us from this town whose people are oppressors! By your grace, give us a protector and helper."'

[34] Collectively known as the Geneva Conventions of 12 August 1949, the four conventions are the Geneva Convention for the Protection of the Wounded and Sick in Armed Forces in the Field, opened for signature 12 August 1949 (hereinafter GC I); the Geneva Convention for the Amelioration of the Condition of the Wounded, Sick, and Shipwrecked Members of the Armed Forces at Sea, opened for signature 12 August 1949 (hereinafter GC II); the Geneva Convention Relative to the Treatment of Prisoners of War, opened for signature 12 August 1949 (hereinafter GC III); and the Geneva Convention Relative to the Protection of Civilian Persons in Time of War, opened for signature 12 August 1949 (hereinafter GC IV). Protocol I: International Committee of the Red Cross (ICRC), Protocol Additional to the Geneva Conventions of 12 August 1949, and relating to the Protection of Victims of International Armed Conflicts (Protocol I), 8 June 1977 (hereinafter AP I). Protocol II: International Committee of the Red Cross (ICRC), Protocol Additional to the Geneva Conventions of 12 August 1949, and relating to the Protection of Victims of Non-International Armed Conflicts (Protocol II), 8 June 1977 (hereinafter AP II); International Conferences (The Hague), Hague Convention (IV) Respecting the Laws and Customs of War on Land and Its Annex: Regulations Concerning the Laws and Customs of War on Land, 18 October 1907; See also the ICRC study on Customary International Humanitarian Law. Available at: <https://www.icrc.org/customary-ihl/eng/docs/v1_cha> (last accessed 25 May 2019).

such as *Al-Qaeda* and ISIS. The study will also examine the validity and effectiveness of the various contemporary counterterrorism measures adopted by the international community and the local authorities in the Islamic world and the other affected countries. It will further highlight the degree of compatibility between the counterterrorism legal framework and the other related branches of international law, such as IHL and international human rights law (IHRL).

Chapter 5 discusses the added value of the interaction between international law and Islamic law. It tackles the challenge of the ambiguity and diverse interpretations of Islamic law texts by explaining their most recognized interpretive methods. Finally, this chapter seeks to provide an integrated approach or partnership between international law and Islamic law. The rationale behind adopting this approach is to attempt to create a pragmatic legal formula, inspired by the common values of international law and Islamic law, which could be used by international lawyers, policy-makers, and international organizations to foster the compliance and commitment of the Islamic Jihadist groups to the laws of war.

1

Islamic Law and the Evolution of Jihad

1. The Tenets of Islamic Law

The word 'Islam' is an Arabic word which means 'submission to the will of God'.[1] This word comes from the same root as the Arabic word *salam*, which means 'peace'. As such, the religion of Islam teaches that in order to attain true peace of mind and surety of heart, one must submit to God and live according to his divinely revealed law 'Islamic law', commonly referred to in Arabic as 'Islamic *Sharia*'.[2] The first part of this chapter will examine the concept of Islamic law and its main sources, while the second part will tackle the evolution of the notion of Jihad throughout Islamic history.

(i) The Concept of Islamic Law

Like the system of common law originally developed in medieval England or the system of civil law that first evolved in ancient Rome, Islamic law should be regarded as a body of law, or a system of law, rooted in history but very much alive today.[3] However, it should be noted that Islamic law mostly sees less need than other legal systems to separate the religious and the secular; legal, ethical, and moral questions; and the public and private aspects of a Muslim's life.[4] Similar to other legal systems, most of Islamic law is the product of rational

[1] UN Office on Drugs and Crime, *Combating Trafficking in Persons in Accordance with the Principles of Islamic Law* (New York, NY: UNODC, 2010). Available at: <https://www.unodc.org/documents/human-trafficking/UNODC_Trafficking_and_Islamic_Law_-Amended.pdf (last accessed 25 May 2019).

[2] *Sharia* is an Arabic word that literally means the 'way to be followed' and technically it stands for the regulation of people's life in a way which is best for them. *Sharia* is the code of law for the Islamic way of life, which God has revealed for mankind and commanded Muslims to follow. See M. Cherif Bassiouni and Gamal M. Badr, 'The Shari'a: Sources, Interpretation, and Rule Making', *UCLA Journal of Islamic and Near Eastern Law* (2002) 135, 135–78, 135.

[3] Hamid Khan, *Practitioner's Guide: Islamic Law* (International Network to Promote the Rule of Law, 2013) 15.

[4] Sharia is an entire code of Islamic law concerning the rights and obligations of Muslims. It prescribes a complete set of laws for the guidance of mankind so that Good (*Ma'ruf*) may triumph and Evil (*Munkar*) may disappears from society. It provides a clear and straight path, which leads to progress and fulfilment in life and the attainment of Allah's pleasure. It is primarily concerned with the methods of

Islamic Jihadism and the Laws of War. Omar Mekky, Oxford University Press. © Omar Mekky 2023.
DOI: 10.1093/oso/9780198888369.003.0002

intellectual exercise and, despite prevalent misconception, it is subject to modifications.[5] It is also noteworthy to clarify that Islamic law is a means to accomplish the higher aspirations and expectations of Islam; it is never an end in and of itself.[6] Consequently, Islamic law as a legal system has been developed in different cultural environments over hundreds of years after the death of Prophet Muhammad in 632, as the Islamic empire expanded to the edge of North Africa in the west and to China in the east.[7] Islamic law, as it is today, is among the recognized legal systems of the world.[8] To mention an illustrative example, the Hague International Conference on Comparative Law of 1932 and 1937 stated that *Sharia* law is independent of other legal systems and that Islamic civilization and jurisprudence are considered to be among the principal legal systems of the world in the sense of Article 9 of the Statute of the Permanent Court of International Justice.[9]

One branch of Islamic law is *Siyar*—literally meaning 'paths'—which is commonly referred to by modern Islamic jurists as Islamic international law. In Islamic law *Siyar* often refers to issues related to the laws of war.[10] This is why some Islamic jurists used the title 'the book of Jihad' rather than 'the book

worship, social principles, law regarding people's relations with each other, the rules and conditions regarding the lawful and unlawful, and similar other problems. The main intention of Sharia is to regulate people's life. Sharia is very comprehensive to the extent that it deals with matters as simple as regulating dress codes to matters that include complex law-making. Sharia is applicable to everyone and anyone, extending from the laymen sweeper to royalty, including noticeably apportioning the dealing of non-Muslims. Ibid.

[5] Ibid.

[6] M. Cherif Bassiouni, 'The Sharia, Islamic Law, and Post Conflict Justice' (not published) 14; Mathew Lippman, 'Islamic Criminal Law and Procedures: Religious Fundamentalism V. Modern Law', *Boston College International and Comparative Law Review* (1989) 12(1) 347–80, 349.

[7] Professor Bassiouni clarified this idea of the development of *Sharia* by describing *Sharia* as a tree with many branches and he mentioned that '[t]he fact that this tree has grown over fourteen hundred years explains the strength of the trunk, and also the diversity of the branches; while the trunk remains unchanged, the branches are constantly expanding in different directions, assuming new shapes and sizes. However, some of these branches fall from the tree or wither away, while other grows stronger, taller, wider, or even move out in different directions.' He also added that seeing this tree entirely is a challenging task and he said 'this is why so few have the full knowledge of the *sharia* multifaceted subjects and their applications over the span of fourteen centuries and across so many cultures in which Islam has taken root. This explains why Muslim reformists have had such difficulties in facing the challenges of progressive development, and why traditional have been more successful in preserving the status quo.' See Bassiouni, 'The Sharia, Islamic Law, and Post Conflict Justice' (n 6) 20.

[8] See Rene David and John E. C. Brierly, *Major Legal Systems in the World Today* (New York, NY: Macmillan, 1978) 421.

[9] Article 9 of the Statute of the International Court of Justice provides that: '[a]t every election, the electors shall bear in mind not only that the persons to be elected should individually possess the qualifications required, but also that in the body as a whole the representation of the main forms of civilization and of the principal legal systems of the world should be assured'. See Sobhi Mahmassani, 'The Principle of International Law in Light of Islamic Doctrine' in *Collected Courses*, Vol. 117 (The Hague: Academy of International Law, 1966) 201–328, 221.

[10] Nasiruddin al-Mutrrazi and Mahmood Fakhori (eds), *Al-Mugrib fi Tartib al-Mu'rib*, Vol. 1 (Syria-Halab: Maktab Usama ibn Zayd, 1979) 227.

of *Siyar*' to describe the laws of war.[11] Muslim jurists began the systematic articulation of the principles of Islamic international law in the ninth century. Muhammad ibn al-Hassan al-Shaybani (d. 805), often called the Hugo Grotius of Islamic international law, was the first to present a systematic approach to international law in his manuscript *The Shorter Book on Muslim International Law* (*Kitab al-siyar al-saghir*).[12] Islamic international law thus is for the most part an accumulation of rules that allow for binding international agreements rather than an imposition of a set of mandatory universal rules.[13] In fact, Islamic international law is a misleading term—in the traditional understanding of the concept of international law—as Islamic international law is not made to regulate the relationship of nation states towards each other, but to provide Muslims with a comprehensive code of conduct. Therefore, its rules, first and foremost, are a source of reference for Muslim individuals.[14]

Despite various attempts to define *Siyar* in Islamic history,[15] in my opinion, the definition provided by Nagib Arminazi is the most comprehensive one. Arminazi defines *Siyar* as:

> the set of rules that are binding on Muslims in their relations with non-Muslims, whether they fight [the Muslim state] or have peaceful relations with them, whether they are individuals or states, and whether they are inside Muslim territory or outside of it. And the set of these rules also include the situation of apostates, rebels and robbers.[16]

[11] Ibid.

[12] See generally Majid Khadduri, *The Islamic Law of Nations: Shaybani's Siyar* (Baltimore, MD: The Johns Hopkins Press, 1966); Muhammad Munir, 'Islamic International Law (Siyar): An Introduction', *Hamdard Islamicus No. 4, International Islamic University Islamabad* (2012) 37–60. Available at: <http://works.bepress.com/cgi/viewcontent.cgi?article=1041&context=muhammad_munir> (last accessed 25 May 2019).

[13] Nahed Samoun, 'Modernized Islamic International Law Concepts as a Third World Approach to International Law' in Rüdiger Wolfrum (ed.), *Max Planck Encyclopedia of Public International Law* (Oxford: Oxford University Press, 2010) 543–77, 546. Available at: <http://www.zaoerv.de/72_2012/72_2012_3_a_543_577.pdf> (last accessed 25 May 2019).

[14] Samoun, 'Modernized Islamic International Law Concepts as a Third World Approach to International Law' (n 13) 546.

[15] Imam Sharkasi (d. 1090) stated that Imam Mohamed Ibn Hassan Al-Shaibany has designed this chapter by 'Siyar' since it describes the behaviour of the Muslims in dealing with the polytheists from among the belligerents as well as those of them who have made a peace treaty (with Muslims) and live either as resident aliens or as non-Muslim citizens (of the Muslim stat)]; in dealing with apostates who are the worst of the infidels, since they renounce (Islam) after acceptance; and in dealing with rebels whose position is less (unworthy) than that of the polytheists, although they be ignorant and in their interpretation on wrong ground. See Muhammad Ibn Ahmad al-Sarakhasi, *Kitab al-Mabsut*, Vol. 10 (Beirut: Dar Ehia al-Tourath al-ʿArabi, 2002) 5.

[16] Muhammad Munir, Islamic International Law (Siyar): An Introduction', *Hamdard Islamicus No. 4, International Islamic University Islamabad* (2012). Available at: <http://works.bepress.com/cgi/viewcontent.cgi?article=1041&context=muhammad_munir> (last accessed 25 May 2019).

Another definition, perhaps slightly closer to the legal framework of the contemporary international law, was provided by the renowned modern Islamic scholar Imam Abu Zahrah. In his introduction to the *Sharh Kitab al-Siyar al-Kabir*, *Siyar* is defined as:

> the rules of Jihad and war, what is allowed in it and what is not, and the rules of [permanent] peace treaties and temporary truce, and the rules of who should be granted alien status and who should not, the rules of war booty, ransom and enslavement, as well as other problems that arise during wars and its aftermath. In short, it designates the rules of international relations between Muslims and other [communities] during peace and war, although most of the discussion is about the war.[17]

It is evident from the language of these definitions that the classical doctrine of *Siyar* divides the world into Muslims and non-Muslims comparable to that of the classical Roman division between Romans and barbarians.[18] Given that classical Islamic law in general was originated and developed in a world divided primarily along religious rather than national boundaries, the majority of Muslim jurists reasoned over international relations as a jurisprudential division of the world into two domains; one of peace (*dar al-islam*) and one of war (*dar al-harb*).[19] The domain of peace is where Islamic law governed and the political power lied with the Muslim community, while the domain of war encompassed territories which were outside the scope of Islamic sovereignty and thus the religious and political rules of Islam were not implemented.[20] The identification and distinction of these two domains, however, has no textual support, either in the *Quran* or in the Prophetic traditions (*Sunnah*). Still, conceptualizing these two domains and analysing and reading their competing interpretations and implications were particularized and heavily debated by jurists of the different Islamic schools of legal thought. These debates revealed

[17] Abu Zahrah, *Introduction to Sharh Siyar al-Kabir* (Cairo: M'atb'at Cairo University, n.d.) 33.

[18] The approach of dividing the world on the basis of 'we and they' or believers and non-believers is hardly novel nor confined to Islam. St Augustine, for instance, proposed a similar construct whereby Christians were divided between areas under the domain of religious law, or *civitas dei* (the city of God), and areas outside that domain and within the *civitas terrenae* (the earthly city). See M. Khadduri, *The Islamic Law of Nations: Shaybani's Siyar* (Baltimore, MD: The Johns Hopkins Press, 1966) vii; James T. Johnson, *The Holy War Idea in Western and Islamic Traditions* (Philadelphia, PA: Pennsylvania State University Press, 1997).

[19] W. Al-Zuhili, 'Islam and International Law', *International Review of the Red Cross* (2005) 87(858), 269–83, 278.

[20] Samoun, 'Modernized Islamic International Law Concepts as a Third World Approach to International Law' (n 13) 546.

various legal understandings as embedded in Islamic history, which reflected the needs and conditions of particular Muslim communities as well as their subsequent Islamic states in a particular period of time.[21]

(ii) The Sources of Islamic Law

Sharia is based on multiple primary sources, which are the *Quran*, *Sunnah*, Consensus (*Ijma*), and analogical reasoning (*Qiyas*).[22] However, the starting point and foundation for it is the Holy *Quran*, which literally means 'reading or recitation'.[23] The *Quran* is considered to be the word of God as revealed to his Prophet Muhammad as a guide for human behaviour and social relations. The *Quran* governs devotional obligations known as *Ibadat*, such as prayer, fasting, alms giving, pilgrimage, or any other religious obligation; it also governs legal relations *Muamalat*, such as family law, contracts, torts, property law, criminal and penal law, and the law of war and peace.[24] Like any legal text, some of the *Quran*'s legal sentiments are highly clear and straightforward; others, instead, are very ambiguous. Islamic scholars divide such verses into 'definitive elements' and 'tentative elements'.[25] Thus, while tentative verses have scope for wider interpretation than definitive verses do, it is important to recognize that both types invite and allow a variety of interpretations.[26] One of the most significant guidelines of interpretation of *Quran* is following the *Sunnah*.

The second source of Islamic law is the *Sunnah*,[27] which literally means a way of life or a rule of behaviour. In a legal context, *Sunnah* refers to the practice of Muhammad expressed in deeds, oral pronouncements, or in concurrence in action by others.[28] *Hadith* is the part of Islamic knowledge that focuses on the

[21] Ibid.

[22] Lippman, 'Islamic Criminal Law and Procedures: Religious Fundamentalism v. Modern Law' (n 6) 56. The *Quran* is about the same length as the New Testament, but in contrast to the New Testament and the Hebrew Bible, which are collections of books written by a number of different persons over centuries, the *Quran* is regarded to have a single source, namely God (Allah in Arabic). The content of the *Quran* is believed by Muslims to have been transmitted from the Archangel Gabriel to Muhammad over the course of twenty-three years (609–32). The *Quran* is divided into 114 *suras* (chapters) and about 6,235 *ayas* (verses). Khan, *Practitioner's Guide: Islamic Law* (n 3) 18. Available at: <http://inprol.org/sites/default/files/publications/2013/islamic_law_guide-july_2013_final_0.pdf> (last accessed 25 May 2019).

[23] Farooq A. Hassan, 'The Sources of Islamic Law', *American Society in International Law Proceedings* (1982) 76, 65–75, 65.

[24] UNODC, *Combating Trafficking in Persons in Accordance with the Principles of Islamic Law* (n 1) 12.

[25] Mohamed H. Kamali, *Sharia Law: An Introduction* (London: Oneworld Publications, 2008) 23.

[26] Khan, *Practitioner's Guide: Islamic Law* (n 3) 19.

[27] The Prophetic *Sunnah* serve as a source of law by invoking various Quranic commandments urging believers to follow the Prophet: 'You who believe, obey God and the Messenger, and those in authority among you' (4:59); and 'Whoever obeys the Messenger obeys God' (4:80).

[28] Bassiouni and Badr, 'The Shari'a: Sources, Interpretation, and Rule Making' (n 2) 150.

oral saying of Muhammad.[29] Therefore, *hadith* is listed under the *Sunnah* because Muhammad's sayings were one of the things that he did and echoed the tradition in verbal form.[30] Muhammad lived his life according to the *Quran*, setting the *Quran* into practice in his own life. All of these details were passed on and recorded, to be referred to in future legal rulings. Many questions concerning personal conduct, community and family relations, political and other matters, were discussed during the lifetime of Muhammad, decided by him, recorded and preserved until now.[31] However, unfortunately for Muslims, the process of searching, compiling, and recording the *hadith* did not start until the ninth century. In other words, it started some two centuries after the source of the story passed away. To address concerns regarding authenticity, each *hadith* included an *isnad*, or a chain of reliable and credible oral transmitters, and had to be traced to the Prophet himself.[32]

The third source of Islamic law is *Ijma*, which is the consensus of Islamic scholars. According to Islamic law, the agreement of Muslim jurists constitutes a rule of law. In cases where Muslims have not been able to find a specific legal ruling in the *Quran* or *Sunnah*, the consensus of the Islamic jurists in the community is sought.[33] *Ijma* is not divine in nature like the *Quran* or the *Sunnah*, as it has not been revealed to Muhammad by God. While *Ijma* is a consensus, it cannot be a consensus that is inconsistent with either the *Quran* or the *Sunnah*. The predominant view within classical Islamic law defined *Ijma* as a consensus reached by the highest order of Islamic jurists concerning a rule or norm for a given time.[34] Modernist Islamic jurists, such as Mohamed Abdu (d. 1905) and Rachid Rida (d. 1935), argued that this role could be played by the

[29] Ibid., 151.

[30] Each *hadith* is linked to the prophet through a chain of authorities (*isnad*); as *hadith* are ranked to their degree of authenticity as sound (*sahih*), good (*hasan*), and weak (*daif*). See Malise Ruthven, *Islam in the World* (Oxford: Oxford University Press, 1984) 148–56.

[31] *Ahadith* (plural of *Hadith*) have been very carefully collected and compiled two centuries after the death of Muhammad. Six collections of *Hadith* are regarded as the most authentic/credible, they are: *Sahih Al-Bukhari, Sahih Muslim, Sunnah Abu Dawud, Sunnah Ibn Majah, Jami At-Tirmidhi*, and *Sunnah An-Nasi*. *Sunnah* is divided into two types: *Mutwatir*, or widely reported by a large number of narrators and thus universally accepted as authoritative, and *Ahad*, or reported by a limited number of narrators. *Hadith* is further divided according to its credibility and the verification of the chain of transmission into 'sound' (*sahih*), 'good' (*hasan*), and 'weak' (*daaif*).

[32] 'The most well-known and well-respected compilations among the Sunni Muslims—mentioned above—are the collections of Muhammad ibn Ismail al Bukhari (d. 870) and Muslim al-Hajjaj (d. 874), whose compilations are popularly known as Sahih Bukhari and Sahih Muslim, respectively)'. See Khan, *Practitioner's Guide: Islamic Law* (n 3) 19.

[33] There are two types of *Ijma*: active *Ijma*, in which all eligible Muslim jurists share the same opinion, and passive *Ijma* in which some jurists express an opinion and others do not dissent.

[34] Wael B. Hallaq, *A History of Islamic Legal Theories: An Introduction to Sunni Usul al-fiqh* Cambridge: Cambridge, 1999) 20, 27–8.

contemporary members of the elected legislative or executive bodies who are best placed to address the needs of the people.[35]

The fourth source of Islamic law is the *Qiyas* or analogical reasoning.[36] *Qiyas* can be carried out only in cases where the solution to a problem cannot be found through *Quran*, *Sunnah*, or *Ijma*.[37] To apply *Qiyas*, four elements should exist: an original subject *asl*, a new subject *far*, a common cause in both *illa*, and a rule derived from *Qiyas*, *hukm*.[38] Moreover, other supplementary sources have been used to elaborate and expand Islamic law, such as *Istislah* or consideration of public interest,[39] *Istihsan* or reasoning based on the best outcome or equity that the jurist prefers,[40] and finally *Urf* or custom and usage that have been invoked to conform the Islamic law to the prevailing practice in a community.[41] Furthermore, the practices of the first four Caliphs as forms of authoritative precedents, the decisions of learned judges, treaties and pacts, contracts, and *Fatwas* or scholarly opinions on legal matters, are also considered as supplemental sources of law to apply wherever the four primary sources are silent on a given issue.[42]

While these diverse sources have pooled to shape the Islamic legal system, they were not sufficient to cover every aspect of social life that Muslim societies over time have come to consider as needing to be regulated by law. The science of *Fiqh* arises to fill this gap. *Fiqh*, which literally means knowledge and understanding, is the science of Islamic law or jurisprudence. However, the intellectual process of discovering the rules of Islamic law and extracting the science of Islamic law from detailed Islamic sources is called *Ijtihad*.[43] Some superlative Islamic jurists have devoted themselves to the task of developing

[35] 'This position is controversial, however, because many Muslim-majority states still adhere to the notion that *ijma* remains the province of jurists rather than the masses.' Muhammad Rashīd Ridā, *Tafsīr al-Qur'ān al-H akīm: Al-Shahīr bi-Tafsīr al-Manār*, 12 Vols (Cairo: Dār al-Manār, 2002).

[36] Mohamed H. Kamali, *Principles of Islamic Jurisprudence*, 3rd edn (Cambridge: Islamic Text Society, 2005) 231.

[37] Ibid., 264.

[38] There is a wide range of how restrictive or extensive analogy can be applied. Literalists will limit analogy to that which is either precisely the same or substantially the same; however, non-literalists, using a policy approach, will extend the reasoning by analogy to that which the Roman law referred to as *jus dem generis*, meaning of the same genre. UNODC, *Combating Trafficking in Persons in Accordance with the Principles of Islamic Law* (n 1) 12; Cherif Bassiouni, 'The Sharia, Islamic Law, and Post Conflict Justice' (n 6) 23.

[39] Majid Khadduri, 'The Maslaha (Public Interest) and Ilta (cause) in Islamic Law', *New York University Journal of International Law & Policy* (1979) 12, 213–17213, 216.

[40] Noel J. Coulson, *The History of Islamic Law* (Edinburgh: Edinburgh University Press, 1964) 60.

[41] Khizr M. Khan, 'Juristic Classification of Islamic Law', 6 *Houston Journal of International Law* (1983) 6, 23–35, 27.

[42] Cherif Bassiouni, 'The Sharia, Islamic Law, and Post Conflict Justice' (n 6) 22.

[43] UNODC, *Combating Trafficking in Persons in Accordance with the Principles of Islamic Law* (n 1) 13. For further detailed discussion on the science of Fiqh (commonly referred to as *Usul al-fiqh*) and *Ijtihad*, see Chapter 5, Section 2.

the jurisprudence of Islamic law and its practices. Among these jurists are the four Sunni fundamental compilers of *Sharia* law, namely Imam Abu Hanifah, Imam Malik, Imam Shafii, and Imam Ibn Hanbal.[44] The various schools of jurisprudence (*Fiqh*), including those established by the aforementioned Islamic jurists, all rank the sources of Islamic law differently[45] and pursue different analytical approaches and methods with respect to its interpretation.

It is worth mentioning that the Shiite school of thoughts, while bearing a resemblance to Sunni Islamic schools, contains some essential differences that arise due to the historical, political, and theological tension between these major two sects of Islam. These differences emerged immediately after the death of Muhammad and revolved around the question of who was empowered to lead the *Ummah*. Shiite schools recognize Ali as Muhammad's cousin, son-in-law, and the first male to convert to Islam as the rightful Caliph or successor to Muhammad. They comprise the Twelvers (Imami school), who acknowledge the existence of twelve Imams in the line of the descendants of Lady Fatima, Muhammad's daughter and Ali's wife; the Isma'ili, followers of Ismail, whom they consider the legitimate seventh Imam; and the Zaydi, whose adherents followed the leadership of Zaid, the fifth Imam.[46] Out of these, the Twelvers are the best known and have the largest percentage of followers in the Islamic world, particularly in Iran and Iraq.[47]

Hence, seeking *Fiqh* or *Ijtihad* is a key process targeting the interpretation of Islamic law, which relies on textual analysis to provide legal opinions. *Ijtihad* is an intellectual endeavour to seek out solutions of day-to-day issues. It is a rational and analytical approach based on the *Quran* and *Sunnah* for interpreting religious issues.[48] Professor Khaled Abou Al-Fadl persuasively argues:

[44] It is noteworthy that those Jurists are the founders of the main four schools of jurisprudence in the Sunni's Society while Shiites have their own schools of jurisprudence, such as Imamis, Druze, Neydi, Ithna Ashari, and Ismaili Alawi. These Sunni schools are relied upon by an estimated 90 per cent of the overall 1.7 billion Muslims throughout the world and the other 10 per cent follow the Shiites' schools.

[45] However, all the schools of jurisprudence agree that the *Quran* is the first source of the *Sharia* and then followed by *Sunnah* but they disagree about the ranking of the rest of the sources.

[46] Mohamed E. Badar, 'Ius in Bello under Islamic International Law', *International Criminal Law Review* (2013) 13, 593–625. Available at <http://nrl.northumbria.ac.uk/13564/1/1_Final_and_Edited_version_-_Ius_in_Bello_under_Islamic_International_Law_-_PDF.pdf> (last accessed 25 May 2019).

[47] Ibid.

[48] 'The work of the interpreter of the text is to ascertain the authenticity of the sources and then: (1) to discover the laws through the interpretation of the sources; (2) extend the laws to new cases that may be similar to the cases mentioned in the sources for which the laws cannot be discovered through literal interpretation; (3) extend the laws to new cases that have not been covered by the previous two methods by looking at the general principles and objectives of the *sharia* (this method is known as *istihsan* or *istislah*—general interests of the community).' See 'Concept of Ijtihad in Islam'. Available at: <http://www.cssforum.com.pk/css-compulsory-subjects/islamiat/islamiat-notes/15108-concept-ijtihad-islam.html> (last accessed 25 May 2019).

> Islamic law is founded on the logic of a Principal who guides through instructions. Those instructions are issued to the agents who have inherited the earth and who are bound to the Principal by a covenant ... [T]he point of the covenant is not to live according to the instructions, but to attempt to do so. Searching the instructions is a core value in itself—regardless of the results, searching the instruction is a moral virtue. This is not because the instructions are pointless, but because the instructions must remain vibrant, dynamic, open, and relevant.... [I]t is impossible for a human being to represent God's Truth—a human being can only represent his or her own efforts in search of this truth. The ultimate and unwavering value in the relationship between human beings and God is summarized in the Islamic statement, 'And, God knows best.'[49]

2. The Evolution of Jihad

Jihadist movements grow out of and are sustained by a pervasive Islamic ideology that is constantly evolving. Such movements are themselves derived from an evolving body of law; namely, Islamic law. Accordingly, this section briefly examines the evolution of the notion of Jihad throughout the Islamic history. The aim of this examination, however, is not to retrace the history of Islam but rather to highlight the evolution of the notion of Jihad from Muhammad's time to that of Abu Bakr al-Baghdadi. Bearing in mind that *Sharia* per se has not been the exclusive focal point for all of Jihadist ideologies, some parts of the ideology are quite political with very slight theological basis. It is ultimately this distinction which makes the contextual studying of the evolution of the notion of Jihad a necessary endeavour.

(i) Jihad in the Prophet Period

One night in 610, while Muhammad was meditating on Mount Hira in the city of Mecca, he had an encounter that would significantly change the face of the earth. It was the moment when Muhammad ceased being a Meccan businessman concerned with societal reforms in order to have a more essential role as a prophet, to use the language of the Abrahamic tradition. At the beginning,

[49] Khaled Abou Al-Fadl, *Speaking in God's Name: Islamic Law, Authority and Women* (London: Oneworld Publications, 2001).

Muhammad was ordered to merely use the Jihad of evidence,[50] by using what would be revealed to him—the *Quran*—to call the unbelievers to Islam.[51] Islamic literature is replete with stories of oppression and persecution that have been imposed on him and his companions by the *Qurayshite* leaders (the most influential tribe in Arabia at the time) as a response to his preachings.[52] This violent campaign did not cease the increasing numbers of supporters that Muhammad was gaining day after day.

The persecution of Muhammad increased after the death of his uncle and protector Abu Talib and his wealthy wife Khadija.[53] Every tribe started attacking their Muslims.[54] When Muhammad saw the increasing tendencies of persecution and torture against his followers and companions, he advised them to immigrate to Abyssinia where the king, the Negus, was a righteous man who would not allow anyone to be oppressed on his territory.[55] Muhammad was then subjected to an attempt of assassination by all the tribes in Mecca,[56] which compelled him and his companions to flee to Yathrib (currently known as Medina). There he met the *Ansar*, literally meaning 'supporters'. That year, 622, will forever be known as year 1 A.H. (After Hijrah—After Immigration) in the Islamic calendar. It is in Medina that the Muslim *Ummah* (nation) was born and where Muhammad's ideas on social reform in Arabia transformed into a universal religious ideology.[57] It was also the birth of what is called 'political Islam'. According to Reza Aslan: 'Muhammad in Medina became the paradigm for the Arab empire that expanded throughout the Middle East after the Prophet's death, and the standard that every Islamic Kingdom and Sultanate struggled to meet during the Middle Ages'. He also added that this 'Medinan

[50] Ibn al-Qayyim al-jawziyya, *Zad al-ma'ad*, Vol. 3 (Cairo: n.p., University Library, n.d) 5.

[51] 'So do not obey the disbelievers, and strive against them with the *Quran* a great striving', *Quran* (25:52); 'Arise and deliver the warning', *Quran* (74:2); 'Invite to the way of your Lord with wisdom and good instruction, and argue with them in a way that is best. Indeed, your Lord is most knowing of who has strayed from His way, and He is most knowing of who is [rightly] guided', *Quran* (16:125). It is worth mentioning that given that the original language of *Quran* is Arabic, most of the English translations I have come across throughout my research are somewhat inaccurate. Therefore, most of the Quranic verses translated in this research are conducted first-hand by the author, periodically using the *Quran*'s English version available at Quran.com for guidance.

[52] Ahmed Al-Dawoody, *The Islamic Law of War: Justifications and Regulations* (New York, NY: Palgrave Macmillan, 2011) 15–17.

[53] Ibn Ishaq, *Al-Sīrah al-Nabawiyyah*. Ed. ʿAbd al-Malik ibn Hishām, annotated by Fu'ād ibn ʿAlī Hāfiz (Beirut: Dār al-Kutub al-ʿIlmiyyah, 2000) 260; A. Guillaume (trans.), *The Life of Mohamed: A Translation of Ibn Ishaq: Sirat Rasul Allah* (Oxford: Oxford University Press, 2002) 159–61.

[54] Guillaume, *The Life of Mohamed* (n 53).

[55] Abdulrahman M. Alsumah, 'The Sunni Concept of Jihad in Classical Fiqh and Modern Islamic Thought' (PHD Thesis presented at University of Newcastle, 1998) 178.

[56] Ibid.

[57] Reza Aslan, *No God But God: The Origins, Evolution and Future of Islam* (New York, NY: Random House Trade, 2011) 52.

ideal' inspired the various Islamic revivalist movements of the eighteenth and nineteenth centuries, all of which strove to return to the original values of the original 'Islamic State'.[58]

Muhammad established the first Islamic state. Biographers agree that Muhammad's biggest achievements in Medina were building a mosque, establishing a brotherhood between the Meccan immigrants (*al-Muhajrin*) and the Medinian Muslims (*al-Ansar*), and concluding a peace treaty with the Jews of Medina.[59] In this year, Muslims were authorized for the first time to fight back or, more precisely, to defend themselves. It was stated in *Quran* as follows: 'Permission [to fight] has been given to those who are being fought, because they were wronged. And indeed, Allah is competent to give them victory.'[60] 'They' were identified as 'those who have been evicted from their homes without right—only because they say, "Our Lord is Allah" '.[61] Another command was then revealed that rather limits this authorization of defensive Jihad.[62] These rules are considered as the *jus ad bellum* of the Muslims during the period from 622 to 632,[63] throughout which Muhammad fought most of his battles (*Ghazwat*) against the idolaters of *Quraysh* and the Jewish tribes who breached the peace treaty.[64]

In the last year of the Medinan Period, one year before Muhammad's death, however, two verses were revealed to create a controversy that persists to this day. These two verses command Muslims to conduct an offensive Jihad to kill the Polytheists and the People of the Book (Jews, Christians, and Sabians) unless they embraced Islam or accepted to pay *Jizya* (protection tax paid by the People of the Book).[65] Chapter 2 will thoroughly discuss the Islamic *jus ad bellum* and in particular the authenticity and the legitimacy of the notion of offensive Jihad.[66]

[58] Ibid.

[59] Mohamed Hammidullah, *The Battlefield of the Prophet Muhammad, with Maps, Illustration and Sketches: A Continuation in Muslim Military History* (New Delhi: Kitab Bhavan, 2003) 16.

[60] See *Quran* (22:39).

[61] See *Quran* (22:40).

[62] 'Fight in the cause of Allah those who fight you but do not transgress. Indeed. Allah does not like transgressors.' *Quran* (2:190).

[63] Niaz A. Shah, 'The Use of Force Under Islamic Law', *The European Journal of International Law* (2013) 24(1), 343–65.

[64] Al-Dawoody, *The Islamic Law of War: Justifications and Regulations* (n 52) 24–9.

[65] 'And when the sacred months have passed, then kill the polytheists wherever you find them and capture them and besiege them and sit in wait for them at every place of ambush. But if they should repent, establish prayer, and give *zakah*, let them [go] on their way. Indeed, Allah is Forgiving and Merciful.' See *Quran* (9:5): 'Fight those who do not believe in Allah or in the Last Day and who do not consider unlawful what Allah and His Messenger have made unlawful and who do not adopt the religion of truth from those who were given the Scripture—[fight] until they give the *jizyah* willingly while they are humbled.' See *Quran* (9:29).

[66] Just to give you a glimpse of the controversy revolves around this topic, Professor Sohail H. Hashmi refutes the idea of the existence of any verse that justify the offensive jihad in *Quran*, considering that

(ii) Jihad in the Rightly Guided Caliphs Period

Following the death of Muhammad, a disagreement ensued in deciding who should serve as the leader of the Islamic nation. A majority of Muslims believed that the head of the Islamic state, the Caliph, should be chosen from the group of companions to Muhammad, as selected by the leadership of the Prophet's tribe, the *Quraysh*.[67] A minority of Muslims, however, believed that only direct kin should follow in the line of succession from the Prophet and that Ali (Muhammad's cousin and son-in-law, who married his daughter Fatima) should be named the first Caliph. In the end, Ali was passed over in favour of Muhammad's long-time follower Abu Bakr, selected in 632 to serve as the first Caliph.[68] The issues surrounding the leadership of Islam continually plagued the early Muslim community and set the foundation for the future sectarian division between Sunni and Shiite today.

In the beginning of the period of the first Caliph, Abu Bakr, a new form of Jihad floated to the surface, namely Jihad against apostasy (*Riddah* wars). As soon as the Prophet was declared dead, many of the Najd's tribes decided not to pay *Zakat* (Muslim taxes) to Abu Bakr, the new Caliph of the Islamic state.[69] Those tribes rejected one of the five pillars of Islam and also obedience to the new governor.[70] Thus, the Caliph prepared the *Ummah* for Jihad and sent a large army under the command of Khalid bin al-Walid.[71] The apostates were

'the Jihad tradition is parallel to the "just war" tradition in the West, acknowledging that violence is evil, but it may be justifiable in certain circumstances. Only two verses, the 'verses of the sword' suggest an interpretation of 'conquering people with the ultimate goal of converting them to Islam'. Hashmi considers that 'scholars after Muhammad death concentrated on [these verses] because they wanted to justify the expansion of Islam as an empire (an expansionist jihad), whereas the *Quran* overwhelmingly speaks of defensive wars only'. See Richard Bonney, *Jihad from Quran to Bin Laden* (New York, NY: Palgrave Macmillan, 2004) 14.

[67] See 'A Concise Summary of the Evolution of Islamic Law (Sharia) from its Inception to the Present'. Available at: <http://www.upenn.edu/emeritus/events/IslamicLaw.pdf> (last accessed 25 May 2019).

[68] Ibid.

[69] Hugh Kennedy, *The Prophet and the Age of the Caliphates: The Islamic Near East from the Sixth to the Eleventh Century* (London: Longman, 1986) 54.

[70] Ibid.

[71] If a group of people abstains from paying *Zakah* though acknowledging its legality, they must be fought until they pay it. This is confirmed by *Abu Hurairah's* narration that '[w]hen the Messenger of Allah (peace be upon him) deceased and Abu Bakr was appointed Caliph, some Arab tribes apostatized. 'Umar said to Abu Bakr, "Why would you fight these people while Allah's Messenger (peace be upon him) said: I have been directed to fight against people till they testify that there is no god but Allah. Whoever professes it is granted full protection of his property and life except for a right cause and his (other) affairs rest with Allah?" Upon this Abu Bakr said, "By Allah, I would definitely fight against those who make a difference between Prayer and *Zakah*, for it is the obligation upon the rich. By Allah, I would fight against them even if they withheld a cord (used for hobbling the feet of a camel) which they used to give to Allah's Messenger (peace be upon him) (as Zakah)." 'Umar said, "Then I became convinced that Abu Bakr was right."' See Obligations and Conditions of Zakat. Available at: <http://www.zakatguide.org/english/condition_zakat.html> (last accessed 25 May 2019).

defeated and agreed to pay *Zakat* and also to be under the control of the Islamic state. Islamic commentators argue that the *Riddah* wars represented Abu Bakr's conscious effort to preserve the unity of the Arabs under the eternal banner of Islam and the centralized unified authority of Medina, and thus to prevent the *Ummah* from falling back into the old tribal system,[72] but this should not be confused with religious wars, as Abu Bakr's war was intended to reinforce the purely political interest of Medina.[73] Still, these *Riddah* wars had the regrettable consequence of perpetually associating 'apostasy (denying the one faith) with treason (denying the central authority of the Caliph)'.[74] Simply because religious affiliations and citizenships were nearly identical terms in seventh-century Arabia, apostasy and treason were considered one and the same.[75] Following this precedent, the Islamic scholar Ibn Taymiyyah (d. 1328) stated that if any group belonging to Islam rejects any of the five pillars of Islam, 'Muslims agrees that they have to face Jihad as Abu Bakr waged it against Najd's tribes'.[76] This is despite the fact that nowhere in the *Quran* is any earthly punishment proscribed for apostasy.

During the reign of Umar (Second Caliph) and Uthman (Third Caliph), wars were a mix between defensive and offensive Jihad against polytheists and the People of the Book. By 641, Umar presided over the rise of Islamic power through military endeavours into modern day Iraq, Syria, Palestine, and Egypt. Islamic historian Karen Armstrong notes that the Muslim wars of expansion were not a 'divine mandate to conquer the world' but rather a desire to further the national interests of the state that were advanced by a unified Islamic community.[77] However, the reign of Uthman witnessed the first large-scale state of rebellion against a Muslim ruler through which he neither used force against the rebels nor gave up power. Uthman's reign was characterized by a lack of strong leadership and a rise in tribal factions, which eventually led to Uthman's assassination in 656.[78]

Uthman's death paved the road for Ali to ascend to the position of the fourth Caliph. Ali came to power in 656 overloaded by two strong emerging

[72] Aslan, *No God But God* (n 57) 121.
[73] Ibid.
[74] Ibid.
[75] Ibid.
[76] Ahmad ibn ʿAbd al-Halīm Ibn Taymiyyah. *Majmūʿ Fatāwā Shaykh al-Islām Ahmad Ibn Taymiyyah*, compiled by ʿAbd al-Rahman ibn Muhammad ibn Qāsim al-ʿĀsimī, Vol. 28 (Cairo: Maktabah ibn Taymiyyah, n.d.) 356.The Five Pillars of Islam are the framework of the Islamic creed, namely: the testimony of faith, prayer, paying alms—*zakat* (support of the needy), fasting during the month of Ramadan, and the pilgrimage to Makkah once in a lifetime for those who are able to do it.
[77] Karen Armstrong, *Islam: A Short History* (New York, NY: Random House Inc., 2002) 27–30.
[78] Rgheb Al-Sergani, *Islamic History Encyclopedia* (Cairo: Iqraa Foundation, 2013) 160–230.

opposition movements that were aggrieved by Ali's failure to bring Caliph Uthman's murderers to justice.[79] The first one led by Aisha, Abu Bakr's daughter and Muhammad's widow, and the second by Muawiyah, the governor of Syria appointed by Uthman, who refused to pledge allegiance to Ali. While Ali's armies were able to withstand the rebellion of Aisha's forces, the first time a Caliph fought against another Muslim army (Battle of the *Camel*), a more serious challenge was posed by Muawiyah.[80]

The battle (Battle of Siffin) between Ali's armies and Muawiyah's armies was long and bloody. When Muawiyah witnessed that Ali's forces were on the brink of victory, he asked his troops to raise copies of *Quran* on theirs spears: a message signalling his desire to surrender for arbitration.[81] Ali, abiding by the Islamic *jus ad bellum*, accepted the arbitration.[82] The arbitration declared Uthman's murder to have been unjust and worthy of retribution. This was a decision that at least on the surface seemed to justify Muawiyah's rebellion.[83] Ali's acceptance to the arbitration had, however, led to the emergence of a new opposition, namely the *kharijites* (splitters) who wanted to continue the fight against Muawiyah's army.[84] Ali was then reluctantly forced to send the army to fight the *kharijites* who seceded from it. They were defeated in the Battle of *Nahrwan*.[85] In 661, a *kharijite* killed Ali to leave the way open to Muawiyah to ascend to the position of the Caliph and proceeded to turn the Islamic empire into a familial monarchy.[86] It is noteworthy to elaborate that *kharijites* were a group that adopted a unique interpretation and understanding of Islamic law. Some modern Islamic scholars argue that the *kharijites* were obsessed with judging who could and could not be considered as a Muslim.[87] According to the *kharijites*, anyone who disobeyed any of the Quranic prescriptions or violated the example of the Prophet in any way was to be considered a *Kafir* (unbeliever), and immediately expelled from the *Ummah*.[88] *Kharijites* can be considered the first Muslim 'extremists' and although the group itself lasted only a few centuries, its ultra-conservative doctrines and ideologies were adopted by succeeding generations of extremists to give religious sanction to their political rebellions against both Muslims and non-Muslims governments.[89]

79 John Esposito, *Islam the Straight Path* (Oxford: Oxford University Press, 2005) 37.
80 Ibid., 38.
81 Aslan, *No God But God* (n 57) 137.
82 'But if they cease, then there is to be no aggression except against the oppressors.' See *Quran* (2:193).
83 Aslan, *No God But God* (n 57) 137.
84 Ibid.
85 Al-Sergani, *Islamic History Encyclopedia* (n 78) 149–56.
86 Esposito, *Islam the Straight Path* (n 79) 38.
87 Aslan, *No God But God* (n 57) 135.
88 Ibid.
89 Ibid.

(iii) Jihad during the Umayyad Caliphate Period (661–750)

Under Muawiyah, the seat of the Caliphate was moved to Damascus and the institutional spheres of the Islamic empire were strengthened.[90] The Umayyad Empire achieved an unprecedented expansion of the Islamic state. By the time Muawiyah became Caliph, Islam had spread to Egypt, Libya, Syria, Iraq, Persia, and the borders of Afghanistan.[91] The expansionary military conquests under the Umayyad Empire additionally led to Islamic control over the Maghreb (North Africa), Spain, and Portugal.[92] It was clear that the offensive Jihad verses in the *Quran*—now commonly referred to as the 'sword verses'—were used by Islamic jurists during this era to support the permissible territorial expansion of the empire.[93]

To deepen the conflict between Sunni and Shiite, after the death of Muawiyah in 680, his son Yazid was named Caliph and inherited a challenge to his power posed by the resurgence of the followers of Ali (Shiite), led by Ali's son Husayn.[94] Husayn, who long refused the legitimacy of the Umayyad Caliphate that rose to power following the death of his father, sustained political support among ethnic Persians who rejected the Arab-dominated Umayyad Empire.[95] Husayn and his outnumbered forces fought against Yazid's army but were massacred on the field of battle, becoming martyrs for their beliefs.[96] The distinction between Sunni and Shiite was significantly cemented by this battle and led to the development of distinct religious, legal, and cultural practices within the two sects that continue to influence the conflicts, boundaries, and politics of the Middle East today.[97]

By 720, the Umayyad Empire lost all the power to withstand the spectre of revolt. Various ethnic and tribal groups significantly challenged and weakened the ruling authority.[98] One notable faction consisted of pious Muslims from various ethnic backgrounds who claimed the Umayyad Empire departed from

[90] 'A Concise Summary of the Evolution of Islamic Law (Sharia) from its Inception to the Present' (n 67) 1.

[91] Esposito, *Islam the Straight Path* (n 79) 40.

[92] Ibid.

[93] Ibid.

[94] Ibid., 33.

[95] Vali Nasr, *The Shia Revival: How Conflicts Within Islam Will Shape the Future* (New York, NY: W.W. Norton & Company Inc., 2007) 40.

[96] Ibid., 41.

[97] Contemporary Shia expert Vali Nasr analogizes the Sunni-Shia split to that of the Protestants and Catholics in Western Christianity, noting that 'just as past intra-Christian politics shaped European politics, so the Sunni Shia conflict continues to shape the history of the Islamic world and the broader Middle East'. Ibid., 34.

[98] Esposito, *Islam the Straight Path* (n 79) 50.

Islamic law, condemning the Umayyads' policies as purely 'un-Islamic innovations'.[99] In 747, a rebel group supported a freed Abbasid slave Abu al-Abbas to lead the opposition against the Umayyads.[100] Backed by the Shiite community, the rebellion led to the fall of the Umayyad Empire. In 750 Abu al-Abbas was named the first Caliph of the Abbasid Caliphate.[101]

(iv) Jihad during the Abbasid Caliphate (750–1258)

Western literature remembers the Abbasid Empire (750–1258) best for its great economic, scientific, and cultural advancements, later viewed as the golden age of the Islamic civilization.[102] By the tenth century, however, the Abbasid Caliphate was unable to maintain sufficient governmental authority over its vast territory, and rebellions spread across its territories.[103] Two groups gained control over the Caliphate: the Buyids (945–1055), a Persian Shiite dynasty, and the Seljuks (1055–1258), a Turkish Sunni dynasty.[104]

The Crusades (1095–1453) began when the Abbasid Seljuk army defeated the Christian army of the Byzantine Empire. In response, Byzantine Emperor Alexius I called on a unification of Christendom to fight the 'infidel' Islamic state and liberate Jerusalem from Muslims' rule.[105] The victory of the First Crusade recaptured Jerusalem under the Byzantine control in 1099, but the brutality that the Christian forces employed was remembered by future generations of Muslims as a means of cultivating anti-Christian sentiment.[106] In this respect, Bernard Lewis notes that although the events of the First Crusade are cited by modern Islamists as an injustice by the Christians, including in the contemporary rhetoric of Usama Bin Laden, the historical record proposes that at the time the Islamic empire was indifferent to the loss of Jerusalem to the Crusaders.[107] Christian rule over Jerusalem following the First Crusade did not last long. In 1187 the famed Islamic military leader Saladin led the effort to recapture the city and return it to Islamic reign.[108] A massive amount of Islamic

[99] Ibid.
[100] Ibid.
[101] Ibid.
[102] Bernard Lewis, *The Crisis of Islam: Holy War and Unholy Terror* (New York, NY: Random House Trade, 2004) 4.
[103] Esposito, *Islam the Straight Path* (n 79) 56.
[104] Richard Martin, 'Political Growth of the Islamic Empire' in Clarice Swisher (ed.), *The Spread of Islam* (San Diego, CA: Greenhaven Press, 1999) 79, 82.
[105] Esposito, *Islam the Straight Path* (n 79) 58–9.
[106] Ibid.
[107] Lewis, *The Crisis of Islam'* (n 102) 47.
[108] Esposito, *Islam the Straight Path* (n 79) 59.

literature has been written on this battle (Battle of *Hattin*).[109] By the thirteenth century, following the successful conquests of Genghis Khan's Mongol Empire throughout Central Asia, China, and Russia, in 1258, the Abbasid Caliphate found itself subjected to the same fate.[110] When the grandson of Ghengis Kahn, Hulagu Kahn, eviscerated the capital of Baghdad and executed the Caliph and his family, the reign of the Abbasid Caliphate officially came to an end.[111]

During this particular phase, however, we cannot omit the rise of the most influential Islamic thinker and ideologue of virtually all the Jihadist movements today, Ibn-Taymiyyah (d. 1328). Ibn-Taymiyyah was the first to issue a *fatwa* against Muslims when he declared that the Mongols (converted to Islam), who were locked in a vicious struggle with the Muslim rulers of Egypt, were apostates due to their failure to implement Islamic law.[112] Ibn-Taymiyyah's labelling of the Mongols as apostates is still used by Jihadist groups until today to draw an analogy to governments run by Muslims who similarly fail to implement Islamic law. He also provided the theological groundwork for allowing the killing of Muslims as 'collateral damage' by saying '[i]f with the Kuffar (unbelievers) there are some pious people from the best of mankind and it is not possible to fight these Kuffar except by killing them, then they are to be killed as well'.[113]

(v) Jihad during the Ottoman Caliphate (1492–1918)

The Ottoman Empire developed out of the vacuum of power left by the successors of Genghis Kahn and maintained a proud Mongol-Turkish tradition that fused militancy and a strong connection to classical Islam.[114] The Ottomans extended their dominance over the Arab Middle East and North Africa.[115] Successive Ottoman military victories also led to the incorporation of Greece, Cyprus, the Balkans, and the majority of Eastern Europe.[116] However, efforts to further the Ottoman's expansionist Jihad were kept in check by the victories

[109] This literature will be discussed in Chapter 3 related to the Islamic *jus in bello*.
[110] Esposito, *Islam the Straight Path* (n 79) 59.
[111] Ibid.
[112] Christopher Henzel, 'The Origins of *Al-Qaeda*'s Ideology: Implications for US Strategy', *Parameters: The US Army War College Quarterly* (2005) 35(1), 69–80, 71.
[113] Abdulla Azzam, 'Defense of Muslim Lands'. Available at <http://www.religioscope.com/info/doc/jihad/azzam_defence_3_chap1.htm> (last accessed 25 May 2019).
[114] Esposito, *Islam the Straight Path* (n 79) 61.
[115] Ibid.
[116] Ibid.

of both Mediterranean Christians in 1580 and Eastern Europeans in Vienna in 1683.[117]

The rapid decline in the power of the Islamic empires enabled some traditionalist Arabian Muslims to gain momentum in their objective to effectuate a return to classical practices and teachings of Islam. Muhammad Ibn-Abd-al-Wahhab (d. 1791), an Islamic legal theologian who endorsed to the ideas of Ibn-Taymiyya and the conservative *Hanbali* school, became the primary revivalist of the early eighteenth century.[118] He called for an Islam 'that returned to its revealed sources'.[119] Like Ibn-Taymiyyah, Ibn-Abd-al-Wahhab called for a literal interpretation of the *Quran*. Ibn-Abd-al-Wahhab was the first to reintroduce the *Kharijite* concept of *takfir*. Derived from the Arabic word for declaring someone to be a disbeliever, *takfir* is the process of declaring another Muslim to be an apostate and, thus, indicating that it is legitimate to kill that person.[120] In helping the al-Saud family take control of the Arabian Peninsula, Ibn-Abd-al-Wahhab was given the opportunity to shape the state's religious beliefs and provide key philosophical rationales for future generations to pursue the global Jihad, thereafter known as the *Wahhabi* Movement.[121] The end of the nineteenth century witnessed the decay of the last Islamic Caliphate and the rise of the Western European powers, which was accompanied by the rise of capitalism. This was, indeed, the first experience of Islam since its inception as being politically and economically subservient to 'Christian' states. A new encounter that paved the way to what is called 'Islamic revivalism'.

(vi) Jihad in the Post World Wars Period (1918–1979)

In 1914, the Ottomans aligned with imperial Germany and the Austro-Hungarian Empire, joining a military alliance known as the Central Powers. Upon the defeat of the Central Powers, the victorious Allied powers of England, France, and Russia administered the international post-war environment that gave rise to four imperative developments in the Islamic world.[122] First, the dissolution of the Ottoman Empire and the consequent creation of a secular Turkish state with the rise of Kamal Ataturk, who instigated an unprecedented

[117] Ibid.
[118] Ibid., 118–19.
[119] Devin R. Springer, James L. Regens, and David N. Edger, *Islamic Radicalism and Global Jihad* (Washington, DC: Georgetown University Press, 2009) 30.
[120] Ibid.
[121] Ibid.
[122] Raj Bhala, *Understanding Islamic Law* (New York: LexisNexis, 2011) 250.

program of economic modernization and religious secularization.[123] Second, the creation of the modern state of Iran in the Persian lands, ruled by the autocracy of Reza Khan, who seized power and proclaimed himself *shah* of Iran in 1925. Unlike Ataturk, Reza Khan did not denounce or untangle the roots of *Shiite* Islam within the state or Iranian civil society.[124] Third, the official recognition of statehood of the Kingdom of Saudi Arabia. In 1924, Abd al-'Aziz Ibn Saud, the leading descendant of the Saudi tradition that embraced the Wahhabi ideology, gained control over the Islamic holy lands of Mecca and Medina.[125] Fourth, the increased immigration of Eastern European Jews to Palestine due to the rise of religious persecution across Europe following the First World War, which fostered the momentum of the Jewish Zionist movement.[126] Moreover, the 1917 Balfour Declaration, which announced British support for the creation of a 'National Home for the Jews in Palestine', had a significant impact on the Islamic world because Britain maintained administrative control over Palestine's majority Muslim population, and the prospect of a Jewish state in Palestine potentially challenged Islamic interests and created the bloodiest, most protracted conflict in the Middle East today.[127]

After the victory of the Allies (the United States, Britain, and the Soviet Union) in the Second World War, Western countries occupied number of Islamic states and some elements of the colonial order remained, especially the presence of the French in North Africa and the British in India and the Middle East. The Muslim communities across the Islamic world suffered political, economic, and social frustration. As a response to the British colonial powers in Egypt and India, two Islamic organizations were created: (i) the Muslim Brotherhood in Egypt, led by Hassan al-Banna (d. 1949) and (ii) the *Jamaat e-Islami* in India led by Abul Ala Maududi (d. 1979). The two groups called for the end of colonization in Islamic countries and for the creation of a unified Islamic nation that is based on Islamic values. The lasting ideological and organizational influence of both groups was self-confessed during the latter half of the twentieth century when both movements spread throughout the larger Islamic world: the Muslim Brotherhood continued to grow throughout Sudan, Syria, Jordan, Palestine, Algeria, Morocco, the Kingdom of Saudi Arabia, and

[123] Bernard Lewis, *The Middle East: A Brief History of the Last 2,000 Years* (New York, NY: Scribner, 1995) 345–6.
[124] Ibid.
[125] Ibid., 344.
[126] Ibid., 348.
[127] Ibid., 348.

Kuwait; while *Jamaat e-Islami* expanded to India, Afghanistan, Kashmir, and Pakistan.[128]

In Egypt, however, the Islamic ideology turned into a dramatically different level of extremism after the former President Gamal Abd al-Nasser rose to power. In 1952, the Muslim Brotherhood supported Nasser and his cronies to launch a military coup that ousted King Farouk. The Brotherhood hoped to establish a predominantly Islamic-based community. However, under Nasser's Arab-nationalist agenda (socialism), Islam was pushed out of the public sphere. The Brotherhood felt betrayed by Nasser and started protesting and campaigning against him. Some claimed that they even tried to assassinate him.[129] The government then allegedly initiated a wide-scale security campaign against the Brotherhood by attacking its headquarters, arresting and torturing its leaders and members, and by launching a severe public defamation campaign against them through the use of state-owned media machinery and propaganda. However, these alleged suppressive measures taken by Nasser's government failed to end its problems with Islamist groups.[130] Throughout the rest of the century, Egypt's leaders resorted to mass arrests, torture, and execution in their battle against political Islam. Many of the men who were arrested and subjected to harsh treatment in Nasser's prison camps were ultimately released after negotiations between the Egyptian government and the Islamists movements.[131] Once released, number of them became the new voices of Islamic extremism, affecting successor generations both inside and outside Egypt. Among the Brotherhood leaders was the outspoken Egyptian Islamist Sayyid Qutb, who is one of the most prominent ideologues for *Al-Qaeda*, ISIS, and many other Jihadist groups today. As mentioned before, Jihadists group interpreted Qutb's ideas, provided in his manuscript 'Milestones', as a justification for Muslims to target secularized societies seen as *Jahili* and thus enemies of Islam.[132] In August 1966, Qutb was hanged along with two of his companions. He died before being able to clarify his concept of *Jahilya* and its various implications. The Jihadists, however, take this concept today in its most literal form. Contrary to the expectations of the Egyptian government, the prisons that hosted members of the Egyptian Muslim Brotherhood served as schools for the indoctrination of the future leaders of the global Jihad, such as Abdullah Azzam and Ayman al-Zawahiri.

[128] Esposito, *Islam the Straight Path* (n 79) 151–3.
[129] Springer, Regens, and Edger, *Islamic Radicalism and Global Jihad* (n 119) 21.
[130] Ibid.
[131] Ibid.
[132] Ibid., 34.

(vii) The Anti-Soviet Union Jihad in Afghanistan (1979–1989)

In 1979, the Soviet Union decided to invade Afghanistan to support its new communist government. At that moment, Afghanis decided to take up arms to resist Soviet forces, which initiated a decade-long conflict. Although the resistance movements were largely composed of Afghani nationals, Muslims from around the world rallied to the call for anti-Soviet Jihad. Palestinian Islamic scholar Abdullah Azzam, and Usama Bin Laden, the son of a wealthy businessman with close ties to the Saudi royal family, were among those who came from the Middle East to participate in the Jihad. Azzam and Bin Laden quickly established a wide facilitation network for providing foreign fighters for the Jihad.[133] Their organization became known as Maktab al-Khidmat (MAK), which literally means the Services Bureau. The MAK created a global network of financiers and recruiters to bring fighters from around the globe, particularly Arab Muslims from the Middle East, to Pakistan and Afghanistan.[134] Once they had arrived there, the foreign fighters were often hosted in MAK guesthouses before traveling to the frontlines. Azzam's *fatwa* characterization of the Jihad in Afghanistan as an individual duty—*fard ayn*—aided the MAK's objectives,[135] given that Jihad has traditionally been recognized as a collective duty—*fard Kifaya*.[136] The MAK brought fighters from around the world and in particular Arabs from the Middle East. For instance, a contingent of Egyptians, including Ayman al-Zawahiri, the Egyptian *Islamic Jihad* group's leader at the time, joined Azzam and Bin Laden.

Azzam, in his influential tract *Join the Caravan*,[137] wrote that one of the reasons for Jihad was to control some territory militarily that could serve as a homeland for the Jihadists and their supporters:

> [The] establishment of the Muslim community on an area of land is a necessity, as vital as water and air. This homeland will not come about without an organized Islamic movement which perseveres consciously and realistically upon Jihad, and which regards fighting as a decisive factor and as a protective

[133] Ibid., 13.

[134] Ibid.

[135] Ibid.

[136] *Fard kifaya* means an obligation that should be carried out by the community and not mandatory for individuals as long as the community sends a sufficient number of individual *Mujahdien*. While *fard ayn* means an obligation to be carried out by every Muslim as a requirement of Islam along with daily prayer and fasting Ramadan and so on. Ibid., 43.

[137] Abulla Azzam, 'Join the Caravan'. Available at: <https://archive.org/stream/JoinTheCaravan/JoinTheCaravan_djvu.txt> (last accessed 25 May 2019).

> cover. The Islamic movement will not be able to establish the Islamic community except through a common people's Jihad which has the Islamic movement as its beating heart and deliberating mind.[138]

After Moscow's announcement in April 1988 that Soviet forces would withdraw from Afghanistan over the next nine months, Azzam and Bin Laden started planning the MAK's future. It was during this time period that *Al-Qaeda* was formally created by Azzam and Bin Laden.[139] Although both of them wanted to preserve the MAK's facilitation network and bring its resources to bear in future Jihadist campaigns, they had two very different visions for its future and thus the future of Jihad in the world.[140] Azzam, who was firmly committed to strengthening Jihadists' control of Afghanistan, preferred to continue the MAK's support to the Afghan resistance.[141] He also expressed an interest in organizing a similar resistance movement against Israel on behalf of the Palestinians. Bin Laden seems to have shared the viewpoint of the Egyptian wing of *Al-Qaeda*, which favoured using *Al-Qaeda* to prepare fighters for conflicts elsewhere—in Bin Laden's view, worldwide.[142] This dispute over the strategic direction of *Al-Qaeda*, in addition to Bin Laden's tendencies to become the unchallenged leader of the group,[143] drove Bin Laden and Azzam apart. Bin Laden was, at this time, already the *amir* (leader) of *Al-Qaeda*. However, Azzam remained an influential figure among foreign fighters. This schism within *Al-Qaeda* and the struggle over its leadership and future direction were resolved while Bin Laden was back in his home country, Saudi Arabia. Azzam and his son were killed by a car bomb in Peshawar, Pakistan, on 24 November 1989. Azzam's assassination remains unsolved but many suspect that the Egyptian wing of *Al-Qaeda*, led by Ayman al-Zawahiri, were involved in this incident, given their desire to see *Al-Qaeda* pursue a global strategy.[144] At this particular time, the stated objective of *Al-Qaeda* shifted its focus on overthrowing Islamic dictators in the Middle East so as to return the Muslim community to the true form of classical Islam.[145]

138 Ibid.

139 Sean P. Wilson, 'The Evolution of *Al-Qaeda*' (unpublished MA thesis, American Military University, 2007). 13.

140 Springer, Regens, and Edger, *Islamic Radicalism and Global Jihad* (n 119) 14.

141 Ibid.

142 Ibid.

143 Wilson, 'The Evolution of *Al-Qaeda*' (n 139) 13.

144 Springer, Regens, and Edger, *Islamic Radicalism and Global Jihad* (n 119) 14.

145 Wilson, 'The Evolution of *Al-Qaeda*' (n 139) 13.

(viii) Jihad in the Middle East and Africa (1989–2001)

After a peace treaty was reached to end the Iran–Iraq War in Saddam Hussein's slim favour, it encouraged the bolstered Iraqi dictator to embark on the annexation of an oil-rich neighbour country, the small Sunni Arab state of Kuwait.[146] In response, Bin Laden offered the *al-Saud* royal family of the Kingdom of Saudi Arabia, which aligned in defence of the sovereignty of the state of Kuwait, the support of *Al-Qaeda* to defend it against the Iraqi acts of aggression.[147] Bin Laden's offer was rejected by the Saudi leadership in favour of US troops, who utilized Saudi military bases within the territory of the Kingdom to efficaciously launch counter-attacks on Iraq in the Gulf War.[148] Furious with this turn of events, Bin Laden and a number of other Saudi Islamists denounced the Saudi royal family's decision to welcome non-Muslim military forces into the land of the two holy mosques (the Kingdom of Saudi Arabia).[149] As a result, Bin Laden was placed under surveillance and subjected to an augmented level of pressure by the Saudi government.[150] In response to the Saudi government's actions, Bin Laden accepted the offer of the Islamist Sudanese political leader Hassan al-Turabi, who had urged him to move his organization to Sudan.[151] Assured that he could freely prepare for future Jihad and manage the group's various business interests, instead of returning to Saudi Arabia after a 1991 trip to Pakistan Bin Laden moved to Sudan.[152]

During this period, *Al-Qaeda* expanded its contacts and global networks across the Middle East and Africa.[153] By this time Bin Laden had become a renowned Islamist in the ideologically influential areas of Egypt, the Arabian Peninsula, and the Afghanistan–Pakistan border region. In 1992, *Al-Qaeda* issued its first *fatwa* against the United States for its occupation of Muslim lands during the Gulf War.[154] Later, in a 1996 *fatwa*, Bin Laden called for a rebellion against the royal family in Saudi Arabia, as well as an attack against all US interests, which he criticized as the backbone of the Muslim governments.[155] In his *fatwa* against Saudi Arabia and the United States, Bin Laden attempted

146 Lewis, *The Middle East* (n 123) 369.
147 Wilson, 'The Evolution of *Al-Qaeda*' (n 139) 14.
148 Ibid.
149 Springer, Regens, and Edger, *Islamic Radicalism and Global Jihad* (n 119) 14.
150 Ibid.
151 Ibid., 14–15.
152 Ibid., 15.
153 National Commission on Terrorist Attacks upon the United States, '*The 9/11 Commission Report*', 86–90. Available at: <http://govinfo.library.unt.edu/911/report/911Report.pdf> (last accessed 25 May 2019).
154 Ibid., 57.
155 Wilson, 'The Evolution of *Al-Qaeda*' (n 139) 64.

to appeal to the larger Islamist cause with the hope that the message of *Al-Qaeda* would surpass ethnic and geographic boundaries of the modern Islamic world.[156] In response to these two fatwas, Sudan suffered significant pressure from Saudi Arabia and the United States to cease acting as a host country to Bin Laden and his *Al-Qaeda* followers and to expel him as soon as possible.[157] In 1996, Bin Laden and his supporters fled Sudan to take refuge with the Taliban in Afghanistan and they recognized Mullah Omar as *amir al-mu'minin* (the Commander of the Believers).[158] Recovering from the financial difficulties and other restrictions from which *Al-Qaeda* suffered in Sudan, Bin Laden and his supporters were given extraordinary protection and autonomy by Mullah Omar and the Taliban.[159] The Taliban allowed thousands of foreigners to enter Afghanistan to train at Bin Laden-sponsored training camps.[160]

In February 1998, Bin Laden issued another statement in which he declared that 'to kill the Americans and their allies—civilians and military—is an individual duty for every Muslim who can do it in any country in which it is possible to do it'.[161] Less than six months later, two car bombs were exploded outside of the American embassies in Nairobi, Kenya, and Dar es Salaam, Tanzania, by *Al-Qaeda* East African cells.[162] In January 2000, *Al-Qaeda* operatives attempted an unsuccessful attack against USS The Sullivans while it was anchored in Yemen.[163] Ten months later, on 12 October 2000, Bin Laden planned and coordinated a subsequent *Al-Qaeda* attack, utilizing explosives loaded on a small fibreglass boat exploded by two suicide bombers. This attack succeeded in severely damaging the USS Cole and resulted in killing seventeen and injuring thirty-seven crew during a port call in the Yemeni port of Aden.[164] At the same time, planning for the 11 September (9/11) attacks was well under way—an event that would change the politics of the world.

[156] Ibid., 64–5.

[157] Springer, Regens, and Edger, *Islamic Radicalism and Global Jihad* (n 119) 15.

[158] Ibid. Bin Laden's arrival coincided with the 1996 capture of Kabul by the Taliban (translated as 'students'), a group of ethnic Pashtun Sunni Muslims led by many individuals who studied at Islamic schools (*madrassas*) and trained in camps created by Bin Laden). See also Patricia Grossman, 'Afghanistan in the Balance', *Middle East Report* (2001) 221(Winter) 8–14. Available at: <http://people.uncw.edu/ricej/SOC490/Afghanistan%20in%20the%20Balance%20by%20Patricia%20Grossman.pdf> (last accessed 25 May 2019).

[159] Springer, Regens, and Edger, *Islamic Radicalism and Global Jihad* (n 119) 15.

[160] Ibid.

[161] The World Islamic Front statement (23 February 1998), in Bruce Lawrence (ed.), *Messages to the World: The Statements of Osama Bin Laden* (London: Verso, 2005) 61.

[162] Springer, Regens, and Edger, *Islamic Radicalism and Global Jihad* (n 119) 16.

[163] Ibid.

[164] Ibid.

(ix) Jihad in the Post-11 September Period

The attacks of 9/11 led to an instantaneous move in President George W. Bush's political agenda from a preliminary focus on domestic projects and policies to eight years presidency consumed by foreign policy, most specifically the 'war on terror'.[165] A pillar to his administration's counterterrorism policy was the enactment of the 'Bush Doctrine' which held, *inter alia*, that terrorist attacks would be treated as 'acts of war' and that the United States would make no distinction between terrorists and the states that harbour them.[166] Within a few weeks of 9/11, the United States waged a fully fledged war on Afghanistan to overthrow the Taliban and capture or kill Bin Laden. While the capital city of Kabul was under the US forces' control by mid-November, the *Al-Qaeda* leader evaded capture in Afghanistan and fled into the familiar, but to US forces, territorially unfriendly, mountainous border region with Pakistan.[167] Following the end of Taliban control in Afghanistan, the Bush administration shifted its attention towards Saddam Hussein, the Iraqi dictator. The primary justification provided by the United States in its case against Saddam Hussein was his alleged possession of weapons of mass destruction (WMD). Although US forces easily secured control of Iraq and captured Hussein in December 2003, the situation in Iraq quickly deteriorated as Iraqi militias representing sectarian Sunni, Shia, and Kurdish interests led the country to the brink of civil war.[168] Following the US invasion of Iraq, Islamist religious leaders, in particular those from Saudi Arabia, issued *fatwas* that called on Muslims to fight a defensive Jihad. This message resonated in particular with the Sunni community in Iraq.[169]

Led by Abu Musab al-Zarqawi, a Jordanian Jihadist who managed to move from Afghanistan to Iraq after the fall of the Taliban, al-Zarqawi's group began operating in Iraq under the name *al-Tawhid wa-al-Jihad* in 2003.[170] A year later, in 2004, Bin Laden approved al-Zarqawi's pledge of allegiance to join *Al-Qaeda*, which caused al-Tawhid wa-al-Jihad to acquire a new name: *Al-Qaeda*

[165] Steven W. Hook, *US Foreign Policy: The Paradox of World Power* (Washington, DC: CQ Press, 2008) 58.
[166] Ibid.
[167] Ibid., 59.
[168] Ibid., 57–61.
[169] Andrew M. Bennet, 'Islamic History & *Al-Qaeda*: A Primer to Understanding the Rise of Islamist Movements in the Modern World', *Pace International Law Review Online Companion* (2013) 3, 316–70, 361. Available at: <http://digitalcommons.pace.edu/cgi/viewcontent.cgi?article=1035&context=pilronline> (last accessed 25 May 2019).
[170] Muhammad al-Ubaydi, Nelly Lahoud, Daniel Milton, and Bryan Price, 'The Group That Calls Itself a State: Understanding the Evolution and Challenges of the Islamic State', *The Combating Terrorism Center at West Point* (2014) 1–102, 12.

in Mesopotamia (*Tanzim Al-Qaeda fi Bilad al-Rafidayn*).[171] The leading objectives of the group were, *in primis*, to further the *Al-Qaeda* narrative that Western countries and their puppet dictators in the Middle East have subjected Islam to war; to unify the various Islamist groups against a common enemy, namely the United States (in their language: the 'head of the snake'); and to provide a sanctuary for *Al-Qaeda* operatives and foreign Jihadists with the ultimate goal of establishing the Islamic Caliphate.[172] In January 2006, al-Zarqawi changed the name of the group to *Majlis Shura al-Mujahdien fi al-Iraq* (The Jihadists' Advisory Council in Iraq), which led to the merging of at least six Sunni militants groups.[173] The killing of al-Zarqawi in June 2006 did not lead his successor—Abu Hamza al-Muhajir—to give up on his plan of rebuilding an Islamic Caliphate. Based on this rationale, Abu Hamza pledged allegiance to Abu Umar al-Baghdadi's newly formed group the 'Islamic State of Iraq' (ISI), a group that both Western and regional media referred to as *Al-Qaeda* in Iraq. While there were indeed links between *Al-Qaeda* in Afghanistan and Pakistan and the fledgling ISI, the latter was from the very beginning never fully subordinate to *Al-Qaeda*.[174] It was evident that ISI did not want to limit its activities to militancy. In April 2007, ISI announced the appointment of ten ministers, including ministers for health, oil, agriculture, and fisheries, through which it clearly assumed the business of governance.[175] This new policy and the declaration of the state as such never met the content of *Al-Qaeda* leaders, as evidenced later in the letters that were captured during the raid of the US Navy SEALs that killed Bin Laden on 2 May 2011 in Pakistan.[176]

In April 2010, US and the Iraqi forces killed Abu Umar and Abu Hamza, leaving the leadership of ISI to Abu Bakr al-Baghdadi.[177] In late 2011, Baghdadi had sent a contingent of fighters to Syria to form a Jihadi group called *Jabhat al-Nusra* ('the Salvation Front'),[178] which quickly grew in popularity as the leading Sunni rebel militant group in the Syrian civil war.[179] In April 2013,

[171] Ibid.
[172] Nelson and Sanderson, 'Al Qaeda in Iraq' (n 169) 361. Available at: <http://digitalcommons.pace.edu/cgi/viewcontent.cgi?article=1035&context=pilronline> (last accessed 25 May 2019).
[173] al-Ubaydi et al., 'The Group That Calls Itself a State' (n 170) 13.
[174] Cole Bunzel, From Paper State to Caliphate: The Ideology of the Islamic State", *Analysis Paper No. 19*, Brookings Project, Center for Middle East Policy (2015), 1–45, 17. Available at: <http://www.brookings.edu/~/media/research/files/papers/2015/03/ideology-of-islamic-state-bunzel/the-ideology-of-the-islamic-state.pdf> (last accessed 25 May 2019).
[175] al-Ubaydi et al., 'The Group That Calls Itself a State' (n 170) 14.
[176] Ibid.
[177] Ibid., 15.
[178] The group is currently called *Hay'at Taḥrīr al-Shām* (Organization for the Liberation of the Levant).
[179] Abū Muhammad al-Jawlānī, *al-I'lān 'an Jabhat al-Nusra* (Minbar al-Tawh: Īd wa'l-Jihād, 2012). Available at: <http:/www.tawhed.ws/dl?i=0308141g> (last accessed 25 May 2019). It should be noted

al-Baghdadi unilaterally proclaimed the founding of the Islamic State in Iraq and Levant (ISIL) by declaring a merger between ISI and *Jabhat al-Nusra* in Syria. However, Abu Muhammad al-Julani, the *Jabhat al-Nusra*'s leader, publicly rejected the merger and pledged allegiance directly to al-Zawahiri, the leader of *Al-Qaeda* since the killing of Bin Laden.[180] It seems that al-Zawahiri sensed that the merger that al-Baghdadi was imposing on *Jabhat al-Nusra* amounted to a coup against *Al-Qaeda*; thus he intervened by annulling ISI's incorporation of Syria and ordered the groups to remain separate units observing separate jurisdictions in Iraq and Syria, respectively.[181] On 15 June, Baghdadi refuted Zawahiri, declaring that 'the Islamic State of Iraq and Sham will endure, so long as we have a vein that pulses and an eye that bats'.[182] In response, *Al-Qaeda* issued a statement officially dissociating itself from the ISIL.[183]

In June 2014, ISIL made a surprise move. The group swept into western Iraq nearly unimpeded, conquering most of the country's Sunni territories, including the city of Mosul. On 29 June, it finally declared itself the Caliphate in a triumphant audio address by Abu Muhammad al-'Adnani.[184] Henceforward, as Adnani announced, the group was no longer to be known 'the Islamic State of Iraq and Sham' but simply as 'the Islamic State' (IS). Its sovereignty was to extend across the entire world, not just Iraq and Syria. Five days later, Abu Bakr al-Baghdadi made his first public appearance, delivering a sermon from the pulpit of the great mosque of Mosul. Quoting the accession speech of the first Sunni Muslim Caliph (Abu Bakr al-Siddiq), he channelled the memory of the early Islamic Caliphate.[185] Here, it is worth mentioning that IS is neither worried about statehood recognition nor membership in the United Nations to be

that Jabhat Al-Nusra was the first Jihadist group to emerge in Syria and in its nascent phase, it was praised even by non-Jihadists for its effective conduct on the battlefield and its dealing with the populace.

[180] Abū Muhammad al-Jawlānī, *Kalima sawtiyya lil-fātih. Abī Muh. Ammad al-Jawlānī* (Mu'assasat al-Manāra al-Bayda, 10 April 2013). Available at: <http://occident2.blogspot.com/2013/04/text-of-jabhat-al-nusras-amir-abu.html> (last accessed 25 May 2019).

[181] Ayman al-Zawāhirī, 'Letter to Abū Bakr al-Baghdādī and Abū Muhammad al-Jawlānī', 23 May 2013. Available at: <http://www.aljazeera.com/news/middleeast/2013/06/2013699425657882.html> (last accessed 25 May 2019).

[182] Speech of Abū Bakr al-Baghdādī, 'Bāqiya fī 'l-'Irāq wa'-l-Shām', *Mu'assasat al-Furqān*, 15 June 2013. Available (in Arabic) at: <https://archive.org/details/glxglx151_yahoo> (last accessed 25 May 2019).

[183] 'Bayān bi-sha'n 'alāqat Jamā'at Qā'idat al-Jihād bi-Jamā'at 'al-Dawla al-Islāmiyya fī 'l-'Irāq wa'l-Shām'. Available (in Arabic) at: <http://www.arrahmah.com/arabic/tnzym-qadt-al-jhad-al-qyadt-al-amt-byan-bshan-alaqt-jmat-qadt-al-jhad-bjmat-ad-dwlt-al-islamyt.html> (last accessed 25 May 2019).

[184] Speech of Abu Muhammad al-Adnānī, 'Hādha wa'd Allāh', 2014. Available (in Arabic) at: <https://archive.org/details/Waad_201408> (last accessed 25 May 2019).

[185] Bunzel, 'From Paper State to Caliphate' (n 174) 31. Available at: <http://www.brookings.edu/~/media/research/files/papers/2015/03/ideology-of-islamic-state-bunzel/the-ideology-of-the-islamic-state.pdf> (last accessed 25 May 2019).

part of the global community of nation states[186] as it believes that the world order is illegitimate. Instead, it seeks to redraw today's world map and create a global Islamic state, a Caliphate, akin to the one that predates the modern state system.[187] In conformity with this objective, the group had intended to pursue the acquisition of additional territories beyond Iraq and Syria. Al-Baghdadi, in his only speech, promised that if the Muslim Mujahidin remain united and commit themselves to being the 'guardians of religion' they 'shall conquer Rome and seize the earth, asserting that the day will come when the Muslim will walk everywhere as master'.[188] These expansionist ambitions, however, faced a significant defeat in late 2017 when IS suffered strategic military setbacks in Iraq and Syria. Islamic State's loss of control over its strongholds in urban areas forced the group to evolve and transform from a hierarchically organized group, focusing on conquering and holding territory, to a networked group, emphasizing 'terror attacks' within and outside the conflict zones.[189] Despite its recent setbacks, 'the group and its affiliates continue to pose a significant and evolving threat around the world', as clearly demonstrated in the recent report of the UN Secretary General on the threat posed by ISIL to international peace and security.[190]

3. Conclusion

This chapter introduced Islamic law as a legal system which is rooted in history but very much alive today, a law that entails a comprehensive set of rules concerning the rights and obligations of Muslims—including rules regulating Muslims' conducts in warfare (commonly referred to by Muslim Jurists as *Siyar*). It further discussed the primary sources of Islamic law which are the *Quran*, *Sunnah*, Consensus (*Ijma*), and analogical reasoning (*Qiyas*). It then highlighted the significant role of the science of *fiqh* in filling the gap regarding the different aspects of social life that Muslim societies over time have come

[186] Abu Bakr Nagi, *Edaret Al-tawahoush* (Syria: Dar al-tamroud, n.d) 195.
[187] Ibid., 195–6.
[188] Damien McElroy, 'Rome will be conquered next, says leader of 'Islamic State', *The Telegraph*, November 2014. Available at: <http://www.telegraph.co.uk/news/worldnews/middleeast/syria/10939235/Rome-will-be-conquered-next-says-leader-of-Islamic-State.html> (last accessed 25 May 2019).
[189] Letter dated 17 January 2018 from the Chair of the Security Council Committee pursuant to resolutions 1267 (1999), 1989 (2011), and 2253 (2015) concerning Islamic State in Iraq and the Levant (Da'esh), Al-Qaida and associated individuals, groups, undertakings, and entities addressed to the President of the Security Council, United Nations, Security Council (27 February 2018), paras 1–6.
[190] Sixth report of the Secretary-General on the threat posed by ISIL (Da'esh) to international peace and security and the range of United Nations efforts in support of Member States in countering the threat, United Nations, Security Council (31 January 2018), para 4.

to consider as needing to be regulated by law. This indicates that Islamic law, similar to other legal systems, is mostly the product of rational intellectual exercise and, despite prevalent misconception, it is subject to modifications as it has been developed in different cultural environments throughout hundreds of years.

This chapter also examined the historical and contextual evolution of the notion of Jihad from the 'Medinan ideal' state of Muhammad to the now collapsed 'state' of Abu Bakr Al Baghdadi and attempted to highlight how every Islamic state or group used or misused the notion of Jihad throughout Islamic history based on various socio-political considerations. Accordingly, it fleshed out the fact that the Jihad during Muhammad's time was predominantly defensive in order to repel actual attacks against Muslims' lands, properties or people. During the Rightly Guided Caliphs period, however, Jihad undertook different forms and shapes that were mainly expansionist to further the national interest of the then growing Islamic empire. This period—particularly during Ali's era—also witnessed the eruption of intra-Islamic conflicts which led to the evolution of the Islamic law of non-international armed conflicts. Afterwards, the rapid decline of the Islamic empires in the early eighteenth century inspired theologians such as Muhammad ibn Abd al-Wahab, who endorsed quite a fundamentalist approach of Islamic law including the concept of *takfir*, with the purpose of reviving the old powerful Islamic state. Later, in the early twentieth century, the dissolution of the last Islamic Caliphate and the Western colonization of many Muslim states led to the creation of a number of mainstream Islamic organizations across the territories of the states of the dissolved Caliphate. The primary purposes of which were to end colonization in Muslim states and to recreate a unified Islamic nation. Finally, the Soviet Union's invasion of Afghanistan in 1979 shifted the Jihadist Movement in the Muslim states to a completely different mode of action, where Muslims from around the world rallied to the call for anti-Soviet Jihad. This also led to the creation of *Al-Qaeda*, which later became the most prominent transnational Jihadist group across the globe. A few years later, particularly after the events of 9/11, the 'global war on terror' intensified military confrontations between many Western states and allied governments in the Islamic world, on the one hand, and *Al-Qaeda* and its offshoots, including ISIS, on the other. During this period, these latter groups would use Jihad to legitimize their armed force against their perceived enemies both domestically and internationally.

2
The Islamic *Jus ad Bellum* from International Law Perspective

1. Military Jihad vs the Use of Force

In recent times, the application of the concept of Jihad by some leaders of Islamic States (Iraq and Afghanistan) or Islamic armed groups (Hamas, *Hezbollah*, *Al-Qaeda*, and ISIS)[1] to justify the use of force has raised questions regarding the compatibility of the notion of Jihad, as conceptualized in Islamic law, with the modern norms of international law, as enunciated in the UN Charter. Hence, this chapter provides a jurisprudential analysis of the concept of Jihad and locates it in the wider framework of Islamic international law (*Siyar*). It also examines the contextual limitations on the applicability of the notion of Jihad and relates this discussion to contemporary norms of the use of force under international law. For the purpose of this study, this chapter will be divided into four sections: Section 1: Military Jihad vs the Use of Force; Section 2: Defensive Jihad vs Right to Self-defence; Section 3: Islamic Law Responsibility to Protect (R2P) vs International Law R2P; and Section 4: Offensive Jihad.

As discussed in Chapter 1, Jihad has historically been used in several contexts, including self-defence against enemies' aggression; pre-emptive self-defence; conquest, revolution, and regime change; political violence; and terrorism. Thus, in order to avoid any misuse, misquotation, misunderstanding, distortion, or manipulative interpretation of the meaning of Jihad, the term itself has to be clearly defined.

Linguistically, the term Jihad is derived from the Arabic word *Juhd* and literally means to 'strive' and 'struggle'. In Islamic law, Jihad has dual religious connotations. First, as an inwardly directed personal struggle intended as a process of self-purification by struggling against the evil in oneself; and second,

[1] By putting these four Islamic armed groups in the same brackets as an example, the author of this study did not intend by any means to infer that they share the exact same ideology or *modus operandi*; in particular, their political objectives and their interpretation of Islamic law are quite distant. The only reason why they are mentioned together is the fact that they are all considered as non-state armed groups that integrate some sort of Islamic ideology according to their own understanding of it.

Islamic Jihadism and the Laws of War. Omar Mekky, Oxford University Press. © Omar Mekky 2023.
DOI: 10.1093/oso/9780198888369.003.0003

as an outwardly directed struggle: a fight in the cause of God against oppression and tyranny.[2] It is, however, claimed by some commentators that the self-purification is the 'greater' form of Jihad, whilst outwardly directed Jihad is the 'lesser' form.[3] This view is based on a statement attributed to Muhammad (*hadith*—prophetic saying), who reportedly said to his companions when they returned from a military campaign (the battle of *Badr*): 'We have come back from the lesser Jihad to the greater Jihad.' His followers questioned: 'Is there any greater Jihad than the Jihad against the idolaters?' Muhammad responded: 'Yes, Jihad against one's self.'[4] Indeed, this *hadith* has raised considerable controversy in the Islamic community. Muslims agree that the outwardly directed Jihad—commonly referred to as 'military Jihad'—cannot take place until one strives and forces oneself to do it.[5] The aforementioned *hadith*, however, is classified by many Islamic jurists as weak and unauthentic[6] because of its questionable chain of transmission from Muhammad. In addition, the *hadith* contradicts the *saheeh* (authentic) *hadith*, which indicates that fighting in the cause of God is the highest degree of Jihad.[7] Furthermore, the former *hadith* has never been mentioned in any of the authentic books of *hadith*.

In any case, Jihad in the second sense, as fighting in the cause of God, is not devoid of the Jihad of one's self in the first sense. Needless to say, in most cases, the self prefers safety, loves life, and hates death. Hence, struggling against personal worldly desires and tendencies is necessary but not as the 'greater' form of Jihad, yet possibly this struggle is an essential step to prepare Muslims for outwardly directed Jihad.[8] Even if this controversial *hadith* were to be authentic, the Prophet reportedly said it after returning back from the battle of *Badr*, which indicates that it was not intended to undermine the notion of military Jihad by any means.[9] It should be also noted that Muhammad in a different

[2] Devin R. Springer, James L. Regens, and David N. Edger, *Islamic Radicalism and Global Jihad* (Washington, DC: Georgetown University Press, 2009) 1. For an overview of the various formulations of Jihad, see generally Paul Heck, 'Jihad Revisited', *The Journal of Religious Ethics* (2004) 32(1) 95–128. Available at: <http://faculty.georgetown.edu/plh2/Jihad.Revisited.pdf> (last accessed 25 May 2019).

[3] Niaz A. Shah, 'The Use of Force Under Islamic Law', *The European Journal of International Law* (2013) 24(1), 343–65, 344.

[4] Sheikh Muhammed and Salih Al-Munajjid, 'Greater and Lesser Jihad', *Fatwa 10455* (2001). Available at: <https://islamqa.info/en/answers/10455/greater-and-lesser-jihaad> (last accessed 25 May 2019).

[5] Manisuli Ssenyonjo, 'Jihad Re-Examined: Islamic Law and International Law', *Santa Clara Journal of International Law* (2012) 10(1), 1–33, 5.

[6] See, e.g., Muhammad Ibn Uthaymeen, *Fataawa Manaar al-Islam* (Riyadh: Dar Al-Watan, 1995/1415) 2:421; Raj K. Pruthi (ed.), *Encyclopedia of Jihad* (New Delhi: Anmol Publications, 2002) 62–3; Muhammed and Al-Munajjid, 'Greater and Lesser Jihad' (n 4) cited in Ssenyonjo, 'Jihad Re-Examined: Islamic Law and International Law' (n 5) 5.

[7] Ssenyonjo, 'Jihad Re-Examined: Islamic Law and International Law' (n 5) 5.

[8] *Manhj Al-Islam fi al-Harb wa al-Salam* (Kuwait: *Mktabat Dar al-Arqam*, 1982) 106.

[9] Ssenyonjo, 'Jihad Re-Examined: Islamic Law and International Law' (n 5) 6.

authentic *hadith* proposed three forms of Jihad that Muslims are obliged to follow to fight evil in society: (i) Jihad with one's hands (physical Jihad) if one has the capabilities to do so; otherwise (ii) Jihad with one's words (speaking out); or, if neither of the previous two options are possible, (iii) Jihad with one's heart (identifying the action as wrongdoing and rejecting it internally).[10] This *hadith* makes it noticeable that Muhammad favoured the 'physical Jihad' as a response to wrongdoings. According to various interpretation, however, it is not clear if the authority of using 'physical Jihad' against wrongdoers is an obligation on every Muslim individual or only an obligation solely on their leaders.[11] Another controversial matter related to the notion of Jihad, as mentioned in Chapter 1, is whether the Quranic Medinian verses that permitted the use of military Jihad were meant to be only for defensive reasons, or offensive (expansionist) purposes as well.

In short, the purpose of this discussion is to shed light on the fact that Jihad is a comprehensive term that is composed of several elements, only one of which involves the use of force. This is supported by the fact that several Quranic Meccan verses made references to Jihad at a time when military Jihad was not yet permitted.[12] As previously stated, the permission to use military Jihad was revealed after the migration of Muhammad from Mecca to Medina in 622, where he established the first Islamic state. Thus, it is worth elaborating that the absolute minimum level of Jihad is to strive against one's own soul and temptations and to control one's worldly desires, whilst the highest level or epitome of Jihad in Islam is to be ever-ready to engage willingly in military Jihad, which may lead to the loss of one's life and property in order to further the cause of God.[13] Nowadays, this latter form of Jihad is the form that raises a variety of questions and controversies due to its contemporary implications on national and international peace and security as well as its level of compatibility with

[10] *Sahih* Muslim, in *Hadith* 1:79 (narrated by Abu Sa'id al-Khudri: 'I heard the Messenger of Allah (PBUH) as saying: "He who amongst you sees something abominable should modify it with the help of his hand; and if he has not strength enough to do that, then he should do it with his tongue; and if he has not strength enough to do even that, then he should (at least abhor it) from his heart; and that is the least of faith." ')

[11] *Hadith*: '*mn ra'a menkom monkaran*', IslamWeb, 2006. Available at: <http://articles.islamweb.net/media/index.php?id=76925&lang=A&page=article> (last accessed 25 May 2019).

[12] 'But verily thy Lord, to those who leave their homes after trials and persecutions, and who thereafter strive and fight for the Faith and patiently persevere, thy Lord, after all this is Oft-Forgiving, Most Merciful.' See *Quran* (16:110). 'O Prophet! Strive hard against the unbelievers and the hypocrites, and be firm against them. Their abode is Hell,–an evil refuge indeed.' See *Quran* (9:73). 'O Prophet! Strive hard against the unbelievers and the hypocrites, and be harsh with them. Their abode is Hell,–an evil refuge (indeed).' See *Quran* (66:9).

[13] Ssenyonjo, 'Jihad Re-Examined: Islamic Law and International Law' (n 5) 16.

international law. Therefore, this chapter focuses exclusively on the notion of 'military Jihad'.

The use of military force is a phenomenon that has always accompanied international relations. Indeed, relations between states has unquestionably been characterized by the use of force with very limited reference to laws and morals.[14] States have historically been free to pursue their own interests by using force wherever they deemed it necessary.[15] As Clausewitz famously put it in the early nineteenth century: 'war is nothing but a continuation of politics with the admixture of other means'.[16] Based on this predominant ideological position, the principal point of view in the theory of international relations is the determination of the role and place of the use of force in international relations.[17] After quite a long history of hostile relations between states and several failure attempts of enacting an explicit prohibition of the use of force,[18] states finally came to the conclusion that the succeeding generations should be saved from the scourge of war.[19] In 1945, the UN Charter was adopted by states with the primary purpose of maintaining international peace and security and ensuring that 'armed force shall not be used'.[20] On the run-up to the contemporary prohibition of the use of force, the majority of the international lawyers' literature was dedicated to Western scholarship and the Christian just war tradition that paved the road to the UN Charter while disregarding any equivalent related Islamic literature. Authors frequently quote St Augustine (d. 430), St Thomas Aquinas (d. 1274), Francisco de Vitoria (d. 1546), Francisco Suarez (d. 1617), and Hugo Grotius (d. 1645) on issues related to the *justum bellum* theory. And yet digging into the Islamic literature in this regard has not been in the interest of the predominant Western-oriented international lawyers and historians, despite the fact that Islamic law had a significant contribution to the concept of *jus ad bellum*.

Islam, unlike Christianity,[21] provided regulations on the use of military Jihad by Muslims in their relations with both Muslims and non-Muslims in

[14] Momir Milojevic, 'Prohibition of the Use of Force and Threats in International Relations, Law and Politics', *Facta Universitatis Series: Law and Politics* (2001) 1(5), 581–604 581.

[15] Iain Scobbie, 'Strange Angel: Reflections on War', *EJIL Analysis*, 2015. Available at: <http://www.ejiltalk.org/strange-angel-some-reflections-on-war/#more-13909> (last accessed 25 May 2019).

[16] '*On War*' (1832–34), Book 8, Ch. 6, sect. B, cited in Iain Scobbie, 'Strange Angel: Reflections on War', *EJIL Analysis* (2015). Available at: <http://www.ejiltalk.org/strange-angel-some-reflections-on-war/#more-13909> (last accessed 25 May 2019).

[17] Milojevic, 'Prohibition of the Use of Force and Threats in International Relations, Law and Politics' (n 14) 581.

[18] For the history of the prohibition of force, see generally Ibid., 581–604.

[19] Paragraph 1 of the preamble of the UN Charter.

[20] Ibid., at paras 6 and 7, and Article 1 of the UN Charter.

[21] One of the major difficulties with the Christian just war tradition is that it has neither a scriptural premise—especially not a New Testament premise—nor any early theological roots, as it

its most sacred scripture—the *Quran*. It is elaborated in several passages in the *Quran* and confirmed by *Sunnah* and other Islamic scholarship that peace should be the foundation of Muslims' relations with others. Accordingly, the majority of Muslim jurists argue that war in Islamic law is an aberration and a means to which Muslims may only resort under unavoidable circumstances.[22] Under the *Quran* and *Sunnah*, Islamic law dictates that Muslims' relations with other nations should be peaceful and non-hostile.[23] This fact is repeated several times in the *Quran*, as exemplified by the following passages: 'Allah does not forbid you from those who do not fight you because of religion and do not expel you from your homes - from being righteous toward them and acting justly toward them. Indeed, Allah loves those who act justly';[24] 'Ye who believe! Enter into peace heartedly, and follow not the footsteps of the evil one, for he is to you an avowed enemy';[25] 'Therefore, if they withdraw from you but fight you not, and (instead) send you (guarantees of) peace, then God hath opened no way for you (to war against them)';[26] 'But if they (the enemy) incline towards peace, do thou (also) incline towards peace, and trust in God: for he is the one that heareth and knoweth (all things).'[27]

It is also recognized that Muhammad, shortly after his arrival in Medina, concluded a document called *Sahifah al-Madinah* which is translated in Western scholarship as the Constitution of Medina.[28] In this document, Muslims made an agreement with a number of Jewish clans by including them in the first Islamic state while ensuring their right to practise their religion.[29] The document also stipulated a collective defence agreement between the Jews and the Muslims in the case of an attack on either of them.[30] Only when the Jewish clans breached this agreement and fought the Muslims did Muhammad

begun to emerge only in the middle of fourth century. Charles W. Amjad Ali, 'Jihad and Just War Theory: Dissonance and Truth', *Dialog* (2009) 48(3), 239–47, 239. Available at: <http://cges.umn.edu/docs/Amjad-Ali.Jihad_and_Just_War_Theory.pdf> (last accessed 25 May 2019).

[22] Abd al-Wahhab Khallaf, *Al-Siyasa al-Shariyya* (Cairo: Dar Al Ansar, 1931/1350), 61–100; Sayyid Qutb, *al-Adala al-Ijtimaiyya* (Cairo: Dar Al Shorouk, 1954) 92, 94–5, cited in Majid Khadduri, *The Islamic Law of Nations: Shaybani's Siyar* (Baltimore, MD: The Johns Hopkins Press, 1966) 293.
[23] Khadduri, *The Islamic Law of Nations* (n 22) 293.
[24] *Quran* (60:8).
[25] Ibid., (2:208).
[26] Ibid., (4:90).
[27] Ibid., (8:61).
[28] Ahmed Al-Dawoody, *The Islamic Law of War: Justifications and Regulations* (New York, NY: Palgrave Macmillan, 2011) 19.
[29] Ibid., 20.
[30] Ibid.

and his army fight back.[31] This sequence of events is commonly used by Islamic jurists to support the exclusive interpretation of Jihad as a form of self-defence.

Another peace treaty was concluded between Muhammad, as the Leader of the Islamic state in Medina, and *Quraysh*, the ruling tribe in Mecca and the most influential tribe in Arabia at that time. The agreement stipulated a ten-year armistice between the two parties and their allies.[32] The aforementioned Islamic references affirm the fact that Muslims are obliged, by virtue of their law and religion, to seek peace in their relations with other nations and not to resort to military Jihad unless to repel the aggressors, as will be elaborated in the following section.

In a similar vein, after some fourteen centuries since the foundation of Islam, the UN Charter codified a specific prohibition on all member states from 'the threat or the use of force against the territorial integrity or political independence of any state.'[33] In fact, the prohibition on the threat or the use of force constitutes one of the fundamentals of the modern international legal order. It is labelled by authors as the 'cornerstone of peace in the charter.'[34] Nonetheless, similar to the controversy surrounding the definition of Jihad, the precise definition of the notion of 'force' under international law inspired significant controversy and debate in the UN General Assembly.[35] While some countries[36] claimed that the prohibition of the use of force comprises political and economic aggression,[37] among other things, this is contradicted by the *travaux préparatoires* of the UN Charter, which illustrate that the prohibition on the use of force is only concerned with military force.[38] Here, it should be taken into consideration that a Brazilian proposal to include economic aggression was rejected at the UN Conference on International Organization in San Francisco.[39] Moreover, the dictates of Article 44 of the UN Charter support the fact that the term 'force' is intended to mean 'armed force.'[40] Therefore, in contemporary

[31] For the details regarding Mohamed's battles against the Jewish clans, specifically; the Battles against Banu Qaynuqaa, Banu al-Nadir, and Banu Qurayzah, Ibid., 26–7.

[32] For a translation of the content of the treaty, see Afzal Iqbal, *Diplomacy in Early Islam* (Pakistan, Institute of Islamic Culture, 1988) 54, cited in Al-Dawoody, *The Islamic Law of War* (n 28) 28.

[33] *Charter of the United Nations*, Article 2(4).

[34] Bruno Simma, Daniel-Erasmus Khan, Georg Nolte, and Andreas Paulus (eds), *The Charter of the United Nations: A Commentary*, 3rd edn, Vol. II (Oxford: Oxford University Press, 2012) 207.

[35] Peter Malanczuk and Michael Akehurst, *Akehurst's Modern Introduction to International Law*, 7th edn (London: Routledge, 1997) 310.

[36] Mainly the developing countries and the formerly Eastern Bloc countries during the cold war. Simma et al. (eds), *The Charter of the United Nations* (n 34) 208.

[37] Ibid., 209.

[38] Ibid.

[39] UN Documents of the Conference on International Organization, UNCIO, Vol. 6, 339, 340, 609.

[40] *Charter of the United Nations*, Article 44: 'When the Security Council has decided to use force it shall, before calling upon a Member not represented on it to provide armed forces in fulfilment of the obligations assumed under Article 43, invite that Member, if the Member so desires, to participate in the

legal literature, it is widely accepted that the term 'use of force' refers to the use of armed force only.[41] It should also be noted that the phrases 'territorial integrity' and 'political independence' stated in Article 2(4) are not intended to restrict the prohibition on the use of force.[42] Thus, an illegal use of force within the meaning of these two phrases is not only triggered if a state's territorial existence or the status of its political independence is threatened or eliminated; rather, these two phrases were meant to encompass any possible type of cross-frontier use of armed force.[43] If any possible gaps are left, these should be filled by the remaining form that outlaws the threat or use of force 'in any manner inconsistent with the purpose of the UN Charter'.[44]

Despite the similarity in the substantial meaning of the prohibition on military Jihad under Islamic law and the use of force under the UN Charter, there are some discrepancies with regard to the scope of application of these two bodies of law. In the dictates of Article 2(4), it is prohibited to use force in interstate relations, but the internal use of force within a state was left totally uncovered. In other words, the Charter neither prevents insurgents from initiating a civil war nor the government from using armed force against them.[45] Nevertheless, this matter is mainly regulated under national laws and other branches of international law, including International Human Rights Law (IHRL) and International Humanitarian Law (IHL), through which the distinction between *jus ad bellum* and *jus in bello* becomes relatively impossible (this will be discussed thoroughly in Chapter 3).[46] Under Islamic law, however, the internal use of force within the Islamic state was deliberately regulated. The

decisions of the Security Council concerning the employment of contingents of that Member's armed forces.'

[41] Yoram Dinstein, *War, Aggression and Self-Defense*, 4th edn (Cambridge: Cambridge University Press, 2005) 86. (Another debate was raised on the issue of 'physical non-armed force', such as cross frontier expulsion of population or the release of large quantity of water down a valley. However, it was agreed that it can be considered as 'use of force' within narrow limits. As there is no need to extend the prohibition of the use of force to such cases as the unlawfulness of these activities are normally regulated by different rules under international law, such as the principle of non-intervention). Simma et al. (eds), *The Charter of the United Nations* (n 34) 210.

[42] ICJ, *Oil Platforms Case*, ICJ Rep., 161f, paras 64 and 72.

[43] Simma et al. (eds), *The Charter of the United Nations* (n 34) 216. For a counter argument, see Leslie Green, *The Contemporary Law of Armed Conflict*, 3rd edn (Manchester: Manchester University Press, 2008) 9.

[44] Simma et al. (eds), *The Charter of the United Nations* (n 34) 216.

[45] Ibid., 214.

[46] ICRC, 'Violence and the Use of Force', 2011. Available at: <http://www.use-of-force.info/images/un/additional-reading/General/ICRC%20Violence%20and%20the%20use%20of%20force%202014.pdf> (last accessed 25 May 2019).

general prohibition on the use of force applies in Muslims' internal relations as it applies within their external relations.[47]

Islamic law had excluded two particular situations from such a prohibition: (i) the war against *al-bughah* (rebels) and (ii) the war against *al-muharibun/qutaa al-tariq* (bandits, highway robbers, and terrorists).[48]

The *jus ad bellum* of the 'war against *al-bughah*' is believed to be treated under the following self-explanatory verse of *Quran*:

> And if two parties or groups among the believers fight each other, then make peace between both of them, but if one of them rebels against the other, then fight you (all) against the one that rebels until it complies with the Command of Allah; then if it complies, then make reconciliation between them justly, and be equitable. Verily! Allah loves those who are equitable.[49]

According to Al-Dawoody, who aptly summarized the opinions of the Muslim jurists regarding the justifications of the use of force in this regard, the question of whether Islamic state authorities or Muslim rebels are permitted to resort to the use of force against each other can be tackled under three considerations, as follows:[50]

(1) Using force as a response to persistent violation of Islamic law. On the one hand, the Islamic state may resort to the use of force against any rebel group under the justification of their persistent violation of Islamic law. On the other hand, the same grounds may justify the rebels' use of force if the state imposes on the citizens an obligation that contradicts Islamic law.[51] It is also unanimously agreed among Muslim jurists that if the

[47] In addition to the previously mentioned verses related to the general prohibition of Military Jihad. It was narrated in *Saheeh Al-Bukhari* (number 1739) and *Mosnad Ahmad* (number 2037) that Mohamed said: 'Truly your blood, your property, and your honor are inviolable.' Accordingly, the life and property of all citizens in the Islamic state are considered sacred, whether the person is Muslim or not.

[48] It should be noted, however, that these are the two principal types of internal conflicts in the Islamic history that were regulated under Islamic law, particularly, in the *Quran*. While there are two other additional types of internal conflicts that were mentioned in the Islamic history but never mentioned in the primary sources of Islamic law (*Quran* and *Sunnah*) as it occurred after the death of Muhammad, namely; *al-Riddah* (apostasies) war that took place during Caliph Abu Bakr reign and the war against *al-kharjjites* (splitters) that took place during Caliph Ali reign. The last two internal conflicts, in my opinion, should be treated and covered under the first category, the war against *al-Bughah* (Rebels). See Al-Dawoody, *The Islamic Law of War* (n 28) 140–1.

[49] *Quran* (49:9).

[50] Al-Dawoody, *The Islamic Law of War* (n 28) 157.

[51] In support of this argument, the *Quran* states: 'O ye who believe! Obey Allah, and obey the messenger and those of you who are in authority; and if ye have a dispute concerning any matter, refer it to Allah and the messenger if ye are (in truth) believers in Allah and the Last Day. That is better and more seemly in the end.' See *Quran* (4:59). An interpretation of this verse clarifies that God and his messenger (Muhammad) should be absolutely obeyed by the believers; however, the people in power

leader of the Islamic state apostasizes, rebels are permitted to use force against him.[52] This position, when received by radical Jihadist groups who adopt the *kharijite* approach of *takfir* (considering other Muslims as non-believers simply on the basis of their behaviour), could broaden the permission to use force not only against the Muslim rulers but also against ordinary Muslim citizens. ISIS has been extensively quoted by Islamic scholars as a *kharijite*-like group for using this approach to legitimize their resort to use of force under Islamic law.[53]

(2) Using force to maintain security and public order within the Muslim state. The Islamic state has the right to use force against rebels to maintain security and public order if the rebels used force after the state has reached the conclusion that their demands are illegal or unjustifiable. The majority of Muslim scholars agreed that in this case, the objective of the use of force shall not, by any means, be intended to eliminate the rebels but rather to bring them into obedience to the ruler and thus prevent the bloodshed of Muslims. Such a statement, if read in light of the contemporary international law rules, implies that Islamic law, in this case, favours the application of IHRL over IHL.[54]

(3) Using force to protect the citizens' rights and freedoms. Only a minority of Muslim jurists allows the use of force for overthrowing an unjust ruler of the Islamic state when the latter ignores rebels' calls to stop his injustice and continues his tyranny. However, according to some of this minority, if overthrowing the ruler will lead to the bloodshed of Muslims, rebels should apply the juristic Islamic principle of 'choosing the lesser of two evils', which means choosing the less harmful option between the consequences of the ruler's injustice and the expected bloodshed of Muslims. Unlike the first case, the majority of Islamic jurists do not permit the use of force against the unjust leader with the rationale of

should always be obeyed only if their rules are in line with *Quran* and *Sunnah*. See the interpretation of the verse, available (in Arabic) at: <http://www.nabulsi.com/blue/ar/art.php?art=1853&id=212&sid=650&ssid=651&sssid=652> (last accessed 25 May 2019).

52 Muhammad Rashīd Ridā, *Tafsīr al-Qur'ān al-Hakīm: Al-Shahīr bi-Tafsīr al-Manār*, 12 Vols (Cairo: Dār al-Manār, 2002) Vol. 6, 367.

53 Hesham A. Hassaballah, 'The Real Name for ISIS Should Be KIL: The Kharijites of Iraq and the Levant'. Available at: <https://www.beliefnet.com/columnists/commonwordcommonlord/the-real-name-for-isis-should-be-kil-the-kharijites-of-iraq-and-the-levant/> (last accessed 25 May 2019); Abu Aaliyah Surkheel, 'Khawarij Ideology, ISIS Savagery: Part One', 2015. Available at: <http://muslimmatters.org/2015/08/24/khawarij-ideology-isis-savagery-part-one/> (last accessed 25 May 2019).

54 This matter will be further elaborated in Chapter 3 concerning the *jus in bello*. See Report of the Special Rapporteur on extrajudicial, summary, or arbitrary executions, written by Philip Alston, A/HRC/14/24/Add.6, 28 May 2010, 11, paras 32 and 33.

avoiding the bloodshed of Muslims, even if the ruler took power by the use of force or *coup d'état*.

As for the *jus ad bellum* of the war against *al-muharibun/qutaa al-tariq*, Islamic law provides the Islamic state the permission to use force against those groups of citizens within the Islamic state who commit the crime of *qat al-tariq* as termed by the *Hanafis* and *Shafiis*; and *al-hirabah* as termed by the *Malikis* and *Hanbalis*.[55] The Muslim jurists commonly agree that this crime is committed by a group of people who, under the threat or usage of arms, attack or intimidate their victims in order to rob, kill, or merely terrorize them overly and coercively.[56] While the sanction stated in the *Quran* for this crime is perhaps the most severe sanction provided by Islamic penal law (either crucifixion, execution, amputation of the limbs on opposite sides, or exile),[57] the elements necessary to constitute the offence are quite ambiguous and remain a source of controversy among Islamic jurists today.[58] This crime has been interpreted to mean highway robbery, piracy, rebellion, sedition, and terrorism.[59] A review of case law, however, suggests, that *hirabah/qat al-tariq* crime in Islamic history amounted to a catch-all category covering crimes related to rebellion, sedition, and any other crime that the Caliph felt threatened the public order of the Islamic state.[60]

In conclusion, Islamic law and international law generally agree on the principle of maintenance of peace and the prohibition of the use of force or military Jihad in international relations between states. The relationship between the two legal regimes is relatively different when it comes to the regulations of *jus ad bellum* in internal conflicts since it has been regulated by Islamic law while left out by the UN charter to be regulated by other predominantly *jus in bello* rules, namely IHRL and IHL. Additionally, as discussed in Chapter 3, international law recognizes various types of internal conflicts,

[55] As previously elaborated in Chapter 1, these are the main four Sunni Islamic School of thoughts. See Al-Dawoody, *The Islamic Law of War* (n 28) 170.

[56] Ibid., 171.

[57] 'Indeed [the] retribution [for] those who wage war [against] Allah and His Messenger and strive in the earth spreading corruption [is] that they be killed or they be crucified or be cut off their hands and their feet of opposite sides or they be exiled from the land. That [is] for them disgrace in the world and for them in the Hereafter [is] a punishment great: except for those who repent before you have overpowered them. Know well that Allah is All-Forgiving, All-Compassionate.' See *Quran* (5:33–34).

[58] Hamid Khan, *Practitioner's Guide: Islamic Law* (International Network to Promote the Rule of Law, 2013) 74.

[59] Sherman Jackson, 'Domestic Terrorism in the Islamic Legal Tradition', *Muslim World* (2001) 91(3-4), 293–310; Khan, *Practitioner's Guide: Islamic Law* (n 58) 74.

[60] Khan, *Practitioner's Guide: Islamic Law* (n 58) 74.

some of which trigger the application of IHL, while others do not reach the required threshold.[61] However, internal conflicts under Islamic law should be understood as any conflict that takes place in one or more Islamic states, without any consideration of the territorial borders between Islamic states. This is evident in the Islamic law arguments used by various Islamic scholars to legitimize the Islamic states' use of force against Saddam Hussein in the Gulf War (1990–1991) to liberate the state of Kuwait from the Iraqi invasion.[62] In this particular incident, Muslim jurists openly called for the application of the Islamic law related to internal conflicts.[63] Finally, Islamic law and international law agree on considering states' right of self-defence to repel other states' aggression as the key exception to the prohibition of the use of force, elaborated further in Section 2 of this chapter.

2. Defensive Jihad vs Right to Self-defence

As the guardian of the international peace and security, the states of the world entitled the UN Security Council (UNSC) to the power to determine the existence of any 'threat to the peace, breach of the peace, or act of aggression' and to decide on the measures that should be taken in accordance with Articles 41 (economic and diplomatic enforcement measures) and 42 (military enforcement), in order to maintain or restore international peace and security.[64] However, recognizing the fact that the SC might not always be capable to react in due course to possible acts of aggression, the drafters of the Charter included an express provision dealing with self-defence.[65] Article 51 of the UN Charter reads as follows:

[61] The types and definitions of armed conflicts and particularly non-international armed conflicts under IHL (common Article 3 of the Geneva Conventions and Article 1 of the Second Additional Protocol) will be elaborated in Chapter 3.

[62] Muhammad Sayyid Tantāwī, 'Al-Hukm al-Shar'ī fī Ahdāth al-Khalīj', *The Islamic Fiqh Council Journal* (1991/1411) 5, 49–100, 68–73; Ahmad 'Umar Hāshim, 'Ma'sāh al-Ghazw al-'Irāqī wa Wājib al-'Arab wa al-Muslimīn', *The Islamic Fiqh Council Journal* (1991/1411) 5, 101–18, 104; Husayn Hāmid Hassān. 'Hukm al-Sharī'ah fī Ghazw al-Irāq lil-Kuwayt', *The Islamic Fiqh Council Journal* (1991/1411) 5, 189–94, 191–3.

[63] They used the Quranic verse that regulates the use of force against *al-bugha*, which states: 'And if two parties or groups among the believers fight each other, then make peace between both of them, but if one of them rebels against the other, then fight you (all) against the one that rebels until it complies with the Command of Allah; then if it complies, then make reconciliation between them justly, and be equitable. Verily! Allah loves those who are equitable.' Ibid.

[64] *Charter of the United Nations*, Articles 39, 41, and 42.

[65] Tom Ryus, *Armed Attack and Article 51 of the UN Charter: Evolutions in Customary Law and Practice* (Cambridge: Cambridge University Press, 2010) 57.

> Nothing in the present Charter shall impair the inherent right of individual or collective self-defense if an armed attack occurs against a Member of the UN, until the Security Council has taken the measures necessary to maintain international peace and security. Measures taken by Members in the exercise of this right of self-defense shall be immediately reported to the Security Council and shall not in any way affect the authority and responsibility of the Security Council under the present Charter to take at any time such action as it deems necessary in order to maintain or restore international peace and security.

In Islamic history, however, the absence of an UNSC-like body made the Islamic state and Muslims the only beneficiaries of the right to self-defence.

Immediately after the migration of Muhammad and his companions to Medina, Muslims were authorized for the first time, finally, to use force to defend themselves. It was stated in the *Quran* as follows: 'Permission [to fight] has been given to those who are being fought, because they were wronged. And indeed, Allah is competent to give them victory.'[66] In conformity with Article 51, it is evident in this verse that the exception to the prohibition on the use of force is limited to cases where Muslims are being fought or, in other words, attacked. However, Islamic law and international law have been equally vague as to whether the occurrence of armed attack is a prerequisite to invoke the right to self-defence.

Article 51 preserves the right to use force in self-defence 'if an armed attack occurs'. Some insist that the right is confined to circumstances in which an actual armed attack has taken place.[67] The contrary position is that states have the right to invoke self-defence in order to avert the threat of an *imminent* attack, commonly referred to as 'anticipatory self-defence', and this is widely accepted in the contemporary international law literature.[68] For proponents of this position, the right to self-defence is a customary right that includes anticipatory self-defence to avert imminent attacks.[69] This position is more logical

[66] *Quran* (22:39).

[67] ICJ, *Case concerning Military and Paramilitary Activities in and against Nicaragua (Nicaragua v. USA)*, Judgment, (Merits, 1986) ICJ Rep., para. 194; ICJ, *Case Concerning Oil Platforms (Islamic Republic of Iran v. United States of America)*, 2003, ICJ Rep., paras 61–64 and 72.

[68] Richard J. Erickson, Legitimate Use of Military Force Against State Sponsored International Terrorism (Alabama: Air University Press, 1989) 138 (listing the members of the expansive school of thought who interpret Article 51 as permitting anticipatory self-defence in response to imminent armed attack). Available at: <http://www.au.af.mil/au/awc/awcgate/au/erickson.pdf> (last accessed 25 May 2019).

[69] Claud H. M. Waldock, 'The Regulation of the Use of Force by Individual States in International Law' in *Collected Courses*, Vol. 81 (The Hague: Academy of International Law, 1952) 455–517, 496–7; Derek W. Bowett, *Self Defense in International Law* (Manchester: Manchester University Press, 1958), cited in: Leo Van Den hole, 'Anticipatory Self-Defence Under International Law', *American University*

than a restrictive reading of Article 51 because the latter would lead to 'manifestly absurd' results when states, before being able to respond, would be forced to suffer a 'first strike', in particular when such strike caused decisive destruction.[70] Similarly, in Islamic law, a restrictive reading of the aforementioned verse would limit Muslims' right to invoke the right to self-defence to circumstances in which Muslims have actually been attacked.[71] A description of the word 'attack' was elaborated in *Quran* as follows: 'those who have been expelled from their homes without just reason—only because they say, "Our Lord is Allah"'.[72] Here, the verse is referring to an 'actual attack' against Muhammad and his followers who had to flee Mecca to Medina after being persecuted and tortured by the tribe of *Quraysh*. Muslim jurists believe that most of the battles that were fought by Muslims during Muhammad's lifetime were fought according to the restrictive meaning of defensive Jihad, in which the Islamic state's lands, properties, or people were actually attacked.[73] However, since the most accepted interpretive method for the *Quran* is *Sunnah*, a review of the justifications and details of the battles led by Muhammad is indispensable in order to explore whether the right to self-defence under Islamic law includes anticipatory self-defence.

In 626, Muhammad was informed that *Banu Al-Mustaliq* (an Arab tribe allied with the tribe of *Quraysh*) was mobilizing an army to fight him under the leadership of Al-Haarith bin Abi Dhiraar.[74] Subsequently, Muhammad sent one of his followers (Buraydah Ibn al-Husayb al-Aslami) to verify the news, who then confirmed that the army was preparing for war against the Islamic state in Medina. Thus, Muhammad decided to mobilize his army to fight them in their lands.[75] Similar preparatory incidents justified fighting two succeeding battles under Muhammad's leadership of the Islamic state, namely the battle of

International Law Review (2003) 19(1), 69–106, 77. In this regard, Judge Schwebel in his dissenting opinion said: 'I wish . . . to make clear that, for my part, I do not agree with a construction of the United Nations Charter which would read Article 51 as if it were worded: "Nothing in the present Charter shall impair the inherent right of individual of collective self-defense if, and only if, an armed attack occurs. . . ." I do not agree that the terms or intent of Article 51 eliminate the right of self-defense under customary international law, or confine its entire scope to the express terms of Article 51.') See *ICJ, Military and Paramilitary Activities*, Judgment, 1986, para. 347.

[70] Such scenarios are likely, especially with the types of highly destructive weapons used in today's wars. Ryus, *Armed Attack and Article 51 of the UN Charter* (n 65) 60; Thomas M. Franck, 'When, if Ever, May States Deploy Military Force Without Prior Security Council Authorization?', *Singapore Journal of International Law* (2000) 4, 362–76, 368.

[71] *Quran* (22:39).

[72] *Quran* (22:40).

[73] Al-Dawoody, *The Islamic Law of War* (n 28) 24–9.

[74] Ibid., 28.

[75] Ibid.

Hunayn and the battle of *Tabuk*.[76] In these three battles, the enemies' preparation to war—more precisely, mobilizing their armies—was an ample reason for Muslims to attack them. This fact confirms that Muhammad interpreted the right to self-defence stated in *Quran* to include anticipatory self-defence.

It is thus self-evident that anticipatory self-defence has more legal ground in Islamic law than in international law. However, despite the controversies surrounding the *de jure* existence of the right of anticipatory self-defence under international law,[77] it is difficult to deny its *de facto* acceptance in international relations today. It is therefore significant to discuss the conditions related to its practice under international law and Islamic law.

The customary international law of anticipatory self-defence is mainly derived from the *Caroline* incident.[78] In the beginning of the nineteenth century, while Canada was still under British rule, an anti-British insurgency was constantly taking place in Canadian territories.[79] At the time, the United States and Great Britain were in a state of peace. There was, however, a ship owned by US nationals (the *Caroline*), which was allegedly providing assistance to the rebels

[76] Ibid., 28. The Battle of *Hunayn* (630): After Mohamed's conquest to Mecca in 630, several clans and tribes (Huwzain, Thaqif, Qais, Nasr, Jusham, Sa'ad b. Bakr, and B. Hilal) marched to fight him in Mecca at Hunayam (three miles from Mecca). When Muhammad heard about their march, he sent one of his followers (Abd Allah ibn Abi hadrat al-Aslami) to verify the news. After he confirmed that their army was dispatched for this purpose, Muhammad met them with his army three miles outside Mecca at Hunayn. The Battle of *Tabuk* (630): After a Syrian trader informed Muhammad that the Byzantines are preparing for war against the Islamic state and that they are camping at al-Balaqi, Muhammad marched with his army, with the support of Quraysh, to confront them.

[77] Professor Andrea Bianchi in his answer to the question 'Is there a customary law in the use of force?' commented on the ICJ decision on *Military and Paramilitary Activities* that concluded 'customary international law continues to exist alongside treaty law'. He said: 'To conceive of a separate and distinctly applicable customary law on the use of force has allowed states to invoke and rely on customary international law rules justifying intervention on humanitarian grounds and anticipatory self-defense.' He elaborated that '[u]nlike in Nicaragua, where customary law was used to complement the law of the Charter by specifying the requirements of necessity and proportionality for the exercise of self-defense and by demanding that the victim of an armed attack expressly ask others to intervene in collective self-defense, arguments based on customary international law have gone as far as to admit of the existence of further exceptions not included in the Charter.' He concluded by stating that '[i]f the idea of the distinct existence and separate applicability of the international customary law regime on the use of force was expedient to overcome the jurisdictional objections and provide the applicable law in the Nicaragua case, to conceive of two distinct lives for the same societal body (virtually all states are parties to the UN Charter) may be difficult. In other words, it is puzzling to see how there can be state practice on the use of force outside the UN Charter. It is enlightening that the ICJ in Nicaragua stated that not all the issues of use of force in international relations are regulated by the UN Charter, but it would have been useful had the Court sketched out where these uncharted waters lie and how a UN member state could freely sail in them without colliding with the 'cornerstone' of the prohibition of the use of force.' See generally Andrea Bianchi, 'The International Regulation of the Use of Force: The Politics of Interpretive Method', *Leiden Journal of International Law* (2009) 22(4), 651–76, 660–1.

[78] Anthony Clark, 'International Law and the Preemptive Use of Military Force', *The Washington Quarterly* (2003) 26(2), 89–103, 90. Available at: <https://doi.org/10.1162/016366003605697 11> (last accessed 25 May 2019); Van Den Hole, 'Anticipatory Self-Defence Under International Law' (n 69) 95.

[79] Clark, 'International Law and the Preemptive Use of Military Force' (n 78) 90. Available at: <https://doi.org/10.1162/016366003605697 11> (last accessed 25 May 2019).

in Canada.[80] On the night of 29 December 1837, while the ship was anchored on the US side of the Niagara River, an armed band under the command of a British officer crossed the river, boarded the ship, and killed several US nationals, set the ship on fire, and cut it loose to float over the Niagara Falls.[81] The British claimed that they were acting in self-defence, but after some heated exchanges with the US Secretary of State, Daniel Webster, the British government eventually admitted culpability and apologized.[82] Nonetheless, over the course of diplomatic communications between the Americans and the British government, three criteria for permissible self-defence, including anticipatory self-defence, were articulated: immediacy, necessity, and proportionality.[83] These criteria are, generally, still relevant in the admissibility of the right to self-defence until today. They were further adopted by the International Court of Justice (ICJ) when it held that 'there is a specific rule whereby self-defence would warrant only measures which are proportional to the armed attack and necessary to respond to it, a rule well established in customary international law'.[84] Islamic law embodies the same criteria in a number of Quranic verses, such as: 'Fight in the cause of Allah those who fight you but do not transgress. Indeed. Allah does not like transgressors';[85] and 'And if they cease (their aggression), then indeed, Allah is Forgiving and Merciful'.[86] The interpretations of these verses are in conformity with the said criteria. Since it provides that Muslims are entitled to take the necessary measures only to repel the aggression of the enemy, once the enemy ceases the hostilities Muslims are not allowed to use force against them any longer. During the battles that took place under the command of Muhammad, it was noticeable that he effectually applied this Quranic command.[87] It has also been proven by *Sunnah* that Muhammad, in his three previously mentioned manifestations of the right of anticipatory self-defence,[88] respected the immediacy criteria. As stated, Muhammad sent one of

80 Ibid.

81 Van Den Hole, 'Anticipatory Self-Defence Under International Law' (n 69) 95.

82 Clark, 'International Law and the Preemptive Use of Military Force' (n 78) 90.

83 A key diplomatic exchange, among others, written by Secretary of State Daniel Webster on 24 April 1841 to the British Government stated that '[i]t will be for that Government (UK) to show a necessity of self-defense, instant, overwhelming, leaving no choice of means, and no moment for deliberation'. See Letter of Mr Webster to Mr Fox (24 April 1841), in 29 British and Foreign State Papers, 1840–41 at 1137–38 (1857) in Van Den Hole, 'Anticipatory Self-Defence Under International Law' (n 69) 96. The British Government accepted the definition of Mr Webster in a letter sent by Lord Ashburton to Mr Webster on 28 July 1842, but disagreed on the facts; Letter of Mr Webster to Lord Ashburton (8 August 1842), in 30 British and Foreign State Papers, 1841–1842, at 196 (1858) in Ibid.

84 *ICJ, Case Military and Paramilitary Activities*, Judgment, 27 June 1986.

85 *Quran* (2:190).

86 *Quran* (2:192).

87 Shah, 'The Use of Force Under Islamic Law' (n 3) 360.

88 The Battles of *Banu Al-Mustaliq*, *Hunayn*, and *Tabuk*. See Al-Dawoody, *The Islamic Law of War* (n 28) 27–8.

his followers to verify if the enemy is posing any threat or planning any attack against the Islamic state.

Another ongoing debate under international law is related to the scope of a state's right to self-defence against an imminent or actual attack by non-state actors who reside in another territorial state. One side of the debate favours the restrictive approach adopted by the ICJ, which stipulates that the right of self-defence can only be invoked 'in the case of armed attack by one State against another State'.[89] Conversely, if an attack is not attributed to a state, the victim state cannot use defensive force against another state. For this purpose, attribution takes place on the basis of the institutional, functional, and agency tests.[90] The institutional test is embodied in Article 4 of the Draft Article of the Responsibility of States (DASR) according to which an attack will be attributed to a state if it has been committed by a *de jure* or a *de facto* organ of that state.[91] According to the functional test, however, an attack will be attributed to a state if it has been committed by an entity that is empowered by that state to exercise governmental authority or is committed by an organ of another state that has been placed at the disposal of the first state.[92] As to the agency test, it requires an *ad hoc* relationship between a state and the non-state actor that commits the attack which is established when the state instructs or directs the non-state actor to attack,[93] or when the state exercises 'effective control' over such non-state actors.[94] The ICJ recognized that 'the sending by or on behalf of a State of armed bands, groups, irregulars or mercenaries' might trigger the right of self-defence under Article 51, commonly referred to as the '*Nicaragua* threshold'.[95] On the other side of the debate stand those who favour the more liberal but also more controversial approach that does not restrict the right to self-defence to attacks by states. This approach instead expands lawful self-defence to attacks

[89] ICJ, Advisory Opinion on the *Legal Consequences of the Construction of a Wall in the Occupied Palestinian Territory*, 9 July 2004, para. 139. The matter came up again in a recent case in the ICJ; the Court stated that in the absence of attribution of the armed force to a state there is no right of self-defence against that State. ICJ, *Case concerning Armed Activities on the territory of the Congo (Democratic Republic of the Congo v. Uganda)*, Merits, 2005, ICJ Rep., paras 146, 147.

[90] Kristen E. Boon, 'Are Control Tests Fit for the Future? The Slippage Problem in Attribution Doctrines', *Melbourne Journal of International Law* 1 (2014) 15(1), 1–48).

[91] ILC, 'Draft Articles on Responsibility of States for Internationally Wrongful Acts, with commentaries', General Assembly Official Records 56th session, supplement no. 10 (A/56/10), Article 4, 2001.

[92] Ibid., Articles 5 and 6

[93] Ibid., Article 8; ICJ, *Case Concerning United States Diplomatic and Consular Staff in Tehran (United States of America v. Iran)*, Judgment, 1980, ICJ Rep., 3, para. 58; ICJ, *Case Concerning Military and Paramilitary Activity in and against Nicaragua Case*, Judgment, 27 January 1986, Separate Opinion of Judge Ago, para. 16.

[94] ICJ, *Military and Paramilitary Activities (Nicaragua. v. U.S.)*, Judgment, 27 June 1986.

[95] Ibid.

by non-state actors.[96] One has to admit that despite the solid legal ground of the restrictive approach, it is no longer the dominant position in the international law literature today.[97] Many international lawyers now cite the contrary practice as evidence that defensive force against non-state actors is, at least sometimes, lawful.[98] These lawyers generally claim that customary international law has been evolving toward this direction, tending to regard the reactions of states and the SC to the 9/11 attacks as an unequivocal confirmation of this view.[99]

On the noon of 12 September 2001, a day after *Al-Qaeda* had killed almost 3,000 civilians, a few miles away of the collapsed twin towers, the members of the UNSC convened at the UN Headquarters in New York.[100] After a brief meeting, the UNSC unanimously adopted Resolution 1368 that affirmed the UNSC's determination 'to combat by all means threats to international peace and security caused by terrorist acts', and recognized, in general terms, 'the inherent right of individual or collective self-defence in accordance with the Charter'.[101] Two weeks after, the UNSC adopted a more legally and politically generous Resolution, Resolution 1373. This document repeated the same concerns and recognized the same right of self-defence.[102] It also embodied a whole list of obligations and recommendations for states in order to tackle international terrorism; a remarkable quasi-legislative action by the UNSC[103] that will be discussed thoroughly in Chapter 4.[104] In response, the UK government conducted its investigations on the attack on 9/11 which concluded that the attacks 'were planned and carried out by *Al-Qaeda*' and affirmed that the group still had 'the will, and the resources, to execute further attacks of similar scale' in the future, targeting the United States or its close allies.[105] In a

[96] Elizabeth Wilmshurst, 'The Chatham House Principles of International Law on the Use of Force in Self-Defense', *International & Comparative Law Quarterly* (2006) 55, 963–72, 964.

[97] Dinstein, *War, Aggression And Self-Defense* (n 41) 206–8; Thomas M. Franck, 'Terrorism and the Right of Self-Defense', *American Journal of International Law* (2001) 95, 839–43; Christopher Greenwood, 'International Law and the Pre-emptive Use of Force: Afghanistan, *Al-Qaeda*, and Iraq', *San Diego International Law Journal* (2003) 4, 7–38, 16–17; Jordan J. Paust, 'Use of Armed Force Against Terrorists in Afghanistan, Iraq, and Beyond', *Cornell International Law Journal* (2002) 35, 533–56, 535.

[98] Ibid.

[99] Ibid.

[100] UN Security Council, Resolution 1368 (2001). Available at: <http://daccess-dds-ny.un.org/doc/UNDOC/GEN/N01/533/82/PDF/N0153382.pdf?OpenElement> (last accessed 25 May 2019).

[101] Ibid.

[102] UN Security Council, Resolution 1371 (2001). Available at: <http://daccess-dds-ny.un.org/doc/UNDOC/GEN/N01/557/43/PDF/N0155743.pdf?OpenElement> (last accessed 25 May 2019).

[103] Paul Szasz, 'The Security Council Starts Legislating', *American Journal of International Law* (2002) 96, 901–5.

[104] Ibid.

[105] UK Press Release, Office of the Prime Minister, 'Responsibility For the Terrorist Atrocities in the United States, 11 September 2001', updated 14 November 2001. Available at: <http://fas.org/irp/news/2001/11/ukreport.html> (last accessed 25 May 2019).

failed attempt to flirt with the '*Nicaragua* threshold', the investigations added to the conclusion the following statement: 'the attacks could not have occurred without the alliance between the Taliban (as Afghanistan's *de facto* government) and Usama Bin Laden (as the leader of *Al-Qaeda*), which allowed Bin Laden to operate freely in Afghanistan, promoting, planning and executing terrorist activity'.[106] A fact later confirmed by the White House.[107] Once the source of the attacks had been established, convincingly enough for them, the United States issued an ultimatum demanding that the Taliban (i) hand over *Al-Qaeda* leaders, (ii) immediately shut down all their training camps, and (iii) allow the United States to verify that these camps were no longer operating.[108] President George W. Bush elaborated that these requests were not subject to negotiation or discussion, adding: 'The Taliban must act and act immediately, they will hand over the terrorists or they will share in their fate.'[109] On 7 October 2001, following a rejection of the ultimatum, the United States and the United Kingdom launched 'Operation Enduring Freedom', reporting to the SC on the exercise of their right of self-defence according to Article 51 of the UN Charter.[110]

Given the wide support that Operation Enduring Freedom received from the international community, some authors wonder why the United States and the United Kingdom did not even attempt to obtain SC authorization for this military operation.[111] Other lawyers suspiciously inquired whether this attitude was inspired by a deliberate strategic policy of seeking to 'overthrow' the *Nicaragua* threshold to liberate the world from such tight shackles.[112] Be that

[106] Ibid.

[107] David E. Sanger, 'A Nation Challenged: The Evidence; White House Approved Data Blair Released', *The New York Times*, 6 October 2001. Available at: <http://www.nytimes.com/2001/10/06/world/a-nation-challenged-the-evidence-white-house-approved-data-blair-released.html> (last accessed 25 May 2019). In this document, the White House acknowledged that it had coordinated and approved Britain's release of details of the case against Osama Bin Laden, even though it had declined, on national security grounds, to publish a similar accounting of the evidence against the suspected mastermind of the attacks on the Pentagon and the World Trade Center.

[108] 'US President address before a joint session of the US Congress', 20 September 2001, cited in Ryus, *Armed Attack and Article 51 of the UN Charter* (n 65) 435.

[109] Ibid.

[110] Ibid.

[111] Jonathan Charney, 'The Use of Force Against Terrorism and International Law', *American Journal of International Law* (2001) 95, 835–9, 838; Greenwood, 'International Law and the Pre-emptive Use of Force' (n 97) 21.

[112] Byres argues that '[a]lthough previous attempts to establish a right to engage in self-defense against terrorists proved largely unsuccessful due to a lack of international support, the situation in the aftermath of 11 September was considerably more conducive. Having seized the opportunity to establish self-defense as an accepted basis for military action against some terrorist attacks, the US will now be able to invoke it again-even when the circumstances are less grave. It is thus plausible to regard the choice of justification as, in part, a strategic decision directed at loosening the legal constraints on the use of force to the ongoing advantage of the US.' See Michel Byers, 'Terrorism, The Use of Force and

as it may, the international community almost unanimously, including the Organization of Islamic Conference (OIC), supported Operation Enduring Freedom,[113] thereby establishing the new doctrine of 'harboring and supporting' under international law, despite its clear departure from the dictates of Article 51 of the Charter and the *Nicaragua* threshold.[114] According to this controversial doctrine, states can only invoke the right of self-defence against an armed attack launched by a non-state actor in another territorial state if that state actively harbours or supports the given actor.[115] Others, instead, consider that it is sufficient to regard the non-state actors' attack as an 'armed attack' within the meaning of Article 51 if the host state lacks control over the area in which non-state actor operates, even if its actions cannot be attributed to the host state.[116] Some go further, by adopting the 'unable or unwilling' standard, by which states can invoke the right of self-defence against an armed attack launched by a non-state actor in another territorial state, even when the state exercises territorial governance over the area where the non-state actor operates and is actively trying to suppress their armed attacks but is, simply, ineffective.[117] This standard, however, is extremely tricky as it risks the political independence and territorial sovereignty of the host state in favour of the interests of the victim states without sufficient regard to the broader prospect for peace and security and the impact of such kind of broad exceptions on the general prohibition of the use of force under the UN Charter. Nevertheless, a number of states, including the United States, Israel, Russia and Turkey, have deliberately invoked the 'unable and unwilling' standard to justify defensive military operations.[118] For instance, the United States recalled this standard to

International Law After 11 September', *International and Comparative Law Quarterly* (April 2002) 51, 401–14, 410.

[113] Ryus, *Armed Attack and Article 51 of the UN Charter* (n 65) 436.

[114] The nexus between Al Qaeda and Taliban fell *prima facie* below the Nicaragua threshold. Based on the information available it was generally accepted that the 9/11 attacks were not attributable to the Taliban within the meaning of the ILC DASR. The Operation was not 'directed or controlled' by the Taliban as envisaged in Article 8 of the DASR, nor did the refusal of the Taliban to extradite Usama Bin Laden amount to 'acknowledging and adopting' of the attacks as their own as provided in Article 11 of the DASR. See Ryus, *Armed Attack and Article 51 of the UN Charter* (n 65) 440.

[115] Franck, 'Terrorism and the Right of Self-Defense' (n 97) 839, 840; Greenwood, 'International Law and the Pre-emptive Use of Force' (n 97) 7, 17.

[116] ICJ, *Armed Activities on the Territory of the Congo* (*Dem. Rep. Congo v. Uganda*), Judgment, 2005, ICJ 168, separate opinion of Simma, J., para. 12 (19 December). Ibid., separate opinion of Kooijmans, J. para. 30.

[117] Monica Hakimi, 'Defensive Force against Non-State Actors: The State of Play', *International Law Studies* (2015) 91(1), 1–32, 13.

[118] Ashley S. Deeks, 'Unwilling or Unable: Toward a Normative Framework for Extraterritorial Self-Defense', *Virginia Journal of International Law* (2012) 52, 483–550, app. I; W. Michael Reisman and Andrea Armstrong, 'The Past and Future of the Claim of Preemptive Self-Defense', *American Journal*

justify its airstrikes against the Islamic State in Iraq and Levant (ISIL).[119] The standard also finds some support in scholarly literature.[120] To conclude: the diversity of these arguments and opinions only reflects and confirms states' reluctance, confusion, and uncertainty about how this area of law stands and how it should be developed in the future.

Islamic law, however, did not provoke the same confliction and complexity in terms of the *ratione personae* of the right of self-defence. According to Islamic law, Muslims have the unlimited right to fight whoever attacks them, be it a state or a group or a tribe. The only limitation, as stated earlier, is that the 'other' has to initiate the first attack or pose an imminent threat of attacking the Islamic state. The question, nevertheless, is who can declare the defensive Jihad? According to the *Quran*, it was Muhammad's responsibility to declare the defensive Jihad. The verse says: 'O Prophet, urge the believers to the fight.'[121] Muslim Jurists unanimously agree that after Muhammad's death this responsibility was burdened strictly on the *Imam*, literally means the leader of the Islamic state.[122] In conformity, Ibn Qudama (a prominent Islamic scholar) stated that Jihad can be called only by the *Imam*, and the *Ummah* has to obey him.[123] Muslim jurists further agree that the fact that the *Imam* is a tyrant or unjust must not be an excuse for Muslims to abandon the *Imam's* call for defensive Jihad.[124] Accordingly, Muslim individuals or groups are not entitled to declare defensive Jihad without the permission of the *Imam* under Islamic law.[125] There are, however, two exceptions to this limitation, where Muslim individuals or groups can declare Jihad without awaiting the permission of the *Imam*. First, if the Islamic state is the victim of an alien military invasion, every Muslims have the right to launch a defensive Jihad against the alien invaders

of International Law (2006) 100, 525–50 cited in Hakimi, 'Defensive Force against Non-State Actors' (n 117) 13.

119 The US report to the Security Council explained that Iraq was 'facing a serious threat of continuing attacks from the Islamic State ... coming out of safe havens in Syria' and that, as 'the Syrian regime has shown that it cannot and will not confront these safe havens effectively itself'. See UN Security Council, Permanent Representative of the United States to the United Nations, Letter dated 23 September 2014 from the Permanent Representative of the United States to the United Nations addressed to the Secretary-General, UN Doc. S/2014/695, 23 September 2014.

120 Wilmshurst, 'The Chatham House Principles of International Law on the Use of Force in Self-Defense' (n 96) 969.

121 *Quran* (8:65).

122 Mohamed Al-Bouti, *Al-Jihad fi-al-Islam* (Beirut: Dar al-fekr, 1993) 112–18.

123 Muwaffaq al-Dīn 'Abd Allah ibn Ahmad Ibn Qudama, *Al-Mughnī: fī Fiqh al-Imām Ahmad Ibn Hanbal al-Shaybānī*, 10 Vols (Beirut: Dār al-Fikr, 1984–1985/1405) Vol. 8, 352.

124 Al-Bouti, *Al-Jihad fi-al-Islam* (n 122).

125 Ibid.

without an authorization from the *Imam*.[126] It is a permission similar to national liberation movements' controversial right to use force in pursuit of self-determination under contemporary international law rules.[127] Second, in the case of a powerful and organized rebel group,[128] if force is used in an internal conflict against the Islamic state and establishes a *de facto* government, the leader of this group is entitled to declare defensive Jihad without the permission of the *Imam* of the *de jure* government.[129] Similarly, if the Muslim rebel group resides in the territories of a non-Islamic state, such as *Hezbollah* in Lebanon, the leader of this group is entitled to declare defensive Jihad, if needed.[130]

3. Islamic Law R2P vs International Law R2P

In the background of the heated debate between the principle of state sovereignty and the principle of humanity sits the victims of human rights violations awaiting, as always, the announcement of the results. The question that this section addresses is whether states can resort to the use of force, under both Islamic law and international law, to prevent massive human rights violations occurring in a foreign state, despite the prohibition laid down in Article 2(4) of the UN Charter and the *Quran*. While this is one of the most controversial subjects under international law, it is less controversial under Islamic law rules. It should be noted, however, that international law clearly distinguishes between the protection of state's own nationals abroad and the protection of foreign nationals abroad, labelling the latter as 'humanitarian intervention'.[131] Thus the two matters will be analysed separately.

The concept of humanitarian intervention has evolved as a subdivision of *jus ad bellum* and rapidly came to compete for an institutional position alongside

[126] Ibid. The *Sunnah* also has dealt with this situation. After the battle of Qurayzah a group of non-Muslims raided the outskirts of Madinah, seized their camels, and killed their shepherds. One of Mohamed's followers fought against the attackers without his authorization; later on, Muhammad approved his action. See Muhammad ibn Abī Bakr Ibn Qayyim al-Jawziyyah, *Zad al-ma'ad*, Vol. 3 (Cairo: University Library, n.d.) 278–9.

[127] For arguments supporting the use of force by the National Liberation Movements, see generally George Abi-Saab, 'Wars of National Liberation in the Geneva Conventions and Protocols' in *Collected Course*, Vol. 169 (The Hague: Academy of International Law, 1981) 353–445, 366–92; General Assembly Resolution 2625, 25 UN GAOR Supp. (No. 28) at 121, UN Doc. A/8028 (1970) (hereinafter Declaration on Friendly Relations).

[128] The elements of 'power' and 'organization' as requirements for a rebel group will be discussed in Chapter 3 under the qualification of conflicts.

[129] Al-Dawoody, *The Islamic Law of War* (n 28) 155, 162; Shah, 'The Use of Force Under Islamic Law' (n 3) 358.

[130] Shah, 'The Use of Force Under Islamic Law' (n 3) 359.

[131] Simma et al. (eds), *The Charter of the United Nations* (n 34) 222.

self-defence and the SC authorization as a legal and legitimate reason for the use of force. Despite its commonality, the question that we are addressing here, namely whether humanitarian intervention is legal under international law, still generates uncertain answers. Many authors agree that the concept of humanitarian intervention appears to violate the prohibition of use of force under the UN Charter and thus should be considered illegal under international law today. However, recent developments in state practice could be taken as evidence of an emerging doctrine in international law that makes humanitarian intervention legal under certain circumstances.[132] Lawyers who are against the concept of humanitarian intervention rest their arguments on the plain language of Article 2(4) that prohibits the use of force by states and leaves no room for consideration for the motives behind the action. In an attempt to narrow down the scope of prohibition, some argue that the use of force that is strictly based on humanitarian justifications is directed neither against the 'territorial integrity' nor the 'the political independence' of the target state and that it is in conformity with the 'most fundamental preemptory norms' of the Charter.[133] As stated earlier, this argument is not supported by the purpose of the prohibition or the *travaux préparatoires* of the UN Charter.[134] Moreover, all the references made to human rights and fundamental freedoms of individuals, which might be read as endorsing a kind of humanitarianism in the UN Charter, are not attached to any legal obligations by states other than 'promoting' and 'reaffirming' those rights and freedoms.[135] Hence, legally speaking, the violations of those obligations may not be interpreted to modify or to make an exception to the general prohibition on the use of force. Had that clause been proposed in San Francisco seventy years ago, that failure of the protection of human rights could trump the prohibition of use of force, the idea would have undoubtedly been defeated by a large majority of the delegations, including the five SC permanent members to be.[136] Along the same lines, some argue that Article 2(4) prohibits humanitarian intervention only to the extent that the UN fulfils its

[132] Antonio Cassese, '*Ex Inuiria Ius Oritur*: Are We Moving towards International Legitimation of Forcible Humanitarian Countermeasures in the World Community?', *European Journal of International Law* (1999) 10, 23–30, 23; Bruno Simma, 'NATO, the UN and the Use of Force; Legal Aspects', *European Journal of International Law* (1999) 10, 1–22, 1.

[133] Michael Riesman and Myres McDougal, 'Humanitarian Intervention to Protect the Ibos' in Simma et al. (eds), *The Charter of the United Nations* (n 34) 222.

[134] For counter arguments, see Section 2 of this chapter.

[135] *Charter of the United Nations*, Preamble, Articles 1 and 55.

[136] Ian Hurd, 'Is Humanitarian Intervention Legal? The Rule of Law in an Incoherent World', *Ethics & International Affairs* (2011) 25(3), 293–313, 299.

role in safeguarding human rights.[137] The opponents of this argument, however, reply that the UN Charter does not provide the 'slightest hint' that validity of Article 2(4) might be by any means 'conditioned by the effectiveness of collective mechanisms for the protection of human rights'.[138]

Others argue that the new developments of international law evolving through state practice accept humanitarian intervention as legal.[139] Many authors agree that the concept of humanitarian intervention might have significantly gained acceptance in the recent years, citing a number of humanitarian interventions, including; the Economic Community of West African States (ECOWAS) interventions in Liberia and Sierra Leone, and the North Atlantic Treaty Organization (NATO) intervention in Kosovo.[140] In addition, the institutionalization of the concept of humanitarian intervention through the concept of the responsibility to protect (R2P) reflects states' willingness to take action in such situations.[141] Pursuant to R2P, governments affirmed their 'collective international responsibility to protect populations from genocide, war crimes, ethnic cleansing and crimes against humanity' and their 'willingness to take timely and decisive collective action for this purpose'.[142] Nevertheless, it stays as a political concept so far as it does not allow the use of force without a prior SC authorization.[143] The SC, however, explicitly endorsed the concept in Resolution 1674 in 2006,[144] and has applied it with varying degrees of ambiguity in relation to Darfur (Res. 1706), Somalia (Res. 1814), Libya (Res. 1973), and elsewhere.[145]

To the contrary, other scholars acknowledge the existence of relevant state practice but claim that there is no evidence of sufficient *opinio juris* to justify humanitarian intervention as a legitimate exception to the prohibition of the

[137] Michael Reisman, *Nullity and Revision. The Review and Enforcement of International Judgments and Awards* (New Haven, VT: Yale University Press, 1971) 850 cited in Simma et al. (eds), *The Charter of the United Nations* (n 34) 222.

[138] Simma et al. (eds), *The Charter of the United Nations* (n 34) 223.

[139] Michael J. Smith, 'Humanitarian Intervention: An Overview of the Ethical Issues', *Ethics & International Affairs* (1998) 12, 63–79 cited in Hurd, 'Is Humanitarian Intervention Legal?' (n 136) 304; Cassese, '*Ex Inuiria Ius Oritur*' (n 132) 23.

[140] Christine Gray, *International Law and the Use of Force*, 2nd edn (Oxford: Oxford University Press, 2004) 99; Sean D. Murphy, *Humanitarian Intervention: The United Nations in an Evolving World Order* (Philadelphia, PA: University of Pennsylvania Press, 1996) 366.

[141] '2005 World Summit Outcome: Fact Sheet', United Nations Department of Public information, September 2005. Available at: <http://www.ipu.org/splz-e/unga05/outcome.pdf> (last accessed 25 May 2019).

[142] Ibid.

[143] Ibid.

[144] 'Importance of Preventing Conflict Through Development, Democracy, Stressed: As Security Council Unanimously Adopts Resolution 1674 (2006)', United Nations, Press Release, 28 April 2006. Available at: <http://www.un.org/press/en/2006/sc8710.doc.htm> (last accessed 25 May 2019).

[145] Hurd, 'Is Humanitarian Intervention Legal?' (n 136) 299.

use of force under customary international law,[146] given that states provide various justifications for their forcible action.[147] Last but not least, some authors argue in favour of the concept of humanitarian intervention but from a completely distinct conceptual and legal perspectives. They argue that the 'normative value of sovereignty is derived from and geared towards humanity', since human rights, freedoms, interests, and security must be respected and protected.[148] The idea behind the humanitarianization of sovereignty suggests that statehood itself is legally dependent on acceptable government behaviour by respecting the human rights of its citizens, such that failure of a government to meet certain minimum standards nullifies its claim to non-interference. In other words, failure to meet such standards suspends that state's right to sovereignty.[149] In the end, no right answer exists in contemporary international law for this question. We find nothing more telling than the statement of Thomas Frank on the legality of the NATO humanitarian intervention in Kosovo, on which he frames it as a

> humane exception', while highlighting, however, that 'law is strengthened when it avoids absurdly rigid absolutes—for example, by requiring passivity in the face of destruction of entire populations—but only if exceptions intended to prevent such *reductio ad absurdum* are clearly understood and applied in a manner consonant with agreed notions of procedural and evidentiary fairness.[150]

Commenting on the same matter, Cassese asked: 'should one remain silent and inactive only because the existing body of international law proves incapable of remedying such a situation? Or rather, should respect for the rule of law be sacrificed on the altar of human compassion?' He, generously, answered the question he posed, by giving a genuine but dual consciousness answer: 'My answer is that from an ethical viewpoint resort to armed force was justified. Nevertheless, as a legal scholar I cannot avoid observing in the same breath that this moral action is contrary to current international law.'[151]

[146] Simma et al. (eds), *The Charter of the United Nations* (n 34) 234.
[147] Ibid.
[148] See generally Anne Peters, 'Humanity as the A and Ω of Sovereignty', *European Journal of International Law* (2009) 20(3), 513–44.
[149] Ibid.
[150] Thomas M. Franck, *Recourse to Force: State Action Against Threats and Armed Attacks* (Cambridge: Cambridge University Press, 2002) 172
[151] Cassese, '*Ex Inuiria Ius Oritur*' (n 132) 25.

On a slightly different front, despite the equal controversy and criticism against states' military operations with the purpose of rescuing state's own nationals abroad, states have managed to stretch the existing body of international law to legalize such conduct. Given the confirmatory state practice over at least the last fifty years, the positive *opinion juris*, the reluctance of other states in condemning or qualifying such operations as illegal, a rule of customary international law is established that allows a 'limited forcible action with the legitimate aim to rescue state's own nationals (and nationals of other states upon their request) in another state's territory without that state's consent and entailing, therewith, an unwritten justification to use armed force'.[152] This justification, however, is admissible in limited circumstances and under well-defined preconditions, as follows: (i) the nationals must be in serious and immediate danger; (ii) the host state must be unable or unwilling to protect the nationals; (iii) the intervening state does not pursue any other purpose on the occasion of the operation; (iv) the acting state may use only such force as is reasonably necessary.[153] Others argue that rescue operations could be justified under the right of self-defence laid down in Article 51 of the UN Charter.[154] As previously discussed, the dictates of Article 51 refer to the right existing whenever an armed attack occurs 'against a Member of the United Nations'; therefore, it would seem difficult to view any claim to self-defence as legitimate in the absence of a specific border or territorial violation.[155]

Under Islamic law, however, it is explicitly stated in the *Quran* that the Islamic state has the authorization to use forcible humanitarian intervention in particular circumstances. In the aftermath of the migration of Muhammad and some of his followers from Mecca to Medina, a considerable number of Muslims stayed in Mecca where they were subjected to oppression and religious persecution by the ruling tribe of Mecca—*Quraysh*.[156] The *Quran* explicitly provided Muhammad the permission to declare Jihad against *Quraysh* in order to 'rescue' the victims of oppression and persecution, who were

[152] Simma et al. (eds), *The Charter of the United Nations* (n 34) 227–8.
[153] Ibid., 228
[154] Bowett, *Self Defense in International Law* (n 69) 117 in Rex Zedalis, 'Protection of Nationals Abroad: Is Consent the Basis of Legal Obligation', *Texas International Law Journal* (1990), 25, 209–70, 235.
[155] Zedalis, 'Protection of Nationals Abroad' (n 154) 235; Simma et al. (eds), *The Charter of the United Nations* (n 34) 226.
[156] Ermin Sinanovic, 'Humanitarian Intervention in International and Islamic Law', *The American Journal of Islamic Social Sciences* (2003) 20(1), 88–106, 100 Available at: <http://www.i-epistemology.net/v1/attachments/695_Ajiss20-1%20-%20Sinanovic%20-%20Humanitarian%20Intervention.pdf> (last accessed 25 May 2019).

living under the clutches of *Quraysh* in a non-Islamic state. The dictate of the verse says:

> How is it that you do not fight in the way of Allah and in support of the helpless—men, women and children—who pray: Our Lord, bring us out of this land whose people are oppressors and appoint for us from Yourself a protector, and appoint for us from Yourself a helper.[157]

While some Muslim jurists, according to a restrictive reading of this verse, suggest that the permission to use forcible humanitarian intervention is limited to the case of supporting oppressed Muslims only, given the context and the rationale behind the revelation of the Quranic verse,[158] others claim that this verse lacks any reference to the oppressed people's religious affiliation and thus should be interpreted universally.[159] They argue that Muhammad was not sent only for a specific nation or nations but for all human beings, as God tells him in *Quran*: 'And We have not sent you but as mercy for all humankind'.[160] According to their arguments, the verse has a universal application irrespective of the religion professed and practised by those who are enduring persecution and oppression.[161] In conformity, the *Quran* says: 'Whoever saves the life of a person is as if he has saved the life of the whole of humankind.'[162] Here, the use of the word 'person' and not 'Muslim or believer' confirms that the scope of the protection responsibility given to the Islamic state should extend to reach any person in need, regardless of his religious adherences.[163]

Another Islamic concept, often cited by authors in this respect, is the concept of doing good (*al-amr bl-marouf*) and denouncing evil (*al-nahy a'n-al-munkar*).[164] As mentioned earlier, it was narrated in *Sunnah* that whoever

[157] *Quran* (4:75).

[158] Al-Dawoody, *The Islamic Law of War* (n 28) 59. It was also narrated by Numan bin Bashir in an authentic *hadith* that Muhammad said: 'The believers in their mutual kindness, compassion and sympathy are just like one body. When one of the limbs suffers, the whole body responds to it with wakefulness and fever', which means that Muslims should stand for each other's rights.

[159] Sinanovic, 'Humanitarian Intervention in International and Islamic Law' (n 156) 100.

[160] *Quran* (21:107).

[161] This is based on a principle in Islamic legal methodology that implies that a verse has universal application even though it was revealed on a specific occasion (*al-'ibrah bi 'umum al-lafz la bi khusus al-sabab*);Sinanovic, 'Humanitarian Intervention in International and Islamic Law' (n 156) 100; Yusuf Al-Qaradāwī, *Fiqh al-Jihād: Dirāsah Muqāranah li-Ahkāmih wa Falsafatih fī Daw' al-Qur'ān wa al-Sunnah*, 2 Vols (Cairo: Maktabah Wahbah, 2009) Vol. 1, 241f, 435f; Vol. 2, 865–71.

[162] *Quran* (5:32).

[163] Shah, 'The Use of Force Under Islamic Law' (n 3) 350.

[164] Sinanovic, 'Humanitarian Intervention in International and Islamic Law' (n 156) 100.

witnesses an evil deed should seek to correct it, if capable, by his hand; if not, then with his words; if this is not possible then at least by despising it in his heart.[165] In the same vein, the *Quran*, addressing Muslims, says: 'You are the best nation produced [as an example] for mankind. [Because] You enjoin what is right and forbid what is wrong and believe in God . . . .'[166] It is significant to note here that Muslim jurists repeatedly recall these sacred texts to confirm the very fact that one Quranic commentator put, by saying: 'one should not sit idle while people are enduring ongoing abuse'.[167] However, some of those jurists did put their own readings and interpretations to the definitions of 'good' and 'evil' to support what is called 'offensive Jihad'.[168] This concept will be discussed in the following section of this chapter.

In another Quranic verse, the Islamic state's right to use force in order to 'support' Muslims abroad was reaffirmed, whilst the exception to limit the authorization of this type of intervention is represented by the presence of a peace treaty between the Islamic state and the host state. In this case, the Islamic state's permission to intervene will be temporarily suspended. The verse says:

> And those who believed but did not migrate (to the Islamic state), you are under no obligation of alliance unless they migrate. And should they seek help from you in the matter of religion, it is incumbent on you to provide help unless it is against people with whom you have a covenant.[169]

In this context, the Islamic state is not permitted to use force against the oppressor as long as the peace treaty is valid. However, it could still decide if the treaty should be terminated, according to the severity of the violation, and thus use force against the host state.[170] In the end, it should be noted that the concept of humanitarian intervention for the protection of nationals/Muslims abroad is equally accepted under Islamic law and international law, whilst the one for foreign nationals/non-Muslims abroad is uncertain and underdeveloped in the jurisprudence of both laws.

[165] *Sahih Muslim*, in *Hadith* 1:79 (narrated by Abu Sa'id al-Khudri).
[166] *Quran* (3:110).
[167] Sayyid Qutb, *Fī Zilāl al-Qur'ān*, Vol. 6, 11th edn (Cairo: Dar Al-Shorouk, 1985); *Quran* (2:708).
[168] Shah, 'The Use of Force Under Islamic Law' (n 3) 354 (referring to Qutb and Mawdudi).
[169] *Quran* (8:72).
[170] Wahba Al- Zuhaylī, *Āthār al-Harb fī al-Islām: Dirāsah Muqāranah*, 3rd edn (Damascus: Dār al-Fikr, 1998/1419) 360.

4. Offensive Jihad

In 631, one year before the death of Muhammad, the last two rules related to *jus ad bellum* were revealed to him.[171] One verse (9:5) addresses Muslims' relationship with the polytheists and the other (9:29) addresses their relationship with the People of the Book. The first verse says: 'So, when the sacred months expire, kill the [polytheists] wherever you find them, and catch them and besiege them and sit in ambush for them everywhere. Then, if they repent and establish [prayer] and pay [poor due], leave their way. Surely, Allah is most Forgiving, Very-Merciful.'[172] The second says: 'Fight those People of the Book who do not believe in Allah, nor in the Last Day, and do not take as unlawful what Allah and His Messenger have declared as unlawful, and do not profess the Faith of Truth; [fight them] until they pay jizya with their own hands while they are subdued.'[173] A restrictive literal reading of these verses, led by some prominent classical Islamic scholars, suggests that Muslims are entitled to use force against the polytheists and the People of the Book if they refuse to accept Islam or submit to Muslim rule.[174] Under this interpretation, offensive Jihad is legitimized as the Islamic *jus ad bellum* rules were revealed to Muhammad in a gradual and progressive manner consisting of three phases.[175] The first during the Meccan period (610–622) in which Muslims were not entitled to use force; the second beginning after the migration to Medina (622–631)[176] at which point Muslims were given the permission to defend themselves under the concept of defensive Jihad;[177] and the last occurring after the Muslim community consolidated itself in Medina (631) in which the aforementioned verses, commonly referred to as the 'sword verses', were revealed to abrogate the 'defensive Jihad' and give Muslims permission to kill polytheists unless they embrace Islam; and kill the People of the Book unless they convert to Islam or pay *Jezya* (protection tax), thereby showing submission to the Muslim rule.[178]

[171] Michel Bonner, *Jihad in Islamic History: Doctrine and Practices* (Princeton, NJ: Princeton University Press, 2006) 26.

[172] *Quran* (9:5).

[173] *Quran* (9:29).

[174] This interpretation founded by Imam al-shafii (d. 820) and maintained by some Hanbali jurists and Ibn Hazm (d. 1064). See Al-Dawoody, *The Islamic Law of War* (n 28) 81.

[175] Shah, 'The Use of Force Under Islamic Law' (n 3) 346.

[176] *Quran* (2:109): '[O Muslims], many among the People of the Book desire to turn you, after your accepting the faith, back into disbelievers—all out of envy on their part, even after the truth has become clear to them. So, forgive and overlook till Allah brings out His command.'

[177] *Quran* (2:190): 'Permission [to fight] has been given to those who are being fought, because they were wronged. And indeed, Allah is competent to give them victory'. See *Quran* (22:39), 'Fight in the way of Allah against those who fight you, and do not transgress. Verily, Allah does not like the transgressors.'

[178] Shah, 'The Use of Force Under Islamic Law' (n 3) 346–7.

Muslims jurists, however, disagree over the very existence of the concept of abrogation in the *Quran*. Those who support its existence usually quote two Quranic verses, the first of which says: 'We do not abrogate a verse or cause it to be forgotten except that We bring forth [one] better than it or similar to it. Do you not know that Allah is over all things competent?'[179] The second says: 'And when We substitute a verse in place of a verse - and Allah is most knowing of what He sends down—they say, "You, [O Muhammad], are but an inventor [of lies]." But most of them do not know.'[180] Conversely, others argue that these verses mean that the *Quran* abrogates earlier revelations, such as the Holy Bible and the Old Testament.[181] In the end, even those who advocate for the existence of the concept of abrogation disagree on its definition and scope of application. They further differ in identifying instances of it.[182]

The majority of the modern Muslim jurists maintain that only defensive Jihad against aggression and persecution (R2P) is permissible and has never been abrogated.[183] The rationale behind their rejection of the gradual progressive approach is that studying Quranic verses must be preceded by a careful determination of the social context in which these verses have been revealed.[184] As Al-Dawoody persuasively points out: 'it goes without saying that Quranic verse on the issue of war must be read in their sociopolitical and linguistic context.'[185] He further elaborated that studying the Quranic verses on war requires two things: (i) defining the meaning of the words and the identity of those to whom the rule is addressed (i.e. the warring parties), and (ii) reconstructing the situation in which the parties involved went to war, including the reasons and justifications for the initiation of a particular act.[186] Hence, in order to prove that the 'sword verses' did not abrogate the defensive Jihad verses, a careful examination of the linguistic meaning and the socio-political context of these verses is inevitable.

At the time of the revelation of Chapter Nine in 630, there were four kinds of polytheists in Medina: (i) those with whom Muslims concluded a peace treaty. In particular, the treaty of *al-hudaybiyya* that allowed the principal parties (Muslims and the tribe of *Quraysh*) to create alliances by accepting the accession of other tribes to the treaty. Accordingly, the tribe of *Banu Bakr* allied

[179] *Quran* (2:106).
[180] *Quran* (16:101).
[181] al-Qaradāwī, *Fiqh al-Jihād* (n 161) Vol. 1, 275–84.
[182] Al-Dawoody, *The Islamic Law of War* (n 28) 52–3.
[183] Ibid., 81.
[184] Shah, 'The Use of Force Under Islamic Law' (n 3) 347.
[185] Ibid., 45.
[186] Ibid.

with *Quraysh* and the other tribe of *Banu Khazag* allied with the Muslims. This treaty was breached after *Banu Bakr*, with the support of *Quraysh*, attacked *Banu Khazag* in violation to the treaty. (ii) Those with whom Muslims had concluded peace treaties for a fixed period of time that were still valid and respected by both sides at the time of the revelation, such as the tribes of *Bani Zamrah* and *Bani Madlej*. (iii) Those with whom Muslims had open-ended peace treaties; and (iv) those with whom Muslims had no peace treaties.[187]

The first three verses in Chapter Nine addressed the polytheists who had breached the treaty of *al-hudaybiyya*[188] and were subsequently given four months of safe passage (*aman*).[189] Verse number 5, however, is one of the so-called sword verses. It states that once the four months have passed, war breaks out against those who breached the peace treaty except those of them who decide to embrace Islam.[190] The subsequent verse obliges Muslims not to kill those who have stopped fighting and asked for safety.[191] Furthermore, two other verses in the same chapter confirm that Muslims must respect the treaties concluded with those who did not support or take part in any attack against them.[192] The other 'sword verse'—verse 29—was revealed to give permission to Muslims to fight the People of the Book until they pay *Jizya* (protection tax) and submit to the rule of Islam.[193] This verse was revealed after news had reached Muhammad that the Byzantines (Romans), Lakhm, Judham, Ghassan, and Amilah—mainly Christian tribes—were preparing to attack Medina.[194] Accordingly, he mobilized his army and camped in *Tabuk* awaiting

[187] Shah, 'The Use of Force Under Islamic Law' (n 3) 348; *Quran Tafsir Ibn Kathir, Surat Al-Tawba* Available at: <http://www.qtafsir.com/index.php?option=com_content&task=view&id=2583&Itemid=64#1> (last accessed 25 May 2019).

[188] al-Qaradāwī, *Fiqh al-Jihād* (n 161) Vol. 1, 244.

[189] '[This is a declaration of] disassociation, from Allah and His Messenger, to those with whom you had made a treaty among the polytheists', see *Quran* (9:1). 'So travel freely, [O disbelievers], throughout the land [during] four months but know that you cannot cause failure to Allah and that Allah will disgrace the disbelievers.' *Quran* (9:2); Shah, 'The Use of Force Under Islamic Law' (n 3) 348.

[190] 'And when the sacred months have passed, then kill the polytheists wherever you find them and capture them and besiege them and sit in wait for them at every place of ambush. But if they should repent, establish prayer, and give poor due, let them [go] on their way. Indeed, Allah is Forgiving and Merciful.' *Quran* (9:5). The *jus in bello* aspects of these types of wars will be discussed in Chapter 3.

[191] 'And if any one of the polytheists seeks your protection, then grant him protection so that he may hear the words of Allah. Then deliver him to his place of safety. That is because they are a people who do not know.' *Quran* (9:6).

[192] 'Excepted are those with whom you made a treaty among the polytheists and then they have not been deficient toward you in anything or supported anyone against you; so complete for them their treaty until their term [has ended]. Indeed, Allah loves the righteous [who fear Him].' *Quran* (9:4). 'How can there be for the polytheists a treaty in the sight of Allah and with His Messenger, except for those with whom you made a treaty at al-Masjid al-Haram? So as long as they are upright toward you, be upright toward them. Indeed, Allah loves the righteous [who fear Him].' *Quran* (9:7).

[193] 'Fight those People of the Book who do not believe in Allah, nor in the Last Day, and do not take as unlawful what Allah and His Messenger have declared as unlawful, and do not profess the Faith of Truth; [fight them] until they pay jizya with their own hands while they are subdued.' *Quran* (9:29).

[194] Al-Dawoody, *The Islamic Law of War* (n 28) 29.

to repel what he thought to be an imminent Byzantine attack. The battle never took place.[195] Hence, the enemy of Muslims in this battle was not all the People of the Book, but rather a hostile group among them.[196] Al-Qaradawi, in this regard, affirmed that there is no justification for going to war against those, whether polytheists or People of the Book, who are not hostile to Muslims.[197]

The rest of the verses of this chapter were revealed after Muslims came back from the Battle of *Tabuk* to deal with those labelled in the *Quran* as 'hypocrites', particularly, those who had announced that they were Muslims but refused to join Jihad to defend Islam.[198] It should also be noted that Muhammad, during his journey to *Tabuk*, concluded a number of peace treaties with Jewish and Christian tribes located near the gulf of *Aqabah*. Therefore, modern Muslim jurists conclude that a careful contextual reading to these verses will only confirm that the 'sword verses' were revealed to address particular groups of people and their relationships with the Muslim at that time.[199] Indeed, the two verses still exist in the Quranic text but they are addressing the Muslims of seventh-century Arabia in the peculiar hostile context in which Arabs were living. In this regard, however, there is no disagreement between Muslim and Western scholarship that war was the normal state of relations between the various tribes in Arabia.[200]

Some of the Quranic verses were revealed to Muhammad not only as the Prophet of God but as the head of the Islamic polity at that particular time of

195 Shah, 'The Use of Force Under Islamic Law' (n 3) 349.

196 Ibid., 65.

197 Al-Qaradāwī, *Fiqh al-Jihād* (n 161) Vol. 1, 296f.

198 See, as mere examples, the following verses: 'O you who have believed, what is [the matter] with you that, when you are told to go forth in the cause of Allah, you adhere heavily to the earth? Are you satisfied with the life of this world rather than the Hereafter? But what is the enjoyment of worldly life compared to the Hereafter except a [very] little.' See *Quran* (9:38). 'If you do not go forth, He [Allah] will punish you with a painful punishment and will replace you with another people, and you will not harm Him at all. And Allah is over all things competent.' *Quran* (9:39). 'Go forth, whether light or heavy, and strive with your wealth and your lives in the cause of Allah. That is better for you, if you only knew.' *Quran* (9:41). 'Had it been an easy gain and a moderate trip, the hypocrites would have followed you, but distant to them was the journey. And they will swear by Allah, "If we were able, we would have gone forth with you," destroying themselves [through false oaths], and Allah knows that indeed they are liars.' *Quran* (9:42). 'May Allah pardon you, [O Muhammad]; why did you give them permission [to remain behind]? [You should not have] until it was evident to you who were truthful and you knew [who were] the liars.' *Quran* (9:43). 'Those who believe in Allah and the Last Day would not ask permission of you to be excused from striving with their wealth and their lives. And Allah is Knowing of those who fear Him.' *Quran* (9:44). 'Only those would ask permission of you who do not believe in Allah and the Last Day and whose hearts have doubted, and they, in their doubt, are hesitating.' *Quran* (9:45). 'And if they had intended to go forth, they would have prepared for it [some] preparation. But Allah disliked their being sent, so He kept them back, and they were told, 'Remain [behind] with those who remain.' *Quran* (9:46). 'Had they gone forth with you, they would not have increased you except in confusion, and they would have been active among you, seeking [to cause] you fitnah. And among you are avid listeners to them. And Allah is Knowing of the wrongdoers.' *Quran* (9:47).

199 Shah, 'The Use of Force Under Islamic Law' (n 3) 349.

200 Al-Dawoody, *The Islamic Law of War* (n 28) 29.

history in order to deal with a specific group of individuals in a specific socio-political context.[201] An analogy from the contemporary rules of international law, although far from being complete, is modern states' decision to include Article 107 in the UN Charter, in San Francisco 1945, given the particularity and the complexity of the socio-political situation of the world order in the post-Second World War period.[202] According to this Article, states that have the responsibility for actions taken or authorized as a result of the Second World War in relation to an 'enemy state' are exempt from the obligations of the Charter as far as these actions are concerned. Of course, that includes the prohibition of the use of force.[203] In this particular context, the principal victorious powers did not want to be restricted by the dictates of the Charter in their actions relating to their war enemies. Thus, states decided to add this provision while keeping it with a 'transitional' nature. In other words, the Article stays valid as long as the context for which it was created still exists. Thus, the Article becomes legally invalid once the consequences of the war with enemy states have been settled and after those states have been admitted as UN members.[204] Today, despite its textual existence in the UN Charter, Article 107 is considered obsolete under international law.[205] By the same logic, modern Muslim jurists, in my opinion, consider the so-called sword verses as obsolete today.

Even if we accept that abrogation is applicable to the Quranic text, this would imply that Muslims are obliged and not just entitled to fight unbelievers until they embrace Islam, whether there is a prior or imminent armed attack or not, as the defensive Jihad rules would have been abrogated in this case. Such an interpretation would be at odds with a number of verses that confirm the principle of freedom of belief in Islam and its peaceful preaching. In this respect, *Quran* says that 'there shall be no compulsion in religion.'[206] It also

[201] Some Quranic verses were revealed to Muhammad even to blame him for making wrong decisions in a particular context. One of the examples relevant to the subject of discussion in this chapter, is when those Muslims—later called 'hypocrites' (pretends that they are Muslims without believing in it)—asked Muhammad for excuse not to join the anticipatory defensive Jihad in the battle of *Tabuk*, he accepted their excuses, then a verse was revealed to blame him, it says: 'May Allah pardon you, [O Muhammad]; why did you give them permission [to remain behind]? [You should not have] until it was evident to you who were truthful and you knew [who were] the liars.' *Quran* (9:43). Quran Tafsir Ibn Kathir. Available at: <http://www.qtafsir.com/index.php?option=com_content&task=view&id=2552&Itemid=64#1> (last accessed 25 May 2019).

[202] 'Nothing in the present Charter shall invalidate or preclude action, in relation to any state which during the Second World War has been an enemy of any signatory to the present Charter, taken or authorized as a result of that war by the Governments having responsibility for such action.' *Charter of the United Nations*, Article 107.

[203] Ibid.

[204] Georg Ress and Jurgen Bröhmer, 'Article 107' in Simma et al. (eds), *The Charter of the United Nations* (n 34) 2124–91.

[205] Simma et al. (eds), *The Charter of the United Nations* (n 34) 219.

[206] *Quran* (2:256).

says: 'And if your Lord had willed, everyone on the face of the earth would have professed the faith. Are you then forcing people to become believers?'[207] 'And if your Lord had willed, He would certainly have made mankind a single nation. Yet they shall continue differ.'[208] Commentators of the *Quran*, such as Ibn Kathir and Rashid Rida, consider the key message of these verses to be the absolute prohibition of compulsion in religion, according to which no-one shall be compelled to embrace Islam, for it would serve no useful purpose for a person to be obliged to embrace Islam while his or her mind and heart are padlocked to Islamic guidance.[209] Rashid Rida adds that 'faith, which is the pillar and essence of religion, implies wilful submission of the self. Faith cannot be attained through coercion and duress; it must be attained through conviction and reasoning.'[210]

In terms of the methods of preaching Islam, the *Quran* says

> Invite (mankind, O Muhammad) to the Way of your Lord (Islam) with wisdom (with the Divine Inspiration and the *Quran*) and fair preaching, and argue with them in a way that is better. Truly, your Lord knows best who has gone astray from His Path, and He is the Best Aware of those who are guided.[211]

The call to the faith, therefore, should be through explanation and persuasion. Once the people are shown what Muslims believe to be the right path, it is their choice whether to take it or leave it. Some Muslim jurists, however, argue that the freedom of religion-related verses were abrogated, as well, by the verses on offensive Jihad.[212] Modern Muslim jurists, on the other hand, claim that the proponents of the abrogation approach lack sound reasoning.[213] They affirm that their argument is inconsistent with the general essence of the *Quran*, especially those related to the freedom of belief and those that assure the respect

[207] *Quran* (10:99).
[208] *Quran* (11:116).
[209] Mohamed H. Kamali, 'Freedom of Religion in Islamic Law', *Capital University Law Review* (1992) 21, 63–81, 77.
[210] Ibid.
[211] *Quran* (16:125). More verses indicated the methods by which Muhammad was assigned to use in preaching Islam, such as: 'If they embraced Islam, they would have found guidance, but if they turned their backs on it, then your only duty is to convey the message.' See *Quran* (3:20). 'Remind them, for you are a reminder, not a holder of power over them.' See *Quran* (88:21). 'And if they turn away, then we have not sent you as a guardian over them. Your duty is no other than conveying the message.' See *Quran* (42:48).
[212] Kamali, 'Freedom of Religion in Islamic Law' (n 209) 81.
[213] Ibid.

given to the previous scriptures and their people.[214] They further argue that it contradicts the practices of Muhammad who, in his first year in Medina, concluded a treaty with the various tribes of different beliefs, Christians and Jews, that guaranteed their freedom to practise their religion.[215]

Muslim jurists, nevertheless, disagree on the interpretation of another verse that fuels the Jihadist movements' ideologies to this day. This verse says: 'And fight them until there is no *fitnah* and [until] the religion, all of it, is for Allah. And if they cease—then indeed, Allah is seeing of what they do.'[216] Here the controversy arises from the interpretation of the Arabic word *fitnah*. Some Muslim jurists interpret *fitnah* as polytheism. According to them, Muslims are required to fight the polytheists until polytheism is eradicated from Mecca and even from the rest of the world, if possible.[217] Other jurists interpret *fitnah* as persecution and thus Muslims are permitted to fight their persecutors until they gain the freedom to practise their religion by repelling the enemy.[218]

These discrepancies between Muslim jurists over the meaning of the term *fitnah* lead to the formulation of two different theories of Jihad.[219] One of these theories advocates for a 'holy war', like offensive Jihad in which Muslims should fight until the enemies believe in Islam or be killed. The other recalls the notion of defensive Jihad or perhaps the principle of humanitarian intervention in Islam in which the legality of the use of force depends on the circumstances.[220] The problem, however, is that even those who interpret *fitnah* as persecution provide different meanings to this term. According to al-Mawdudi (d. 1979), colonialism has committed the 'biggest *fitnah*' by imposing man-made laws instead of *Sharia* law in the Islamic countries, affirming that Muslims should fight the colonial power until they retreat.[221] Qutb (d. 1966), however, stated

[214] 'We revealed the Torah in which there is guidance and light.' *Quran* (5:46). 'And in their footsteps We sent Jesus the son of Mary confirming the law that was revealed before him; We sent him the Gospel in which there is guidance and light and it confirms the law that had come before him, a guidance and admonition to those who fear God. Let the followers of the Gospel judge by what God has revealed therein, and whoever refuses to judge by what God has revealed are transgressors.' *Quran* (5:49–50). 'Say: We believe in God and in what has been revealed to us and what was revealed to Abraham, Ishmael, Isaac, Jacob and the Tribes, and in the scriptures that God sent Moses and Jesus and the Prophets. We make no distinction between them.' *Quran* (3:84).

[215] Ssenyonjo, 'Jihad Re-Examined: Islamic Law and International Law' (n 5) 25.

[216] See *Quran* (8:39).

[217] Muhammad ibn 'Umar Al-Rāzī, *Al-Tafsīr al-Kabīr aw Mafātīhal-Ghayb*, 32 Vols (Beirut: Dār al-Kutub al-'Ilmiyyah, 2000/1421) Vol. 15, 131; Al-Qaradāwī, *Fiqh al-Jihād* (n 161) Vol. 1, 257, 259–63.

[218] Muhammad ibn Jarīr Al-Tabarī, *Jāmi' al-Bayān 'an Ta'wīl Āy al-Qur'ān*, 30 Vols (Beirut: Dār al-Fikr, 1984–1985/1405) Vol. 9, 248–50; Muhammad ibn 'Alī ibn Muhammad Al-Shawkānī, *Fath al-Qadīr: Al-Jāmi' bayn Fannay al-Riwāyah wa al-Dirāyah min 'Ilm al-Tafsīr*, 5 Vols (Beirut: Dār al-Fikr, n.d.) Vol. 2 308; Ahmad Mustafā Al-Marāghī, *Tafsīr al-Marāghī*, 30 Vols (Cairo: Mustafā al-Bābī al-Halabī, 1946/1365) Vol. 9, 207.

[219] Al-Dawoody, *The Islamic Law of War* (n 28) 63.

[220] Ibid.

[221] Ahmed Abd Al-rahman, *Al-Islam w-al-qital* (Cairo: Dar al-Sharq Al-Awsat Lel-Nashr, 1990) 46.

that *Fitnah* could take place through an armed attack by the enemy or by simply creating the condition to corrupt the Islamic society, highlighting the fact that Muslims should fight whoever stands as an obstacle to the path of Allah or those who restrict Muslims' freedom of belief.[222] According to this verse, both al-Mawdudi and Qutb see Jihad as a permanent revolutionary struggle to abolish oppressive regimes.[223] Now that all the Muslim countries have been liberated from colonial powers, except the complicated case of Palestine, and oppression in their view is mainly being committed by Islamic countries against their own people, the new concept of Jihad against the 'near enemy' was developed and adopted by Jihadist movements.[224] This new concept of Jihad arguably finds its roots in Qutb's writings on *Jahili* society, meaning barbarism and ignorance of the pre-Islamic Arabia. Qutb argues that Muslims are 'surrounded by *Jahiliyya* today which is of the same nature as it was during the first period of Islam, perhaps a little deeper'.[225] He further claims that Muslims' foremost objective should be to change the *Jahiliyya* system at its very roots; a system which is fundamentally at variance with Islam and which, with the help of force and oppression, keeps Muslims from living the life demanded by God.[226] Finally, Qutb contends that Jihad against the current oppressive political systems is not intended to compel anyone to convert to Islam; it is rather designed to create a conducive environment for people to be free to choose if they want to believe or not.[227] Hence, for Qutb and his followers, Jihad is not a defensive movement in the narrow sense which today is technically called a defensive war. It is rather a movement 'to wipe out tyranny and to introduce true freedom to mankind, using resources according to the actual human situation, and it had definite stages, for each of which it utilized new methods'.[228]

In recent times, stemming from al-Mawdudi and Qutb neo-interpretations of the Islamic text, Jihad has increasingly been used by many Islamic Jihadist groups to justify the use of force against what they refer to as the 'far enemies'

222 Qutb, *Fī Zilāl al-Qur'ān* (n 167) Vol. 1, 189 cited in ibid.
223 Al-Qaradāwī, *Fiqh al-Jihād* (n 161) Vol. 1, 393–404; Shah, 'The Use of Force Under Islamic Law' (n 3) 352.
224 Al-Dawoody, *The Islamic Law of War* (n 28) 63.
225 Sayyid Qutb, *Ma'alem Ala al-tariq* (Milestones) (Cairo: Dar Al-Shrouk, 1973).
226 Ibid., 7.
227 'It is not the intention of Islam to force its beliefs on people, but Islam is not merely "belief". As we have pointed out, Islam is a declaration of the freedom of man from servitude to other men. Thus it strives from the beginning to abolish all those systems and governments which are based on the rule of man over men and the servitude of one human being to another. When Islam releases people from this political pressure and presents to them its spiritual message, appealing to their reason, it gives them complete freedom to accept or not to accept its beliefs.' Ibid., 33.
228 Ibid., 37.

and 'near enemies' of Islam. The 'far enemies' are, in particular, the United States and its Western allies, while the 'near enemies' are most of the governments in the Islamic world, and particularly in the Arab world, who are perceived by Jihadists as puppets at the hands of the Western powers. This is evident from statements made by Usama Bin Laden in 1996 and 1998, in which he declared war against the United States, whether civilians or combatants,[229] as well as in statements from ISIS leaders and other *fatwas* from various Islamic Jihadist groups.

Bassiouni commented on the recent evolution of the notion of Jihad by pointing out that:

> what characterized these doctrinal developments in internal Muslim power struggles is the search for the legitimization of armed force against perceived enemies, domestic and foreign. This has brought about new unorthodox exegeses of Quranic and *hadith* texts. The blatant politicization of the permissible use of force under contemporary political Jihad doctrine, which was developed selectively by politically-motivated clerics and leaders of radical movements advocating violence, is also accompanied by a rejection of traditional *Sharia* limitations on the ways and means of conducting warfare.[230]

He added that: 'self-characterization of legitimate violence is not enough to justify the unlawful use of violence by any party to a conflict, no matter how legitimate the cause may be.'[231]

[229] Osama Bin Laden, 'Fatwa: Background and Declaration of War Against the Americans Occupying the two Holy Places' (1996). Available at: <http://www.mideastweb.org/osamabinladen1.htm> (last accessed 25 May 2019); Osama Bin Laden, 'Declaration of the World Islamic Front for Jihad against the Jews and the Crusaders' (23 February 1998). Available at: <http://www.mideastweb.org/osamabinladen2.htm> (last accessed 25 May 2019).

[230] M. Cherif Bassiouni, 'Evolving Approaches to Jihad: From Self Defense to Revolutionary and Regime Change—Change Political Violence', *Chicago Journal of International Law* (2007) 8(1), 119–46, Article 8, 138. Available at: <http://chicagounbound.uchicago.edu/cjil/vol8/iss1/8> (last accessed 25 May 2019).

[231] Ibid. Professor Bassiouni argues that: 'Since World War II, there have been a number of conflicts in which impermissible violence was used by state and non-state actors. The latter, because of the military imbalance and power asymmetry between non-state actors and the occupying power or the established regimes, have resorted to unlawful use of violence as a means of redressing that imbalance. In conflicts of a non-international character, which include de-colonization, regime-change and wars of national liberation, the opposing sides have always advanced the legitimacy of their causes through labels which connote legitimacy. Thus, what is jihad to some is terrorism to others, and what is self-defense to some is terrorism to others.'

5. Conclusion

This chapter tackled the *jus ad bellum* from international law and Islamic law perspectives, whether in international or non-international armed conflicts. Its main purpose is to shed light on the commonalities and differences between these two existing legal paradigms because they are, in the main, the norms regulating the initiation of wars by and against the Islamic Jihadist movements in our contemporary world. It started with defining the different meanings of the concept of Jihad under Islamic law, highlighting that this research will focus only on the concept of military Jihad which raises a variety of questions and controversies due to its contemporary implications for national and international peace and security as well as its level of compatibility with international law. It further discussed the particularities of the prohibition on the use of force as articulated in the UN Charter. Accordingly, it was concluded that both international and Islamic laws, generally speaking, agree on the principles of the maintenance of peace and the prohibition of the use of force or military Jihad in international relations between states—and within one state according to Islamic law.

These two bodies of law also share the same exception on the use of force in self-defence—if an actual armed attack has taken place or to avert a threat of imminent attacks (the latter is commonly referred to as anticipatory self-defence)—and they adopt similar criteria for a permissive exercise of this right, namely immediacy, necessity, and proportionality. It is also apparent that the principle of humanitarian intervention for the protection of nationals/ Muslims abroad is equally accepted under Islamic law and international law, whilst protection of foreign nationals/non-Muslims abroad is uncertain and underdeveloped in the jurisprudence of both laws.

Last but not least, this chapter evaluated thoroughly the positions and debates of Muslim jurists *vis-à-vis* the notion of offensive Jihad, highlighting the risk of adopting any interpretation that supports such a theory. It emphasized the fragility of the position of those who supported the existence of the concept of abrogation or the so called 'gradual progressive approach' in the *Quran*, not only because it contradicts the opinion of the majority of the modern Muslim jurists, who rejected this approach because—for them—interpreting Quranic verses must be preceded by a careful determination of the social context in which these verses have been revealed but also because the applicability of such concept or approach would be at odds with a number of verses that confirm the principle of freedom of belief in Islam and its peaceful preaching. Nonetheless, one must admit, especially after reviewing al-Mawdudi and Qutb neo-interpretations of the Islamic text, that the ambiguity and indeterminacy of some of the Quranic verses in addition to the absence of any authoritative doctrinal body of interpretation on the subject, would often lead to a diversification of legal interpretations, notions, and practices, as will be discussed in Chapter 5.

3

The Islamic *Jus in Bello* from International Law Perspective

1. The Classification of Conflicts

In recent armed conflicts in the Middle East, the concept of Jihad has arguably been central in the legal and political debate among experts, analysts, and policy-makers. The term 'Jihad' was often used to cast doubts on the compatibility of Islam with modern norms of International Humanitarian Law (IHL). In such debates, Islam has been equated, by many, with radicalism, fanaticism, terrorism, intolerance, and aggression. Islam was usually labelled as a threat to humanitarian values and as an enemy of Western civilization. In this regard, questions have been raised about the validity of the regionalization of IHL or the Islamic particularism. Much of the confusion stems from the fact that the Islamic *jus in bello* has not received due attention in Western legal scholarship. Islam is frequently judged by the massive targeting of civilians in spectacular attacks that have occurred since 2001 or the daily massacres taking place in armed conflicts in the Middle East today. Thus, this chapter seeks to clarify the rules regulating the conduct of hostilities in both international and non-international armed conflicts under Islamic law. It attempts to draw lines between the Islamic law rules and those of contemporary IHL, while bearing in mind that thirteen centuries separate the births of these two legal regimes. For the purpose of this study, the chapter will be divided into three sections: Section 1: the Classification of Conflicts; Section 2: the Protected People and Objects; and Section 3: the Means and Methods of Warfare.

The rapid progress and evolution of the nation state in seventeenth-century Europe, beginning with the Peace of Westphalia (1648) and the ostensible decline of traditional religious authority in the Western world, led to the creation of a new body of law to regulate the complex and hostile relationship between states in times of war, a law that was predominantly drafted in the absence of any mighty Islamic power. IHL was created, mainly by Western states to regulate the conduct of hostilities of the warring parties in order to alleviate the

Islamic Jihadism and the Laws of War. Omar Mekky, Oxford University Press. © Omar Mekky 2023.
DOI: 10.1093/oso/9780198888369.003.0004

scourge of warfare. It is also referred to as the law of war or the law of armed conflict—*jus in bello* in Latin. The rules of IHL intend to preserve humanitarian values during armed conflicts by (i) protecting those who do not or no longer directly participate in hostilities, and (ii) restricting the right of parties to the conflict to use particular means and methods of warfare.[1] Similarly, the Islamic *jus in bello* seeks, under the same humanitarian grounds, to regulate the conduct of hostilities of Muslims by protecting non-combatants (be they Muslims or non-Muslims) and to limit their rights to use certain weapons and military tactics.[2] Both bodies of law apply only in times of armed conflict, and they distinguish between two generic types of armed conflicts, namely armed conflicts of an international character and armed conflicts of non-international character. Each type of armed conflict is subject to distinct sets of rules under IHL and Islamic law.

It is worth mentioning, however, that the classification methodologies and underlying motivations and interests vary a great deal from one body of law to the other. On the one hand, when codifying the rules of IHL, nation states were extremely cautious not to jeopardize the cardinal legal principle of sovereignty and therefore they adopted a more limited range of rules applicable during non-international armed conflicts.[3] On the other hand, in developing Islamic law, the Islamic community was keen to extend the rights and obligations derived from the law to all the *Ummah* members. As a result, Muslim jurists in their discussion on 'rebellion' provided even more protection to rebels than the one provided under international law, as elaborated in this section.[4] Hence, one can fairly say that IHL was developed along sovereignty-based interests while Islamic law evolved along community-based interests. In this regard, Vanhullebusch said that 'the categorization of the applicable law to different contexts of warfare shows proof of such distinction based on the nature of the belligerent parties as defined along the lines of presence or absence of respectively state-hood in IHL or Muslim-hood in ILW (Islamic law)'.[5] To understand the rationale behind such rules, and to define the moment when the *jus in bello*

[1] ICRC, 'What Is International Humanitarian Law?'. Available at: <https://www.icrc.org/eng/assets/files/other/what_is_ihl.pdf> (last accessed 25 May 2019).

[2] Mohamed E. Badar, 'Ius in Bello under Islamic International Law', *International Criminal Law Review* (2013) 13, 593–625.

[3] Matthias Vanhullebusch, *War and Law in the Islamic World* (Leiden: Brill Nijhoff, 2015) 5, 6.

[4] Nesrine Badawi, 'Islamic Jurisprudence and The Regulation of Armed Conflict', *Humanitarian Policy and Conflict Research at Harvard University* (2009) 1–13, 5, 6. Available at: <http://reliefweb.int/sites/reliefweb.int/files/resources/8FC97823516EEEDA4925762E001ABDA8-Harvard_Feb2009.pdf> (last accessed 25 May 2019).

[5] Vanhullebusch, *War and Law in the Islamic World* (n 3) 6.

becomes applicable in each context, it is necessary to clarify the different criteria of conflict classifications.

(i) Armed Conflicts of an International Character

Despite the explicit states' prohibition of the use of force against any other sovereign state, interstate warfare and armed conflicts are still a sad reality of our world today.[6] While some of these armed conflicts might amount to the crime of aggression, others are legitimized in exercise of states' inherent right of individual or collective self-defence or by the United Nations Security Council authorizations.[7] IHL, however, at least theoretically, applies with equal force to all the parties in an armed conflict irrespective of which party was responsible for initiating the conflict or of the legality or illegality of the use of force. This fact stems from the understanding and pragmatic assumption that armed conflicts are an enduring and probably inevitable feature of the international system and that rules to regulate such a complicated phenomenon must exist irrespective of which party is responsible for its initiation.[8] It is also irrelevant whether the parties to the conflict consider themselves to be in a state of war with each other and how they describe the conflict.[9]

The International Criminal Tribunal for the former Yugoslavia (ICTY), in conformity, held in the *Tadić* case that an international armed conflict exists whenever there is 'resort to armed force between States'.[10] This reading is in line with the so-called first shot theory, according to which IHL applies from the first moment that force is used by one state against the other state, regardless of any intensity or duration considerations.[11]

[6] *Charter of the United Nations*, Article 2(4): 'All Members shall refrain in their international relations from the threat or use of force against the territorial integrity or political independence of any state, or in any other manner inconsistent with the purposes of the United Nations.' By prohibiting the use of force rather than war, this provision avoids debate about whether a particular conflict constitutes war.

[7] *Charter of the United Nations*, Article 39–42 and Article 5.

[8] Steven Haines, 'The Developing Law of Weapons' in Andrew Clapham and Paola Gaeta (eds), *The Oxford Handbook of International Law in Armed Conflicts* (Oxford: Oxford University Press, 2014) 278.

[9] *Common Article 2 to Geneva Conventions*. It states that IHL applies to 'all cases of declared war or of any other armed conflict which may arise between two or more of the High Contracting Parties, even if the state of war is not recognized by one of them'.

[10] ICTY, *Prosecutor v Tadić*, Decision on the Defence Motion for Interlocutory Appeal on Jurisdiction, Appeals Chamber, 2 October 1995, para. 70.

[11] This opinion was supported by ICRC in its commentaries to the four Conventions. It provides: 'any difference arising between two States and leading to the intervention of armed forces is an armed conflict within the meaning of Article 2, even if one of the Parties denies the existence of a state of war. It makes no difference how long the conflict lasts, or how much slaughter takes place.' ICRC, 'The Geneva Conventions and their Commentaries', Common Article 2, paragraph 236, Available at: <https://www.icrc.org/en/war-and-law/treaties-customary-law/geneva-conventions> (last accessed 13 June 2023). A minority view argues that minor border clashes or other small incidents should be excluded from the

IHL of international armed conflicts also applies to all cases of total or partial military occupation, even if this occupation meets no armed resistance.[12] Once the territory of one state is placed under the authority of a hostile state's army, it is considered that an international armed conflict exists and thus IHL becomes applicable.[13] The occupation, however, extends only to the territory where such authority has been established and can be exercised, which is governed by the facts on the ground.[14] The last type of international armed conflicts is the so-called national liberation wars, in which people are fighting against 'colonial domination', 'alien occupation', or 'racist regimes', in the exercise of their right to self-determination.[15] This type has very limited relevance to the contemporary armed conflicts. It has also been argued that its field of application was intended to be quite restricted.[16]

The Islamic *jus in bello*, however, sees international armed conflicts with relatively different lenses. Islam was born in the seventh century in a hostile environment of tribal warfare in the Arabian Peninsula. The power, as eloquently put by Okan, 'was asserting itself in all walks of life and was absolute. The societies of the day had little or no social or economic structure. Any notion of state, territory, frontier, nationality, organized relations, information or communications was either lacking or unknown.'[17] At the time, people's identity was often based on their religious affiliations. Thus, the Islamic *jus in bello* was revealed and developed in a world divided primarily along religious rather than national boundaries. In other words, the Islamic *jus in bello*, unlike IHL which is made by sovereign states to protect states' interests, evolved along the Muslim community interests' in order to regulate Muslims' relations with

definition, as the notion of armed conflict would require a certain intensity; Andreas Paulus and Mindia Bashakmadze, 'Asymmetrical War and the Notion of Armed Conflict: A Tentative Conceptualization', *International Review of the Red Cross* (2009) 91(873), 95–12595ff., 101.

[12] Common Article 2 to the Geneva Conventions (GCs), para. 2.

[13] Article 42, Fourth Geneva Convention (GC IV), respecting the Laws and Customs of War on Land and its annex: Regulations concerning the Laws and Customs of War on Land. The Hague (18 October 1907). It provides that: 'Territory is considered occupied when it is actually placed under the authority of the hostile army. The occupation extends only to the territory where such authority has been established and can be exercised.'

[14] Ibid.; ICJ, *Legal Consequences of the Construction of a Wall in the Occupied Palestinian Territory*, Advisory Opinion, ICJ Reports 2004, 167, paras. 78; Ibid., 172, para. 89; ICJ, *Case Concerning Armed Activities on the Territory of the Congo (DR Congo v Uganda)*, judgment, 19 December 2005, para. 172.

[15] Article 1(4), First Additional Protocol to the Geneva Conventions.

[16] Harold Albert Wilson, *International Law and the Use of Force by National Liberation Movements* (Oxford: Clarendon Press, 1988) 168 in Deiter Fleck (ed.), *The Handbook of International Humanitarian Law*, 3rd edn (Oxford: Oxford University Press, 2013).

[17] Etin O. Okon, 'Islam, War and International Humanitarian Law', *European Scientific Journal* (2014) 16(14), 100–15, 106.

non-Muslims and among Muslims themselves.[18] Accordingly, the majority of Muslim jurists reasoned over international relations as a jurisprudential division of the world in two domains: one of peace (*dar al-islam*) and one of war (*dar al-harb*).[19] The domain of peace is where Islamic law governed and the political power lay with the Muslim community, and the domain of war encompassed territories which were outside the scope of Islamic sovereignty and, thus, where the religious and political rules of Islam were not implemented.[20] Accordingly, some classical Muslim jurists argue that Muslims are always at a state of war against the non-Muslim communities unless there is a peace treaty signed, which is often referred to as the domain of conciliation (*dar al-sulh*).[21] They reached this conclusion based on the fact that the Islamic *Ummah* has expansionist ambitions in order to propagate Islam, which resonates with the theory of offensive Jihad.[22] While this argument might have significant implications on the applicability of the Islamic *jus ad bellum*, it does not really impact the applicability of the Islamic *jus in bello*, which applies in any case once the actual use of force is initiated between any Muslim 'state' and a non-Muslim one. The criteria here are not subjective but rather objective. The fact that the Jihad is defensive, offensive, or undertaken on 'humanitarian intervention' grounds, justified or unjustified, is irrelevant. Under all circumstances, the Islamic *jus in bello* of international armed conflicts applies on all Muslims' conflicts that have at least one non-Muslim party. The case, however, becomes relatively different if the two parties to the conflict are Muslims.

(ii) Armed Conflicts Not of an International Character

During the past half century, non-international armed conflicts have far outnumbered those that are international in character. With the multiplicity of organized armed groups on the ground, especially in the Middle East, many Muslim states are involved in non-international armed conflicts in the region today. These states are often supported by a coalition of Western states to help them fight their internal enemies. Indeed, the prevalence of non-international

[18] Majid Khadduri, *The Law of War and Peace in Islam: A Study in Muslim International Law* (London: Luzac & Co., 1946) 118–120.

[19] Wahba Al-Zuhili, 'Islam and International Law', *International Review of the Red Cross* (2005) 87(858), 269–83, 278.

[20] Nahed Samour. 'Modernized Islamic International Law Concepts as a Third World Approach to International Law' in Rüdiger Wolfrum (ed.), *Max Planck Encyclopedia of Public International Law* (Oxford: Oxford University Press, 2010) 543–77.

[21] Vanhullebusch, *War and Law in the Islamic World* (n 3) 21.

[22] Ibid.

armed conflicts also has been ensured by a legal approach that views only state-on-state conflict as 'international' in character. In other words, a foreign intervention in support of a sovereign state in its fight against 'rebels' does not make a conflict international. According to IHL instruments,[23] there are two definitions for non-international armed conflicts and both differ from the definition provided for international armed conflicts.

A non-international armed conflict is defined under Common Article 3 as an: 'armed conflict not of an international character occurring in the territory of one of the High Contracting Parties'.[24] Given the ambiguity of the definition, a significant contribution was provided by the ICTY in the *Tadić* case in order to elaborate its tenets. The Court held that 'the central legal question is whether there is sufficiently intense armed violence between an organized armed group and a state or another organized armed group'.[25] Accordingly, two basic requirements are conditioned in order to classify an armed conflict as non-international, namely: (i) the parties must be sufficiently organized and (ii) the armed violence must be of sufficient intensity. In other words, it is not enough for a conflict to comprise dispersed individuals who do not possess the minimum level of organization that enable them to engage in military activities of a certain intensity, and not enough that the conflict consists of only sporadic acts of violence, such as terrorist attacks.[26] According to this definition, violence can take place, as in the classical scenarios of insurgencies, between one organized non-state armed group on one side, and the governmental forces on the other, or between organized non-state armed groups. The latter situation may occur when the state is unwilling or unable to intervene, or where there is no more government in place, as in the 'failed state' scenario.[27]

Additionally, a more restrictive definition of non-international armed conflict was adopted by the Second Additional Protocol, which provides that the Protocol applies to armed conflicts

> which take place in the territory of a High Contracting Party between its armed forces and dissident armed forces or other organized armed groups

[23] Common Article 3 of the Geneva Conventions; Article 1, Second Additional Protocol to the Geneva Conventions.
[24] Ibid.
[25] ICTY, The *Prosecutor v. Dusko Tadic*, Judgment, IT-94-1-T, 7 May 1997, paras 561–568; ICTY, The *Prosecutor v. Fatmir Limaj*, Judgment, IT-03-66-T, 30 November 2005, para. 84.
[26] International Institute of Humanitarian Law, 'The Distinction Between International and Non-International Armed Conflicts: Challenges for IHL?', *38th Sanremo Round Table* (Sanremo, 3–5 September 2015). Available at: <http://www.iihl.org/wp-content/uploads/2015/12/Pedrazzi.pdf> (last accessed 25 May 2019).
[27] Ibid.

> which, under responsible command, exercise such control over a part of its territory as to enable them to carry out sustained and concerted military operations and to implement this Protocol.[28]

This definition includes two specific elements that are distinctly not requested by the former definition of Common Article 3, namely (i) a requirement of territorial control, by providing that the non-state organized armed groups must exercise sufficient territorial control 'as to enable them to carry out sustained and concerted military operations'; and (ii) the fact that this Protocol applies only to conflicts between the state and non-state organized armed groups, and not those conflicts only involving organized armed groups. In this context, it must be noted that the definition of the Second Additional Protocol 'develops and supplements' Common Article 3 'without modifying its existing conditions of application.'[29] This means that this restrictive definition is relevant for the application of the Second Additional Protocol only, and does not extend to the law of non-international armed conflicts in general. In this regard, Article 8(2)(f) of the Rome Statute confirms the existence of a definition of a non-international armed conflict not fulfilling the criteria of the Second Additional Protocol.[30]

Despite the apparent simplicity of the definition of non-international armed conflicts, its application faces multiple layers of complexities in order to classify armed conflicts on the ground, based on which IHL becomes either applicable or inapplicable. Among the legal complexities is the determination of the standards that should be followed to assess the level of organization and the level of intensity as two indispensable factual criteria for classifying a situation of violence as non-international armed conflict. Indeed, the assessment of these elements depends on a factual examination of events on the ground that are often complex, inaccessible, and lack clarity. In an attempt to solve this legal dilemma, the ICTY jurisprudence put forward indicative factors on the basis of which the 'organization' and 'intensity' criteria may be assessed.[31] But

[28] Article 1, Second Additional Protocol to the Geneva Conventions, 1977.

[29] Ibid.

[30] Article 8(2)(f), *Rome Statute*. The article provides that '[i]t applies to armed conflicts that take place in the territory of a State when there is protracted armed conflict between governmental authorities and organized armed groups or between such groups' without any mention of the 'territorial control' aspect.

[31] As for the level of organization, the court held that '[a]s for armed groups, Trial Chambers have relied on several indicative factors, none of which are, in themselves, essential to establish whether the "organization" criterion is fulfilled. Such indicative factors include the existence of a command structure and disciplinary rules and mechanisms within the group; the existence of a headquarters; the fact that the group controls a certain territory; the ability of the group to gain access to weapons, other military equipment, recruits and military training; its ability to plan, coordinate and carry out military operations, including troop movements and logistics; its ability to define a unified military strategy and use military tactics; and its ability to speak with one voice and negotiate and conclude agreements

despite all the jurisprudence offered by the international tribunals, the recent evolution of warfare and the variety of the factual scenarios of armed conflicts and its parties have led to the emergence of various types of non-international armed conflicts that are rather more complex. Recent or emerging extra-conventional types of non-international armed conflicts include:[32]

(1) The 'Spill Over Scenario': non-international armed conflicts originating within the territory of a single state between government armed forces and one or more non-state organized armed groups have also been known to 'spill over' into the territory of neighboring states;
(2) The 'Multinational Scenario': the last decade, in particular, has seen the emergence of what may be called 'multinational non-international armed conflicts'. These are armed conflicts in which multinational armed forces are fighting alongside the armed forces of a 'host' state in its territory, against one or more non-state organized armed groups. As the armed conflict does not oppose two or more states, as all the state actors are on the same side, the conflict must be classified as non-international, regardless of the international components existent on the ground, which can at times be significant;
(3) The 'Cross-border Scenario': in this scenario, the armed forces of a state are engaged in hostilities against a non-state organized armed group and operating from the territory of a neighbouring host state without that state's control or support;
(4) The 'Transitional Scenario': these are armed conflicts taking place across multiple states in which one state or a coalition of states' are fighting one non-state organized armed group and its affiliates. This particular scenario was brought into existence after the attacks of 9/11, when the Bush Administration waged the 'war on terror'. The United States declared that *Al-Qaeda* and its affiliates comprise a global network active

such as cease-fire or peace accords.' As for the level of intensity, the court provides indicative factors for assessment including 'the number, duration and intensity of individual confrontations, the type of weapons and other military equipment used, the number and calibre of munitions fired, the number of persons and types of forces partaking in the fighting, the number of casualties, the extent of material destruction, and the number of civilians fleeing combat zones'. ICTY, *Prosecutor v. Ramush Haradinaj, Idriz Balaj and Lahi Brahimaj*, Trial Judgment, IT-04-84-T, 3 April 2008, para. 49.

[32] ICRC, 'International Humanitarian Law and the Challenges Of Contemporary Armed Conflicts Report', *31st International Conference of the Red Cross and the Red Crescent* (Geneva: ICRC, 2011) 9–10 (hereinafter ICRC Challenges Report); Marco Sassoli, 'The Role of Human Rights and International Humanitarian Law in New Types of Armed Conflicts' in Orna Ben-Naftali (ed.), *International Humanitarian Law and International Human Rights Law* (Oxford: Oxford University Press, 2011) 34–94.

> in numerous states and because of this it might be necessary to conduct hostilities wherever the *Al-Qaeda* fighters are present. By this, the US government confirmed that this conflict is neither an international armed conflict governed by the Geneva Conventions, because *Al-Qaeda* was not a state party, nor a non-international armed conflict because it exceeded the territory of one state.[33] This opinion was domestically superseded by the US Supreme Court, which ruled in the 2006 *Hamdan* case that the armed conflict in question was at least governed by Common Article 3 as a matter of US treaty obligation, and thus implying that the situation was a non-international armed conflict in nature.[34] The International Committee of the Red Cross (ICRC) announced, with respect to this particular question, that it does not believe that there was, or is, an armed conflict of global dimensions of any kind taking place; it adopted a case-by-case approach to analysing and classifying legally the various situations of violence that have taken place in the fight against 'terrorism'.[35]

Islamic law, however, offers an equivalent level of complexity in respect to the assessment of the factual criteria on the ground in order to classify the conflict as non-international. Under Islamic law, there are two main sources predominantly cited for the rules applicable in non-international conflicts, namely the *Quran*,[36] and the precedents set by the Fourth Caliph Ali ibn Abi Talib in his conflicts with those who rebelled against him in the battles of the *Camel* (656) and *Siffin* (657). It is noteworthy that *Sunnah* did not refer to any rules related to non-international armed conflicts due to the fact that the first

[33] White House Memorandum on the 'Humane Treatment of Taliban and Al Qaeda Detainees', 7 February 2002. Available at: <http://www.pegc.us/archive/White_House/bush_memo_20020207_ed.pdf> (last accessed 25 May 2019). Indeed, subsequent US administrations have taken a different position and instead refer to an armed conflict of the United States with *Al-Qaeda* and its associated forces. See, e.g., H. H. Koh, Legal Adviser, US Department of State, Address to the Annual Meeting of the American Society of International Law: The Obama Administration and International Law (25 March 2010), <<http://www.state.gov/s/l/releases/remarks/139119.htm> (last accessed 25 May 2019).

[34] United States Supreme Court, *Hamdan v. Rumsfeld* (hereafter the Hamdan case), 548 US 557, 2006, pp. 628–31.

[35] 'International Humanitarian Law and the Challenges of Contemporary Armed Conflicts', *ICRC Report presented at the 28th International Conference of the Red Cross and Red Crescent* (03/IC/09), 2–6 December 2003, 18; 'International Humanitarian Law and the Challenges of Contemporary Armed Conflicts', *ICRC Report presented at the 30th International Conference of the Red Cross and Red Crescent* (30IC/07/8.4), 26–30 November 2007, 7.

[36] 'And if two parties or groups among the believers fight each other, then make peace between both of them, but if one of them rebels against the other, then fight you (all) against the one that rebels until it complies with the Command of Allah; then if it complies, then make reconciliation between them justly, and be equitable. Verily! Allah loves those who are equitable.' *Quran* (49:9).

non-international armed conflict in Islamic history took place after the death of Muhammad.

Under Islamic law, to put it in the simplest terms, a non-international armed conflict exists when a Muslim group fights against any other Muslim entity. However, similar to IHL, Muslim jurists developed specific criteria and thresholds that must be met for the Islamic *jus in bello* of non-international armed conflicts to be applicable. The only type of such conflicts that trigger the applicability of the Islamic *jus in bello* is the war against *al-bughah* (rebels).[37] The word '*baghy*' (to rebel) in Arabic, means to demand, or to transgress, or commit injustice.[38] The word is not value-neutral, yet Muslim jurists consistently affirm that the term, legally, does not connote censure or blame.[39] Some other jurists insist that *baghy* is an offence that leads only to the destruction of life and property.[40] Muslim jurists do agree on particular criteria that should be fulfilled in any 'rebel' group in order to be legally qualified as a party to a non-international armed conflict, namely 'a group of Muslims that possesses some power and organization (*shawkah*) and that gathers, under the command of a leader, to fight against a just ruler claiming, whether rightly or wrongly, that they have a *ta'wīl* (just cause, plausible interpretation) for their rebellion, secession or non-compliance with an obligation.'[41]

[37] Sadia Tabassum, 'Combatants, Not Bandits: The Status of Rebels in Islamic Law', *International Review of the Red Cross* (2011) 93(881) 121–39.

[38] Khaled Abu Al-Fadl, *Rebellion and Violence in Islamic Law* (Cambridge: Cambridge University Press, 2001) 32.

[39] Ibid.

[40] Ibid.

[41] Zayd al-Dīn Ibn Najīm, *Al-Bahr al-Rā'iq Sharh Kanz al-Daqā'iq*, 2nd edn, 8 Vols (Beirut: Dār al-Ma'rifah, n.d.) Vol. 5, 151; 'Abd Allah ibn Mahmūd Ibn Mawdūd, *Al-Ikhtiyār li-Ta'līl al-Mukhtār*, ed. 'Abd al-Latīf Muhammad 'Abd al-Rahman, 3rd edn, 5 Vols (Beirut: Dār al-Kutub al-'Ilmiyyah, 2005/1426) Vol. 4, 160; al-Shaykh Niẓām and a group of Indian scholars, *Al-Fatāwā al-Hindiyyah: Fī Madhhab al-Imām al-A'zam Abī Hanīfah al-Nu'mān*, 6 Vols (n.p.: Dār al-Fikr, 1991/1411) Vol. 2, 283; Muhammad Amīn ibn 'Umar Ibn 'Ābidīn, *Hāshiyah Radd al-Muhtār 'alā al-Durr al-ukhtār: Sharh Tanwīr al-Absār Fiqh Abū Hanīfah*, 8 Vols (Beirut: Dār al-Fikr, 2000/1421) Vol. 4, 261; Muhyī al-Dīn ibn Sharaf al-Nawawī, *Al-Majmū': Sharh al-Muhadhdhab*, ed. Mahmūd Matrajī, 22 Vols (Beirut: Dār al-Fikr, 2000) Vol. 20, 337; Alī ibn Muhammad ibn Habīb al-Māwardī, *Nasīhah al-Mulūk*, ed. Khidr Muhammad Khidr (Al-Safah, Kuwait: Maktabah al-Falāh, 1983/1403) 254; Muhammad al-Khatīb al-Shirbīnī, *Mughnī al-Muhtāj ilā Ma'rifah Ma'ānī Alfāz al-Minhāj*, 4 Vols (Beirut: Dār al-Fikr, n.d.) Vol. 4, 123; Muwaffaq al-Dīn 'Abd Allah ibn Ahmad Ibn Qudāmah, *'Umdah al-Fiqh*, ed. 'Abd Allah Safar al-'Abdalī and Muhammad Dughaylib al-'Utaybī (Taif: Maktabah al-Tarafayn, n.d.) 149; and Al-Mughnī, Vol. 9, 5; al-Mirdāwī, 'Al-Inṣāf', Vol. 10, 311; Mansur Ibn Yunus Ibn Salah Al-Din al-Buhūtī, *Al-rawd al-murbi' sharh zad al-mustaqni'* (Turath For Solutions, 2013) Vol. 3, 335; Mansur Ibn Yunus Ibn Salah Al-Din al-Buhūtī, *Kashshāf al-Qinā' 'an Matn al-Iqnā'*, ed. Hilāl Misīlhī Mustafā Hilāl (Beirut: Dār al-Fikr, 1981–1982/1402) Vol. 6, 159, 161; Ibn Muflih, *Al-Furū'*, ed. Abī al-Zahrā' Hāzim al-Qādī (Beirut: Dār al-Kutub al-'Ilmiyyah, 1997/1418) Vol. 6, 147; Ibn Muflih, 'Al-Mubdi'', Vol. 9, 159; Mustafā al-Suyūtī al-Rahaybānī, *Matālib Ulī al-Nuhā fī Sharh Ghāyah al-Muntahā* (Damascus: Al-Maktab al-Islāmī, 1961) Vol. 6, 262; 'Alī ibn Ahmad ibn Sa'īd Ibn Ḥazm, *Al-Muhallā* (Beirut: Dār al-Āfāq al-Jadīdah, n.d.) Vol. 11, 97; Muhammad ibn 'Alī ibn Muhammad al-Shawkānī, *Al-Sayl al-Jarrār al-Mutadaffiq 'alā Hadā'iq al-Azhār*, ed. Mahmmūd Ibrāhīm Zāyid (Beirut: Dār al-Kutub al-'Ilmiyyah, 1984–1985/1405) Vol. 4, 558; Muhammad Abū Zahrah, *Al-Jarīmah wa al-'Uqūbah fī al-Fiqh al-Islāmī: al-Jarīmah* (Cairo: Dār

According to this definition, Islamic armed groups should meet three requirements to be qualified as a rebel group under Islamic law. First, they must be a powerful organized group (*Shawkah*). Muslim jurists have different views on how to assess the power and the organization of the group. Some claim that it should depend on the rebel numbers,[42] while others are in favour of their ability to exercise territorial control.[43] The majority, however, stipulate that the situation should be sufficiently intense for the state to deploy the armed forces to control it instead of the police.[44] In addition, some jurists point out that the group should have a leader and chain of command.[45] Second, the group must have a just cause (*ta'wil*) or a legitimate reason to rebel, at least from their own perspective. This could be for any injustice inflicted upon them by the government. Their justification may be based on religious or political foundations.[46] The majority of Muslim jurists also agree that the rebels' justifications do not have to be valid from the Muslim state's perspective.[47] The rationale behind this view is not to leave the assessment of the validity of the rebels' justifications for rebellion in the hands of their opponents.[48] Third, the group must use force (*Khuruj*) against the other party to the conflict. In other words, peaceful demonstrations and sit-ins do not trigger the application of the Islamic *jus in bello* of non-international armed conflicts.

al-Fikr al-ʿArabī, 1998) 125ff.; ʿAbd al-Qādir ʿAwdah, *Al-Tashrīʿ al-Jināʾī al-Islāmī: Muqāranā bi-al-Qānūn al-Wadʿī* (Beirut: Dār al-Kitāb al-ʿArabī, n.d.) Vol. 2, 674; and *Criminal Law of Islam*, trans. Zakir Aijaz (New Delhi: Kitab Bhavan, reprint, 2005) Vol. I, 113ff., 182, cited in Ahmed Al-Dawoody, *The Islamic Law of War: Justifications and Regulations* (New York, NY: Palgrave Macmillan, 2011) 150.

[42] Al-Shirbīnī, *Mughnī al-Muhtāj ilā Maʿrifah Maʿānī Alfāz al-Minhāj* (n 41) Vol. 4, 123; Muhammad ibn Idrīs al-Shāfiʿī, *Al-Umm*, 2nd edn (Beirut: Dār al-Maʿrifah, 1973/1393) Vol. 4, 218; Al Fadl, *Rebellion and Violence in Islamic Law* (n 38) 151; Alī ibn Sulaymān Al-Mirdāwī, *Al-Insāf fī Maʿrifah al-Rājih min al-Khilāf ʿalā Madhhab al-Imām Ahmad Ibn Hanbal*, ed. Muhammad Hamid al-Fiqī (Beirut: Dār Ihyāʾ al-Turāth al-ʿArabī, n.d.) Vol. 10, 311; Ibn Mufl ih, *Al-Furūʿ* (n 41) Vol. 6, 147 cited in Al-Dawoody, *The Islamic Law of War* (n 41) 159.

[43] Abū al-ʿAbbās Šihāb-ad-Dīn al-Bakīr Al-Anṣārī, *Asnā al-maṭālib šarḥ rawḍ aṭ-ṭālib* (Cairo: Dār al-Fikr, 2008) Vol. 4, 112; al-Shirbīnī, *Mughnī al-Muhtāj ilā Maʿrifah Maʿānī Alfāz al-Minhāj* (n 41) Vol. 4, 123; Muhammad ibn Abī al-ʿAbbās Ahmad ibn Hamzah al-Ramlī, *Nihāyah al-Muhtāj ilā Sharh al-Minhāj* (Beirut: Dār al-Fikr, 1984/1404) Vol. 7, 403; Muhammad al-Khatīb Al-Shirbīnī, *Al-Iqnāʿ fī Hall al-Fāz Abī Shujāʿ*, ed. Maktab al-Buhūth wa al-Dirasāt (Beirut: Dār al-Fikr, 1994–5/1415) Vol. 2, 547, cited in Al-Dawoody, *The Islamic Law of War* (n 41) 159.

[44] Al-Qarāfī, 'Al-Dhakhīrah', Vol. 12, 6; al-Rahaybānī, *Matālib Ulī al-Nuhā fī Sharh Ghāyah al-Muntahā* (n 41) Vol. 6, 161 cited in Al-Dawoody, *The Islamic Law of War* (n 41) 159.

[45] Al-Nawawī, *Al-Majmūʿ* (n 41) Vol. 20, 348ff.; al-Shirbīnī, *Al-Iqnāʿ fī Hall al-Fāz Abī Shujāʿ* (n 43) Vol. 2, 547; al-Ghazālī, 'Al-Waṣīt', Vol. 6, 415ff.; al-Mirdāwī, *Al-Insāf fī Maʿrifah al-Rājih min al-Khilāf ʿalā Madhhab al-Imām Ahmad Ibn Hanbal* (n 42) Vol. 10, 312; Ibn Muflih, *Al-Furūʿ* (n 41) Vol. 6, 147; ʿAwdah, *Al-Tashrīʿ al-Jināʾī al-Islāmī: Muqāranā bi-al-Qānūn al-Wadʿī* (n 41) Vol. 2, 680 cited in Al-Dawoody, *The Islamic Law of War* (n 41) 159.

[46] Al Fadl, 'Political Crime in Islamic Jurisprudence and Western Legal History', *U.C. David Journal of International Law and Policy* (1998) 4, 1–26, 16.

[47] Al-Dawoody, *The Islamic Law of War* (n 41) 160.

[48] Ibid.

Hence, one might comfortably infer that the similarities between the classification criteria under Islamic law and IHL are rather evident. Both bodies of law require a sufficient level of organization of the armed groups or rebels and a sufficient level of intensity of the armed violence. The only Islamic law criteria that might slightly contradict with IHL is the *t'awil* (just cause) requirement. Under IHL, the underlying motivations of non-state organized armed groups, including religious and political ideologies, are irrelevant to the legal determination of whether they are involved in a non-international armed conflict or not.[49] Under Islamic law, however, the rebels should have at least a belief in the justness of their cause to benefit from the Islamic *jus in bello* of non-international armed conflicts. Along the same lines, in Islamic law, an armed group that satisfies the two previously mentioned thresholds (a powerful, organized group that uses force on a large scale) but lacks the *t'awil* requirement becomes part of a different type of a non-international conflict that does not trigger the applicability of the Islamic *jus in bello*.[50] This type of conflict is commonly referred to as the war against *al-muharibun/qutaa al-tariq* (bandits, highway robbers, and terrorists), as previously explained in the context of the legal permissibility afforded to the Islamic state to use force against those citizens who committed this offence.[51] Islamic law treats this situation the way international law treats 'internal disturbances and tensions, such as riots, isolated and sporadic acts of violence and other acts of a similar nature, as not being armed conflicts'.[52] In this respect, Muslim bandits are to be punished for their violations under the ordinary Islamic law rules.[53] As for the rights and obligations of Muslim rebels and combatants under the Islamic *jus in bello* of international and non-international armed conflicts, this is addressed in the following section of this chapter.

2. The Protected People and Objects

While IHL establishes a comprehensive legal framework to protect those who do not or no longer directly participate in hostilities from the effects of military operations, this stands in stark contrast to the situation that civilians in conflict-affected areas encounter on the ground nowadays, especially in the

49 ICRC Challenges Report (n 32).
50 Tabassum, 'Combatants, Not Bandits' (n 37) 10.
51 For more details about this type of conflict please review Chapter 2, Section 1.
52 Article 1(2), Second Additional Protocol of the Geneva Conventions.
53 For more details about this type of conflict please review Chapter 2, Section 1.

Middle East. Civilians, in particular, account for a high proportion of the victims in most contemporary armed conflicts, whether as an unintended result of the fighting or because they are deliberately targeted by belligerents as part of the warring parties' military strategies. As an example of the latter, some Islamic Jihadist groups brag openly about the killing of innocent civilians and the destruction of their properties on a daily basis, while other Muslim states deliberately target civilians after accusing them of having ties with radical Islamic terrorist groups. Hence, this study finds that it is crucial to examine the rules related to the protection of people and objects under the Islamic *jus in bello* in comparison to those embodied in IHL. The main aim is to familiarize the reader with what is permissible and what is forbidden under Islamic law concerning the lives and properties of enemies during the actual conduct of hostilities, while making a distinction between international and non-international armed conflicts, where necessary.

(i) Protection of Non-Combatants

The principle of distinction is the core principle of IHL in international and non-international armed conflicts.[54] It requires the warring parties to distinguish between civilians and combatants. While attacks may be directed against combatants, civilians should not be directly attacked under any circumstances. Combatants are, mainly, the members of armed forces and persons participating in a *levée en masse* in an international armed conflict.[55] Civilians are those who do not belong to these two categories. Combatants alone have the right to kill, injure, or destroy without being held accountable for their acts, provided that they fight within the limitations of IHL. This category of persons may also be targeted by the armed forces of the adverse party. Civilians, however, do not have such a right to take a direct part in hostilities. Thus, the non-involvement of civilians in hostilities is a precondition of the principle of distinction according to which the civilian population shall be protected from military operations in all circumstances. A civilian who 'directly

[54] The principle of distinction is now codified in Articles 48, 51(2), and 52(2) of Additional Protocol I, to which no reservations have been made. According to Additional Protocol I, 'attacks' means 'acts of violence against the adversary, whether in offence or in defence'. Moreover, Article 13(2) of Additional Protocol II prohibits making the civilian population as such, as well as individual civilians, the object of attack. See also Rule 1, ICRC Customary IHL Study. Available at: <https://ihl-databases.icrc.org/customary-ihl/eng/docs/v1_cha_chapter1_rule1#refFn_74_3> (last accessed 25 May 2019).

[55] Article 4A, GC III; Article 43, First Additional Protocol to the Geneva Conventions.

participate in hostilities'[56] loses their protection for the duration of each specific act amounting to direct participation.[57] Moreover, persons accompanying the armed forces, or those who are in the service of armed forces without being members thereof, are considered to be civilians. They are also not entitled to take a direct part in military operations,[58] yet in case of capture they are to be treated as if they were prisoners of war.[59] Furthermore, wounded, sick, and shipwrecked, whether civilians or combatants, should be respected and protected, as long as they do not take part in hostilities.[60] Similarly, medical and religious personnel shall be respected and protected in all circumstances.[61]

The Islamic *jus in bello* clearly echoes the principle of distinction as spelled out in IHL. Under Islamic law, Muslims are allowed to target only combatants, whereas non-combatants should be spared as long as they do not participate in hostilities. This principle was articulated explicitly in the *Quran*, where it says: 'And fight in the way of God those who fight against you and do not transgress, indeed God does not like transgressors.'[62] The principle of distinction has been also reiterated by Muhammad in several *Ḥadīths*, including: 'Do not kill an aged, a young child or a woman'; 'Do not kill children or the clergy'; and 'Do not kill children or *'usafā* (hired men at the service of the army)'.[63] Following his guidance, Abu Bakr and Umar recommended to the leaders of

[56] According to the Interpretive Guidance on the Notion of Direct Participation in Hostilities under International Humanitarian Law three cumulative criteria must be met in order to qualify an act as a direct participation in hostilities: (i) the act must be likely to adversely affect the military operations or military capacity of a party to an armed conflict or, alternatively, to inflict death, injury, or destruction on persons or objects protected against direct attack (threshold of harm); (ii) there must be a direct causal link between the act and the harm likely to result either from that act, or from a coordinated military operation of which that act constitutes an integral part (direct causation); and (iii) the act must be specifically designed to directly cause the required threshold of harm in support of a party to the conflict and to the detriment of another (belligerent nexus). See Nils Melzer, *Interpretive Guidance on the Notion of Direct Participation in Hostilities under International Humanitarian Law* (Geneva: ICRC, 2009) 16.

[57] Article 51, para. 3, First Additional Protocol to the Geneva Conventions; Article 13, para. 3, Second Additional Protocol to the Geneva Conventions.

[58] Article 4A, GC III.

[59] Ibid.

[60] Articles 12, para. GC I; Article 35, para. 1, GC I; Article 12, para. 1, GC II; Article 3, para. 1 No. 2, GC III; Article 16, GC IV; Article 10, para. 1, First Additional Protocol to the Geneva Conventions; Article 7, para. 1, Second Additional Protocol to the Geneva Conventions.

[61] Articles 24 and 25, GC I; Articles 36 and 37, GC II; Article 15, First Additional Protocol to the Geneva Conventions; Article 9, Second Additional Protocol to the Geneva Conventions.

[62] *Quran* (2:190).

[63] Al-Sāʿatī, Aḥmad ʿAbd al-Raḥmān al-Bannā, *Badā'iʿ al-Manan fi Jamiʿ wa Tartīb Musannad al-Shafi'i wa al-Sanan: Mudhayla bi-al-Qawl al-Ḥasan Sharaḥ Badā'iʿ al-Manan*, 2nd edn (Cairo: Maktabah al-Furqān, 1983) Vol. 2, 12; *Abū al-Ṭayyib, Sadīq ibn Ḥasan ibn 'Ali al-Ḥusseini al-Qannūji al-Bukhārī, Al-Rawḍah al-Nadiyyah Sharaḥ al-Durar al-Munīryyah* (Cairo: Idārah al-Ṭibāʿah al-Munīrīyah, n.d.) Vol. 2, 339, cited in Ahmed Al-Dawoody, *The Islamic International Humanitarian Law: Between Theory and Practice* (Geneva: ICRC, 2017) 245. Available (in Arabic) at: <https://www.icrc.org/ar/publication/IHL-contemporary-conflicts> (last accessed 25 May 2019).

the Islamic army in several occasions not to kill women, children, and aged people.[64] According to these Islamic sources, Muslim jurists developed a distinction of two categories of enemy: *Al-muqatilah, ahl Al-qitall, al-muharibah* (combatants, fighters, warriors), and *Ghayr al-muqatilah, ghayr al-muharibah* (non-combatants, non-fighters, and non-warriors).[65] Al-Zuhayli, in this respect, states that the legal rationale for not killing civilians in wartime is that they cannot fight back or harm Muslims.[66] He further explains that the verb *qatila* (to fight) is reciprocal and therefore someone who is not participating in a fight is disarmed and should not be attacked under Islamic law.[67] Along the same lines, the majority of the Muslim jurists agree that the justifications for the unanimous agreement on the protection of women from being targeted in war is the fact that women traditionally do not engage in the conduct of hostilities.[68] Children, similarly, enjoy non-combatant immunity for the same reason. Muslim jurists classify anyone who has not reached puberty or who is under the age of fifteen as a child.[69] This does not mean, however, that the protection of women and children is absolute. Muslim jurists affirm that both will lose their protection once they participate in hostilities. Al-Dawoody examined a few cases related to the jurists' opinions on this matter.[70] For example, the jurists discussed the permissibility of killing a woman if she kills Muslim soldiers; throws stones at them to kill them; stands guard over enemy armies or strongholds; or if the woman is queen of her country; or if she is a wealthy women and spends her money to incite the army to fight in the battlefield; and similarly, if a child is king of their country. On this issue, the jurists disagree, with some authorizing the targeting of women and children in the aforementioned cases and others classifying it as undesirable. They also disagree on whether or not an aged person could be targeted if they entered the battlefield to support the enemy in planning war operations.[71]

[64] Muhammad ibn Jarīr Al-Tabarī, *Tārīkh al-Tabarī: Tārīkh al-Umam wa al-Mulūk*, 6 Vols (Bierut: Dār al-Kutub al-'Ilmiyyah, 2001/1422) Vol. 4, 46–7.

[65] Badar, 'Ius in Bello under Islamic International Law' (n 2) 606.

[66] Wahbah Al-Zuhayli, *Āthār al-Harb fī al-Islām: Dīrāsah Muqāranah*, 3rd edn (Damascus: Dār al-Fikr, 1998/1419) 500–1.

[67] Ibid.

[68] Muwaffaq al-Dīn 'Abd Allah ibn Ahmad Ibn Qudāmah, *Al-Mughnī: fī Fiqh al-Imām Ahmad Ibn Hanbal al-Shaybānī* (Beirut: Dār al-Fikr, 1984–1985/1405) Vol. 9, 250.

[69] Ibid., 248; al-Khiraqī, *Mukhtasar al-Khiraqī min Masā'il al-Imām Ahmad Ibn Hanbal*, ed. Zuhayr al-Shāwīsh, 3rd edn (Beirut: Al-Maktab al-Islāmī, 1982) 132; Sobhi Mahmassani, *Al-Qānūn wa al-'Alāqāt al-Dawliyyah fī al-Islām* (Beirut: Dār al-'Ilm lil-Malāyīn, 1972/1392) 239.

[70] Al-Dawoody, *The Islamic International Humanitarian Law: Between Theory and Practice* (n 63) 245.

[71] Ibid.

The Islamic *jus in bello* also provides protection to other groups as long as they are not taking part in the hostilities. For example, Muslim jurists agree that the sick, blind, and incapacitated should not be targeted in wartime,[72] with one exceptional opinion that permitted the targeting of the incapacitated if they are still physically able to fight or support the enemy.[73] Also, clergies (religious personnel) should not be targeted according to *hadith*, Abu Bakr's commands, and the majority of Muslim jurists.[74] In this respect, Ibn Taymyah indicates that the reason for prohibiting the targeting of clergies during war is that they are confined to their monasteries and do not engage in acts of hostility against Muslims. He adds that the jurists agree that if clergies support the army of the enemy, they lose their immunity.[75] Moreover, *al-asif* (a hired man at the service of the army), being a non-combatant, should not also be targeted.[76] This Arabic term refers to someone who is paid by the enemy to do work for them during a war as Al-Shawkani put it 'to mind the belongings and the animals but not engage in fighting'.[77] By analogy, targeting medical personnel and war reporters who are accompanying the armed forces is prohibited under IHL.[78]

Under IHL applicable in non-international armed conflicts, civilians (or persons taking no active part in the hostilities) must be treated humanely and shall not to be subjected to any violence against their lives.[79] However, defining civilians negatively in non-international armed conflicts is rather complicated.

[72] Caliph Abū Bakr prohibited targeting *al-mariḍ* (the sick). See Alā al-Dīn al-Kāsānī, *Badā'i' al-Sanā'i' fī Tartīb al-Sharā'i'*, 2nd edn (Beirut: Dār al-Kitāb al-'Arabī, 1982) Vol. 7, 101; Ibn Qudāmah, *Umdah al- Fiqh* (n 41) 153; Ibn Mufl ih, *Al-Furū'* (n 41) Vol. 6, 197; Mansur Ibn Yunus Ibn Salah Al-Din al-Buhūtī, *Sharh Muntahā al-Irādāt al-Musammā Daqā'iq 'Ulī al-Nuhā Li-Sharh al-Muntahā*, 2 edn (Beirut: 'Ālam al-Kutub, 1996) Vol. 1, 624ff.; Mansur Ibn Yunus Ibn Salah Al-Din al-Buhūtī, *Kashshāf al-Qinā' 'an Matn al-Iqnā'*, ed. Hilāl Misīlhī Mustafā Hilāl (Beirut: Dār al-Fikr, 1981–1982/1402) Vol. 3, 50; al-Rahaybānī, *Matālib Ulī al-Nuhā fī Sharh Ghāyah al-Muntahā* (n 41) Vol. 2, 517ff.; Ihsān al-Hindī, *Ahkām al-Harb wa al-Salām fī Dawlah al-Islām* (Damascus: Dār al-Numayr, 1993/1413) 178.

[73] 'Abd al-'Azīz Ṣaqr, *'Al-'Alāqāt al-Dawliyyah fī al-Islām Waqt al-Harb: Dirāsah lil- Qawā'id al-Munazzimah li-Sayr al-Qitāl*, Mashrū' al-'Alāqāt al-Dawliyyah fī al-Islām 6 (Cairo: Al-Ma'had al-'Ālamī lil-Fikr al-Islāmī, 1996) 48.

[74] *Hadīth* number 965 in Anas Ibn Mālik, *Muwatta' al-Imām Mālik*, ed. Muhammad Fū'ād 'Abd al-Bāqī, 2 Vols (Cairo: Dār Ihyā' al-Turāth al-'Arabī, n.d.) Vol. 2, 447; *hadīths* numbers 9375 and 9377 in 'Abd al-Rāziq ibn Hammām al-Ṣana'ānī, *Al-Musannaf*, ed. Habīb al-Rahman al-A'zamī, 2nd edn (Beirut: Al-Maktab al-Islāmī, 1982–3/1403) Vol. 5, 199ff.; al-Nawawī, *Al-Majmū'* (n 41) Vol. 21, 58; Ibn Anas, *Al-Mudawwanah*, Vol. 3, 7; Mahmassani, *Al-Qānūn wa al-'Alāqāt* (n 69) 262.

[75] Ahmad ibn 'Abd al-Halīm Ibn Taymiyyah, *Majmū' Fatāwā Shaykh al-Islām Ahmad Ibn Taymiyyah*, compiled by 'Abd al-Rahman ibn Muhammad ibn Qāsim al-'Āsimī (Cairo: Maktabah ibn Taymiyyah, n.d.) Vol. 28, 660; al-Hindī, *Ahkām al-Harb wa al-Salām fī Dawlah al-Islām* (n 72) 178; Abdulrahman M. Alsumaih, 'The Sunni Concept of Jihad in Classical Fiqh and Modern Islamic Thought' (PhD Thesis presented at University of Newcastle, 1998) 119.

[76] *Hadiths* numbers 2841 and 2842 in Muhammad ibn Yazīd Ibn Mājah, *Sunan Ibn Mājah*, ed. Muhammad Fū'ād 'Abd al-Bāqī (Beirut: Dār al-Fikr, n.d.).

[77] Al-Shawkānī, *Al-Sayl al-Jarrār al-Mutadaffiq 'alā Hadā'iq al-Azhār* (n 41) Vol. 4, 532.

[78] Al-Dawoody, *The Islamic International Humanitarian Law: Between Theory and Practice* (n 63) 245.

[79] Common Article 3 to the Geneva Conventions.

Civilians, in non-international armed conflicts, are those who are not members of the state armed forces and the non-state organized armed groups.[80] While it could be simple to determine who falls under the first category, the determination of the membership of the organized armed groups requires further investigation. Some non-state armed groups are organized similarly to state armed forces, comprising both fighting forces and supportive segments of the civilian population, such as political and humanitarian wings.[81] What makes the process of determining the membership of state armed forces more feasible is the fact that it is regularly 'defined by domestic laws and expressed through formal integration into permanent units distinguishable by uniforms, insignia and equipment'.[82] This is not the case with the membership of organized armed groups, which has no basis in domestic laws and is not consistently expressed through uniforms, fixed distinctive signs, or identification cards. Thus it is particularly difficult to distinguish between a non-state organized armed group and its armed forces given the fact that most of the organized armed groups have informal, flexible, and clandestine structures. Hence, one cannot depend on abstract affiliation (political or religious) or family ties to determine the membership of the group. Rather, 'the decisive criterion for individual membership in an organized armed group is whether a person assumes a continuous function for the group involving his or her direct participation in hostilities'.[83] It should be pointed out, however, that this 'continuous combat function' does not imply *de jure* entitlement to combatant privilege. In other words, members of the armed forces of state-like organized armed groups do not have the right to participate directly in hostilities with immunity from domestic prosecution for lawful acts of war, which is provided only to members of the armed forces of parties to an international armed conflict (except medical and religious personnel) as well as to participants in a *levée en masse*.[84]

Under the Islamic *jus in bello*, however, rebels who form part of an Islamic organized armed group, as explained in Section 1, are not to be held accountable for the damage to life and property that they have caused during their rebellion.[85] In other words, rebels, in non-international armed conflicts, are entitled

[80] Melzer, *Interpretive Guidance on the Notion of Direct Participation in Hostilities under International Humanitarian Law* (n 57) 31–2.

[81] For the purpose of applying the principle of distinction in non-international armed conflicts, the term 'organized armed group' refers exclusively to the armed or military wing of a non-state party: its armed forces in a functional sense—not the supportive segments, such as the political or humanitarian wings of the organized armed groups. Ibid.

[82] Ibid.

[83] Ibid., 33.

[84] Ibid.

[85] Badawi, 'Islamic Jurisprudence and the Regulation of Armed Conflict' (n 4) 8.

to combatant privilege.[86] Muslim jurists agree that the Islamic state armed forces should seek peace, reconciliation, and negotiations with the rebels before they use force against them.[87] However, if force has to be used against the rebels, the jurists agree that the objective of the use of force should not be to eliminate them but to bring them into obedience to the ruler.[88] Muslim jurists also affirm that rebels should only be targeted as long as they are taking active part in hostilities, but if they lay down their arms for any reason they should be protected.[89] The jurists, finally, agree that non-combatants accompanying the rebels during wars should not be targeted, such as women, children, and the wounded.[90]

(ii) Protection of Prisoner of Wars

Under IHL, the purpose of captivity of enemy combatants is not defined as such in the Third Geneva Convention relative to the Treatment of Prisoner of Wars. However, one can easily deduce from the dictates of the convention's

[86] The Hanafi jurist Abu Bakr al-Sarakhasi says: 'they should not be asked to compensate for the damage they caused to the life and property [of the adverse party]. He means to say: when they caused this damage after they had organized their group and had attained mana'ah. As for the damage they caused before this, they should be asked to compensate it. See Muhammad Ibn Ahmad Al-Sarakhasi, *Kitab al-Mabsut*, Vol. 10 (Beirut: *Dar Ehia al-Tourath al-'Arabi*, 2002) 136.

[87] Ibid. Al-Dawoody, *The Islamic Law of War* (n 41) 162.

[88] Ibn Qudāmah, *Al-Mughnī* (n 68) Vol. 9, 5; al-Anṣārī, 'Asnā al-Maṭālib', Vol. 4, 113; Abū Zahrah, *Al-Jarīmah wa al-'Uqūbah fī al-Fiqh al-Islāmī: al-Jarīmah* (n 41) 130; 'Awdah, *Al-Tashrī' al-Jinā'ī al-Islāmī: Muqāranā bi-al-Qānūn al-Waḍ'ī* (n 41) Vol. 2, 690; Awdah, *Criminal Law of Islam* (n 41) Vol. I, 118; Mahmassani, *Al-Qānūn wa al-'Alāqāt* (n 69) 198; Anna K. S. Lambton, *State and Government in Medieval Islam* (Oxford: Oxford University Press, 1981) 210ff.; Nik Wajis, *The Crime of Ḥirāba in Islamic Law* (PhD Thesis, Glasgow Caledonian University, 1996) 153; Alsumaih, 'The Sunni Concept of Jihad in Classical Fiqh and Modern Islamic Thought' (n 75) 80; Al Fadl, 'Political Crime in Islamic Jurisprudence and Western Legal History' (n 46) 11ff.; Al Fadl, *Rebellion and Violence in Islamic Law* (n 38) 157; Sohail H. Hashmi, 'Islam, Sunni' 219, cited in Al-Dawoody, *The Islamic Law of War* (n 41) 157.

[89] al-Shāfi'ī, *'Al-Umm* (n 42) Vol. 4, 218; al-Nawawī, *Al-Majmū'* (n 41) Vol. 20, 343 f.; Ibrāhīm ibn 'Alī ibn Yūsuf al-Shirāzī, *Al-Muhadhdhab: Fī Fiqh al-Imām al-Shāfi'ī*, ed. Zakariyyā 'Imīrat (Beirut: Dār al-Kutub al-'Ilmiyyah, 1995/1416) Vol. 3, 250–2; al-Anṣārī, *Asnā al-maṭālib šarḥ rawḍ aṭ-ṭālib* (n 43) Vol. 4, 114; and Manhaj *al-Ṭullāb*, 124; al-Shirbīnī, *Mughnī al-Muhtāj ilā Ma'rifah Ma'ānī Alfāz al-Minhāj* (n 41) Vol. 4, 127; al-Māwardī, *Nasīhah al-Mulūk* (n 41) 255; al-Ramlī, *Nihāyah al-Muhtāj ilā Sharh al-Minhāj* (n43) Vol. 7, 407; Ibn 'Abd al-Barr, *'Al-Kāfī fī Fiqh Ahl al-Madīnah'*, 222; Ibn Qudāmah, *Umdah al- Fiqh* (n 41) 149; Ibn Qudāmah, *Al-Mughnī* (n 68) Vol. 9, 9; al-Mirdāwī, *Al-Insāf fī Ma'rifah al-Rājih min al-Khilāf 'alā Madhhab al-Imām Ahmad Ibn Hanbal* (n 42) Vol. 10, 314ff.; al-Buhūtī, *Al-rawd al-murbi' sharh zad al-mustaqni'* (n 41) Vol. 3, 336ff.; Ibn Muflih, *Al-Furū'* (n 41) Vol. 6, 149ff.; al-Rahaybānī, *Matālib Ulī al-Nuhā fī Sharh Ghāyah al-Muntahā* (n 41) Vol. 6, 269; Abū Zahrah, *Al-Jarīmah wa al-'Uqūbah fī al-Fiqh al-Islāmī: al-Jarīmah* (n 41) 128; 'Awdah, *Al-Tashrī' al-Jinā'ī al-Islāmī: Muqāranā bi-al-Qānūn al-Waḍ'ī* (n 41) Vol. 2, 690; Mahmassani, *Al-Qānūn wa al-'Alāqāt* (n 69) 198; Wajis, 'The Crime of Ḥirāba in Islamic Law' (n 88) 153; Al Fadl, *Rebellion and Violence in Islamic Law* (n 38) 152, 160. Cited in Al-Dawoody, *The Islamic Law of War* (n 41) 163.

[90] al-Kāsānī, *Badā'i' al-Sanā'i' fī Tartīb al-Sharā'i'* (n 72) Vol. 7, 141; Ibn Najīm, *Al-Bahr al-Rā'iq Sharh Kanz al-Daqā'iq* (n 41) Vol. 5, 152ff.; Ibn Mawdūd, *Al-Ikhtiyār li-Ta'līl al-Mukhtār* (n 41) Vol. 4, 162.

provisions that the main purpose of captivity is to neutralize the threat posed by enemy combatants, which is expressed by their participation in the military operations against the detaining power. Accordingly, the humane treatment of prisoners of war (POWs) derives from the conviction that captured enemy combatants no longer pose any threat to the lives of persons nor to the detaining power, as articulated by Jean-Jacques Rousseau more than four centuries ago.[91] Rousseau made the following statement in his work *The Social Contract or Principles of Political Right* that reportedly influenced the attitude of the Western states toward the conduct of warfare:

> War then is a relation, not between man and man, but between State and State, and individuals are enemies only accidentally, not as men, nor even as citizens, but as soldiers; not as members of their country, but as its defenders . . . The object of the war being the destruction of the hostile State, the other side has a right to kill its defenders while they are bearing arms; but as soon as they lay them down and surrender they become once more merely men, whose life no one has any right to take.[92]

In international armed conflicts, captured enemy combatants and other groups of persons, such as the authorized war correspondents and supply contractors, as defined in Article 4 of the Third Geneva Convention and Article 43 of the First Additional Protocol, enjoy POW status.[93] Based on this status, they may not be prosecuted for lawful acts of violence committed in the course of hostilities (combatant privilege), which clearly does not include IHL violations.[94] Moreover, detained persons must in all circumstances be treated humanely and shall not be subjected to torture, injury, medical experiments, intimidation, or insult.[95] In the words of the Third Geneva Convention: 'Any unlawful act or omission by the Detaining Power causing death or seriously

[91] Sandra Kräehenmann, 'Protection of Prisoners in Armed Conflict' in Fleck (ed.), *The Handbook of International Humanitarian Law* (n 14), 359–412.

[92] Jean-Jacques Rousseau, *The Social Contract or Principles of Political Right*, translated by H. J. Tozer (Hertfordshire: Wordsworth Editions, 1998) Book I, chapter 4.

[93] Article 4, GC III; Article 43, First Additional Protocol to the Geneva Conventions. It is also noteworthy to mention that should any doubt arise as to whether the captured person qualify as a POW or not, the person should be treated as a POW until a competent tribunal arrives at a determination regarding that person's status; Article 5 para. 2, GC III; Article 45 paras 1 and 2, First Additional Protocol to the Geneva Conventions.

[94] Sandra Kräehenmann, 'Protection of Prisoners in Armed Conflict', 367 cited in Fleck (ed.), *The Handbook of International Humanitarian Law* (n 14).

[95] 'Prisoners of war are in the hands of the enemy Power, but not of the individuals or military units who have captured them. Irrespective of the individual responsibilities that may exist, the Detaining Power is responsible for the treatment given them.' Article 12, GC III.

endangering the health of a prisoner of war in its custody is prohibited, and will be regarded as a serious breach of the present Convention.'[96]

Along the same lines, detaining powers are prohibited from resorting to reprisals against POWs in all circumstances, even if the enemy has committed grave breaches against their POWs.[97] It is also worth mentioning that should the detaining powers decide to put the POWs in camps, they should not be situated in dangerous zones.[98] The rationale behind stipulating this obligation is not only to protect the lives of the POWs but also to prohibit the detaining powers from using the camps as shields to secure military advantage.[99] It should not be necessary to state that the detaining powers have an obligation to provide POWs with sufficient food,[100] clothing,[101] and medical attention.[102] POWs should also be allowed to write to their families and correspond regularly with their relatives.[103] Ultimately, POWs should be released and repatriated without delay after the cessation of active hostilities unless they are the subject of criminal proceedings for an indictable offence, in which case they may be detained until the end of such proceedings and, if necessary, until the completion of the punishment.[104]

The principle of humane treatment is not limited to POWs in international armed conflicts. Even those persons captured in the context of a non-international armed conflict, who do not qualify for POW status, should be treated humanely.[105] Both states and non-state organized armed groups are responsible for the humane treatment of those whom they capture in a non-international armed conflict.[106]Additionally, the principle of humane treatment is enshrined in international human rights law, which provides an additional layer of protection for all detainees.[107]

[96] Article 13 of the GC III.

[97] Article 13 para. 3, GC III.

[98] Articles 19 para. 1, GC III; Article 21 para. 1, GC III.

[99] The camps shall meet certain minimum requirements of hygiene and health (Article 22 para. 1, GC III). They shall be provided with shelters against air raids and other hazards of war (Article 23 para. 2, GC III). Whenever the military situation permits, prisoner-of-war camps shall be marked by the letters PG (*prisonniers de guerre*) or PW (prisoners of war), clearly visible from the air (Article 23, para. 4, GC III).

[100] Article 26, GC III.

[101] Article 27, GC III.

[102] Articles 29–31, GC III.

[103] Articles 70 and 123, GC III.

[104] Articles 118 and 119 paras 5, GC III.

[105] Common Article 3 of the Geneva Conventions.

[106] Common Article 3 of the Geneva Conventions; Article 5, Second Additional Protocol to the Geneva Conventions.

[107] Article 10, International Covenant of Civil and Political Rights (ICCPR); General Comment No. 21: Humane Treatment of Persons Deprived of their Liberty (Article 10), UN Doc. HRI/GEN1/Rev. 9 (Vol. 1) 202, Human Rights Council, 6 April 1992.

In the Islamic *jus in bello*, both the *Quran* and *Sunnah* legitimize the taking of captives. The permission for Muslims to capture enemy combatants as POWs is reflected in several passages in the *Quran*, such as: 'take them captives and besiege them',[108] and 'then tighten their bonds'.[109] The rules regarding the treatment of POWs, however, stem from the incident of the Battle of *Badr* (624). This was the first battle fought by Muslims when Muslim fighters, under the leadership of Muhammad, managed to capture seventy enemy combatants.[110] Muslims at the time did not have any rules regulating the treatment of POWs and the first challenge they faced was where to shelter the captured enemy. Muhammad ordered his companions to accommodate some of the enemy in the Mosque and the other within his companions' houses, which were the safest places in Medina at the time.[111] He then instructed them to treat the captives humanely, saying: 'Observe good treatment towards the prisoners.'[112] In conformity, the majority of Muslim jurists agree that POWs should not be subjected to torture, regardless of whether military information is needed from them.[113] One of the POWs of *Badr* narrates how the Muslims treated him back then:

> I was with a number of the *Ansar* when they (Muslim fighters) brought me from Badr, and when they ate their morning and evening meals they gave me the bread and ate the dates themselves in accordance with the orders that the apostle had given about us. If anyone had a morsel of bread he gave it to me. I felt ashamed and returned it to one of them but he returned it to me untouched.[114]

Other prisoners from *Badr* affirmed that they had received the same treatment from their captors.[115] Along the same lines, the *Quran* says on providing food to POWs: 'And they feed the needy, the orphans and the captives [out

[108] *Quran* (9:5).
[109] *Quran* (47:4).
[110] Al-Dawoody, *The Islamic Law of War* (n 41) 138–9.
[111] Al-Zuhaylī, *Āthār al-Ḥarb fī al-Islām* (Damascus: Dār al-Fikr, 1998/1419) 409; al-Zayd, *Al-Qānūn al-Dawlī al-Insānī* (Cairo: ICRC, 2004) 65; Malik Abdulazeez al-Mubarak, 'Warfare in Early Islam' (PhD thesis, University of Glasgow, 1997) 204.
[112] Alfred Guillaume (trans.), *The Life of Mohamed: A Translation of Ibn Ishaq: Sirat Rasul Allah* (Oxford: Oxford University Press, 2002) 309; Alsumaih, 'The Sunni Concept of Jihad in Classical Fiqh and Modern Islamic Thought' (n 75) 147.
[113] Saleem Marsoof, 'Islam and International Humanitarian Law', *Sri Lanka Journal of International Law* (2003) 15, 23–8, 25; Christopher G. Weeramantry, *Islamic Jurisprudence: An International Perspective* (London: Palgrave Macmillan, 1988) 125.
[114] Guillaume, *The Life of Mohamed* (n 112) 309; Alsumaih, 'The Sunni Concept of Jihad in Classical Fiqh and Modern Islamic Thought' (n 75) 147.
[115] al-Zuhaylī, *Āthār al-Harb fī al-Islām* (n 66) 413; Mahmassani, *Al-Qānūn wa al-'Alāqāt* (n 69) 257.

of their] food, despite their love for it [or also interpreted as: because of their love for God]. Indeed, we feed you for the sake of pleasing God: we don't wish reward or gratitude from you.'[116] It is also understood from the practice of Muhammad that clothing POWs is necessary if needed. It was narrated by one of his companions that 'when it was the day (of the battle) of Badr, prisoners of war were brought including Al-ʿAbbās, who was undressed. The Prophet looked for a shirt for him. It was found that the shirt of ʿAbdullah ibn Ubaī would do, so the Prophet let him wear it.'[117] Furthermore, the majority of jurists believe that the POWs should not be separated from their families who are also captured, such as separating parents from their children.[118]

Despite a great level of similarity between IHL and the Islamic *jus in bello* in terms of the treatment of the POWs, the rules related to the termination of the captivity differs from one body of law to the other. As previously stated, under IHL, all POWs shall be released and repatriated without delay after the cessation of active hostilities, unless they are the subject of ongoing criminal proceedings.[119] Under Islamic law, however, due to the ambiguity of the text and the limited volume of prophetic practices (*Sunnah*), there is a disagreement among Muslim jurists regarding the fate of the POWs. One thing that Muslim jurists agree on is that the POWs' fate is left to the political authority (the Caliph or the head of state) to decide as he sees fit in the best interest of the Muslim *Ummah*.[120] However, they diverge regarding the choices available to the Muslim leader to terminate their captivity.[121] The majority of Muslim jurists agree that the Muslim leader has the following five options: (i) to execute some or all of the prisoners; (ii) to enslave them; (iii) to set them free as an act of grace; (iv) to set them free after asking for ransom; or (v) to exchange them for Muslim POWs.[122] These choices were agreed upon by the majority of Muslim jurists despite the fact that *Quran* stipulates only two options, namely (i) to set POWs free as an act of grace, or (ii) to set them free after asking for ransom.[123] The elimination of the three other choices is not only supported

[116] *Quran* (76:8).

[117] Muḥammad ibn Ismāʿīl Al-Bukhārī, *Mukhtaṣar Ṣaḥīḥ al-Imām al-Bukhārī*, ed. Muḥammad Nāsr al-Albānī (Riyadh: Maktabah al-Maʿarif, 2002), Vol. 2, 318.

[118] Weeramantry, *Islamic Jurisprudence* (n 113) 135; Badar, 'Ius in Bello under Islamic International Law' (n 2) 619.

[119] Articles 118 and 119, para. 5, GC III.

[120] Muhammad Munir, 'The Layha for the Mujahideen: An Analysis of the Code of Conduct for the Taliban Fighters Under Islamic Law', *International Review of the Red Cross* (2011) 93(881), 81–102, 89.

[121] Ibid.

[122] Ibid.; Al-Dawoody, 'The Islamic International Humanitarian Law: Between Theory and Practice' (n 63) 245.

[123] 'When you meet the disbelievers in battle, strike them in the neck, and once they are defeated, bind any captives firmly--later you can release them by grace or by ransom--until the toils of war have ended'. *Quran* (47:4).

by the Quranic text but also by the instructions of Muhammad while conquering Mecca (630), when he said 'slay no wounded person, pursue no fugitive, execute no prisoners, and whosever closes his door is safe'.[124] Accordingly, a number of Muhammad's companions affirmed that POWs shall not be executed.[125] Many Muslim jurists, however, argue that the permissibility of execution is based on the fact that Muhammad executed three POWs during his lifetime.[126] These three POWs were (i) 'Uqbah ibn Mu'ayṭ, who was captured at the battle of *Badr* (624) along with seventy others and was executed for his crimes against Muslims in Mecca;[127] (ii) Abū 'Azzah al-Jumaḥī, who was captured at the battle of *Uḥud* (625) and set free after the battle of *Badr* on condition that he would not fight the Muslims again, but was subsequently executed after he was captured again fighting Muslims at Uhud;[128] and (iii) 'Abdullah B. Khatal, who was captured immediately after Muslims had conquered Mecca and was executed for killing innocent Muslim during his stay in Medina and for fighting with the enemy against Muslims.[129] Consequently, the three who were executed during Muhammad's lifetime were penalized for the unlawful acts that they committed against Muslims prior to their captivity and not simply because they were POWs. This is evidenced by the fact that all other prisoners captured in battle were not executed. The Islamic *jus in bello* in this case is not too dissimilar from IHL in that the detaining power is allowed to prosecute and sentence POWs under their own laws for acts committed prior to capture, which may include sentencing them to death.[130]

(iii) Protection of Civilian Objects

As stated previously, the principle of distinction is the cornerstone of IHL. It requires the warring parties to distinguish between civilians and combatants and between civilian objects and military objectives. According to this principle, civilian population and civilian objects shall not be the object of attacks. In the first part of this section, the negative definition of civilians was tackled

[124] Abu al-Abas Ahmad b. Jabir al Baladhuri, *Kitab Futuh al-Buldan*, trans. Philip Khuri Hitti, Vol. 1 (New York, NY: Columbia University, 1916) 66.
[125] Abul Walid Muhammad Ibn Rushd, *The Distinguished Jurist's Primer*, trans. Imran Nyazee (Reading: Garnet Publishing Ltd, 1994) Vol. 1, 456.
[126] Al-Dawoody, *The Islamic Law of War* (n 41) 138.
[127] Munir, 'The Layha for the Mujahideen' (n 120) 90.
[128] Al-Dawoody, *The Islamic Law of War* (n 41) 138.
[129] Badar, 'Ius in Bello under Islamic International Law' (n 2) 617.
[130] Articles 85 and 101, GC III; Jean Pictect, 'ICRC Commentary to the Third Geneva Convention' on Article 85.

via explaining the definition of combatants and direct participation in hostilities. Using the same approach, civilian objects are defined negatively under IHL as any object that does not constitute a military objective. It is therefore necessary to determine the definition and scope of a military objective under IHL. To this end, Article 52(2) of the First Additional Protocol states that 'military objectives are limited to those objects which by their nature, location, purpose or use make an effective contribution to military action and whose total or partial destruction, capture or neutralization, in the circumstances ruling at the time, offers a definite military advantage'.[131] Under this definition, an object must cumulatively fulfil two elements to be a military objective. The first element is the nature, location, purpose, or use of the object that makes an effective contribution to military action. This element clarifies that military objects are not only the objects of a military nature that are used directly by the armed forces, such as weapons, equipment, and fortifications. Rather, objects which by their nature have no military function but which, by virtue of their location, make an effective contribution to military action, such as bridges.[132] Furthermore, there are two other criteria: 'purpose', which is concerned with the intended future use of an object, and 'use' which is concerned with its present function, such as school grounds that are used for military purposes.[133] The second element is that the object's total or partial destruction, capture, or neutralization, in the circumstances ruling at the time, offers a definite military advantage. Accordingly, it is not legitimate to attack an object that only offers potential or indeterminate advantages.[134] Moreover, military advantage is anticipated from the whole and not from isolated or particular parts of the attack. Therefore, the person ordering or executing the attack must have sufficient information available to take this element into account. It is evident that the drafters of this definition tried to avoid overly broad interpretations of what constitutes a military objective by excluding indirect contributions and possible advantages.[135] Without this restriction, the limitation to 'military' objectives could be too easily undermined.[136] One of the challenges, however,

[131] Article 52(2), First Additional Protocol to the Geneva Conventions.

[132] ICRC, 'Commentary on the First Additional Protocol of 1977', para. 2021. Available at: <https://ihl-databases.icrc.org/applic/ihl/ihl.nsf/Comment.xsp?action=openDocument&documentId=5F27276CE1BBB79DC12563CD00434969> (last accessed 25 May 2019).

[133] Ibid., para. 2022.

[134] Ibid., para. 2024.

[135] Marco Sassoli, 'Legitimate Targets of Attacks Under International Humanitarian Law', *International Humanitarian Law Research Initiative, Humanitarian Policy and Conflict Research* (2004) 3. Available at: <http://www.hpcrresearch.org/sites/default/files/publications/Session1.pdf> (last accessed 25 May 2019).

[136] Ibid.

is that some object could have dual use. It could serve both civilian and military purposes, such as factories, bridges, electric power grids, railways, or any other facility that dedicates its service to both military and civilian purposes. In this case, if it is proven that the object fulfils these two elements, despite being used for civilian purposes too, it becomes a legitimate military objective.[137] However, if the expected harm inflicted on civilians as a result from the attack against a dual-used object is excessive in relation to the concrete and direct military advantage anticipated by targeting the object, that attack will be considered unlawful under the principle of proportionality.[138]

In addition to the rules governing the conduct of hostilities, IHL also protects the property that falls into the adversary's hands from destruction or appropriation not justified by imperative military necessity.[139] Without this justification, the adversary has an obligation not to cause any damage to the protected property under its control or to seize it without the owner's consent. IHL treaty norms explicitly regulate situations when a belligerent party may invoke a justification of military necessity to destroy or appropriate public or private, movable and immovable, property.[140] Any other violent act committed beyond these envisaged exceptions would amount to a violation of IHL.[141] Such unlawful acts include demolition and arson of civilian households, as well as acts of pillage.[142] Extensive destruction or appropriation of property, not justified by military necessity and carried out unlawfully and wantonly, is listed among the grave breaches of Geneva Conventions.[143]

Similarly, the Islamic *jus in bello* instructs Muslims to avoid the destruction of enemy property such as houses, trees, and animals. The *Quran* prohibits on

[137] Ibid., 7.

[138] 'Launching an attack which may be expected to cause incidental loss of civilian life, injury to civilians, damage to civilian objects, or a combination thereof, which would be excessive in relation to the concrete and direct military advantage anticipated, is prohibited.' ICRC, Customary International Humanitarian Law Study (n 54) Rule 14. Proportionality in Attack. Article 51(5) b, First Additional Protocol to the Geneva Conventions.

[139] Article 15, Lieber Code; Article 23(g), The Hague Regulations of 1907; Article 53, GC IV. The Lieber Code defines that military necessity 'consists in the necessity of those measures which are indispensable for securing the ends of the war, and which are lawful according to the modern law and usages of war'. Article 14, Lieber Code.

[140] The Hague Regulations of 1907; Article 53, GC IV.

[141] Destruction or appropriation of the enemy's property 'unless such destruction or seizure be imperatively demanded by the necessities of war' may amount to a war crime committed in either international or non-international armed conflict, Articles 8(2)(b)(xiii) and 8(2)(e)(xii) of the ICC Rome Statute.

[142] Jean Pictet (ed.), *Commentary on the Fourth Geneva Convention relative to the Protection of Civilian Persons in Time of War* (Geneva: ICRC, 1958) 244; *The Prosecutor v. Germain Katanga*, Trial Chamber II, Judgment pursuant to Article 74 of the Statute, Case No. ICC-01/04-01/07, 7 March 2014, para. 891.

[143] Article 50, GC I; Article 51, GC II; Article 147, GC IV.

several occasions causing mischief, corruption, or disorder in enemy territories. For example, it dictates: 'And when he goes away, he strives throughout the land to cause corruption therein and destroy crops and animals. And Allah does not like corruption.'[144] In conformity with this verse, many Muslim scholars advocate that it is prohibited for Muslims to commit any sort of wanton destruction during the course of hostilities in enemy territories because that is considered as mischief or corruption and God does not like mischief and corruption.[145] Muhammad also said: 'Do not destroy the villages and towns, do not spoil the cultivated fields and gardens, and do not slaughter the cattle.'[146] Along the same lines, Abu Bakr (the first Caliph) in his ten commands to his army commander stated: 'do not cut down fruit-bearing trees; do not destroy buildings; do not slaughter a sheep or a camel except for food; do not burn or drown palm trees'.[147] Muslim scholars, however, unanimously agree that it is permitted to attack enemy property if required by military necessity.[148] This based on the practice of Muhammad, when he ordered the Muslims to cut down the palm trees of the tribe of Banu al-Nadīr in 625 to make them surrender during a bloodless siege that lasted for six nights and ended without fighting.[149] In this incident, the people of Medina, the Bani Quraizah, and the Banu al-Nadir themselves raised a clamour, saying that, on the one hand, Muhammad prohibited spreading disorder in the world but on the other, fruit trees were being cut down by his command, which amounted to spreading disorder in the world.[150] God revealed a verse in *Quran* to settle this controversy and to satisfy Muslims who doubted the morality of Muhammad's command, which says: 'Whatever trees you cut down, or whatever you left standing, your neither act was unlawful, but it had Allah's permission.'[151] The legal ruling that is derived from this verse is that the destruction caused for the sake of military necessity does not come under spreading mischief and corruption in the world.[152] However,

144 *Quran* (2:205).

145 Muhammad ibn al-Hasan Al-Shaybānī, *Al-Siyar al-Kabīr*, ed. Salāh al-Dīn al-Munjid, 5 Vols (Cairo: Maʿhad al-Makhtūtāt, n.d.) Vol. 1, 32–3.

146 Majid Khadduri, *War and Peace in the Law of Islam* (Baltimore, MD: The Johns Hopkins Press, 1940) 102–7.

147 *Hadīth* number 965 in Ibn Mālik, *Muwatta' al-Imām Mālik* (n 74) Vol. 2, 447; Karima Bennoune, 'As-Salamu Alaykum? Humanitarian Law in Islamic Jurisprudence', *Michigan Journal of International Law* (1994) 15, 605–43, 626; M. Cherif Bassiouni, *Manual on International Humanitarian Law and Arms Control Agreements* (New York, NY: Transnational Publishers, 2000) 9.

148 Al-Dawoody, 'The Islamic International Humanitarian Law: Between Theory and Practice' (n 63) 245.

149 Badar, 'Ius in Bello under Islamic International Law' (n 2) 614; Al-Dawoody, *The Islamic Law of War* (n 41) 126–7.

150 Towards Understanding the Quran. Available at: <http://www.islamicstudies.info/tafheem.php?sura=59&verse=1&to=5> (last accessed 25 May 2019).

151 *Quran* (59:5).

152 Towards Understanding the Quran (n 150).

'an army under the fit of war hysteria should intrude into the enemy territory and start destroying the crops, cattle, gardens, houses and everything in its way without any reason' and this can be defined as spreading disorder.[153] Accordingly, the majority of the jurists permitted this sort of destruction provided it was dictated by military necessities—for instance, when trees prevent the army from conducting military operations or if the enemy is taking shelter behind them, especially inside fortifications.[154] It is worth noting, however, that the dual use of objects for civil and military purposes has been a challenge in the implementation of the Islamic *jus in bello* as well. According to the Arab socio-economic system of that time, they did not have a standing army and thus Arab tribes would deploy all their resources for military purposes during times of war.[155] In this case, similar to IHL, Muslims should apply the principle of proportionality. This principle is clearly articulated in several verses of the *Quran*.[156] However, one verse elaborates its tenets aptly given the context of its revelation, by affirming: 'if you take retribution, then do so in proportion to the wrong done to you. But if you can bear such conduct with patience, indeed that is best for the steadfast.'[157] This verse was revealed to prohibit Muslims from committing any disproportionate harm against the enemy during war time. It was revealed when Hamza, the paternal uncle of Muhammad, known in the Islamic society as 'Allah's Lion', was killed and mutilated during the battle of Uhud (625). The person who killed him opened his stomach and brought his liver to Hind bint Utbah, the wife of Abu Sufyan who was the leader of the *Quraysh* army. Hind chewed Hamza's liver and then spat it out. Muhammad swore that he would kill thirty, and some scholars say seventy, people in retaliation. When the Muslim fighters heard Muhammad saying this, they became furious and swore to cut their enemies into pieces. On this occasion, the verse was revealed to prohibit Muslims from committing such disproportionate harm.[158] This verse was also interpreted to prohibit mutilation.

[153] Ibid.
[154] Al-Dawoody, *The Islamic Law of War* (n 41) 128.
[155] Niaz A. Shah, *Islamic Law and the Law of Armed Conflict: The Armed Conflict in Pakistan* (New York, NY: Routledge, 2011) 49.
[156] *Quran* (16:126, 40:40, 42:40).
[157] *Quran* (16:126).
[158] Shah, *Islamic Law and the Law of Armed Conflict: The Armed Conflict in Pakistan* (n 155) 49.

(iv) Protection from Mutilation

Mutilation is prohibited under IHL even before the conclusion of the very first Geneva Convention in 1864. The Lieber Code prohibited inflicting any suffering against POWs by mutilation or any other barbarity.[159] This prohibition was then reflected in Common Article 3 of the Geneva Conventions, which provides that mutilation of persons taking no active part in the hostilities, including members of armed forces who have laid down their arms and those placed *hors de combat* by sickness, wounds, detention, or any other cause is prohibited at any time and in any place whatsoever.[160] Mutilation of POWs and civilians is also prohibited by specific provisions of the Third and Fourth Geneva Conventions.[161] Furthermore, the prohibition on mutilation is reflected as a fundamental guarantee for civilians and persons *hors de combat* in the First and the Second Additional Protocols.[162] Mutilation also constitutes a war crime in both international and non-international armed conflicts under the Statute of the International Criminal Court.[163] These treaties, in addition to state practice, established a norm of customary IHL that applies to both international as well as non-international armed conflicts.[164] It should also be noted that mutilation is prohibited whether the protected person is alive or dead. Several IHL treaties dictate that the warring parties must take all possible measures to prevent the dead from being despoiled, affirming that mutilation

[159] Article 56, Lieber Code, 1863. The Liber Code is instruction for the government of armies of the United States in the field, prepared by Francis Lieber, promulgated as General Order No. 100 by President Abraham Lincoln, Washington, DC, 24 April 1863.

[160] Common Article 3 to the Geneva Conventions, para. 1(a).

[161] 'No prisoner of war may be subjected to physical mutilation or to medical or scientific experiments of any kind which are not justified by the medical, dental or hospital treatment of the prisoner concerned and carried out in his interest.' Article 13, GC III; 'This prohibition applies not only to murder, torture, corporal punishment, mutilation and medical or scientific experiments not necessitated by the medical treatment of a protected person, but also to any other measures of brutality whether applied by civilian or military agents.' Article 32, GC IV.

[162] 'The following acts are and shall remain prohibited at any time and in any place whatsoever, whether committed by civilian or by military agents: ... (iv) mutilation'; Article 75 para. 2(iv), I AP, 8 June 1977; '1. All persons who do not take a direct part or who have ceased to take part in hostilities, whether or not their liberty has been restricted, are entitled to respect for their person, honour and convictions and religious practices. They shall in all circumstances be treated humanely, without any adverse distinction. It is prohibited to order that there shall be no survivors. 2. Without prejudice to the generality of the foregoing, the following acts against the persons referred to in paragraph 1 are and shall remain prohibited at any time and in any place whatsoever: (a) violence to the life, health and physical or mental well-being of persons, in particular murder as well as cruel treatment such as torture, mutilation or any form of corporal punishment.' Article 4 II AP, 8 June 1977.

[163] Article 8(2)(b)(x) and (e)(xi), Rome Statute.

[164] 'Mutilation, medical or scientific experiments or any other medical procedure not indicated by the state of health of the person concerned and not consistent with generally accepted medical standards are prohibited.' Rule 92, ICRC Customary IHL Study (n 54).

of dead bodies is prohibited.[165] This was also reflected as a norm of customary IHL that applies equally in international as well as non-international armed conflicts.[166] IHL goes further by obliging the warring parties to ensure the burial or cremation of the dead according to the rites of the religion to which they belonged.[167]

Under the Islamic *jus in bello*, however, the majority of Muslim jurists interpreted the verse of the *Quran* that was revealed to Muhammad after the mutilation of his uncle's body as a prohibition of mutilation against the enemy.[168] As Muhammad and his companions had initially vowed to mutilate the enemy in retaliation for Muhammad's uncle,[169] Muhammad was quoted instructing Muslim fighters: 'don't betray and don't mutilate'.[170] This instruction was then followed by Abu Bakr, who wrote to one of his governors in Hadramaut, Yemen, instructing him to 'beware of mutilation, because it is a sin and a disgusting act'.[171] It was also narrated that Muhammad prohibited the mutilation even if it was the body of al- *kalb al-ʿaqūr* (rabid dog), which confirms the absolute prohibition of mutilation under Islamic law.[172] Some Muslim jurists, however, hold that mutilation is reprehensible rather than totally prohibited. They argue that Muslims can mutilate the enemy only if the enemy mutilates the bodies of Muslims or if it is justified by military necessity.[173] They based their argument on the fact that back in the days it was common for Muslims to carry the head of the enemy's military leaders back to their Muslim territories. Al-Dawoody

[165] Article 15 para. 1, GC I; Article 18 para. 1, GC II; Article 16 para. 2 GC IV; Article 34 para. 1 IAP; Article 8 II AP.

[166] Rule 113, ICRC Customary IHL Study (n 54).

[167] Article 17, GC I.

[168] Shah, *Islamic Law and the Law of Armed Conflict* (n 155) 50; Al-Dawoody, *The Islamic Law of War* (n 41) 120.

[169] Badar, 'Ius in Bello under Islamic International Law' (n 2) 620.

[170] *Hadīth* number 966 in Ibn Mālik, *Muwatta' al-Imām Mālik* (n 74) Vol. 2, 448; *hadīths* numbers 1408 and 1617 in Muhammad ibn ʿIsā al-Tirmidhī, *Al-Jāmiʿ al-Sahīh Sunan al-Tirmidhī*, ed. Ahmad Muhammad Shākir et al. (Beirut: Dār Ihyā' al-Turāth al-ʿArabī, n.d.) Vol. 2, 22; Vol. 4, 162; *hadīth* number 2857 in Ibn Mājah, *Sunan Ibn Mājah*, ed. Muhammad Fū'ād ʿAbd al-Bāqī (Beirut: Dār al-Fikr, n.d.) Vol. 2, 953; *hadīth* number 2613 in Abū Dāwūd, *Sunan Abī Dāwūd*, ed. Muhammad Muhyī al-Dīn ʿAbd al-Hamīd (n.p.: Dār al-Fikr, n.d.) Vol. 3, 37; *hadīth* number 1731 in Muslim ibn al-Hajjāj al-Qushayrī, *Sahīh Muslim* (ed. Muhammad Fū'ād ʿAbd al-Bāqī, Beirut: Dār Ihyā' al-Turāth al-ʿArabī, n.d.), Vol. 3, 1357; *hadīths* numbers 9428 and 8430 in al-Ṣanaʿānī, *Al-Musannaf* (n 74) Vol. 5, 218, 220. See also for the prohibition of mutilation, *hadīth* numbers 2342 and 5197 in Muhammad ibn Ismāʿīl al-Bukhārī, *Al-Jāmiʿ al-Sahīh al-Mukhtasar*, ed. Mustafā Dīb al-Baghā, 3rd edn (Beirut: Dār ibn Kathīr, 1987/1407) Vol. 2, 875, Vol. 5, 2100 cited in Al-Dawoody, *The Islamic Law of War* (n 41) 120.

[171] Ṣaqr, *'Al-ʿAlāqāt al-Dawliyyah fī al-Islām Waqt al-Harb: Dirāsah lil- Qawāʿid al-Munazzimah li-Sayr al-Qitāl* (n 73) 57; Badar, 'Ius in Bello under Islamic International Law' (n 2) 620.

[172] Muhammad ibn Ahmad ibn Abī Sahl al-Sarakhsī, *Kitāb al-Mabsūt* (Beirut: Dār al-Maʿrifah, n.d.) Vol. 9, 135 and 196; Vol. 10, 129, 131; Vol. 16, 145; Vol. 26, 145.

[173] Muhammad ibn ʿAlī ibn Muhammad al-Shawkānī, *Nayl al-Awtār: Min Ahādīth Sayyid al-Khyār Sharh Muntaqā al-Akhbār* (Beirut: Dār al-Jīl, 1973) Vol. 8, 74; Ibn Qudāmah, *Al-Mughnī* (n 68) Vol. 9, 261.

says that '[i]t seems that this was a practice known in the wars between the Persians and the Byzantines, intended as a sign of victory'.[174] Al-Zhuri, however, affirms that this practice has never been conducted during Muhammad's lifetime.[175] In conformity, when this practice happened during Abu Bakr reign, he rejected it furiously. In this incident, when the head of the commander of the Levantine army *Yannāq al-Biṭrīq* was brought to Abu Bakr, he condemned this as a heinous act and labelled it as *Sunnah al-'ajam* (literally: a practice followed by non-Muslim foreigners). The Muslim fighter argued that this was merely an act of reciprocity because the enemy had done the same to Muslims. Abu Bakr replied frowningly: 'Are we going to follow the Persians and the Romans? We have what is enough: the book [*Quran*] and the *Sunnah*.'[176] Similar to IHL, the Islamic *jus in bello* prohibits the mutilation of dead bodies and obliges Muslims to bury their enemies. Muslim jurists hold the opinion that leaving a body to rot without a burial tantamount to mutilation.[177] It was also reported that Muhammad used to bury the dead once the hostilities had ceased, regardless of whether they were Muslims or non-Muslims.[178] Muhammad would also hand-over the enemies' dead bodies to the enemy if they requested it.[179]

3. The Means and Methods of Warfare

The rapidly developing nature of modern warfare, due in part to the introduction of new weapons, guerilla tactics, and the use of urban centres in the theatre of war has arguably weakened any attempt by the international community to mitigate the horrors of the contemporary wars, particularly in the

[174] Al-Dawoody, *The Islamic Law of War* (n 41) 120.

[175] Ibn Qudāmah, *Al-Mughnī* (n 68) Vol. 9, 261; Yūsuf al-Qaraḍāwī, *Fiqh al-Jihād: Dirāsah Muqāranah li-Ahkāmih wa Falsafatih fī Daw' al-Qur'ān wa al-Sunnah* (Cairo: Maktabah Wahbah, 2009) Vol. 1, 738.

[176] Al-Shaybānī, *Al-Siyar al-Kabīr* (n 145) Vol. 1, 79.

[177] Ahmed Abou-El-Wafa, *Islam and The West: Coexistence or Clash?* (Cairo: Dar Al-Nahda, 2006) 269–70.

[178] *Hadīth* number 1568 in Ibn Abī 'Āṣīm al-Dahhāk, *Al-Āhād wa al-Mathānī* (Riyadh: Dar Alrayah, 1991) Vol. 3, 211; Muhammad ibn Yūsuf al-Ṣālihī, *Subul al-Hudā wa al-Rashād fī Sīrah Khayr al-'Ibād*, ed. 'Ādil Ahmad 'Abd al-Mawjūd and 'Alī Muhammad Mu'awwad (Beirut: Dār al-Kutub al-'Ilmiyyah, 1993/1414) Vol. 4, 85.

[179] At the Battle of the Trench (627), Nawfal Ibn Abd Allah Ibn Al-Mughirah died when he attempted to jump the trench with his horse. When the Meccans offered payment for receiving the body of Nawfal, Muhammad gave them the body but refused the payment. See Ibn Hajar al-'Asqalānī, *Fath al-Bārī Sharh Sahīh al-Bukhārī*, ed. Muhib al-Dīn al-Khatīb (Beirut: Dār al-Ma'rifah, n.d.), Vol. 6, 283; *hadīth* number 30102 in Alā al-Dīn Ibn Husām al-Dīn, *Kanz al-'Ummāl fī Sunan al-Aqwāl wa alAf'āl*, ed. Mahmūd 'Umar al-Dumyātī (Beirut: Dār al-Kutub al-'Ilmiyyah, 1998/1419) Vol. 10, 206; *hadīths* numbers 18135; hadith number 1715 in al-Tirmidhī, *Al-Jāmi' al-Sahīh Sunan al-Tirmidhī* (Beirut: Dār Ihyā' al-Turāth al-'Arabī, n.d.) (n 170) Vol. 4, 214.

Middle East. The asymmetric nature of warfare, with significant disparities between the military capacities of the warring parties, often implies that the weaker party may do whatever it takes to find a way around the adversary's military strength. These tactics (also called methods of warfare) may include mingling combatants and military objectives with the civilian population and civilian objects and using civilians as human shields. Such practices evidently increase the risk of incidental civilian casualties and damage. The use of particular weapons (also called means of warfare), such as artillery shelling or aerial bombardments against military objectives that are located in the cities in proximity to the civilian population and civilian objects, can equally exacerbate the suffering of the civilian population.

Despite the bumpy road from Grotius' work in *De iure belli ac pacis* (1625), passing by the Hague Regulations (1907) and the First Additional Protocol (1977), to some more recent weapons conventions, one could comfortably argue today that IHL provides a relatively comprehensive legal framework regulating the use of particular means and methods of warfare with the ultimate purpose of humanizing war to the greatest possible extent. This section, however, aims at clarifying whether the Islamic *jus in bello* has devoted any specific rules to regulate Muslims' rights to deploy particular means and methods of warfare, while bearing in mind the basic types of weapons used during the early stage of Islamic wars, such as swords, lances, and arrows. Hence, this study finds it significant to discuss this poorly researched part of the Islamic *jus in bello* in order to explore the level of compatibility between IHL and Islamic law, if any.

(i) Methods of Warfare

The 'limited warfare' approach, which dominates the modern laws of war, requires every belligerent to strike a balance between the conflicting concerns of humanity and military necessity. Article 35 of the First Additional Protocol, echoing this principle, dictates that 'in any armed conflict, the right of the Parties to the conflict to choose methods or means of warfare is not unlimited'.[180] It prohibits the employment of weapons and methods of warfare that might cause 'superfluous injury or unnecessary suffering' or 'which are intended, or may be expected, to cause widespread, long-term and severe damage to the natural environment'.[181] Article 35 thus represents a fundamental

180 Article 35, AP I.
181 Ibid.

maxim of humanitarian rules regulating the means and methods of warfare by rejecting the concept of 'total war' in favour of the 'limited war' approach.[182]

The principles of distinction and proportionality—under both IHL and Islamic law—provide the foundations for the regulations of the means and methods of warfare. As previously elaborated (in Section 2), the principle of distinction requires the warring parties to distinguish between civilians and civilian objects on the one hand, and combatants and military objectives on the other hand. While attacks may be directed against combatants and military objectives, civilians and civilian objects should not be directly attacked under any circumstances. Accordingly, indiscriminate attacks are prohibited, whether:

> (a) those which are not directed at a specific military objective or; (b) those which employ a method or means of combat which cannot be directed at a specific military objective or; (c) those which employ a method or means of combat the effects of which cannot be limited ... and consequently, in each such case, are of a nature to strike military objectives and civilians or civilian objects without distinction.[183]

Along the same lines, the principle of proportionality prohibits 'an attack which may be expected to cause incidental loss of civilian life, injury to civilians, damage to civilian objects, or a combination thereof, which would be excessive in relation to the concrete and direct military advantage anticipated'.[184] The two principles of distinction and proportionality are explicitly echoed in the Islamic *jus in bello*, which reflects the same restrictions and prohibitions on the warring parties.[185]

The principle that adds a third layer of protection to protected persons and objects is the principle of precautions, which requires the warring parties 'to take all feasible precautions in the choice of means and methods of attack with a view to avoiding, and in any event to minimizing, incidental loss of civilian life, injury to civilians and damage to civilian objects'.[186] Many states have interpreted the obligation to take all 'feasible precautions' as being limited to those precautions which are practicable or practically possible, taking into account all circumstances ruling at the time, including humanitarian and

[182] Fleck (ed.), *The Handbook of International Humanitarian Law* (n 14) 122.
[183] Article 51(4), AP I.
[184] Ibid., para. (5).
[185] See generally Section 2 of this chapter.
[186] Article 57(2), AP I.

military considerations.[187] For example, the financial cost of precisely targetable weapons and munitions makes their usage notably infrequent, even at the hands of superpowers. Hence, warring parties retain considerable discretion with regard to the implementation of this obligation, which will be exercised primarily according to military considerations, within the framework of operational priorities, along with the humanitarian considerations.[188]

The Islamic *jus in bello*, likewise, shows a high level of consideration to the principle of precaution. This could be deducted from the discussion the Muslim scholars had with regard to *al-Bayat* (literally meaning night attacks). As fighting at night using the traditional basic weapons of the time (swords, lances, and arrows) was once almost impossible, the warring parties used to use mangonels (catapults) and similar indiscriminate weapons; hence the risk of killing non-combatants was relatively high. It was reported that 'whenever the Prophet reached a people by night, he never started an attack until it was morning'.[189] But despite the fact that Muhammad never attacked the enemy at night, it was reported in a different *hadith* that 'the Prophet was asked if it was permissible to attack the enemy by night which may result in casualties among women and children. Then the Prophet replied that they (women and children) belong to them (the enemy warriors).'[190] According to this *hadith*, the majority of the Muslim scholars permitted the night attacks,[191] while others maintained that it was reprehensible.[192] Nonetheless, the majority of Muslim scholars agree that casualties from the enemies' women and children are justified only as collateral damage.[193]

Under IHL, the principle of precaution further adds that 'effective advance warning shall be given of attacks which may affect the civilian population, unless circumstances do not permit'.[194] This should be conducted with

[187] See 'the practice of Algeria (Ibid., § 147), Argentina (Ibid., § 160), Australia (Ibid., § 161), Belgium (Ibid., § 148), Canada (Ibid., §§ 149, 162, and 168), France (Ibid., §150), Germany (Ibid., §§ 151 and 169), India (Ibid., § 170), Ireland (Ibid., § 152), Italy (Ibid., §§ 153 and 171), Netherlands (Ibid., §§ 154, 163, and 172), New Zealand (Ibid., § 164), Spain (Ibid., § 155), Turkey (Ibid., § 174), United Kingdom (Ibid., § 157), and United States (Ibid., § 175)', cited in The ICRC Customary IHL Study (n 54), Rule 15.

[188] Fleck (ed.), *The Handbook of International Humanitarian Law* (n 14) 179.

[189] *Hadith* 2785 in Mohammad Ibn Isma'il Al-Bukhari, *Al-Jami' Al-Sahih Al-Mukhtasar*, ed. Mustafa Dib Al-Bagha, 3rd edn, Vol. 3, 1077 cited in Badar, 'Ius in Bello under Islamic International Law' (n 2) 619.

[190] *Hadith* 2850 in ibid., 620.

[191] al-Shāfi'ī, *Al-Umm* (n 42) Vol. 4, 252; al-Shirāzī, *Al-Muhadhdhab* (n 89) Vol. 3, 278ff.; Ibn Qudāmah, *Al-Mughnī* (n 68) Vol. 9, 230; Ibn Ḥazm, *Al-Muhallā* (n 41) Vol. 7, p.296; al-Shawkānī, *Nayl al-Awtār* (n 173) Vol. 8, 71ff.; al-Sayyid Sābiq, *Fiqh alSunnah* (Cairo: Al-Fath lil-I'lām al-'Arabī, n.d.) Vol. 3, 45 cited in Al-Dawoody, *The Islamic Law of War* (n 41) 119.

[192] Al-Tirmidhī, *Al-Jāmi' al-Sahīh Sunan al-Tirmidhī* (n 170) Vol. 4, 121, cited in Al-Dawoody, *The Islamic Law of War* (n 41) 119.

[193] Al-Shawkānī, *Nayl al-Awtār: Min Ahādīth Sayyid al-Khyār Sharh Muntaqā al-Akhbār* (n 173) Vol. 8, 71.

[194] Fleck (ed.), *The Handbook of International Humanitarian Law* (n 14) 179.

the purpose of allowing an opportunity to the enemy to evacuate the civilian population, or at least to place the population in specifically protected locations. However, as the rule indicates, warnings are not required when circumstances do not permit, such as in cases where the surprise factor is essential to the success of an operation or to the security of the attacking forces.[195]

Islamic law, in this regard, does not explicitly contain any identical obligation for the Muslim armies to give advance warning before attacking the enemy. However, it dictates that Muslim armies are not entitled to initiate acts of hostility except as a third alternative after the enemy refused to accept Islam or to conclude a peace treaty with the Muslim and pay the *Jizya*.[196] Several incidents that occurred in early Islamic history confirm that this procedure has been understood by Muslims and non-Muslims as an obligation to give advance warning before attacking the enemy.[197] For example, it was narrated that the Samarkand people had complained to the Omayyad Caliph Omar Ibn Abdul Aziz of the Muslim commander Qutayba's injustice when he invaded Samarkand without any prior warning.[198] Omar sent his judge to settle the issue and it was held that Muslims had to withdraw from the occupied territory and go back to their camps, unless a new reconciliation pact was concluded or the invasion had taken place after due warning.[199] It should be underlined here that under Islamic law, even if the element of surprise was essential for the success of the military operation, the Muslim army is still obliged to give advance warning in the aforementioned form.[200]

[195] As indicated in Rule 20 of the ICRC Customary IHL Study, this fact is reflected in several treaties, soft law documents, agreements, manuals, and the state practice of many states, including: Article 26 of the Hague Regulations; Article 57(2)(c) of AP I; Article 16 of Brussels Declaration; Article 33 of Oxford Manual; Memorandum of Understanding on the Application of IHL between Croatia and the Socialist Federal Republic of Yugoslavia; Agreement on the Application of IHL between the Parties to the Conflict in Bosnia and Herzegovina; practice of Australia, Belgium, Benin, Cameroon, Canada, Croatia, Ecuador, France, Germany, Italy, Kenya, Madagascar, Netherlands, New Zealand, South Africa, Spain, Switzerland, Togo, United Kingdom, United States, and Yugoslavia, and the reported practice of Israel. The ICRC Customary IHL Study (n 54), Rule 20.

[196] Muhammad Abū Zahrah, *Tanzīm al-Islām lil-Mujtama'* (Cairo: Dār al-Fikr al-'Arabī, n.d.) 48ff.; Khadduri, *War and Peace in the Law of Islam* (n 146) 94–101; al-Hindī, *Ahkām al-Harb wa al-Salām fī Dawlah al-Islām* (n 72) 147–52; Umar Ahmad al-Firjānī, *Usūl al-'Alāqāt al-Dawliyyah fī al-Islām*, 2nd edn (Tripoli: Dār Iqra', 1988/1397) 102–4.

[197] Muslim jurists, however, disagree whether warnings should be given to any non-Muslim adversarial army in general or only those who have not been informed about Islam. Muslim jurists incline to extend the warning obligation before any attack to all their wars, regardless the enemy is informed about Islam or not. See 'Abd al-'Azīz Saqr, *'Al-'Alāqāt al-Dawliyyah fī al-Islām Waqt al-Harb: Dirāsah lil- Qawā'id al-Munazzimah li-Sayr al-Qitāl*, Mashrū' al-'Alāqāt al-Dawliyyah fī al-Islām 6 (Cairo: Al-Ma'had al-'Ālamī lil-Fikr al-Islāmī, 1996) 25–8.

[198] Shiekh Wahbah al-Zuhili, 'Islam and International Law', *International Review of the Red Cross* (2005) 87(858) 269–83, 274.

[199] Ibid., 275.

[200] Al-Dawoody, *The Islamic Law of War* (n 41) 119.

This should not, however, be interpreted to mean that the Islamic *jus in bello* prohibits ruses of war. On the contrary, ruses of war are allowed and even encouraged under Islamic law.[201] It was reported that Muhammad used to say that war is *Kheda'a*, which literally means the art of deceiving the enemy.[202] In several battles, Muhammad orchestrated strategic tricks against the enemy that led to the victory of the Muslim army.[203] In the same vein, the permissibility of ruses of war has been implied in several verses of *Quran*, such as: 'And whoever turns his back to them on such a day, unless it is for a tactic in the battle or joining [another] company, has certainly turns with wrath from Allah, and his abode is Hell.'[204] This verse permits Muslims to operate ruses of war and condemns showing cowardice in the battlefield. Nevertheless, ruses of war should not be confused with perfidy, which is absolutely prohibited under Islamic law. *Quran* explicitly forbids treachery and perfidious acts.[205] It was also reported that Muhammad said that 'every perfidious will be singled out on the Judgment day' in order to receive the appropriate punishment of God.[206] Similarly, IHL prohibits killing, injuring, or capturing an adversary by resort to perfidy.[207] This prohibition is considered by the international community as a customary IHL rule that is applicable in both international and non-international armed conflicts.[208] IHL, in line with the Islamic *jus in bello*, allows ruses of war that intend to mislead the enemy or to induce them to act recklessly, so long as it does not infringe any other international law rule applicable in armed conflict, including the prohibition on perfidy.[209]

201 Shah, *Islamic Law and the Law of Armed Conflict* (n 155) 51.

202 Bukhari (2008: 277); Muslim (2008: 630) cited in Shah, *Islamic Law and the Law of Armed Conflict* (n 155) 51.

203 Shah, *Islamic Law and the Law of Armed Conflict* (n 155) 51.

204 *Quran* (8:16).

205 'If you [have reason to] fear from a people betrayal, throw [their treaty] back to them, [putting you] on equal terms. Indeed, Allah does not like traitors.' *Quran* (8:58). 'And do not argue on behalf of those who deceive themselves. Indeed, Allah loves not one who is a habitually sinful deceiver.' *Quran* (4:107).

206 Bukhari (6966) and Muslim (1736), 'Al Hila w Al Khidaa Fi Al Harb'. Available at: <https://islamqa.info/ar/10138> (last accessed 25 May 2019).

207 '1. It is prohibited to kill, injure or capture an adversary by resort to perfidy. Acts inviting the confidence of an adversary to lead him to believe that he is entitled to, or is obliged to accord, protection under the rules of international law applicable in armed conflict, with intent to betray that confidence, shall constitute perfidy. The following acts are examples of perfidy: (a) the feigning of an intent to negotiate under a flag of truce or of a surrender; (b) the feigning of an incapacitation by wounds or sickness; (c) the feigning of civilian, non-combatant status; and (d) the feigning of protected status by the use of signs, emblems or uniforms of the United Nations or of neutral or other States not Parties to the conflict.' Article 37, AP I.

208 ICRC, The ICRC Customary IHL Study (n 54), Rule 65. Available at: <https://ihl-databases.icrc.org/customary-ihl/eng/docs/v1_rul_rule65> (last accessed 25 May 2019).

209 Article 37 (2) AP I; ICRC, The ICRC Customary IHL Study (n 54), Rule 57. Available at: <https://ihl-databases.icrc.org/customary-ihl/eng/docs/v1_rul_rule57> (last accessed 25 May 2019).

Having said that, one might wonder what the position of Islamic law is *vis-à-vis* suicide attacks; that is, whether they are to be regarded as acts of perfidy or martyrdom. Through his research into the legal history of suicide attacks, Bernard Freamon argues that the Shiite scholars reinterpreted the martyrdom of Husayn as extreme self-sacrifice and revived it in a way that eventually led to self-annihilatory violent behaviour, namely, suicide attacks.[210] According to his view, this has fundamentally transformed the Shiite conception of the religious law of martyrdom.[211] He highlighted that this transformation of religious doctrine—championed by the Shiite scholars and emulated first by *Hezbollah*, then borrowed by Palestinians and later by *Al-Qaeda*—resulted in the emergence of a new norm of 'Jihadist battlefield behavior'.[212]

Today suicide attacks are carried out in many armed conflicts around the world and have become a common feature of warfare, particularly in the Middle East. On the legality of suicide attacks, Al-Shaybani (commonly referred to as the 'Grotius' of Islamic International Law) said: 'It is permissible for a person to plunge into a group of enemy forces, or to attack them in cases where he hopes that he will be saved in the end, or—if there is no such hope—in cases where he will inflict damage on the enemy, and demoralize them, or will encourage his own combatants, or due to an extraordinary power he might feel.'[213] As indicated, Al-Shaybani in his ruling permitted suicide attacks provided that the attacker is a combatant who is targeting a group of enemy forces (combatants) in order to achieve a military advantage for his own combatants even if the attacker will lose their life. Moreover, according to Ibn Taymiyyah, the four leading jurists of the Sunni Schools affirm that a Muslim soldier is entitled to penetrate the enemy's lines even if the soldier knows that they will definitely be killed, provided that this would be advantageous for the Muslim army.[214] In all the previously stated cases, suicide attacks are permitted, and even praised, because it is a Muslim soldier who is executing the attack against enemy soldiers by scarifying his life to achieve an advantage for the Muslim army. However, if a suicide bomber pretends to be a civilian to benefit from the non-combatant immunity and then blows themself up to kill members of the enemy's armed forces, it would undoubtedly constitute a perfidious act that

[210] Bernard K. Freamon, 'Martyrdom, Suicide, and the Islamic Law of War: A Short Legal History', *Fordham International Law Journal* (2003) 27(299), 299–369, 299.

[211] Ibid.

[212] Ibid.; Muhammad Munir, 'Suicide Attacks and Islamic Law', *International Review of the Red Cross* (2008) 90(869), 71–89, 71–78.

[213] M. Ibn Al-Hasan Al-Shaybani, 'Syar Al-Kabir', cited in Ibid., 80.

[214] Ahmad ibn 'Abd al-Halīm Ibn Taymiyah, *Majmū' Fatāwā Shaykh al-Islām Ahmad Ibn Taymiyyah*, Vol. 25 (Cairo: Maktabah ibn Taymiyyah, n.d.) 540.

is prohibited by the Islamic *jus in bello* and IHL.[215] Likewise, suicide attacks against civilians are absolutely prohibited, because of the protection to which they are entitled in both bodies of law, as elaborated in Section 2.

Another method of warfare that has developed in the context of contemporary asymmetric warfare is human shielding. Confronted with overwhelming technological superiority, weaker parties have incorporated the use of human shields as a fighting method designed to counter attacks against which they cannot effectively defend using the weaponry and troops at their disposal.[216] Human shielding is basically using non-combatants—who are protected under IHL and Islamic law—to prevent attacks on combatants and military objectives. Such conduct is absolutely prohibited under IHL. Article 51(7) of the First Additional Protocol broadly provides that:

> the presence or movements of the civilian population or individual civilians shall not be used to render certain points or areas immune from military operations, in particular in attempts to shield military objectives from attacks or to shield, favor or impede military operations. The Parties to the conflict shall not direct the movement of the civilian population or individual civilians in order to attempt to shield military objectives from attacks or to shield military operations.[217]

In conformity, several provisions in the Geneva Conventions mirror the same prohibition.[218] However, despite the lack of any textual prohibition on human shielding in armed conflicts of non-international character, state practice establishes this prohibition as a norm of customary IHL applicable in both international and non-international armed conflicts.[219] Here, one might wonder what would the obligations of the attacker be should the enemy violate the law by using human shields. Or, as Michael Schmitt put it: 'To what extent does the prohibition of human shielding by a defender affect the attacker's operations as a matter of law?'[220] In this regard, the only explicit provision bearing on the attacker's obligations in shielding situations is Article 51(8) of Additional Protocol I, which provides that '[a]ny violation of these prohibitions shall not release the Parties to the conflict from their legal obligations

[215] Munir, 'Suicide Attacks and Islamic Law' (n 212) 82.
[216] Michael N. Schmitt, 'Human Shields in International Humanitarian Law', *Columbia Journal of Transitional Law* (2009), 47, 292–383, 297.
[217] Article 51(7), AP I.
[218] Article 23 GC III; Article 28 GC IV; Article 19 GC I, Article 12(4) AP I.
[219] The ICRC Customary IHL Study (n 54), Rule 97.
[220] Michael N. Schmitt, 'Human Shields in International Humanitarian Law' (n 216) 323.

with respect to the civilian population and civilians, including the obligation to take the precautionary measures provided for in Article 57'.[221] In other words, the attacker should respect the principles of distinction, proportionality, and precautions while attacking the human-shielded object. Scholars, however, distinguish between voluntary and involuntary shields. While most scholars agree that the previously mentioned principles should apply if the enemy uses involuntary shields (such as hostages), they disagree whether this should be the case if the attacker is facing voluntary shields.[222] Regarding the latter, they argue that voluntary shields should be treated as people who directly participate in hostilities and thus they do not merit any considerations, at least with respect to the proportionality and precautions tests.[223]

Unlike IHL, the Islamic *jus in bello* is silent about Muslims' usage of human shielding. It is not clear if this is due to the fact that the Muslim army did not use human shielding as a warfare tactic or because Islamic law dignified the lives of non-combatant Muslims and thus it was an unimaginable scenario for Muslims to use their citizens as human shields. The Islamic *jus in bello*, nevertheless, regulates the Muslim army's obligations in targeting an enemy that uses human shielding. As in the early history of Islam, many tribes used to build forts for their protection in times of war and they would use non-combatants as human shields by holding them out of the walls of the fort so that the Muslim army stopped targeting them with arrows or mangonels.[224] This practice is referred to in Islamic law as *tatarrus*. Here, despite slight disagreement, the majority of the Muslim scholars broadly agree that it is permissible to attack the enemy because of military necessity, provided that the Muslim army intends to direct its attack against the combatants and avoid human shields as much as they can.[225] In other words, collateral damage is allowed in this case, providing that the Muslim army made every possible effort to avoid killing non-combatants.[226]

[221] Article 51(8), AP I.

[222] Schmitt, 'Human Shields in International Humanitarian Law' (n 216) 323–33.

[223] Ibid.

[224] Shah, *Islamic Law and the Law of Armed Conflict* (n 155) 35.

[225] According to Al-Dawoody: 'The jurists strongly disagree over what exactly constitutes the military necessity that would justify an attack on human shields in this context. For al-Māwardī and al-Shirāzī, the military necessity in this case would arise from the risk of a Muslim defeat. On this point, certain jurists add that attacking human shields in this case is a matter of protecting the rest of the Muslims, because if Muslims did not attack the shield and the Muslim army was defeated as a result, many Muslims would be killed. In the view of al-Qurtubī, military necessity in this instance meant avoiding 'enemy capture of all Muslims." Al-Dawoody, 'The Islamic International Humanitarian Law: Between Theory and Practice' (n 63) 245.

[226] Shah, *Islamic Law and the Law of Armed Conflict* (n 155) 35.

(ii) Means of Warfare

The *Quran* and *Sunnah* do not say much about the permissibility of using particular types of weapons. Given the early stage of the Islamic history and the types of weapons used at the time, there was no need for any regulation in this regard. War consisted mainly of one-to-one fights and the weapons used were mainly swords, lances, and arrows,[227] hence, the general Islamic *jus in bello* principles of distinction, proportionality, and precautions were sufficient to regulate the conduct of hostilities. As time passed, Muslim scholars started discussing the use of new types of weapons that had not been used during Muhammad's lifetime.[228] For example, they discussed the permissibility of using poison-tipped arrows. Some scholars prohibited their use and others permitted it as it was more effective in deterring the enemy.[229] Additionally, in contexts other than one-to-one combat where the enemy retreats inside fortifications, Muslim scholars discussed the use of three specific weapons that were at their disposal back then, namely mangonels, fire, and flooding. These weapons were usually used to force the enemy to surrender and ensure the victory of the Muslim army—despite the likelihood of causing casualties among the non-combatant community (as collateral damage).[230] The majority of Muslim scholars permit targeting the fortification with mangonels.[231] This is based on the precedent from the last battle Muhammad attended, *al-Taif* (630), in which Muhammad allowed the Muslim army to use mangonels to target the fortification behind which the Al-Thaqif tribe were hidden.[232] Although its usage was permitted by Muhammad, the Muslim army did not manage to use this newly introduced weapon at the time.[233] It must be noted, however, that this permission has to be considered in light of the general principles of the Islamic *jus in bello*. In other words, the targeting should be directed at the fortifications as military objectives and the civilian casualties and damages should be calculated within the proportionality test.

227 Haykal, 'Al-Jihād wa al-Qitāl', Vol. 2, 1343.

228 Khalīl ibn Ishāq ibn Musā al-Jundī, *Mukhtasar Khalīl fī Fiqh Imām Dār alHijrah*, ed. Ahmad 'Alī Harakāt (Beirut: Dār al-Fikr, 1994–5/1415), 102; Muhammad ibn Yūsuf ibn Abī al-Qāsim al-'Abdarī, *Al-Tāj wa al-Iklīl: Sharh Mukhtasar Khalīl*, 2nd edn (Beirut: Dār al-Fikr, 1977–8/1398) Vol. 3, 352.

229 Ibid.; Al-Shaybānī, *Al-Siyar al-Kabīr* (n 145) Vol. 4, 1475; Alsumaih, 'The Sunni Concept of Jihad in Classical Fiqh and Modern Islamic Thought' (n 75) 115.

230 Al-Dawoody, *The Islamic Law of War* (n 41) 123.

231 Ibid.

232 al-Shaybānī, *Al-Siyar al-Kabīr* (n 145) Vol. 4, 1468.

233 Guillaume, 'The Life of Muhammad' (n 112) 589–91; Ismā'īl ibn 'Umar ibn Kathīr, *Al-Sīrah al-Nabawiyyah* (Beirut: Dār al-Kitāb al-'Arabī, 1997) Vol. 4, 622ff.; Haykal, 'The Life of Muhammad', 423.

Regarding the use of fire as a weapon, the majority of Muslim scholars prohibits the use of fire against enemy combatants. As it was reported that Muhammad said: 'don't punish the creatures of God with the punishment of God'.[234] However, they disagreed about using fire to target enemy fortifications. Some consider it prohibited,[235] or find it merely reprehensible,[236] while others permit it pursuant to the doctrine of military necessity,[237] or that it can only be used in reciprocity if it has been used first by the enemy.[238] By the same token, flooding as a mean of warfare was prohibited by the majority of the Muslim scholars, as it will likely cause indiscriminate casualties among the enemy's population.[239] However, they permitted flooding the enemy fortifications only in case of military necessity; that is, 'when it is the only way to overcome the enemy'.[240]

Unlike Islamic law, IHL today has a relatively comprehensive body of law that regulates the means of warfare. The St. Petersburg Declaration of 1868 was the first instrument to outlaw specific weapons. This Declaration, that has the force of law, confirms the customary rule according to which the use of arms, projectiles, and material of a nature to cause unnecessary suffering is prohibited.[241] This rule was later on embodied in Article 23(e) of the Hague Regulations on Land Warfare of 1899 and 1907. The Preamble of this Declaration sets the foundation and rationale of this whole body of law. It reads:

> that the progress of civilization should have the effect of alleviating as much as possible the calamities of war; that the only legitimate object which States should endeavor to accomplish during war is to weaken the military forces of the enemy; that for this purpose it is sufficient to disable the greatest possible number of men; that this object would be exceeded by the employment of

[234] *Hadīths* numbers 2854 and 6524 in al-Bukhārī, 'Al-Jāmi' al-Ṣah. Īh. al-Mukhtaṣar', Vol. 3, 1098; Ibid. Vol. 6, 2537.

[235] Al-Shawkānī, *Al-Sayl al-Jarrār al-Mutadaffiq 'alā Hadā'iq al-Azhār* (n 41) Vol. 4, 534; Al-Qaraḍāwī, *Fiqh al-Jihād* (n 175) Vol. 1, 595ff.

[236] Al-Shawkānī, *Nayl al-Awtār: Min Ahādīth Sayyid al-Khyār Sharh Muntaqā al-Akhbār* (n 173) Vol. 8, 76.

[237] Al-Shaybānī, *Al-Siyar al-Kabīr* (n 145) Vol. 4, 154; Ibn 'Ābidīn, *Hāshiyah Radd al-Muhtār 'alā al-Durr al-ukhtār* (n 41) Vol. 4, 129; Ibn Qudāmah, *Al-Mughnī* (n 68) Vol. 9, 230.

[238] Muhammad ibn Ahmad ibn Muhammad Ibn Rushd, *Bidāyah al-Mujtahid wa Nihāyah al-Muqtasid*, 2 Vols (Beirut: Dār al-Fikr, n.d.) Vol. 1, 281.

[239] Al-Shaybānī, *Al-Siyar al-Kabīr* (n 145) Vol. 4, 1554.

[240] Ibid.

[241] *Declaration Renouncing the Use, in Time of War, of Explosive Projectiles Under 400 Grammes Weight*, St Petersburg, 29 November–11 December 1868. Available at: <https://ihl-databases.icrc.org/ihl/INTRO/130?OpenDocument> (last accessed 25 May 2019). In the words of the ICJ in its Advisory Opinion on Nuclear Weapons, 'unnecessary suffering' stands for 'a harm greater than that unavoidable to achieve legitimate military objectives'. See ICJ, Nuclear Weapons, ICJ Reports 1996, 257 (para. 78).

> arms which uselessly aggravate the sufferings of disabled men, or render their death inevitable; that the employment of such arms would, therefore, be contrary to the laws of humanity.[242]

This was the same rationale used to prohibit the use of the bullets which expand or flatten easily in the human body (Dum Dum bullets).[243] According to IHL, it is also prohibited to use any weapon the primary effect of which is to injure by fragments which in the human body escape detection by X-rays.[244] Moreover, in order to counter the indiscriminate effects of land mines and their long-lasting impairments of civil life, the Ottawa Convention on the Prohibition of the Use, Stockpiling, Production, and Transfer of Anti-Personnel Mines and on their Destruction was adopted in 1997.[245]According to this Convention, states are prohibited from using, developing, producing, acquiring, stockpiling, retaining or transferring to anyone, directly or indirectly, anti-personnel mines.[246] It also obliges states to destroy or ensure the destruction of all anti-personnel mines in their possession.[247] However, with respect to the mines in general (landmines), booby traps and other devices, it is prohibited under the 1996 Amended Protocol II to the Convention on Certain Conventional Weapons 'in all circumstances to use any mine, booby-trap or other device which is designed or of a nature to cause superfluous injury or unnecessary suffering.'[248] A careful reading to Article 3 of this Protocol, entitled 'General Restrictions', reveals that this Protocol only reaffirms the principles of distinction, proportionality and precautions.[249] These principles were also reflected in the Protocol on Prohibitions or Restrictions on the Use of Incendiary

[242] *Declaration Renouncing the Use, in Time of War, of Explosive Projectiles* (n 241).

[243] William H. Boothby, *Weapons and the Law of Armed Conflict* (Oxford: Oxford University Press, 2009) 73. This prohibition applies also to the use of a shotgun, since its shot causes similar suffering unjustified from the military point of view. It is also prohibited to use projectiles of a nature to burst or deform while penetrating the human body; to tumble early in the human body; or to cause shock waves leading to extensive tissue damage or even lethal shock. (Articles 35, paras 2 and 51, para. 4, lit. c, AP I; Article 23, lit. e, Hague Regulations). See Fleck (ed.), *The Handbook of International Humanitarian Law* (n 14) 134.

[244] Protocol I to the Convention on Certain Conventional Weapons, 10 October 1980; ICRC, Customary IHL Study (n 54) Rule 79.

[245] *Convention on the Prohibition of the Use, Stockpiling, Production and Transfer of Anti-Personnel Mines and on their Destruction* (hereafter *Ottawa Convention*), 18 September 1997. Available at: <https://ihl-databases.icrc.org/ihl/INTRO/580 (last accessed 25 May 2019).

[246] Article 1(1), *Ottawa Convention*, 18 September 1997.

[247] Article 1(2), *Ottawa Convention*, 18 September 1997.

[248] Article 3(3), *Protocol on Prohibitions or Restrictions on the Use of Mines, Booby-Traps and Other Devices* (Protocol II to the 1980 CCW Convention), as amended on 3 May 1996. Available at: <https://ihl-databases.icrc.org/ihl/INTRO/575> (last accessed 25 May 2019).

[249] Ibid; Fleck (ed.), *The Handbook of International Humanitarian Law* (n 14) 138. For more details about the relevant obligations, such as recording of the placement of landmines, removal or neutralization procedures and sharing information, see ICRC, Customary IHL Study (n 54) Rules 81–83.

Weapons.[250] This Protocol not only prohibits direct attacks against civilians and civilian objects, it also prohibits attacking military objectives located in a civilian-concentrated area 'by air-delivered incendiary weapons.'[251] Similarly, it prohibits any attack against military objectives located within a concentration of civilians 'by means of incendiary weapons other than air-delivered incendiary weapons, except when such military objective is clearly separated from the concentration of civilians and all feasible precautions are taken.'[252] It further prohibits to make forests or other kinds of plant cover the object of attack by incendiary weapons except when it is used to cover, conceal or camouflage combatants or other military objectives, or are themselves military objectives.[253] Protocol IV to the 1980 Convention on Certain Conventional Weapons prohibits employing blinding laser weapons[254] and is considered to be the first instrument after the 1868 St. Petersburg Declaration prohibiting a weapon of military interest before it had been used on the battlefield.[255] Additionally, the international community, after decades of seeing civilians suffer with each new use of cluster munitions,[256] adopted a new convention to prohibit using or developing, producing, acquiring, stockpiling, retaining, or transferring to anyone, directly or indirectly, cluster munitions.[257] It also obliges states to co-operate in munition clearance and destruction, victim assistance, and risk education programs.[258]

With regard to the Weapons of Mass Destruction (WMD), IHL absolutely prohibits the use of chemical and biological weapons. The 1899 Hague Declaration concerning Asphyxiating Gases was the first treaty to outlaw the use of gas in warfare.[259] Likewise, they were prohibited as poisoned weapons in the Hague Regulations.[260] This prohibition was reaffirmed after the wide

[250] Article 2, *Protocol on Prohibitions or Restrictions on the Use of Incendiary Weapons (Protocol III)*, 10 October 1980. For the definition of incendiary weapons see Ibid., Article 1.

[251] Ibid., Article 2 paras 1 and 2.

[252] Ibid., para. 3.

[253] Ibid.

[254] Article 1, *Protocol on Blinding Laser Weapons (Protocol IV to the 1980 Convention)*, 13 October 1995.

[255] Boothby, *Weapons and the Law of Armed Conflict* (n 243) 209.

[256] The definition of cluster munitions is: 'means a conventional munition that is designed to disperse or release explosive submunitions each weighing less than 20 kilograms, and includes those explosive submunitions'. Article 2, *Convention on Cluster Munitions*, 30 May 2008.

[257] Ibid., Article 1.

[258] Ibid., Articles 3, 4, and 5.

[259] 'The contracting Powers agree to abstain from the use of projectiles the sole object of which is the diffusion of asphyxiating or deleterious gases.' *Declaration (IV, 2) concerning Asphyxiating Gases*, The Hague, 29 July 1899.

[260] Article 23, *Convention (IV) respecting the Laws and Customs of War on Land and its annex: Regulations concerning the Laws and Customs of War on Land*, The Hague, 18 October 1907.

usage of poisonous gases in World War 1 in the 1925 Geneva Gas Protocol.[261] Afterwards, a comprehensive prohibition was adopted against using, developing, acquiring, producing, stockpiling, retaining, transferring, directly or indirectly, chemical weapons to anyone; or 'to engage in any military preparations to use chemical weapons.'[262] It also obliges states to destroy chemical weapons or chemical weapons production facilities it owns or possesses, or that are located in any place under its jurisdiction or control.[263] A similar initiative yielded the Biological Weapons Convention of 1972 that was initially prohibited in the 1925 Geneva Gas Protocol.[264] The Convention prohibits developing, producing, stockpiling, acquiring or retaining any 'microbial or other biological agents or toxins' or 'weapons, equipment or means of delivery designed to use such agents or toxins for hostile purposes or in armed conflicts.'[265] As to nuclear weapons, a number of multilateral and bilateral treaties already exist which were designed to prohibit the proliferation of nuclear weapons, to restrict the testing of nuclear weapons, to prohibit the stationing of nuclear weapons, to provide for nuclear weapon-free zones, to limit the scope of nuclear armament, and to prevent the outbreak of nuclear war.[266] However, the question of whether the use of nuclear weapons is permissible under international law had not been addressed in a treaty until very recently. Prior to this, the question of the legality of the threat or use of nuclear weapons had been vaguely and controversially answered in 1996 by the International Court of Justice (ICJ) advisory opinion upon the request of the UN General

[261] *Protocol for the Prohibition of the Use of Asphyxiating, Poisonous or Other Gases, and of Bacteriological Methods of Warfare*, 17 June 1925.

[262] Article 1, *Convention on the prohibition of the development, production, stockpiling and use of chemical weapons and on their destruction*, 13 January 1993.

[263] Ibid.

[264] *Protocol for the Prohibition of the Use of Asphyxiating, Poisonous or Other Gases, and of Bacteriological Methods of Warfare*. Geneva, 17 June 1925 ('agree to extend this prohibition to the use of bacteriological methods of warfare').

[265] Article 1, *Convention on the Prohibition of the Development, Production and Stockpiling of Bacteriological (Biological) and Toxin Weapons and on their Destruction*, 10 April 1972.

[266] These includes: *Treaty on the Non-Proliferation of Nuclear Weapons* (NPT) of 1 July 1968; *Treaty Banning Nuclear Weapon Tests in the Atmosphere, in Outer Space, and under Water (Partial Nuclear Test Ban Treaty)*, 5 August 1963; *Treaty on Principles Governing the Activities of States in the Exploration and Use of Outer Space, including the Moon and Other Celestial Bodies (Outer Space Treaty)*, 27 January 1967; *Treaty on the Prohibition of the Emplacement of Nuclear Weapons and Other Weapons of Mass Destruction on the Seabed and the Ocean Floor and the Subsoil Thereof* (Seabed Treaty), 11 February 1971; *Treaty for the Prohibition of Nuclear Weapons in Latin America (Treaty of Tlatelolco)*, 14 February 1967; *South Pacific Nuclear-Free Zone Treaty (Treaty of Rarotonga)*, 6 August 1985; *Treaty on the Elimination of American and Soviet Intermediate-Range and Shorter-Range Missiles*, 8 December 1987; *Treaty on the Southeast Asia Nuclear Weapon-Free Zone* (Treaty of Bangkok) 15 December 1995; *African Nuclear-Weapon-Free Zone Treaty (Treaty of Pelindaba)*, 11 April 1996; *Comprehensive Nuclear-Test-Ban Treaty*, 24 September 1996; *Treaty on a Nuclear-Weapon-Free Zone in Central Asia (Treaty of Semipalatinsk)*, 8 September 2006; cited in Fleck (ed.), *The Handbook of International Humanitarian Law* (n 14) 153.

Assembly.[267] The Court decided that: 'there is in neither customary nor conventional international law any specific authorization of the threat or use of nuclear weapons.'[268] It further ruled: 'A threat or use of nuclear weapons should also be compatible with the requirements of the international law applicable in armed conflict, particularly those of the principles and rules of international humanitarian law.'[269] The Court most interestingly recognized that the use of nuclear weapons 'would generally be contrary' to IHL rules; yet it concluded that, given the current state of international law and the facts at its disposal, it 'cannot conclude definitively whether the threat or use of nuclear weapons would be lawful or unlawful in an extreme circumstance of self-defense, in which the very survival of a State would be at stake.'[270] Be that as it may, eleven years later, 120 states adopted a landmark treaty banning nuclear weapons,[271] basing itself on the principles of distinction, proportionality and precaution, as stated in its Preamble, the treaty prohibits developing, testing, producing, manufacturing, acquiring, possessing, stockpiling, using, or transferring nuclear weapons or other nuclear explosive devices.[272] It further includes various provisions on declarations, international cooperation, victims' assistance, and environmental remediation.[273]

On the Islamic front, however, the use of WMD under the Islamic *jus in bello* has grasped the attention of very few modern Muslim scholars.[274] Al-Dawoody justified this lack of scholarship and interest by two facts, namely: first, unlike Europe and parts of Asia, the Muslim world has not experienced any large scale human catastrophe as a result of the use of WMD; second, the westernization

[267] UN General Assembly, Res. 49/75 K on request for an advisory opinion from the International Court of Justice on the legality of the threat or use of nuclear weapons, 15 December 1994.

[268] ICJ, *Nuclear Weapons case*, Advisory Opinion, 8 July 1996, para. 105. The Court notes as a reasoning for this decision that: 'The Court notes that the treaties dealing exclusively with acquisition, manufacture, possession, deployment and testing of nuclear weapons, without specifically addressing their threat or use, certainly point to an increasing concern in the international community with these weapons; the Court concludes from this that these treaties could therefore be seen as foreshadowing a future general prohibition of the use of such weapons, but they do not constitute such a prohibition by themselves.' Para. 62. The court also used in its reasoning that: '[T]he Members of the international community are profoundly divided on the matter of whether non-recourse to nuclear weapons over the past fifty years constitutes the expression of an *opinio juris*. Under these circumstances the Court does not consider itself able to find that there is such an *opinio juris*.' Para. 67.

[269] Ibid., para. 105.

[270] Ibid.

[271] Historic agreement banning nuclear weapons a 'victory for our shared humanity', ICRC Website. Available at: <https://www.icrc.org/en/document/historic-agreement-banning-nuclear-weapons-victory-our-shared-humanity-icrc-says> (last accessed 25 May 2019).

[272] Article 1, Draft Treaty on the Prohibition of Nuclear Weapons, 7 July 2017. Available at: <http://www.undocs.org/en/a/conf.229/2017/L.3/Rev.1> (last accessed 25 May 2019).

[273] Ibid., Articles 2, 3, 4, 5, 6, and 7.

[274] See generally Sohail H. Hashmi (ed), *Islamic Political Ethics: Civil Society, Pluralism, and Conflict* (Princeton, NJ: Princeton University Press, 2002).

(secularization) of the legal systems in the Muslim world (except on family law issues) created less interest in engaging Islamic scholars in these type of scholarly work.[275] Nevertheless, in the Islamic Republic of Iran, as one of the very few living theocracies in the Muslim world where Muslim jurists have the power to directly engage in the decision making process, the debate on the permissibility of possessing and using nuclear weapons under Islamic law is quite advanced.

In 2003, the Supreme Leader of Islamic Republic of Iran, Ayatollah Ali Khamenei, had issued a *fatwa* (Islamic legal opinion) that 'the production, stockpiling, and use of nuclear weapons are forbidden under Islam and that the Islamic Republic of Iran shall never acquire these weapons.'[276] It was also reported that he said, referring to the context of the Iran-Iraq war: 'We are even against chemical weapons. Even when Iraq attacked us by chemical weapons, we did not produce chemical weapons.'[277]In conformity, the ex-Minister of Foreign Affairs, Kamal Kharazi, said that Iran considers: 'using biological, chemical and nuclear weapons as an act of *haram* (illegal/un-Islamic).'[278] The Islamic law reasoning behind this *fatwa* was the fact that nuclear weapons cause indiscriminate effects and might lead to the killing of non-combatants and inflict unnecessary suffering and destruction.[279] Many Sunni scholars agree with this position.[280] Others are of the opinion that, while using nuclear weapons is prohibited, possessing it for deterrence considerations is absolutely allowed.[281] In support of their deterrence argument, those scholars often quote a verse from *Quran* that reads: 'And prepare against them whatever you are able of power and of steeds of war by which you may terrify the enemy of Allah and your enemy and others besides them whom you do not know [but] whom Allah knows. And whatever you spend in the cause of Allah will be fully repaid

[275] Al-Dawoody, *The Islamic Law of War* (n 41) 125.

[276] Iran's Statement at IAEA Emergency Meeting. Available at: <https://fas.org/nuke/guide/iran/nuke/mehr080905.html> (last accessed 25 May 2019).

[277] Ibid; Michael Eisenstadt and Mehdi Khalaj, 'Nuclear Fatwa: Religion and Politics in Iran's Proliferation Strategy', *Policy Focus 115*, The Washington Institute for Near East Policy, September 2011. Available at: <https://www.washingtoninstitute.org/uploads/Documents/pubs/PolicyFocus115.pdf> (last accessed 5 May 2019).

[278] 'Nuclear weapons forbidden by Islam says Iranian minister', *The Irish Times*. Available at: <https://www.irishtimes.com/news/nuclear-weapons-forbidden-by-islam-says-iranian-minister-1.481354 (last accessed 25 May 2019).

[279] Eisenstadt and Khalaj, 'Nuclear Fatwa' (n 277) 14.

[280] Ibrāhīm Yahyā al-Shihābī, *Mafhūm al-Harb wa al-Salām fī al-Islām: Sirā'āt wa Hurūb 'am Tafā'ul wa Salām?* (n.p.: Manshūrāt Mu'assasah Maī, 1990/1399) 76; See generally Muhammad'Arafah, 'AlKhatar al-Nawawī fī Mirāh 'Ālim 'Āzharī', supplement to *Majalah al-Azhar* (June 2004/Rabī' al-Ākhir 1425); Shmuel Bar, *Warrant for Terror: Fatwās of Radical Islam and the Duty of Jihād* (Lanham, MD: Rowman & Littlefield, 2006) 72.

[281] al-Zuhaylī, *Āthār al-Harb fī al-Islām* (n 66) 48.

to you, and you will not be wronged.'[282] Along the same lines, Khalaji observed that Khamenei's latest statements in 2009/2010 attempt to drop the possession and stockpiling part of his *fatwa* and focus on merely the prohibition of using nuclear weapons,[283] considering it an Islamic pragmatic shift for Iran to enter the game of power in international relations to change the power equation in the region.[284] As a matter of reciprocity, other Muslim scholars argue that Muslims may possess or use any WMD only if their enemies possess or use them.[285] Some of them even say that not possessing or using particular weapons used by the enemy is tantamount to committing suicide, which is prohibited under Islamic law: 'do not throw yourselves into destruction.'[286]

Hence, examining these rulings, it is evident that the bulk of the Muslim jurists, when it comes to the permissibility of using means and methods of warfare, favour the principle of military necessity and/or reciprocity to override the humanitarian restrictions embodied in the text, be it *Quran* or *Sunnah*. The fact that the primary sources of Islamic law are sometimes ambiguous or even silent on some contemporary issues opens the door to various scholarly interpretations as well as misinterpretations. This issue, however, will be discussed thoroughly in Chapter 5.

4. Conclusion

This chapter tackled the *jus in bello* from international law and Islamic law perspectives, whether in international or non-international armed conflicts. Its main purpose is to shed the light on the commonalities and differences between these two existing legal paradigms as they are, mainly, the norms regulating the conducts of hostilities by and against the Islamic Jihadist movements in our contemporary world. It started with how these two bodies of law define the *jus in bello*. To this end, it was concluded that they both define it in the same way with the aim of protecting those who do not or no longer directly

[282] *Quran* (8:60).
[283] Eisenstadt and Khalaj, 'Nuclear Fatwa' (n 277) 14.
[284] Ibid.
[285] Muhammad Abū Zahrah, *Al-'Alāqāt al-Dawliyyah fī al-Islām* (Cairo: Al-Dār al- Qawmiyyah lil-Tbā'ah wa al-Nashr, 1964/1384) 102; Ahmad Ghunaym, *Al-Jihād al-Islāmī: Dirāsah 'Ilmiyyah fī Nusūs al-Qur'ān wa Sihāh al-Hadīth wa Wathā'iq al-Tārīkh* (Cairo: Dār al-Hammamī, 1975/1394) 80; al-Khayyāṭ, 'Abd al-'Azīz. 'Al-Islām Dīn al-Salām: Mafhūm al-Harb wa al-Salām fī al-Islām', *Islam and the 21st Century*, Researches and Facts, the Tenth General Conference of the Supreme Council for Islamic Affairs (Cairo: Supreme Council for Islamic Affairs, 1999/1420) 334; al-Qaraḍāwī, *Fiqh al-Jihād* (n 175) Vol. 1, 591, 602ff., 726.
[286] *Quran* (2:1195); Al-Dawoody, *The Islamic Law of War* (n 41) 126.

participate in hostilities and by restricting the rights of parties to the conflict to use particular means and methods of warfare. It further, pointed out the fact that the two bodies of law apply only in armed conflicts while distinguishing between the respective rules that are applicable to international and non-international armed conflicts.

This chapter, however, made it evident that the two bodies of law vary a great deal in terms of the conflicts' classification methodologies and the underlying motivations of such process. On one hand, international law draws on sovereignty and territorial based interests (statehood) to justify its classification of conflicts, while, on the other hand, Islamic law conflict classification is determined by community-based interests (Muslim-hood). Accordingly, each of them adopted quite different criteria to determine the typology of the armed conflicts. Nonetheless, one must say that the substantial rules related to the protection of the victims of armed conflict are quite similar, including the protection of civilians, civilian objects, wounded, sick, medical personnel, the prohibition of mutilation, and the treatment of POWs and detainees, with a flagrant exception of the rules related to the termination of captivity, to which Muslim jurists have a wide range of diversified opinions.

It was further highlighted throughout this chapter that the principles of distinction, proportionality, and precaution—as the core *jus in bello* principles—are equally treasured under Islamic law and international law. However, with regard to the means and methods of warfare, one can only notice the massive gap between the regulatory rules embodied under the two bodies of law. Clearly, international law provides a relatively comprehensive legal framework to regulate the warring parties' rights to use particular means and methods of warfare during armed conflicts, while the Islamic *jus in bello* paid little attention to this subject. This is mostly due to the basic types of weapons used in the early stages of Islamic wars, yet the legality of using some context-related means and methods of warfare has still been debated among Muslim jurists, such as the legality of using suicide attacks, human shields, WMD, among others.

4

Contemporary Islamic Jihadism from a Counterterrorism Perspective

1. The UN General Assembly and the Dilemma of the Definition of Terrorism

Despite the fact that the ambiguous word 'terrorists' has commonly been used to name and shame different groups of people throughout history, since the late twentieth century it has predominantly—and nearly exclusively—been used to label and often to dehumanize any Islamic Jihadist group. Almost all non-state Islamic armed groups operating in different battlefields today are listed under the UN Security Council (UNSC) sanctions lists as terrorist groups.[1] To mention the most recent example, the Islamic State of Iraq and the Levant (ISIL) and *Al-Qaeda* sanction list contains the names of 257 individuals and eighty-two entities subjected to targeted sanctions, including assets freezes, travel bans, and arms embargoes.[2] Along the same lines, pursuant to other UNSC Resolutions,[3] more than 140 governments, many of which are those of Islamic countries, have passed counterterrorism legislation to criminalize what is often referred to as 'terrorist acts' committed by those groups.[4]

The United States, after the 9/11 attacks in 2001 in New York and Washington, managed to turn this catastrophic event into a unique opportunity to mobilize the international community, including the UN, to wage a coordinated campaign against Islamic Jihadism under the slogan of the 'global war on terror'. In

[1] Consolidated United Nations Security Council Sanctions List, generated on 19 May 2018. Available at: <https://scsanctions.un.org/fop/fop?xml=htdocs/resources/xml/en/consolidated.xml&xslt=htdocs/resources/xsl/en/consolidated.xsl> (last accessed 25 May 2019).

[2] ISIL (Da'esh) & Al-Qaida Sanctions List (pursuant to Security Council res. 1267/1989/2253), Generated on 19 May 2018. Available at: <https://scsanctions.un.org/fop/fop?xml=htdocs/resources/xml/en/consolidated.xml&xslt=htdocs/resources/xsl/en/al-qaida.xsl> (last accessed 25 May 2019).

[3] 'Ensure that any person who participates in the financing, planning, preparation or perpetration of terrorist acts or in supporting terrorist acts is brought to justice and ensure that, in addition to any other measures against them, such terrorist acts are established as serious criminal offences in domestic laws and regulations and that the punishment duly reflects the seriousness of such terrorist acts'. United Nations Security Council, Res. 1373, 28 September 2001.

[4] 'In the Name of Security: Counterterrorism Laws Worldwide Since September 11', Human Rights Watch Report, June 2012. Available at: <https://www.hrw.org/report/2012/06/29/name-security/counterterrorism-laws-worldwide-september-11 (last accessed 25 May 2019).

Islamic Jihadism and the Laws of War. Omar Mekky, Oxford University Press. © Omar Mekky 2023.
DOI: 10.1093/oso/9780198888369.003.0005

this context, the United States led NATO member states and a few other countries into two protracted wars in the Islamic world', one in Afghanistan 2001 against the Taliban government and *Al-Qaeda*, and the second in Iraq 2003 to dispose Saddam Hussein and his government. Since then, the wars have not stopped in this part of the world. In the same vein, today we are witnessing a number of military interventions against ISIL in Iraq, Syria, and Libya, not to mention the war waged by the Saudi-led Arab coalition against the *Houthi* rebels in Yemen.

In this ongoing 'global war on terror', the UNSC played and continues to play a leading role. It issued dozens of legally binding resolutions requiring states to implement measures against 'terrorists' and 'terrorist acts', many of which are targeted specifically at non-state Islamic armed groups. Prior to 9/11 and the subsequent UNSC Resolutions, the lack of definition of the term 'terrorism' was legally inconsequential as the word did not trigger any international rights or obligations. Currently, the term 'terrorism' and its derivatives have legal consequences that cannot be ignored. Defining terrorism is indispensable in order to confine the term and limit the chances of its abuse.[5] Otherwise, we risk blurring the lines between acts that deserve triggering counterterrorism measures and those that should be regulated by other branches of international law. As Ben Saul rightly put it: 'the absence of definition enables States to unilaterally and subjectively determine what constitutes terrorist activity, and to take advantage of the public panic and anxiety engendered by the designation of conduct as terroristic to pursue arbitrary and excessive counterterrorism responses'.[6] It is simply the risk of states not to know what is 'terrorism', who is a 'terrorist', and why.

This chapter focuses on exploring the legal implications of fighting contemporary Islamic Jihadism under the evolving counterterrorism frameworks and is divided into the following sections: Section 1: the UN General Assembly and the Dilemma of the Definition of Terrorism; Section 2: the Emerging Role of the Security Council in Combating Terrorism; Section 3: the Organization of Islamic Cooperation Approach and International Terrorism; Section 4: Fighting Contemporary Islamic Jihadism and *Jus ad Bellum* Limitations; and Section 5: Fighting Contemporary Islamic Jihadism and *Jus in Bello* Limitations.

The despair of reaching a consensus over the definition of the crime of terrorism made a leading international lawyer once say: 'Terrorism is a term without any legal significance. It is merely a convenient way of alluding to activities, whether of states or individuals, widely disapproved of and in which

[5] Ben Saul, *Defining Terrorism in International Law* (Oxford: Oxford University Press, 2006) 5.
[6] Ibid.

either the methods used are unlawful, or the targets protected, or both.'[7] The word 'terrorism' means different things to different people, and even those meanings change over time.[8] While there is agreement on its core meaning, its edges leave a considerable margin for genuine debate about whether particular acts really fit within the meaning of the word.[9] 'Terrorism' literally means extreme fear and fright.[10] This literal meaning, however, is not instructive in refining a legal concept of terrorism since every form of violence is potentially terror-inspiring to its victim.[11] The term 'terrorism' is quite dangerous and politically loaded since it can easily be used to stigmatize, delegitimize, and dehumanize those at whom it is directed, including legitimate political opponents.[12] Yet its existence is indispensable as it tackles a real and pressing phenomenon that undermines fundamental human rights, disturbs states' public order, and possibly threatens international peace and security. Hence, objecting to the misusage of the term 'terrorism' is insufficient and doing so will neither resolve the problem nor overcome the word's inherent ambiguity. The word 'terrorism' will continue to be used antagonistically in public spheres as long as it remains undefined.[13] The phenomenon should be addressed by careful legislation because a clear definition can shape states' understanding of the problem, limit their responses to it, and help to distinguish lawful from unlawful responses.

However, since most of the violent physical manifestations of terrorism are already defined and criminalized by existing domestic legislation, why is it important to classify particular acts as terrorist offences rather than as ordinary national crimes, such as murder and assault?[14] In this regard, it must be elaborated that beyond the violent physical manifestations of terrorism lie its unique and distinguishing characteristics, such as the specific intent to terrorize, intimidate, or coerce, and, if required, the existence of a political motive.[15] These additional elements are not sufficiently reflected in either domestic or international criminal law. Thus, defining terrorism as a discrete crime is of great

[7] Rosalyn. Higgins, 'The General International Law of Terrorism' in Rosalyn Higgins and Maurice Flory (eds), *International Law and Terrorism* (1997) 13–29, 13.

[8] Adam Roberts, 'Countering Terrorism: A Historical Perspective' in Andrea Bianchi and Alexis Keller (eds), *Counterterrorism: Democracy's Challenge* (Oregon, OR: Hart Publishing 2008) 3–43, 5.

[9] Ibid.

[10] *English Oxford Living Dictionaries*. Available at: <https://en.oxforddictionaries.com/definition/terror> (last accessed 25 May 2019).

[11] M. Cherif Bassiouni, 'A Policy-Oriented Inquiry into the Different Forms and Manifestations of "International Terrorism"' in M. Cherif Bassiouni (ed.), *Legal Responses to International Terrorism* (Dordrecht: Martinus Nijhoff, 1988) i–liii, xv.

[12] Saul, *Defining Terrorism in International Law* (n 5) 3.

[13] Ibid., 22.

[14] John Murphy, 'United Nations Proposals on the Control and Repression of Terrorism' in M. Cherif Bassiouni (ed.), *International Terrorism and Political Crimes* (Springfield, IL: Charles C Thomas, 1975) 493–506, 493, 503.

[15] Saul, *Defining Terrorism in International Law* (n 5) 25.

significance not only to regulate a disastrous phenomenon that has the potential to threaten international peace and security but also to express symbolically the community's condemnation of the offence and the offenders.

The first time the term 'terrorism' was used as a legal concept in international juristic circles was in 1931 at the Third Conference for the Unification of Penal Law at Brussels,[16] and then once again at the Sixth Conference in Copenhagen in 1935,[17] where it was defined rather vaguely and loosely.[18] The first concrete step for the international community to work collectively on the prohibition of terrorist acts took place at the League of Nations by drafting the Convention for the Prevention and Punishment of Terrorism.[19] The draft convention tackled only transnational terrorism perpetrated by non-state actors while avoiding the controversy of the acts of terrorism committed by states by excluding it from the definition.[20] It defined 'acts of terrorism' as 'criminal acts directed against a State and intended or calculated to create a state of terror in the minds of particular persons, or a group of persons or the general public'.[21] Although this convention never entered into force because of its broad definition,[22] it served as a point of reference for later discussions.[23]

[16] Venkateshwara Subramaniam Mani, 'International Terrorism-Is a Definition Possible?', *Indian Journal of Internal Law* (1978) 18, 206, 207; Bogdan Zlataric, 'History of International Terrorism and its Legal Control' in Bassiouni (ed.), *International Terrorism and Political Crimes* (n 14) 474–484, 474.

[17] Zlataric, 'History of International Terrorism and its Legal Control' (n 16) 481–2.

[18] The proposed definition of an act of terrorism at the Third Conference for the Unifications of Penal Law at Brussels (1931): '[T]he intentional use of means capable of producing a common danger that represents an act of terrorism on the part of anyone making use of crimes against life, liberty or physical integrity of persons or directed against private or state property with the purpose of expressing or executing political or social ideas.' Additionally, Article 1 of the text adapted in the Sixth Conference in Copenhagen (1935) defined terrorism as follows: 'International acts directed against the life, physical integrity, health or freedom of a head of state or his spouse, or any person holding the prerogatives of a head of state, as well as crown princes, members of governments, people enjoying diplomatic immunity, and members of the constitutional, legislative or judicial bodies [if the perpetrator creates] a common danger, or a state of terror that might incite a change or raise an obstacle to the functioning of public bodies or a disturbance to international relations.' Zlataric, 'History of International Terrorism and its Legal Control' (n 16) 481–2.

[19] Draft Convention for the Prevention and Punishment of Certain Acts of International Terrorism to the General Assembly, UN Doc. A/C.6/L.850, 1972.

[20] Articles 1(2) and 2, Draft Convention for the Prevention and Punishment of Certain Acts of International Terrorism.

[21] Ibid., Article 1(1).

[22] Only twenty-four countries signed the draft convention, namely Albania, Argentina, Belgium, Great Britain, Bulgaria, Cuba, Dominican Republic, Egypt, Ecuador, Spain, Estonia, France, Greece, Haiti, Monaco, India, Norway, The Netherlands, Peru, Romania, Czechoslovakia, Turkey, USSR, Venezuela, and Yugoslavia. Only the state of India ratified it. The broad definition of terrorism contributed to the low number of signatures and ratifications. See Reuven Young, 'Defining Terrorism: The Evolution of Terrorism as a Legal Concept in International Law and Its Influence on Definitions in Domestic Legislation', *Boston College International and Comparative Law Review* (2006) 29(23) 23–105, 37.

[23] UN Counter-Terrorism Committee Executive Directorate, 'The United Nations in the Fight Against Terrorism: Five Years After 9/11'. Available at: <https://www.un.org/sc/ctc/wp-content/uploads/2017/01/2006_01_26_cted_lecture.pdf> (last accessed 25 May 2019).

The attack on Israel's Lod Airport in May 1972 and the kidnapping and killing of eleven Israeli athletes at the Munich Olympic Games in September 1972 alerted the UN General Assembly (UNGA) to address the issue of terrorism once again.[24] However, the polarization of the political positions resulting from the division of the world at the time into the West, the Soviet Bloc, and the Non-Aligned States made reaching a consensus over a definition of terrorism extremely difficult.[25] States directly interested and involved in national liberation wars and self-determination struggles sought to exclude acts committed in such context from any definition of terrorism,[26] in line with the logic of the oft-cited statement 'one person's terrorist is another person's freedom fighter'. In 1972, the first UNGA Resolution on international terrorism was adopted,[27] and the title of the resolution itself reflected the level of polarization and division of the world at the time. The resolution is entitled:

> Measures to prevent international terrorism which endangers or takes innocent human lives or jeopardizes fundamental freedoms, and study of the underlying causes of those forms of terrorism and acts of violence which lie in misery, frustration, grievance and despair and which cause some people to sacrifice human lives, including their own, in an attempt to effect radical changes.[28]

Paragraph 4 of the Resolution went even further to condemn 'the continuation of repressive and terrorist acts by colonial, racist and alien regimes in denying peoples their legitimate right to self-determination and independence and other human rights and fundamental freedoms'.[29]

The UNGA's failure to define 'terrorism' did not halt its continuing attempts to address serious aspects of the threat posed by terrorism. The international community, primarily through the UNGA, moved toward a pragmatic piecemeal approach, often referred to as a 'sectoral approach'. The strategy was to deal with specific criminal conduct that is largely perceived by states to be terrorist in nature rather than addressing the more general notion of 'terrorism' in order to

[24] John Norton Moore, 'Towards Legal Restraints on International Terrorism', *American Society of International Law Proceedings* (1973) 67(88), 87–94.
[25] Young, 'Defining Terrorism' (n 22) 37.
[26] Ibid.
[27] United Nations, General Assembly, Resolution 3034 (XXVII), 18 December 1972.
[28] Ibid.
[29] Ibid.

fill the normative gaps in the regulation of certain activities while avoiding confronting the contentious question of a general definition.[30] Accordingly, from 1963 to 2005, twelve international treaties and five protocols were concluded to address specific types of violent acts proposed by number of states as being terrorist in nature. These are: the Convention on Offences and Certain Other Acts Committed On Board Aircraft;[31] the Convention for the Suppression of Unlawful Seizure of Aircraft;[32] the Convention for the Suppression of Unlawful Acts against the Safety of Civil Aviation;[33] the Convention on the Prevention and Punishment of Crimes Against Internationally Protected Persons;[34] the International Convention against the Taking of Hostages;[35] the Convention on the Physical Protection of Nuclear Material;[36] Amendments to the Convention on the Physical Protection of Nuclear Material;[37] the Protocol for

[30] M. Cherif Bassiouni, 'A Policy-Oriented Inquiry into the Different Forms and Manifestations of "International Terrorism"' in Bassiouni (ed.), *Legal Responses to International Terrorism* (n 6) xxii, xxx.

[31] 'Applies to acts affecting in flight safety; authorizes the aircraft commander to impose reasonable measures, including restraint, on any person he or she has reason to believe has committed or is about to commit such an act, where necessary to protect the safety of the aircraft; and requires contracting States to take custody of offenders and to return control of the aircraft to the lawful commander.' Convention on Offences and Certain Other Acts Committed On Board Aircraft (Aircraft Convention), 1963.

[32] 'Requires State Parties to make it an offence for any person on board an aircraft in flight to "unlawfully, by force or threat thereof, or any other form of intimidation, [to] seize or exercise control of that aircraft" or to attempt to do so.' Convention for the Suppression of Unlawful Seizure of Aircraft (Unlawful Seizure Convention), 1971.

[33] 'Requires State Parties to make it an offence for any person unlawfully and intentionally to perform an act of violence against a person on board an aircraft in flight, if that act is likely to endanger the safety of the aircraft; to place an explosive device on an aircraft; to attempt such acts; or to be an accomplice of a person who performs or attempts to perform such acts.' Convention for the Suppression of Unlawful Acts against the Safety of Civil Aviation (Civil Aviation Convention), 1971.

[34] 'Defines an "internationally protected person" as a Head of State, Minister for Foreign Affairs, representative or official of a State or international organization who is entitled to special protection in a foreign State, and their family; and requires parties to criminalize and make punishable "by appropriate penalties which take into account their grave nature" the intentional murder, kidnapping or other attack upon the person or liberty of an internationally protected person, a violent attack upon the official premises, the private accommodations, or the means of transport of such person; a threat or attempt to commit such an attack; and an act "constituting participation as an accomplice".' Convention on the Prevention and Punishment of Crimes Against Internationally Protected Persons (Diplomatic agents Convention) (1974).

[35] 'Provides that "any person who seizes or detains and threatens to kill, to injure, or to continue to detain another person in order to compel a third party, namely, a State, an international intergovernmental organization, a natural or juridical person, or a group of persons, to do or abstain from doing any act as an explicit or implicit condition for the release of the hostage commits the offence of taking of hostage within the meaning of this Convention".' International Convention against the Taking of Hostages, GA Res. 34/146 (XXXIV) (1979); (Hostages Convention).

[36] 'Criminalizes the unlawful possession, use, transfer or theft of nuclear material and threats to use nuclear material to cause death, serious injury or substantial property damage.' Convention on the Physical Protection of Nuclear Material (1979) (Nuclear Materials Convention) (deposited with the International Atomic Energy Agency)

[37] 'Makes it legally binding for States Parties to protect nuclear facilities and material in peaceful domestic use, storage as well as transport; and provides for expanded cooperation between and among States regarding rapid measures to locate and recover stolen or smuggled nuclear material, mitigate any radiological consequences or sabotage, adds new offences against nuclear facilities, and includes

the Suppression of Unlawful Acts of Violence at Airports Serving International Civil Aviation;[38] the Convention for the Suppression of Unlawful Acts against the Safety of Maritime Navigation;[39] the Protocol to the Convention for the Suppression of Unlawful Acts against the Safety of Maritime Navigation;[40] the Protocol for the Suppression of Unlawful Acts Against the Safety of Fixed Platforms Located on the Continental Shelf;[41] the Protocol to the Protocol for the Suppression of Unlawful Acts against the Safety of Fixed Platforms Located on the Continental Shelf;[42] the Convention on the Marking of Plastic Explosives for the Purpose of Detection;[43] the International Convention for the Suppression of Terrorist Bombings;[44] the International Convention for the

prevention and combat-related offences.' Amendments to the Convention on the Physical Protection of Nuclear Material (2005).

[38] 'Extends the provisions of the Montreal Convention (see above) to encompass criminal acts at airports serving international civil aviation.' Protocol for the Suppression of Unlawful Acts of Violence at Airports Serving International Civil Aviation, supplementary to the Convention for the Suppression of Unlawful Acts against the Safety of Civil Aviation (Airport Protocol) (deposited with the International Civil Aviation Organization).

[39] 'Establishes a legal regime applicable to acts against international maritime navigation that is similar to the regimes established for international aviation; and makes it an offence for a person unlawfully and intentionally to seize or exercise control over a ship by force, threat, or intimidation, to perform an act of violence against a person on board a ship if that act is likely to endanger the safe navigation of the ship, to place a destructive device or substance aboard a ship, and other acts against the safety of ships.' See Convention for the Suppression of Unlawful Acts against the Safety of Maritime Navigation (Maritime Convention) (deposited with the International Maritime Organization).

[40] 'Criminalizes the use of a ship as a device to further an act of terrorism; criminalizes the transport on board a ship of various materials knowing that they are intended to be used to cause, or in a threat to cause, death or serious injury or damage to further an act of terrorism; criminalizes the transporting on board a ship of persons who have committed an act of terrorism; and introduces procedures for governing the boarding of a ship believed to have committed an offence under the Convention.' See Protocol to the Convention for the Suppression of Unlawful Acts against the Safety of Maritime Navigation (1988) (deposited with the International Maritime Organization).

[41] 'Establishes a legal regime applicable to acts against fixed platforms on the continental shelf that is similar to the regimes established for the protection of international aviation.' See Protocol for the Suppression of Unlawful Acts Against the Safety of Fixed Platforms Located on the Continental Shelf, 1678 UNTS 304; 27 ILM 685 (1988) (Fixed Platform Protocol) (deposited with the International Maritime Organization).

[42] 'Adapts the changes to the Convention for the Suppression of Unlawful Acts against the Safety of Maritime Navigation to the context of fixed platforms located on the continental shelf.' See Protocol to the Protocol for the Suppression of Unlawful Acts against the Safety of Fixed Platforms Located on the Continental Shelf (2005) (deposited with the International Maritime Organization).

[43] 'Designed to control and limit the use of unmarked and undetectable plastic explosives (negotiated in the aftermath of the 1988 Pan Am flight 103 bombing); parties are obligated in their respective territories to ensure effective control over unmarked plastic explosives.' See Convention on the Marking of Plastic Explosives for the Purpose of Detection (1991) (Plastic Explosives Convention) (deposited with the International Civil Aviation Organization).

[44] 'Creates a regime of universal jurisdiction over the unlawful and intentional use of explosives and other lethal devices in, into, or against various defined public places with intent to kill or cause serious bodily injury, or with intent to cause extensive destruction of the public place.' See International Convention for the Suppression of Terrorist Bombings (Terrorist Bombing Convention) (deposited with the Secretary-General of the United Nations).

Suppression of the Financing of Terrorism;[45] and the International Convention for the Suppression of Acts of Nuclear Terrorism.[46]

While the adoption of these sectoral conventions and protocols criminalized most of the physical conduct widely considered as terrorist in nature and made it punishable, it did not do much to solve the dilemma of arriving at a general definition. As these treaties were being developed to criminalize terrorist-related acts, a landmark Resolution was issued by the UNGA in 1994 constituting a declaration on measures to eliminate terrorism.[47] The declaration condemned 'all acts, methods and practices of terrorism, as criminal and unjustifiable, wherever and by whomever committed'.[48] In using the formula 'by whomever committed', the UNGA Resolution attempted to establish that any person committing certain criminal acts—with particular intentions—must be 'considered everyone's terrorists even if he or she is someone's freedom fighter or someone else's law-enforcement agent'.[49] It further states that '[c]riminal acts intended or calculated to provoke a state of terror in the general public, a group of persons or particular persons for political purposes are in any circumstance unjustifiable, whatever the considerations of a political, philosophical, ideological, racial, ethnic, religious or any other nature that may be invoked to justify them'.[50] In this paragraph, the declaration required *mens rea* with respect to the criminal act's consequences, precisely the intention 'to

[45] 'Requires parties to take steps to prevent and counteract the financing of terrorists, whether direct or indirect; commits States to hold legal persons which finance terrorism civilly or administratively liable and individuals criminally liable for such acts; extends criminal liability also to individuals, civil and administrative liability to legal persons; and provides for the identification, freezing and seizure of funds allocated for terrorist activities, as well as for the sharing of the forfeited funds with other States on a case-by-case basis. Bank secrecy is no longer adequate justification for refusing to cooperate.' International Convention for the Suppression of the Financing of Terrorism (Terrorist Financing Convention) (deposited with the Secretary-General of the United Nations).

[46] 'Covers a broad range of acts and possible targets, including nuclear power plants and nuclear reactors; deals with both crisis situations (assisting States to solve the situation) and post-crisis situations (rendering nuclear material safe through the International Atomic Energy Agency (IAEA)).' See International Convention for the Suppression of Acts of Nuclear Terrorism (2005) (Nuclear Terrorism Convention) (deposited with the Secretary-General of the United Nations).

[47] GA Res. 49/60, UN Doc. A/RES/49/60 (9 December 1994). The declaration is an outcome of informal consultations related to the work of the Sixth Committee in the early 1990s that were undertaken in an effort to overcome some of the obstacles facing the committee on its work. See Virginia Morris and M. Christiane Bourloyannis-Vrailas, 'The Work of the Sixth Committee at the Fifty Ninth Session of the UN General Assembly', *American Journal of International Law* (1995) 89, 542–54.

[48] GA Res. 49/60, UN Doc. A/RES/49/60, 9 December 1994.

[49] Christian Walter, 'Defining Terrorism in National and International Law' in Christian Walter, Silja Vöneky, Volker Roeben, and Frank Schorkopf (eds), *Terrorism as a Challenge for National and International Law: Security versus Liberty?* (Berlin: Springer-Verlag, 2004) 23–45, 37.

[50] GA Res. 49/60, UN Doc. A/RES/49/60, 9 December 1994.

provoke a state of terror ... for political purposes'. It also excluded any possible justification—'just causes'—for terrorist activities. However, the declaration was not adequately clear about the 'criminal acts' to which it referred. Was it referring to ordinary national crimes or the sectoral offences stated in the previously mentioned treaties and protocols? Be that as it may, it is fairly evident that the declaration represents as close to a comprehensive definition of terrorism as the General Assembly has come during the many years of negotiations on a variety of international legal instruments.[51] Indeed, the content of the declaration was never expressly presented as a definition, yet it implicitly served that function, at least as a working premise.[52] In any case, UNGA Resolutions are not legally binding, unlike those issued by the Security Council.

2. The Emerging Role of the Security Council in Combating Terrorism

The Security Council is a political organ that triggers legal consequence by virtue of its authority to adopt resolutions that bind UN member states.[53] Under Chapter VII of the UN Charter, the Security Council can take enforcement measures to maintain or restore international peace and security. Article 25 of the Charter states that '[t]he Members of the United Nations agree to accept and carry out the decisions of the Security Council in accordance with the present Charter'.[54] Along the same lines, Article 48 states that '[t]he action required to carry out the decisions of the Security Council for the maintenance of international peace and security shall be taken by all the Members of the United Nations or by some of them, as the Security Council may determine'.[55]

Prior to 9/11, the issue of terrorism was predominantly entrusted to the UNGA rather than the Security Council. Nonetheless, it does not take much effort to observe how this has changed over time. In the 1970s, despite various terrorist-like attacks, such as hostage taking and aircraft hijacking, the SC

[51] Jane Boulden, 'The United Nations General Assembly and Terrorism' in Ben Saul (ed.), *Research Handbook on International Law and Terrorism* (Cheltenham/Northampton: Edward Elgar Publishing, 2014) 555–72, 568.

[52] Saul, *Defining Terrorism in International Law* (n 5) 209.

[53] Marc Perrin de Brichambaut, 'The Role of the United Nations Security Council in the International Legal System' in Michael Byers (ed.), *The Role of International Law in International Politics* (2001) 269–76, 269.

[54] Article 25, Charter of the United Nations.

[55] Article 48, Charter of the United Nations.

treated such acts within the different existing international legal frameworks on the use of force, diplomatic and consular immunities, state responsibility, and international civil aviation, without any explicit reference to the term 'terrorism' in order to avoid the political and ideological disputes surrounding it.[56] In 1985, however, the UNSC used the term 'terrorism' for the first time in a resolution in response to the increasing phenomenon of hostage taking and flight hijacking, including the hijackings of a Kuwaiti aircraft in December 1984; a Jordanian aircraft, a Middle East Airlines flight, and a TWA flight in June 1985; an Egyptair flight in November 1985; the seizure of the Achille Lauro in October 1985; and the seizure of twenty-five Finnish UN soldiers by the South Lebanon Army in June 1985.[57] Resolution 579 condemned 'all acts of hostage-taking and abduction' and labelled them precisely as 'manifestations of international terrorism'.[58] It is evident, however, that 'terrorism' as stated in this Resolution does not require any political motives or intent to instil fear. Instead, it is objectively defined by the prohibited methods of hostage taking and abduction, even if the acts are committed for private ends. By the same token, in the context of detecting plastic explosives, Resolution 635 called upon 'all States to co-operate in devising and implementing measures to prevent all acts of terrorism, including those involving explosives',[59] yet it did not explicitly provide any definition to the 'acts of terrorism' mentioned in the Resolution.

Another, rather controversial Resolution issued by the SC in the aftermath of the 1991 Gulf War is Resolution 687.[60] After Iraq's invasion of Kuwait, the Resolution required 'Iraq to inform the Council that it will not commit or support any act of international terrorism or allow any organization directed towards commission of such acts to operate within its territory and to condemn unequivocally and renounce all acts, methods and practices of terrorism'.[61] The Resolution did not specify which Iraqi acts constitute 'terrorism' and whether it really intended by using the words 'not commit' to admit state-sponsored

[56] UN Security Council, Resolution 262 (1968) (Israel attacked Beirut airport); UN Security Council, Resolution 286 (1970) (appealing for the release of hostages held in hijackings and calling on States to prevent hijackings); Security Council, Resolution 457 (1979); UN Security Council, Resolution 461 (1979) (calls on the government of Iran to release immediately the personnel of the Embassy of the United States of America being held in Teheran, to provide them protection and to allow them to leave the country).

[57] Ben Saul, 'Definition of Terrorism in the UN Security Council: 1985–2004', *Chinese Journal of International Law* (2005) 4(141), 141–66, 144.

[58] UN Security Council, Resolution 579 (1985), paras 1 and 5; UN Security Council, Press Statement, 9 October 1985.

[59] UN Security Council, Resolution 635 (1989), para. 2.

[60] UN Security Council, Resolution 687 (1991).

[61] Ibid., para. 32.

terrorism and to create individual criminal liability for state terrorism by Iraq. Along the same lines, in the context of the destruction of a civilian airline (Pan Am Flight 103) over Lockerbie in Scotland, the UNSC issued a number of terrorism-related resolutions.[62] The most relevant among these is Resolution 748 that requested Libya to 'cease all forms of terrorist action and all assistance to terrorist groups' and 'demonstrate its renunciation of terrorism'.[63] This was an implicit acceptance that states could commit terrorism, but again without providing a definition of 'terrorism' itself, other than the clear indication that violence against civil aviation is considered an act of terrorism. A few UNSC Resolutions have also been issued with regard to the war in the former Republic of Yugoslavia in the late 1990s, which tackled terrorism mainly as a non-state activity.[64] On the one hand, the Resolutions largely condemned 'all acts of terrorism by the Kosovo Liberation Army or any other group or individual', while on the other hand, the violence of the Serbian police against civilians was condemned only as 'the use of excessive force'.[65] Resolution 1244, however, provided that state forces may also commit terrorism, by condemning 'all terrorist acts by any party'.[66]

After the 1998 United States embassy bombings by *Al-Qaeda* in Nairobi and Dar-es-salam, UNSC Resolution 1189 condemned the acts of international terrorism and 'emphasized the need for the international community to deal effectively with all such criminal acts'.[67] Needless to say, labelling terrorism for the first time as a 'criminal act' has come with no reference either to the definition of the term or to the specific body of criminal law, be it national or international. Soon after, in the context of the war in Afghanistan, the UNSC issued a number of resolutions demanding 'the Afghan factions to refrain from harboring and training terrorists and their organizations'—especially in the Taliban-controlled areas,[68] and to 'cooperate with efforts to bring indicted terrorists to justice'.[69] Resolution 1267 insisted that:

> the Taliban, which also calls itself the Islamic Emirate of Afghanistan, comply promptly with its previous resolutions and in particular cease the provision

[62] UN Security Council, Resolution 731 (1992); UN Security Council, Resolution 748 (1992); UN Security Council, Resolution 883 (1993); UN Security Council, Resolution, 1192 (1998); UN Security Council, Resolution 1506 (2003).

[63] UN Security Council, Resolution 748 (1992), para. 2.

[64] UN Security Council, Resolution 1199 (1998), 1203 (1998), and 1160 (1998).

[65] UN Security Council, Resolution 1160 (1998), preamble.

[66] UN Security Council, Resolution 1244 (1999), preamble.

[67] UN Security Council, Resolution 1189 (1998).

[68] UN Security Council, Resolution 1193 (1998), para. 15.

[69] UN Security Council, Resolution 1214 (1998), para. 13.

of sanctuary and training for international terrorists and their organizations, take appropriate effective measures to ensure that the territory under its control is not used for terrorist installations and camps, or for the preparation or organization of terrorist acts against other States or their citizens.[70]

It further demanded the Taliban to turn over Usama Bin Laden to 'appropriate authorities' in a country where he has been indicted or would be surrendered or criminally prosecuted for his involvement in bombing the US embassies in Nairobi and Dar-es-salam and for conspiring to kill US nationals outside the United States.[71] The Taliban had one month to comply, after which aircraft and financial sanctions would be imposed, monitored by a committee which is often referred to as '*Al-Qaeda* Sanctions Committee' or 'the 1267 Committee', or, pursuant to the more recent SC Resolution 2253, the 'ISIL and *Al-Qaeda* Sanctions Committee'.[72] Following the Taliban's failure to comply, subsequent Resolutions imposed further aircraft, financial, military, and diplomatic sanctions as well as arms embargoes and travel bans.[73] After the removal of the Taliban government, the military and diplomatic sanctions were dropped as elaborated in Resolution 1989.[74] Hence, according to the current sanctions regime, states should impose a travel ban, arms embargo, and assets freeze on individuals and entities listed on the *Al-Qaeda* Sanctions List.[75] The list is drawn up by the *Al-Qaeda* Sanctions Committee, which is composed of all fifteen members of the UNSC and is responsible for monitoring the

[70] UN Security Council, Resolution 1267 (1999), para. 1.

[71] UN Security Council, Resolution 1267 (1999), para. 2.

[72] UN Security Council, Resolution 1267 (1999), paras 3, 4, and 6; UN Security Council, Resolution 2253 (2015), para 1.

[73] UN Security Council, Resolution 1333 (2000), paras 5, 6, 7, 8, 9, 10, and 11; UN Security Council, Resolution 1989 (2011).

[74] UN Security Council, Resolution 1989 (2011), para. 1.

[75] According to the most updated resolution (1989/2011) on *Al-Qaeda* Sanction Regime with regard to the measures that should be taken by states against the individuals and entities listed on the *Al-Qaeda* Sanctions List, they are as follow: '(a) Freeze without delay the funds and other financial assets or economic resources of these individuals, groups, undertakings and entities, including funds derived from property owned or controlled directly or indirectly, by them or by persons acting on their behalf or at their direction, and ensure that neither these nor any other funds, financial assets or economic resources are made available, directly or indirectly for such persons' benefit, by their nationals or by persons within their territory; (b) Prevent the entry into or transit through their territories of these individuals, provided that nothing in this paragraph shall oblige any State to deny entry or require the departure from its territories of its own nationals and this paragraph shall not apply where entry or transit is necessary for the fulfilment of a judicial process or the Committee determines on a case-by-case basis only that entry or transit is justified; (c) Prevent the direct or indirect supply, sale, or transfer to these individuals, groups, undertakings and entities from their territories or by their nationals outside their territories, or using their flag vessels or aircraft, of arms and related materiel of all types including weapons and ammunition, military vehicles and equipment, paramilitary equipment, and spare parts for the aforementioned, and technical advice, assistance or training related to military activities.' UN Security Council, Resolution 1989 (2011), para. 1.

implementation of the sanctions. Any state may request that the Committee add names to the list. Once the name of an individual or an entity is placed on the list, upon the initiative of one SC member and the approval of the rest, states are obliged to implement the sanctions embodied in the Resolutions against that individual or entity.[76]

The sanctions regime was still in place when the United States was attacked on 9/11 2001, but it was transformed from a traditional territorial regime into a global sanction regime.[77] Resolution 1390 widened the category of the addressees of the 1267 Resolution, from targeting a few political or military leaders (such as Usama Bin Laden and Taliban officials) in a particular context (such as Afghanistan) to targeting a worldwide terrorist organization. Under this Resolution, the sanctions are applicable to 'Usama Bin Laden, members of the *Al-Qaeda* organization and the Taliban and other individuals, groups, undertakings and entities associated with them'.[78] Furthermore, it is within the full power and authority of the Committee to decide who should be listed and on what basis.[79] This was further aggravated by the fact that listing decisions were often made on the basis of the vague notion of 'association with' coupled with the undefined notion of terrorism.[80] Additionally, the Resolution does not respond to a particular threat in a particular country but rather to 'acts of international terrorism' in general. Such wording helped the UNSC avoid limiting itself to any temporal or territorial restraints.[81] This gives the UNSC, represented by the Committee, the authority to sanction any individual or entity in any place and at any time, which many might interpret it as a quasi-judicial power.[82] Even this self-given quasi-judicial role lacked any avenues for individuals and entities to challenge mistaken listings. This unchallenged sanctions regime, however, has gradually improved in response to the growing criticism of its procedural shortcomings. Among many other UNSC Resolutions that have improved the Committee's listing and delisting processes, relatively speaking,[83] Resolution 1904 established an Office of the Ombudsperson to receive requests

[76] Lisa Ginsborg, 'The United Nations Security Council's Counter-Terrorism Al-Qaida Sanctions Regime: Resolution 1267 and the 1267 Committee' in Saul (ed.), *Research Handbook on International Law and Terrorism* (n 51) 608–26, 609.

[77] Ibid., 610.

[78] UN Security Council, Resolution 1390 (2002), para. 2.

[79] Ginsborg, 'The United Nations Security Council's Counter-Terrorism Al-Qaida Sanctions Regime' (n 76) 611.

[80] Ibid., 613.

[81] Jeremy Matam Farrall, *United Nations Sanctions and the Rule of Law* (Cambridge: Cambridge University Press, 2007) 201.

[82] Erika de Wet, *The Chapter VII Powers of the United Nations Security Council* (Oxford: Hart Publishing, 2004) 352–4.

[83] UN Security Council, Resolution 1735 (2206); UN Security Council, Resolution 1822 (2008); and UN Security Council, Resolution 1988 (2011).

from individuals and entities seeking to be removed from the Consolidated List.[84]

On 12 September 2001, the morning after the terrorist attacks on the United States, the UNSC issued Resolution 1368, which condemned in the strongest terms the 'horrifying terrorist attacks' qualifying 'such acts, like any act of international terrorism, as a threat to international peace and security',[85] a qualification that has since been reiterated after the occurrence of every single 'terrorist' attack.[86] The post 9/11 UNSC practices evidently reflect the fact that international terrorism as such is regularly considered as a threat to international peace and security, which may trigger the powers of Chapter VII.[87] The Resolution further called states to work together 'to bring to justice the perpetrators, organizers and sponsors of these terrorist attacks' as well as those who aided, supported, or harboured them.[88] Two weeks later, the UNSC issued Resolution 1373 that lays down a series of general obligations that states must fulfil. This was the first UNSC Resolution, under Chapter VII, to call states to take or refrain from specific actions in a general scope without being connected to any specific situation. The obligations include, *inter alia*, the prevention and repression of the financing of terrorist acts;[89] enacting domestic legislation that criminalizes the raising of funds and financing of terrorist acts;[90] refraining from providing any form of support to entities or persons involved in terrorist acts, including suppressing recruitment of members of terrorist groups and eliminating the supply of weapons to terrorists;[91] denying safe haven to those who finance, plan, support, or commit terrorist acts;[92] ensuring that any person who participates in the financing, planning, preparation, or perpetration of terrorist acts or in supporting terrorist acts is brought to justice, and to ensure that, in addition to any other measures against them, such terrorist acts are established as serious criminal offences in domestic laws and regulations and that the punishment duly reflects the seriousness of such terrorist acts;[93] assisting each other in connection with criminal investigations or

[84] UN Security Council, Resolution 1904 (2009).
[85] UN Security Council, Resolution 1368 (2001), para. 1.
[86] Andrea Bianchi, 'International Law, Counterterrorism and the Quest for Checks and Balances: Why the Calling Sirens of Constitutionalism Should be Resisted' in Bianchi and Keller (eds), *Counterterrorism: Democracy's Challenge* (n 8) 395–424, 404.
[87] Ibid.; ICJ, *Israel Wall Advisory Opinion*, ICJ Case 131, 9 July 2004, para. 35 (sep. op. Kooijmans J).
[88] UN Security Council, Resolution 1368 (2001), para. 3.
[89] UN Security Council, Resolution 1373 (2001), para. 1(a).
[90] Ibid., para. 1(b).
[91] Ibid., para. 2(a).
[92] Ibid., para. 2 (c).
[93] Ibid., para. 2(e).

criminal proceedings;[94] and preventing the movement of terrorists or terrorist groups.[95] The Resolution also established the Counterterrorism Committee (CTC) to monitor the implementation of the obligations embodied in it.[96] The CTC responsibilities include: (i) evaluating the implementation reports presented by the member states; (ii) boosting the ratification of the international counterterrorism—sectoral—conventions; and (iii) providing technical assistance to states that are in need of it.[97] The challenges encountered by the CTC in discharging its mandate pushed the UNSC to issue Resolution 1535, by which a CTC Executive Directorate was established, with a view to improving the capacity of the CTC to continue monitoring the implementation of Resolution 1373 and to assist states in their capacity building efforts.[98]

It is worth mentioning that the obligations imposed by Resolution 1373 and monitored by the CTC are of the variety 'usually contained only in treaties developed through the normal treaty-making process.'[99] The Resolution clearly departed from the business-as-usual language of 'calls upon' and 'urges', and instead embodied mandatory instructions in a style characteristic of legislation, such as 'all states shall . . .'[100] Professor Bianchi commented on this matter by saying:

> If one takes the main elements of the definition of legislative acts given by E. Yemin, that is that they be 'unilateral in form, that they create or modify some element of a legal norm, and the legal norm in question is general in nature, that is directed to indeterminate addressees and capable of repeated application in time', it would be difficult indeed not to characterize Resolution 1373 as a piece of legislation.[101]

The question of whether the UNSC is entitled to act as law-maker by issuing states obligations of general character is highly debated among scholars.[102]

[94] Ibid., para. 2(f).
[95] Ibid., para. 2(g).
[96] Ibid., para. 6.
[97] Luis Miguel Hinojosa-Martinez, 'A Critical Assessment of United Nations Security Council Resolution 1373' in Saul (ed.), *Research Handbook on International Law and Terrorism* (n 51) 631.
[98] Bianchi, 'International Law, Counterterrorism and the Quest for Checks and Balances' (n 86) 404; UN Security Council, Resolutions 1536 (2004).
[99] Young, 'Defining Terrorism' (n 22) 43.
[100] Ibid.
[101] Bianchi, 'International Law, Counterterrorism and the Quest for Checks and Balances' (n 86) 405. The quotation stated in Edward Yemin, *Legislative Powers in the United Nations and Specialized Agencies* (Leiden: Sijyhof, 1969) 6.
[102] See the elaborative discussion of Professor Bianchi on the legitimacy of the Action of the SC as 'world law-maker' in 'Assessing the Effectiveness of the UN Security Council's Anti-Terrorism Measures: The Quest for Legitimacy and Cohesion', *European Journal of International Law* (2006) 17, 881–919, 885–892.

Nevertheless, one must admit that despite the UNSC's uneven representation and its lack of legal expertise and transparency, it is the only existing body that can react to situations that need a timely normative response.[103] International law in general, including treaty law and customary law, is not well equipped to produce legislation in short time span.[104]

Notwithstanding the fact that Resolution 1373 mentions the words 'terrorism' and 'terrorists' forty times, it did not define these terms. The CTC also expressed explicitly that it will not even attempt to define 'terrorism'.[105] Thus, states were left free to define 'terrorism' in their national legislation as they see appropriate, without any legal boundaries set by the international community. This omission permitted divergent implementation of Resolution 1373 at the national level. Analysis of the states' reports to the CTC reveals that national counterterrorism laws are widely divergent with some very broad or vague definitions in play.[106] Some states provide overly general definitions of 'terrorism' and 'terrorist groups'.[107] This could manifest itself in different ways, including expanding the notions of 'participation' or 'providing support to international terrorism', and so forth.[108] Some states went even further by deploying the international legitimacy conferred by the UNSC authorization to define terrorism in order to repress or de-legitimize political opponents and to conflate them with *Al-Qaeda*.[109] The fact of the matter is that the devolution of discretionary power for states to fight terrorism, without defining it, led them to fight 'different terrorisms'.[110] The uncertainty and ambiguity created by the absence of definition subjected the Resolution's obligations to opportunistic and bad-faith implementation.

Not until October of 2004, three years after Resolution 1373 imposed its mandatory obligations and following the reactionary counterterrorism legislations of many states, did the UNSC give a clear indication of how it considers

[103] Bianchi, 'International Law, Counterterrorism and the Quest for Checks and Balances' (n 86) 406.
[104] Andrea Bianchi, 'Enforcing International Law Norms Against Terrorism: Achievements and Prospects' in Andrea Bianchi (ed.), *Enforcing International Law Norms Against Terrorism* (Oxford: Hart Publishing, 2004) 491–534, 516–17.
[105] Chair of the Counter-Terrorism Committee (Ambassador Jeremy Greenstock), 'Combating International Terrorism: The Contribution of the United Nations', Presentation to Symposium, Vienna, 3–4 June 2002.
[106] Saul, 'Definition of Terrorism in the UN Security Council' (n 57) 160.
[107] Bianchi, 'Assessing the Effectiveness of the UN Security Council's Anti-terrorism Measures' (n 102) 899.
[108] Ibid.
[109] Saul, 'Definition of Terrorism in the UN Security Council' (n 57) 160.
[110] Walter Laqueur, *The New Terrorism: Fanaticism and the Arms of Mass Destruction* (Oxford: Oxford University Press, 2001), cited in Saul, 'Definition of Terrorism in the UN Security Council' (n 57) 161.

terrorism should be defined. Resolution 1566, after urging all states to fight international terrorism, recalls:

> that criminal acts, including against civilians, committed with the intent to cause death or serious bodily injury, or taking of hostages, with the purpose to provoke a state of terror in the general public or in a group of persons or particular persons, intimidate a population or compel a government or an international organization to do or to abstain from doing any act, which constitute offences within the scope of and as defined in the international conventions and protocols relating to terrorism, are under no circumstances justifiable by considerations of a political, philosophical, ideological, racial, ethnic, religious or other similar nature, and calls upon all States to prevent such acts and, if not prevented, to ensure that such acts are punished by penalties consistent with their grave nature.[111]

In this Resolution, evidently the UNSC came very close to adopting a definition of terrorism but ultimately fell back on a reference to acts that constitute offences within the scope of existing international conventions and protocols.[112] It is also worth mentioning that the Resolution did not tackle explicitly the issue of whether military targets (persons and objects) can be the subject of terrorist attacks or not. However, careful reading of the text shows that the Resolution implicitly refers to the issue by using the words 'criminal acts, including against civilians', which means that further targets fall within the provided definition.[113] In any case, this has been presented by the UNSC only as a working definition without any explicit call or request to states to ensure that their national counterterrorism legislation conforms with its requirements. Nevertheless, the Resolution was understood by states as establishing soft guide posts for the implementation of the earlier Resolution 1373.[114]

Another unique role of the UNSC came into play after the assassination of the former Lebanese Prime Minister Rafik Al-Hariri in February 2005. Following the failed attempts of the Lebanese Parliament to ratify an agreement between the UN and the Lebanese government, despite the request of the Lebanese Prime Minister,[115] the UNSC, acting under Chapter VII, adopted

[111] See SC Resolution 1566.

[112] Ian Johnstone, 'The UN Security Council, Counterterrorism and Human Rights' in Bianchi and Keller (eds), *Counterterrorism: Democracy's Challenge* (n 8) 346.

[113] Young, 'Defining Terrorism' (n 22) 46.

[114] Ben Saul, 'The Emerging International Law of Terrorism', Legal Studies Research Paper No. 10/108, Sydney Law School. Available at: <http://ssrn.com/abstract=1699568> (last accessed 25 May 2019).

[115] United Nations, Security Council Authorizes Establishment of Special Tribunal to Try Suspects in Assassination of Rafiq Hariri, UN Meetings Coverage and Press Releases. Available at: <https://www.

Resolution 1757 authorizing the creation of the Special Tribunal for Lebanon (STL).[116] The STL Statute provides jurisdiction to the tribunal over the *Hariri* attacks and more restrictively other 'connected cases'.[117] It lists 'acts of terrorism' among the offences over which the tribunal has jurisdiction, as recognized and sanctioned by the Lebanese Criminal Code.[118] In February 2011, the STL's Appeal Chamber issued a decision, pursuant to quasi-advisory powers, determining that a crime of 'international terrorism', at least in times of peace, was recognized under customary international law and was relevant to defining and interpreting the crime of 'terrorism' provided for in the Statute.[119] According to the decision, this customary rule requires the following three key elements:

> (i) the perpetration of a criminal act (such as murder, kidnapping, hostage-taking, arson, and so on), or threatening such an act; (ii) the intent to spread fear among the population (which would generally entail the creation of public danger) or directly or indirectly coerce a national or international authority to take some action, or to refrain from taking it; (iii) when the act involves a transnational element.[120]

However, this extraordinary decision was received with a mixture of scepticism and disapproval as most international law scholars believe that neither state practice nor *opinio juris* support the findings of the Tribunal.[121]

un.org/press/en/2007/sc9029.doc.htm> (last accessed 25 May 2019); United Nations Security Council, Resolution 1664 (2006).

[116] United Nations Security Council, Resolution 1757 (2007) para. 1(a).

[117] 'The Special Tribunal shall have jurisdiction over persons responsible for the attack of 14 February 2005 resulting in the death of former Lebanese Prime Minister Rafiq Hariri and in the death or injury of other persons. If the Tribunal finds that other attacks that occurred in Lebanon between 1 October 2004 and 12 December 2005, or any later date decided by the Parties and with the consent of the Security Council, are connected in accordance with the principles of criminal justice and are of a nature and gravity similar to the attack of 14 February 2005, it shall also have jurisdiction over persons responsible for such attacks. This connection includes but is not limited to a combination of the following elements: criminal intent (motive), the purpose behind the attacks, the nature of the victims targeted, the pattern of the attacks (modus operandi) and the perpetrators.' *Statute of the Special Tribunal for Lebanon*, Article 1.

[118] *Statute of the Special Tribunal for Lebanon*, Article 1.

[119] Guenael Mettraux, 'The United Nations Special Tribunal for Lebanon: Prosecuting Terrorism' in Saul (ed.), *Research Handbook on International Law and Terrorism* (n 51) 651–66, 652.

[120] Special Tribunal for Lebanon, *Interlocutory Decision on the Applicable Law: Terrorism, Conspiracy, Homicide, Perpetration, Cumulative Charging* (document reference: STL-11-01/I/AC/R176bis), 16 February 2011, 49–50.

[121] Stefan Kirsch and Anna Oehmichen, 'Judges Gone Astray: The Fabrication of Terrorism as an International Crime by the Special Tribunal for Lebanon', *Durham Law Review Online* (2011) 1, 1–20. Available at: <http://www.academia.edu/11365795/Judges_gones_astray_The_fabrication_of_terrorism_as_an_international_crime_by_the_Special_Tribunal_for_Lebanon (last accessed 25 May

In June 2014, ISIL's power reached its peak by declaring itself as the Islamic Caliphate and controlling more than 30 per cent of the territory of Syria and Iraq.[122] In response, the UNSC, under Chapter VII, unanimously adopted a leading Resolution (2170), expressing its 'gravest concern' that part of the Iraqi and Syrian territories are under ISIL and Al Nusra Front's (ANF) control and the negative impact of their violent extremist ideology and actions on the stability of Iraq, Syria, and the region.[123] The Resolution began by condemning 'in the strongest terms the terrorist acts of ISIL and its violent extremist ideology, and its continued gross, systematic and widespread abuses of human rights and violations of international humanitarian law'.[124] It further emphasized that 'ISIL, ANF and all other individuals, groups, undertakings and entities associated with *Al-Qaeda*' should be held accountable for the violations they committed, while urging all parties to prevent such violations and cooperate to bring the perpetrators to justice.[125] States were also requested to take national measures to suppress the flow of foreign terrorist fighters from travelling from their soil to join the previously mentioned groups, reiterating obligations under previous counterterrorism Resolutions to prevent the movement of terrorists, as well as their supply with arms or financial support.[126] Moreover, the Council highlighted its concerns about the groups' control over oilfields and related infrastructures which could possibly support them financially and strengthen their operational capability to carry out further terrorist attacks. Accordingly, the UNSC condemned any direct or indirect trade with such groups,[127] a point which was reiterated in a separate UNSC Resolution a year later.[128] Last but not least, the UNSC expressed its readiness to consider listing individuals, groups, undertakings, and entities providing support to ISIL or to

2019). Ben Saul, 'Legislating from a Radical Hague: The United Nations Special Tribunal for Lebanon Invents an International Crime of Transnational Terrorism', *Leiden Journal of International Law* (2011) 24(3) 677–700; Kai Ambos, 'Judicial Creativity at the Special Tribunal for Lebanon: Is There a Crime of Terrorism under International Law', *Leiden Journal of International Law* (2011) 24(3), 655–75; Mettraux, 'The United Nations Special Tribunal for Lebanon: Prosecuting Terrorism' (n 119). For supporters of the definition, see Manuel Ventura, 'Terrorism According to the STL's Interlocutory Decision on the Applicable Law: A Defining Moment or a Moment of Defining?', *Journal of International Criminal Justice* (2011) 9(5), 1021–42.

122 Matthew G. Olsen (Director, National Counterterrorism Center), 'Remarks for the Brookings Institution', 3 September 2014. Available at: <https://www.dni.gov/files/documents/2014-09-03%20Remarks%20for%20the%20Brookings%20Institution.pdf> (last accessed 25 May 2019).

123 United Nations Security Council, Resolution 2170 (2014), preamble.

124 Ibid., para. 1.

125 Ibid., paras 3 and 5.

126 Ibid., paras 8, 9, and 10.

127 Ibid., paras 13 and 14.

128 United Nations Security Council, Resolution 2199 (2015).

ANF to the *Al-Qaeda* Sanction List, bearing in mind that ISIL and ANF were already listed.[129]

Another phenomenon that has captured much of the UNSC's attention is the rapidly growing threat posed by the so-called Foreign Terrorist Fighters (FTFs). The UNSC Resolution defined FTFs as the 'individuals who travel to a State other than their States of residence or nationality for the purpose of the perpetration, planning, or preparation of, or participation in, terrorist acts or the providing or receiving of terrorist training, including in connection with armed conflict'.[130] According to the UNSC, terrorist groups such as ISIL, *Al-Qaeda*, and their associated groups, have attracted over 30,000 FTFs from over 100 states.[131] Thus, Resolution 2178 obliges all states to prevent FTFs recruitments, funding, and movements and ensure that any FTF who participates in the financing, planning, preparation, or perpetration of terrorist acts or in supporting terrorist acts is brought to justice.[132] It further requires states to deal with these violations as 'serious criminal offences' under domestic laws and regulations.[133] In 2017, the same obligations have been detailed in Resolution 2390.[134] Although the Resolution calls on governments to uphold human rights, it left them without any limitations on what 'terrorism' means. This again opens the door for the unequal application of the law in which any state may selectively criminalize fighting by its nationals alongside parties to a conflict whom that state opposes but not fighting by its nationals with parties it supports, even if both sides are engaged in unlawful conduct or listed as terrorist organizations.[135]

In March 2015, concerned about the deterioration of the political and humanitarian situation in Libya—especially since two armed groups pledged

[129] United Nations Security Council, Resolution 2170 (2014), paras 18 and 19.

[130] United Nations Security Council, Resolution 2178 (2014), preamble.

[131] 'Foreign Terrorist Fighters', Security Council Counter-Terrorism Committee. Available at: <https://www.un.org/sc/ctc/focus-areas/foreign-terrorist-fighters/> (last accessed 25 May 2019).

[132] United Nations Security Council, Resolution 2178 (2014), para 2, 3, 5, and 6.

[133] Ibid., para 6.

[134] United Nations Security Council, Resolution 2390 (2017)

[135] 'The UN Working Group on Mercenaries has expressed concern over the potential for governments to selectively apply the "FTF" label to foreign fighters', Office of the High Commissioner for Human Rights (OHCHR), Annual Report of the Working Group on the use of mercenaries as a means of violating human rights and impeding the exercise of the right of peoples to self-determination (A/70/330), paras 56 and 56; cited in Human Rights Watch, 'Foreign Terrorist Fighter' Laws Human Rights Rollbacks Under UN Security Council Resolution 2178, December 2016. (Just to mention one example, the fighters from the United States, United Kingdom, Canada, and Australia, among few other countries, have travelled to northern Syria to join the Kurdish People's Protection Units (YPG) forces fighting ISIL. The international coalition against ISIL, which includes these four countries, backs the YPG. Yet the YPG is affiliated with the Kurdistan Workers Party (PKK), a Kurdish militant group that these and other countries list as a terrorist organization. The question here is whether those fighters are considered as FTFs under Resolution 2178.

allegiance to ISIL in the two Libyan cities of Benghazi and Derna, namely Ansar Al-Charia in Benghazi and Derna—the UNSC adopted Resolution 2214 requesting states to combat these groups by all means and encouraged states to submit listing requests to the *Al-Qaeda* Sanction Committee of individuals and entities supporting those groups operating in Libya.[136] A few months later, the name of the Committee was changed by Resolution 2253 to the 'ISIL (Da'esh) and *Al-Qaeda* Sanctions Committee'.[137] Later in 2015, after a series of terrorist attacks took place on 26 June 2015 in Sousse, 10 October 2015 in Ankara, 31 October 2015 over Sinai, 12 November 2015 in Beirut, and 13 November 2015 in Paris, the UNSC adopted Resolution 2249 in which it expressed its determination 'to combat by all means this unprecedented threat to international peace and security'.[138]

In 2016, in response to the rapidly spread and heavily reported phenomenon of selling women and children by ISIL and other 'terrorist' groups,[139] the UNSC adopted Resolution 2331 to condemn all acts of trafficking in persons, particularly the sale or trade of women and children for the purpose of sexual slavery, sexual exploitation, and forced labour.[140] It further recognizes the importance of collecting and preserving evidence relating to such acts in order to ensure that those responsible can be held accountable, while expressing the Council's intention to consider targeted sanctions for individuals and entities involved in trafficking persons in areas affected by armed conflict, as well as persons involved in conflict-related sexual violence.[141] Likewise, the UNSC, noticing the destruction and trafficking of cultural heritage and the income generated by ISIL and other 'terrorist' groups resulted from the illegal excavation, looting, and smuggling of cultural property that is being used to support their recruitment efforts and to strengthen their operational capability to carry out terrorist attacks,[142] issued Resolution 2347 to condemn such violations and

[136] United Nations Security Council, Resolution 2214 (2015), paras 1, 3, and 4.

[137] United Nations Security Council, Resolution 2253 (2015), para. 1.

[138] United Nations Security Council, Resolution 2249 (2015); United Nations, 'Security Council "Unequivocally" Condemns ISIL Terrorist Attacks, Unanimously Adopting Text that Determines Extremist Group Poses "Unprecedented" Threat', Meetings Coverage and Press Releases. Available at: <https://www.un.org/press/en/2015/sc12132.doc.htm> (last accessed 25 May 2019).

[139] UN News, 'New UN report lays bare widespread ISIL "atrocities" committed against Yazidis in Iraq', 18 August 2016. Available at: <https://news.un.org/en/story/2016/08/536922-new-un-report-lays-bare-widespread-isil-atrocities-committed-against-yazidis> (last accessed 25 May 2019). United Nations Iraq, 'UN report details testimony of Yezidi survivors of ISIL atrocities in Iraq', 18 August 2016. Available at: <http://www.uniraq.org/index.php?option=com_k2&view=item&id=6002:un-report-details-testimony-of-yezidi-survivors-of-isil-atrocities-in-iraq&lang=en> (last accessed 25 May 2019).

[140] United Nations Security Council, Resolution 2331 (2016), para. 11.

[141] Ibid., paras 11 and 12.

[142] United Nations Security Council, Resolution 3247 (2017), preamble.

encourage states to suppress and prevent such acts.[143] It further invited states to submit listing requests for individuals and entities involved in such acts to the ISIL (Da'esh) and *Al-Qaeda* Sanctions Committee.[144]

Finally, the UNSC adopted the more generic 'wrap-up' Resolutions 2364 and 2368.[145] The first Resolution implements a document entitled 'Comprehensive International Framework to Counter Terrorist Narratives', drafted by the CTC, with recommended guidelines and good practices to counter effectively the ways that ISIL, *Al-Qaeda*, and associated groups and individuals use their narratives to encourage, motivate, and recruit others to commit terrorist acts.[146] While the document focuses on preventing the incitement of terrorist acts, it tackles three core elements to counter terrorist narratives: (i) the already existing legal and law enforcement measures in accordance with obligations under international law and relevant UN resolutions; (ii) public–private partnerships; and (iii) the development of counter-narratives.[147] The second Resolution comprises thirty three-pages and 105 paragraphs detailing the past decisions and all types of sanctions already imposed on ISIL, *Al-Qaeda*, and associated groups and individuals.[148] It also expresses its concerns to states, as well as the Committees, about the lack of implementation of Resolutions 1267, 1989, 2199, and 2253, including the insufficient reporting by states to the ISIL and *Al-Qaeda* Sanctions Committee.[149]

To conclude, a careful reader of the recent counterterrorism-related UNSC Resolutions will realize that the vast majority are determined to combat the threat and terror posed by ISIL, *Al-Qaeda*, and the other associated Islamic Jihadist groups. The Resolutions, generally, require states to prevent, suppress, and prosecute their terrorist acts and to impose sanctions on them. Regardless of the legitimacy question of the UNSC as the world law-maker, states seized this controversial yet powerful international legitimacy to enact national counterterrorism legislation to criminalize these group's terrorist activities. Unfortunately, as observed in the states' reports to the CTC, the national counterterrorism laws are widely divergent, with some very broad or vague definitions of 'terrorism' at play. The absence of a clear definition of terrorism

[143] Ibid., paras 1, 2, 3, 4, 8, and 9.

[144] Ibid., para. 10.

[145] United Nations Security Council, Resolution 2364 (2017); United Nations Security Council, Resolution 2368 (2017).

[146] United Nations Security Council, Resolution 2364 (2017), para. 1.

[147] Comprehensive International Framework to Counter Terrorist Narratives, Letter dated 26 April 2017 from the Chair of the Security Council Committee established pursuant to resolution 1373 (2001) concerning counter-terrorism addressed to the President of the Security Council, S/2017/375.

[148] United Nations Security Council, Resolution 2368 (2017).

[149] Ibid.

has permitted states to interpret the various UNSC Resolutions, especially Resolution 1373, in light of their internal political interests. In my opinion, associating most of the prohibited acts embodied in the Resolutions with an undefined phenomenon has done more harm than good. The preventive and repressive measures that were once taken to defend society from evil could have negative effects on the members of the society they were meant to protect.[150] Widening the scope of counterterrorism unjustly creates a breeding ground for terrorism. It offers more excuses to disenfranchised youths to resort to violence, whether as internal fighters or FTFs. This tragic spiral of frustration and resentment should be broken, not nurtured.[151] A definition of terrorism, even if imposed by the UNSC, could fix a legal standard against which we can test and constrain political and ideological abuses of the term. Admittedly, having effective counterterrorism measures is indispensable in the fight against terrorism, but it is equally important to know what terrorism is and what is not, when it starts, and when it stops.[152]

3. The Organization of Islamic Cooperation Approach and International Terrorism

The Organization of Islamic Cooperation (OIC) is the second-largest intergovernmental organization after the United Nations with a membership of fifty-seven states spread over four different continents.[153] The OIC, at least theoretically, is the 'collective voice of the Muslim world'.[154] Its unique characteristic is that its members share a common background of Islamic identity, values, and objectives, which is a membership requirement according to the OIC Charter.[155] The Organization was created right after the tragic 'criminal

[150] Bianchi, 'International Law, Counterterrorism and the Quest for Checks and Balances' (n 86) 414.

[151] Human Rights Watch, 'No to Terrorism, Yes to Human Rights: Letter to Tunisians', 28 April 2016. Available at: <https://www.hrw.org/news/2016/04/28/no-terrorism-yes-human-rights> (last accessed 25 May 2019).

[152] On the same day (14 May 2018) when I was writing these words sixty Palestinians protestors (including six children) were shot dead by the Israeli Defence Forces in Gaza. Israel's Prime Minister, Benjamin Netanyahu, joined the US government in blaming Hamas (designated by many Western countries as a terrorist group) for the deaths. Certainly, in this context, I am not in a place to judge the IDF's law enforcement's behaviours but I guess we are all able to raise questions related to the interpretation of the term 'terrorism' and how far it can reach. See 'Global protests grow after Israeli killing of Palestinian demonstrators', *The Guardian*, 15 May 2018. Available at: <https://www.theguardian.com/world/2018/may/15/palestinians-to-bury-58-people-killed-in-us-embassy-protests> (last accessed 25 May 2019).

[153] See the Organization of Islamic Cooperation website, History. Available at: <https://www.oic-oci.org/page/?p_id=52&p_ref=26&lan=en> (last accessed 25 May 2019).

[154] Ibid.

[155] *Organization of Islamic Cooperation Charter*, Article 3.

arson' of Al-Aqsa Mosque in Jerusalem in August 1969, two years after the military defeat of Arabs against Israel in the Six Days War.[156] In September 1969, the first Islamic Summit Conference was convened in Rabat in the Kingdom of Morocco.[157] Between March 1970 and March 1972 a series of conferences took place, at the level of the states' foreign ministers, leading to the formulation of a Charter for the organization and creation of the OIC itself.[158] The Preamble of the Charter provides that the member states will be 'guided by the noble Islamic values of unity and fraternity, and affirming the essentiality of promoting and consolidating the unity and solidarity among the Member States in securing their common interests at the international arena'.[159] It further adds that the member states are committed to the principles of the UN Charter, the OIC Charter, and international law.[160] Most importantly, the Preamble affirms that the member states will:

> support the struggle of the Palestinian people, who are presently under foreign occupation, and to empower them to attain their inalienable rights, including the right to self-determination and to establish their sovereign state with Al-Quds Al-Sharif as its capital, while safeguarding its historic and Islamic character, and the holy places therein.[161]

These commitments, *inter alia*, have also been reiterated as the objectives of the organization under Article 1 of the Charter, in addition to cooperation in combating terrorism in all its forms and manifestations.[162]

As Palestine was the catalyst behind the creation of the OIC, it also influenced much of the organization's terrorism-related legal responses both within its own law-making context as well as at the UN. The self-determination of the Muslim *Ummah*, particularly within Palestine, has always been at the top of the OIC agenda. The organization adopted hundreds of resolutions reaffirming the right to self-determination of the Palestinian people and to support their cause.[163] There are many historical, political, and regional factors behind the

[156] See the Organization of Islamic Cooperation website, History (n 153)
[157] Ibid.
[158] Hasan Moinuddin, *The Charter of the Islamic Conference and Legal Framework of Economic Cooperation Among its Member States: A Study of the Charter, the General Agreement for Economic, Technical and Commercial Co-operation and the Agreement for Promotion, Protection and Guarantee of Investments Among Member States of the OIC* (Oxford: Clarendon Press, 1987) 70.
[159] *Organization of Islamic Cooperation Charter*, preamble.
[160] Ibid.
[161] Ibid.
[162] Ibid., Article 1.
[163] See e.g., the output of every Council of Foreign Ministers (CFM) meeting; Resolutions on the Cause of Palestine, Al-Quds Al-Sharif, and the Arab-Israeli Conflict, 45th Session of the Council of

reasons why the Palestinian cause has been so central to the OIC, but the religious one is the most relevant to this study. In Chapter 2, we discussed the right of Muslims to repel the aggression of the enemy if the Islamic state's lands, properties, or persons were attacked.[164] We also noted that Muslims, in the context of alien invaders or occupation, are authorized to launch defensive Jihad without seeking the permission of the *Imam*,[165] and that Islamic states are encouraged to use forcible humanitarian intervention in order to protect oppressed people.[166] Be that as it may, the OIC state members predominantly recognize Palestine as occupied land and Palestinians as oppressed people. Accordingly, there have been many explicit as well as implicit references to the notion of Jihad in the OIC resolutions and declarations, especially with regard to the Palestinian cause. For instance, Resolution No. 2/5-P(IS) on the city of Al-Quds Al-Sharif (Jerusalem) adopted in the Fifth Islamic Summit Conference in 1987 states: 'confirming continued Islamic solidarity with the people of Palestine and the unwavering commitment of Islamic States to the declaration of Jihad for the liberation of the City of AI-Quds Al-Sharif, the deliverance of Al-Aqsa Mosque and the restoration of the inalienable national rights of the Palestinian people'.[167] Although the OIC, evidently, toned down this language in more recent resolutions and declarations, the Palestinians' rights to self-determination is still fully incorporated in every resolution.

For the same cause, the OIC has resulted in the definitional impasse in relation to the supposedly ongoing negotiations to finalize the text of the draft UN Comprehensive Convention on International Terrorism. In 2002, the UN Ad Hoc Committee, established by the UNGA Resolution 51/210 and mandated to promote the adoption of a comprehensive convention on international terrorism,[168] reached an agreement on most of the twenty-seven articles in the

Foreign Ministers. Available at: <https://www.oic-oci.org/docdown/?docID=1867&refID=1078> (last accessed 25 May 2019).

[164] See Chapter 2, Section 1.
[165] See Chapter 2, Section 1.
[166] See Chapter 2, Section 1.
[167] Fifth Islamic Summit Conference held in Kuwait, the State of Kuwait, Resolution No. 2/5-P(IS) on the city of Al-Quds Alsharif (Jerusalem), 26–29 January 1987. Available at: <http://ww1.oic-oci.org/english/conf/is/5/5th-is-sum(political).htm> (last accessed 25 May 2019). ('We affirm our resolve to confront this aggression and pressure with all the means at our disposal to prepare ourselves for Jihad in order to liberate the occupied Palestinian and Arab territories and the holy places and to recover the incontrovertible rights of the Palestinian people as recognized by International Law and the UN.'); *The Mecca Declaration of the Third Islamic Summit Conference* (Mecca, the Kingdom of Saudi Arabia), 26–28 January 1981. Available at: <http://ww1.oic-oci.org/english/conf/is/3/3rd-is-sum.htm> (last accessed 25 May 2019).
[168] United Nations General Assembly, Resolution 51/210 (1996).

Draft Convention.[169] While there was a basic consensus on the definition of offences, disagreement floated to the surface when Malaysia, on behalf of the OIC, submitted a proposal seeking exemptions for 'people's struggle including armed struggle against foreign occupation, aggression, colonialism, and hegemony, aimed at liberation and self-determination'.[170] Article 18(2) of the Draft Convention provides that:

> [t]he activities of armed forces during an armed conflict, as those terms are understood under international law, which are governed by that law, are not governed by this Convention, and the activities undertaken by the military forces of a State in the exercise of their official duties, inasmuch as they are governed by other rules of international law, are not governed by this Convention.[171]

The aim of the OIC proposal was to balance the exclusion of the activities of state armed forces by also excluding national liberation forces,[172] having in mind the struggle of the Palestine Liberation Organization (PLO), Hamas, and others. The OIC proposed using the word 'parties' rather than 'armed forces' as it is a well-defined and well-understood term under International Humanitarian Law (IHL).[173] However, this was unsurprisingly opposed by Western states, which seem to be unwilling to accept that non-state actors such as PLO, Hamas, *Hezbollah*, and others could be excluded from the scope of this convention. The key debate revolves around the question of whether IHL should apply to non-state actors (organized armed groups) engaged in self-determination struggles, as provided in Article 1(4) of the First Additional Protocol;[174] or should this matter be covered by the scope of the Comprehensive Convention. It must be noted here that the OIC is not seeking impunity for such entities where, for example, violations of IHL occur; instead, it is seeking

[169] United Nations General Assembly, 'Measures to Eliminate International Terrorism: Working Group Report' (A/C.6/57/ L.9, Annex II, 7–8), Ad Hoc Committee Report no. 38 (57th Session) (6th Committee), 16 October 2002.

[170] Saul, *Defining Terrorism in International Law* (n 5) 85–186.

[171] Draft Comprehensive Convention on Terrorism, Article 18(2).

[172] Saul, *Defining Terrorism in International Law* (n 5) 185–186.

[173] Report of the Ad Hoc Committee established by General Assembly resolution 51/210 of 17 December 1996 Eighth session (28 June–2 July 2004), General Assembly Official Records Fifty-ninth Session Supplement No. 37 (A/59/37) 11.

[174] With regard to the scope of application of the Protocol, see Article 1 (4), AP I. ('The situations referred to in the preceding paragraph include armed conflicts in which peoples are fighting against colonial domination and alien occupation and against racist régimes in the exercise of their right of self-determination, as enshrined in the Charter of the United Nations and the Declaration on Principles of International Law concerning Friendly Relations and Co-operation among States in accordance with the Charter of the United Nations.')

to exclude from the scope of the Comprehensive Convention acts of resistance which are commonly understood not to constitute IHL violations.[175] Despite twenty years having passed since this debate started, the Ad Hoc Committee and the UNGA Sixth Committee have failed to bring the negotiations to completion. Katja Samuel commented on the proposal of OIC in this regard by saying: 'such a stance is most probably influenced by the collective religious obligations accompanying the Islamic peremptory norm of Jihad, making it non-negotiable on religious grounds'.[176]

The same approach has been reflected in the only OIC Convention on Combating International Terrorism adopted in Ouagadougou in 1999.[177] The Convention starts by defining 'terrorism' as:

> any act of violence or threat thereof notwithstanding its motives or intentions perpetrated to carry out an individual or collective criminal plan with the aim of terrorizing people or threatening to harm them or imperiling their lives, honor, freedoms, security or rights or exposing the environment or any facility or public or private property to hazards or occupying or seizing them, or endangering a national resource, or international facilities, or threatening the stability, territorial integrity, political unity or sovereignty of independent States.[178]

It further defines 'terrorist crime' as: 'any crime executed, started or participated in to realize a terrorist objective in any of the Contracting States or against its nationals, assets or interests or foreign facilities and nationals residing in its territory punishable by its internal law'.[179] Additionally, it lists offences in twelve international counterterrorism sectoral conventions as 'terrorist crimes'.[180]

[175] Katja Samuel, 'The Legal Response to Terrorism of the Organization of Islamic Cooperation' in Saul (ed.), *Research Handbook on International Law and Terrorism* (n 51) 727.

[176] Ibid.

[177] *Convention on the Organization of the Islamic Cooperation (OIC) on Combating International Terrorism*. Available at: <http://ww1.oic-oci.org/english/convenion/terrorism_convention.htm (last accessed 25 May 2019).

[178] Ibid., Article 1(2) (The definition is quite similar to the Arab Convention on the Suppression of Terrorism: 'Any act or threat of violence, whatever its motives or purposes, that occurs in the advancement of an individual or collective criminal agenda and seeking to sow panic among people, causing fear by harming them, or placing their lives, liberty or security in danger, or seeking to cause damage to the environment or to public or private installations or property or to occupying or seizing them, or seeking to jeopardize a national resource'.); *Arab Convention on the Suppression of Terrorism*, Article 1(2), 1998.

[179] Ibid., Article 1(3).

[180] Ibid., Article 1(4).

The definition, clearly, is broad and ambiguous. The severity of the 'act of violence' and the credibility of the 'threat' are not determined or illustrated in the definition in anyway. The definition introduces several subjective and vague elements to be attributed to the perpetrators, such as harming or imperilling people's 'lives, honor, freedoms, security or rights', yet it is not clear what level of harm or imperilment is required. It is also not obvious what amounts to exposing the environment or any facility or property to a 'hazard'. In addition, given that this definition makes any violent act amount to the crime of terrorism if perpetrated in pursuit of 'individual or collective criminal plan' and provided that the aforementioned ambiguous aim exists, this makes it difficult to ascertain the difference between an ordinary criminal offence and the crime of terrorism. Accordingly, the definition lacks the distinctive elements and threshold requirements necessary to differentiate between the aggravated crime of terrorism from ordinary criminal offences. Along the same lines, the most dangerous and ambiguous part of the definition is the last sentence, which defines the impact of terrorism as 'threatening the stability, territorial integrity, political unity or sovereignty of independent States'. The Convention neither defined any of these terms nor elaborated about the credibility of the threat. The definition is therefore vulnerable to wide and opportunistic interpretation and abuse.

In line with the OIC efforts in the UN negotiations on the Comprehensive Convention, the OIC Convention also embodied an article that provides people struggling for self-determination and liberation as an exception to the applicability of this convention. Article 2(a) states: 'Peoples' struggle, including armed struggle against foreign occupation, aggression, colonialism, and hegemony, aimed at liberation and self-determination in accordance with the principles of international law shall not be considered a terrorist crime.'[181] Yet this paragraph contradicts the definition of 'terrorism' stated in Article 1, which expresses that the motives and intentions of the perpetrators are irrelevant.

Despite several faultless Articles on extradition and judicial cooperation,[182] the OIC Convention on Combating International Terrorism is only of symbolic value. It does not exceed a mere gesture of opposition by Islamic states to acts of terror in general. The Convention entered into force in November 2002, once the required seven member states had ratified it in accordance with Article 40(1). Today, this number has only doubled to become fourteen out of fifty-seven OIC member states, reflecting a general unwillingness of Islamic

[181] Ibid., Article 2(a).
[182] Ibid., Articles 5–13.

states to engage with the OIC on legally binding matters. The same fourteen OIC member states ratified a number of other international counterterrorism-related conventions under UN auspices, in addition to their legal responses to the UNSC Resolution 1373 and the CTC. One must say, however, that the organization is still active at the diplomatic and political levels. At least, since the events of 9/11 in the United States, the Council of Foreign Ministers meetings adopted numerous resolutions and final communiques in every meeting to condemn and to look into measures to combat terrorism. One must not forget that member states also had an institutional urgency to distance Islam and *Sharia* from terrorist attacks. For instance, one month after the 9/11 attacks, the Ninth Extra-ordinary Session of the Islamic Conference of Foreign Minster in Doha stated in its Final Communique: 'such shameful terrorist acts are opposed to the tolerant message of Islam which spurns aggression, calls for peace, co-existence, tolerance and respect among people, highly prizes the dignity of human life and prohibits killing of the innocent'.[183] It further rejected 'any attempts alleging the existence of any connection or relation between the Islamic faith and the terrorist acts as such are not in the interest of the multilateral efforts to combat terrorism and further damage relations among peoples of the world'.[184] It stressed the need 'to undertake a joint effort to promote dialogue and create links or contacts between the Islamic world and the west in order to reach mutual understanding and building bridges of confidence between the two civilizations'.[185]

4. Fighting Contemporary Islamic Jihadism and *Jus ad Bellum* Limitations

In recent years, ISIL has emerged as the most powerful Islamic Jihadist group posing 'a global and unprecedented threat to international peace and security'.[186] Its presence, attacks, and often territorial control in different states, particularly in Iraq and Syria, triggered a number of military interventions by the international community. Every state or coalition of states justified their military interventions differently, while they all shared the same objective: fighting terrorism. As previously discussed in Chapter 2, *jus ad*

[183] Islamic Conference of Foreign Ministers, Final Communiqué of the Ninth Extraordinary Session (Doha, Qatar), 10 October 2001.
[184] Ibid.
[185] Ibid.
[186] United Nations Security Council, Resolution 2249 (2015).

bellum (the international law on the use of force) is found in the UN Charter. The Charter includes a general prohibition on the threat or use of force.[187] However, it refers explicitly to two circumstances in which the prohibition does not apply, namely (i) forcible measures taken or authorized by the UNSC under Chapter VII, and (ii) the use of force in self-defence, as stated in Article 51.[188] There is also the controversial exception of using force to avert an overwhelming humanitarian catastrophe.[189] Last but not least, if a state invites or consents to another state's use of force on its territory it does not constitute an unlawful use of force, often referred to as 'intervention by invitation' or 'consensual intervention'.

The UNSC, as elaborated in Section 2 of this chapter, adopted numerous Resolutions under Chapter VII to condemn, suppress, and prevent terrorism, and to impose sanctions on terrorist groups. Nonetheless, the practice of the UNSC in the recent years shows that it has not been willing to authorize the use of force under Article 42 of the Charter.[190] Thus states were left with two legal arguments to justify their use of force against terrorist groups: interventions by invitations, and their inherent right of individual or collective self-defence. And yet, in the context of the contemporary fight against 'terrorism', these legal arguments have not always stood up to legal scrutiny.

A quick glance at the recent theatre of military operations in the world today demonstrates that military intervention by invitations or consent is the most common legal argument invoked by states—validly or not—to justify their use of force against a non-state actor perceived by them and/or the international community as a terrorist group. For example, the airstrikes against ISIL in Iraq and Syria, the Saudi Coalition intervention in Yemen, the Egyptian intervention in Libya, the French intervention in Mali, and the US interventions in Pakistan and Afghanistan have all been justified on this basis. One might wonder, why is it permissible to use force by invitation or consent if using force is generally prohibited? In this regard, we must go back to the dictates of Article 2(4) of the UN Charter, which specifies that states 'shall refrain in their international relations from the threat or use of force against the territorial integrity or political independence of any state'.[191] Accordingly, when a state or a

[187] Charter of the United Nations, Article 2(4).

[188] Ibid., Articles 42 and 51.

[189] See Chapter 2, Section 3.

[190] Michael Wood, 'The Role of the UN Security Council in Relation to the Use of Force Against Terrorists' in Larissa van den Herik and Nico Schrijver (eds), *Counterterrorism Strategies in a Fragmented International Legal Order: Meeting the Challenges* (Cambridge: Cambridge University Press, 2013) 317–33, 317, 332.

[191] Charter of the United Nations, Article 2(4).

coalition of states use force in the territory of another state in circumstances in which it is not acting against the latter's 'territorial integrity or political independence', it shall not amount to a violation of Article 2(4), and as such can serve as an exception to the prohibition on the use of force.[192] Consent is a manifestation of the 'sovereign equality' of states, which is the underlying principle of the UN as enshrined in Article 2(7) of the Charter.[193] In conformity, Article 20 of the Draft Articles on Responsibility of States for Internationally Wrongful Acts (DASR) provides: 'Valid consent by a State to the commission of a given act by another State precludes the wrongfulness of that act in relation to the former State to the extent that the act remains within the limits of that consent.'[194] In accordance with this Article, consent by a state to a particular action by another state precludes the wrongfulness of that act in relation to the consenting state.[195] While states are 'non-physical juridical entities', governments are 'the exclusively legally coercive organizations for making and enforcing certain group decisions'.[196] Hence, governments speak for states and act on their behalf and it is therefore crucial for consent to be valid and for the consenting government to be legitimate.[197]

To begin with, in an internal conflict, rebels are precluded from consenting to foreign military assistance on the territory of the state against which they are fighting, a principle confirmed by the International Court of Justice (ICJ) in *Nicaragua*.[198] The Court ruled:

[192] This argument is supported by the definition of the crime of aggression under the Rome Statute, and as stated in the UNGA Resolution 3314 (1974), when they exclude from the term 'aggression' the following actions: '[t]he use of armed forces of one State which are within the territory of another State with the agreement of the receiving State, in contravention of the conditions provided for in the agreement or any extension of their presence in such territory beyond the termination of the agreement'. This means that these two key documents recognize, albeit indirectly, that the international law of the use of force permit the use of force undertaken in accordance with the agreement of the 'receiving' state. See United Nations General Assembly, Resolution 3314 (1974); The Crime of Aggression, Article 8bis(g), Resolution RC/Res. 6, RC/11 (11 June 2010).

[193] 'Nothing contained in the present Charter shall authorize the United Nations to intervene in matters which are essentially within the domestic jurisdiction of any state.' Charter of the United Nations, Article 2(7).

[194] ILC, Draft Articles on Responsibility of States for Internationally Wrongful Acts, with commentaries (2001), General Assembly Official Records 56th session, supplement no. 10 (A/56/10), Article 20.

[195] Ibid., DASR Commentary, Article 20 para. 1.

[196] Edward H. Robinson, 'The Distinction between State and Government', 7/8 Geography Compass, No. 556, 561 (2013) cited in Max Byrne, 'Consent and the Use of Force: An Examination of 'Intervention by Invitation' as a Basis for US Drone Strikes in Pakistan, Somalia and Yemen', *Journal on the Use of Force and International Law* (2016) 3, 97–125, 100.

[197] Ibid., 107.

[198] ICJ, *Military and Paramilitary Activities in and Against Nicaragua* (*Nicaragua v. United States of America*), ICJ Reports 14, 1986, para. 246.

> the principle of non-intervention derives from customary international law. It would certainly lose its effectiveness as a principle of law if intervention were to be justified by a mere request for assistance made by an opposition group in another State... Indeed it is difficult to see what would remain of the principle of non-intervention in international law if intervention which is already allowable at the request of the government of a State, were also to be allowed at the request of the opposition. This would permit any State to intervene at any moment in the internal affairs of another State, whether at the request of the government or at the request of its opposition. Such a situation does not in the Court's view correspond to the present state of international law.[199]

Another question often raised in this regard is whether a government must exert *de facto* or *de jure* control over the state in order to be perceived as legitimate. On this matter, there have been different practices, scholarly opinions, and interpretations.[200] Nonetheless, it appears that the predominant interpretation is that a government is to be considered legitimate, and may therefore consent to intervention, 'either by exercising effective control or, in the absence of such control, if it is recognized by the international community and has not yet been replaced by another entity'.[201]

In the same vein, consent should be provided by an official who represents the consenting government. The ILC adopted a contextual approach with regard to this matter, stating in the commentary to the DASR that '[d]ifferent officials or agencies may have authority in different contexts, in accordance with the arrangements made by each State and general principles of actual and ostensible authority'.[202] One might find the rationale to suggest that the significance of consenting to the use force should require the highest levels of the government, such as the head of state or the head of government or the minister of

[199] Ibid.

[200] For further information about this legal debate see, e.g., *Dreyfus Case* [1901] Traités du XXe Siècle, 394. Translation provided in Bin Cheng, *General Principles of International Law as Applied by International Courts and Tribunals* (Cambridge: Cambridge University Press, 2006) 188; Louise Doswald-Beck, 'The Legal Validity of Military Intervention by Invitation of the Government', *British Yearbook of International Law* (1985) 56(1), 189–252, 194; International Law Association Committee on the Use of Force, Washington Conference 'Report on Aggression and the Use of Force', 2014. Available at: <http://www.ila-hq.org/download.cfm/docid/DA12E88E-5E44-4151-9540DC83D4A0EA78> (last accessed 25 May 2019); David Wippman, 'Military Intervention, Regional Organizations, and Host-State Consent', *Duke Journal of Comparative & International Law* (1996) 7, 209–39, 209, 220; Christine Gray, *International Law and the Use of Force*, 2nd edn (Oxford: Oxford University Press, 2004), cited in Byrne, 'Consent and the Use of Force' (n 196) 108–9.

[201] Ibid., 109.

[202] International Law Commission, Draft Article on State Responsibility (DASR) with Commentaries, Article 20, para. 6.

foreign affairs, as provided in Article 7 of the Vienna Convention of the Law of Treaties (VCLT).[203] As for the validity of the consent, the ILC provides in the commentary to Article 20 of the DASR that consent 'must be freely given and clearly established. It must be actually expressed by the State rather than merely presumed on the basis that the State would have consented if it had been asked. Consent may be vitiated by error, fraud, corruption or coercion.'[204] The same has been reiterated when it comes to the application of Article 45, which provides injured states with the right to waive either the breach itself (e.g. the use of force by external state), or its consequences in terms of responsibility, which is basically an *ex post facto* consent.[205] The commentary to Article 45 of DASR states: '[a]lthough it may be possible to infer a waiver from the conduct of the States concerned or from a unilateral statement, the conduct or statement must be unequivocal.'[206]

Worried about the fall of Baghdad, right after ISIL took control of the ancient city of Mosul, the government of Iraq sent a letter to the UN Secretary General highlighting the increasing threat posed by the terrorist group.[207] In this letter, the government of Iraq requested the UN's and the international community's urgent 'support in order to defeat ISIL' and to protect the Iraqi people and territory from the growing threat.[208] Concerned about its legitimacy after losing control over significant swaths of its lands, the letter started with two paragraphs that stress the authority of the Iraqi government to send this intervention request. It states:

> the people of Iraq, with a great sense of national resolve that was witnessed by the entire world, defied the terrorists and went to the ballot box in great numbers in order to elect its representatives in the new Council of Representatives and choose a new Government, in accordance with the Constitution and in order to sustain its commitment to the political and democratic process. The Independent Electoral Commission, with the assistance of the United Nation

[203] 'In virtue of their functions and without having to produce full powers, the following are considered as representing their State: (a) Heads of State, Heads of Government and Ministers for Foreign Affairs, for the purpose of performing all acts relating to the conclusion of a treaty.' *Vienna Convention on the Law of Treaties*, Article 7(2), 1969.

[204] International Law Commission, Draft Article on State Responsibility (DASR) with Commentaries, Article 20, para. 6.

[205] The Article dictates: 'The responsibility of a State may not be invoked if: (a) the injured State has validly waived the claim.' ILC, DASR, Article 45(a).

[206] ILC, DASR with Commentaries, Article 45 para 5.

[207] United Nations, Letter dated 25 June 2014 from the Permanent Representative of Iraq to the United Nations addressed to the Secretary-General (Doc. S/2014/440), 25 June 2014.

[208] Ibid.

> Assistance Mission for Iraq, then announced the results, which were recently certified by the Federal Supreme Court.[209]

Two months later, in response to this request, the US led coalition-initiated airstrikes against ISIL in Iraq. In his statement, President Obama explicitly affirmed that these airstrike campaigns were launched 'at the request of the Iraqi government' in order to help the Iraqi forces defeat ISIL.[210] Nine states participated in these airstrikes, namely the United States, the United Kingdom, France, Belgium, Canada, the Netherlands, Denmark, Australia, and Jordan.[211] The Iraqi government confirmed its 'express consent' to the military interventions by the US-led coalition in a letter sent to the SC in September 2014, which reads:

> in accordance with international law and the relevant bilateral and multilateral agreements, and with due regard for complete national sovereignty and the Constitution, have requested the United States of America to lead international efforts to strike ISIL sites and military strongholds, with our express consent. The aim of such strikes is to end the constant threat to Iraq, protect Iraq's citizens and, ultimately, arm Iraqi forces and enable them to regain control of Iraq's borders.[212]

Unlike the US-led airstrikes to which Iraq consented and authorized, the Iraqi government rejected the Turkish deployment of hundreds of soldiers and a number of tanks and armoured vehicles near the ISIL-controlled city of Mosul.[213] Along the same lines, the coalition spokesman, Steven Warren, affirmed that the deployment of Turkish military forces in Iraq was not a part of the US-led coalition and that Turkish forces are in Iraq on their 'own mission'.[214] Accordingly, the government of Iraq, in a letter to the UNSC president, highlighted that:

[209] Ibid.

[210] President, The White House, Statement, 7 August 2014. Available at: <http://www.whitehouse.gov/the-press-office/2014/08/07/statement-president> (last accessed 25 May 2019).

[211] US Department of Defense, 'Operation Inherent Resolve: Targeted Operations Against ISIL Terrorists'. Available at: <http://www.defense.gov/News/Special-Reports/0814_Inherent-Resolve> (last accessed 25 May 2019).

[212] Permanent Representative of Iraq to the United Nations, Letter addressed to the President of the UNSC (UN Doc. S/2014/691), 22 September 2014.

[213] Permanent Representative of Iraq to the United Nations, Letter addressed to the President of the UNSC (UN Doc. S/2015/963), 14 December 2015.

[214] Sputnik International, 'Turkey Not Part of US-Led Coalition in Iraq—Coalition Spokesman', 2 February 2016. Available at: <https://sputniknews.com/middleeast/201602021034091107-turkey-us-led-coalition-iraq/#ixzz3zUitAmx1> (last accessed 25 May 2019).

> [t]hose actions were taken without prior coordination or consultation with the federal Government of Iraq and are therefore in flagrant violation of the provisions and principles of the Charter of the United Nations. They also violate the territorial integrity and sovereignty of the Iraqi State, which are guaranteed by the provisions of the Charter, the principles of international law and the relevant Security Council resolutions, which reaffirm the independence, sovereignty and territorial unity and integrity of Iraq. The entry of Turkish forces, including heavy combat equipment and a large number of troops, deep into Iraq territory is an act of provocation and violates international law. Those military movements are an act of aggression under the Charter and the relevant provisions of international law.[215]

Iraq also reserved its right to defend itself and take all measures required to put an end to this act of aggression.[216] Turkey, in response, withdrew its troops, reiterated 'its support for Iraq's sovereignty and territorial integrity', acknowledged 'the miscommunication with the Government of Iraq', and expressed its readiness 'to cooperate with Iraq to more closely coordinate joint efforts to defeat and destroy the terrorist group DAESH [the Arabic translation of ISIL]'.[217] Interestingly, Turkey did not try to state any legal justification for their forcible intervention.

Similarly, the Egyptian Air Force launched airstrikes against ISIL in Libya in coordination with the Libyan Air Force.[218] In a later session in the UNSC, Libya announced that it requested Egypt's support in its fight against 'Ansar Al-Charia and ISIS', and the letter emphasized that 'in view of the lack of international support the Libyan Government has called on brotherly Egypt to support the Libyan army in confronting terrorism'.[219] In the same vein, the United States executed a targeted killing operation in the city of Derna against Abu Nabil, also known as Wissam Najm Abd Zayd al Zubaydi, an Iraqi national who was a longtime *Al-Qaeda* operative and the senior ISIL leader in Libya.[220]

[215] Permanent Representative of Iraq to the United Nations, Letter addressed to the President of the UNSC (UN Doc. S/2015/963), 14 December 2015.

[216] Ibid.

[217] Republic of Turkey Ministry of Foreign Affairs, Press Release Regarding the Bashiqa/Zelikan Training Camp (No. 313), 19 December 2015. Available at: <http://www.mfa.gov.tr/no_-313_-19-december-2015_-press-release-regarding-the-bashiqa_zelikan-training-camp.en.mfa> (last accessed 25 May 2019).

[218] Daily News Egypt, 'Airstrikes hit 3 coastal Libyan cities: Egypt and Libya coordinated attacks, says Libyan Air Force commander', 16 February 2015. Available at: www.dailynewsegypt.com/2015/02/16/airstrikes-hit-3-coastal-libyan-cities/> (last accessed 25 May 2019).

[219] United Nations Security Council, 7387th meeting, 'The Situation in Libya' (UN Doc. S/PV.7387), 18 February 2015, 5.

[220] US Department of Defense, 'Statement from Pentagon Press Secretary Peter Cook on U.S. strike in Libya', 14 February 2015. Available at: <http://www.defense.gov/News/News-Releases/News-Rele

The Pentagon's statement disclosed that this was not the first US strike against terrorists in Libya, but confirmed that it was the first strike against an ISIL leader in Libya, thereby demonstrating that the United States was willing to go after ISIL leaders wherever they operate.[221] The United States, however, did not provide a legal justification for either of the airstrikes in Libya. At the same time, the absence of protest by the Libyan government could be interpreted as a 'passive consent' of such airstrikes. This interpretation finds support in the ICJ ruling in the *Uganda v. DRC* case in which the Court inferred the DRC's consent to the presence of Ugandan troops on its soil from the absence of any objection to such a presence.[222]

In Syria, however, the situation is slightly different. The Syrian conflict is complicated and has often been described as a proxy war between regional and international powers. For instance, Russia, *inter alia*, intervened militarily 'in response to a request from the President of the Syrian Arab Republic, Bashar al-Assad, to provide military assistance in combating the terrorist group Islamic State in Iraq and the Levant (ISIL) and other terrorist groups operating in Syria'.[223] This intervention was openly welcomed by the Syrian government several times.[224] On the contrary, the airstrikes of the US-led coalition against ISIL in Syria did not receive the same type of reaction by the Syrian government. In September 2014, President Obama delivered a statement indicating the intent of the United States to 'hunt down terrorists who threaten our country, wherever they are ... that means I will not hesitate to take action against ISIL in Syria, as well as Iraq'.[225] Ten states have participated in these US-led airstrikes in Syria, namely the United States, the United Kingdom, Australia, Bahrain, Canada, France, Jordan, Saudi Arabia, Turkey, and the

aseView/Article/628954/statement-from-pentagon-press-secretary-peter-cook-on-us-strike-in-libya> (last accessed 25 May 2019).

[221] Ibid. The White House, 'Statement by the President on ISIL', 10 September 2014. Available at: <http://www.whitehouse.gov/the-press-office/2014/09/10/statement-president-isil-1> (last accessed 25 May 2019).

[222] ICJ, *Case concerning Armed Activities on the territory of the Congo (Democratic Republic of the Congo v. Uganda)* 2005, para. 46.

[223] Permanent Representative of the Russian Federation to the United Nations, Letter addressed to the President of the Security Council (UN Doc. S/2015/792), 15 October 2015.

[224] 'Syria's ambassador to Russia urges all countries to join Syria and Russia against terrorism', *Syrian Arab News Agency (SANA)* (1 October 2015). Available at: <https://sana.sy/en/?p=56454> (last accessed 25 May 2019), cited in Karine Banniler-Chirstakis, 'Military Interventions against ISIL in Iraq, Syria and Libya, and the Legal Basis of Consent', *Leiden Journal of International Law* (2016) 29, 743–75, 761.

[225] The White House, 'Statement by the President on ISIL', 10 September 2014. Available at: <http://www.whitehouse.gov/the-press-office/2014/09/10/statement-president-isil-1> (last accessed 25 May 2019).

United Arab Emirates (UAE).[226] The government of Syria responded to their intervention by a letter to the UN Secretary General (SG) and the President of the UNSC, emphasizing that:

> the United States, Britain, France, Canada and Australia have sought to justify their intervention in Syria by citing the fight against ISIL. They have invoked Article 51 of the Charter of the United Nations, but have not consulted with the Syrian Government. That course of action distorts the provisions of the Charter and manipulates international law. Such an assault on Syrian sovereignty will merely give terrorism a freer hand. The only productive way to combat terrorism remains the establishment of an effective international coalition within the framework of international law and with the participation of concerned States, particularly Syria, which is the main party confronting terrorism in the region.[227]

This letter made it clear that the government of Syria did not consent to the US-led airstrikes and thus left no space for any 'intervention by consent' argumentation. As stated in the letter, the United States, like many of its allies, invoked its right to individual and/or collective self-defence. In a letter addressed to the UN SG, the United States emphasized that:

> ISIL and other terrorist groups in Syria are a threat not only to Iraq, but also to many other countries, including the US and our partners in the region and beyond. States must be able to defend themselves, in accordance with the inherent right of individual and collective self-defense, as reflected in Article 51 of the Charter of the United Nations, when, as is the case here, the government of the State where the threat is located is unwilling or unable to prevent the use of its territory for such attacks. The Syrian regime has shown that it cannot and will not confront these safe-havens effectively itself. Accordingly, the US has initiated necessary and proportionate military actions in Syria in order to eliminate the ongoing ISIL threat to Iraq.[228]

[226] US Department of Defense, 'Operation Inherent Resolve: Targeted Operations Against ISIL Terrorists'. Available at: <http://www.defense.gov/News/Special-Reports/0814_Inherent-Resolve> (last accessed 25 May 2019), and cited in Banniler-Chirstakis, 'Military Interventions against ISIL in Iraq, Syria and Libya, and the Legal Basis of Consent' (n 224) 766.

[227] Permanent Representative of the Syrian Arab Republic to the United Nations, Identical letters addressed to the Secretary-General and the President of the Security Council (UN Doc. S/2015/719), 21 September 2015.

[228] Permanent Representative of the US of America to the United Nations, Letter addressed to the Secretary-General (UN Doc. S/2014/695), 23 September 2014.

Similarly, Turkey, Canada, Australia, France, and the United Kingdom justified their intervention relying on the right of self-defence, while only Turkey, Canada, and Australia specifically highlighted the 'unwillingness and inability' of the Syrian government to suppress the use of its territory for such terrorist attacks.[229]

It is evident that in this case the legal issue at stake is not the classical attribution test found in the law on state responsibility to prove the validity of invoking the right of self-defence by the US-led coalition.[230] The attacks perpetrated by ISIL are not attributable to the state of Syria under international law.[231] The US triggered the so-called unable or unwilling test to argue that a victim state is entitled to use defensive force against a non-state actor operating in the territory of another state, providing that the territorial state is either unwilling or unable to prevent the non-state actor from launching further attacks. The rationale behind this argument is that states have the primary responsibility to prevent and suppress non-state attacks from within their territory, but if they are unable or unwilling to fulfil such obligation, the victim state is entitled to take action in self-defence against the non-state actor.[232]

First and foremost, we must confirm that this broad interpretation of invoking the right of self-defence is not supported by any UNSC Resolutions related to counterterrorism. Almost all the SC Resolutions issues in this regard reaffirmed that fighting terrorism should be in full compliance with the Charter of the United Nations, international law obligations, and with respect for the sovereignty, territorial integrity, and political independence of all states.[233] In the Syrian situation, the government of Syria did not even instigate, acquiesce to, or tolerate ISIL activities, which might have been considered a violation of the prohibition on the use force,[234] but rather it was blamed for having not

[229] Charge d'affaires a.i. of the Permanent Mission of Turkey to the United Nations, Letter addressed to the President of the Security Council (UN Doc. S/2015/563), 24 July 2015; Permanent Representative of Australia to the United Nations, Letter addressed to the President of the Security Council (UN Doc. S/2015/693), 9 September 2015; Permanent Representative of the United Kingdom of Great Britain and Northern Ireland, Letter UN Doc. S/2015/688, 7 September 2015; Permanent Representative of France to the United Nations, Identical Letters addressed to the Secretary-General and the President of the Security Council (UN Doc. S/2015/745), 8 September 2015; Chargéd'affaires a.i. of the Permanent Mission of Canada to the United Nations, Letter to the President of the Security Council (UN Doc. S/2015/221), 31 March 2015.

[230] See Chapter 2, Section 1.

[231] See Chapter 2, Section 1.

[232] Nicholas Tsagourias, 'Self-Defence against Non-state Actors: The Interaction between Self-Defence as a Primary Rule and Self-Defence as a Secondary Rule', *Leiden Journal of International Law* (2016) 29, 801–25, 809.

[233] United Nations Security Council, Resolution 2178 (2014); United Nations Security Council, Resolution 2195 (2014); United Nations Security Council, Resolution 2249 (2015).

[234] United Nations General Assembly, Resolution 2625 (XXV), 1970; ICJ, *Military and Paramilitary Activities Case* (*Nicar. v. US*), Judgment, 1986, paras 98–101; ICJ, *Legal Consequences of the Construction*

succeeded in defeating this terrorist group. To accept using the 'unable or unwilling' test to justify the use of force against ISIL in Syria, as claimed by the United States and others, would mean that Article 2(4) of the UN Charter entails not only an obligation of conduct, that is an obligation to take any reasonable measure against an irregular group, but also an obligation of result, namely an obligation to effectively suppress the activities of this group.[235] This evident lowering of the threshold of the prohibition on the use of force is in flagrant contradiction with the current state of international law and particularly the rulings of the ICJ that held that the inability to put an end to irregular activities is not equivalent to a violation of Article 2(4) of the Charter.[236] Furthermore, international law has made a clear distinction between the mere 'use of force' and an 'armed attack' that entitles states to invoke the right of self-defence.[237] In this regard, the ICJ held that:

> while the concept of an armed attack includes the dispatch by one State of armed bands into the territory of another State, the supply of arms and other support to such bands cannot be equated with armed attack. Nevertheless, such activities may well constitute a breach of the principle of the non-use of force and an intervention in the internal affairs of a State, that is, a form of conduct which is certainly wrongful, but is of lesser gravity than an armed attack.[238]

This case confirms that Article 51 requires a higher threshold than Article 2(4). Accordingly, the inability of a state to defeat an irregular group operating in its territory cannot be used as a justification for another state to use force

of a Wall in the Occupied Palestinian Territory, Advisory Opinion, 9 July 2004, ICJ Rep. 136, 171, para. 87.

[235] Olivier Corten, 'The "Unwilling or Unable" Test: Has it Been, and Could it be, Accepted?', *Leiden Journal of International Law* (2016) 29, 777–99, 792.

[236] 'During the period under consideration both anti-Ugandan and anti-Zairean rebel groups operated in this area. Neither Zaire nor Uganda were in a position to put an end to their activities. However, in the light of the evidence before it, the Court cannot conclude that the absence of action by Zaire's Government against the rebel groups in the border area is tantamount to "tolerating" or "acquiescing" in their activities. Thus, the part of Uganda's first counter-claim alleging Congolese responsibility for tolerating the rebel groups prior to May 1997 cannot be upheld.' ICJ, *Armed Activities on the Territory of the Congo*, Judgment (n 222) 268, para. 301

[237] ICJ, Case concerning Military and Paramilitary Activities in and against Nicaragua (*Nicaragua v. USA*), Judgment, 1986, para. 195; *Rome Statute of the International Criminal Court*, Article 8bis; Assembly of State Parties, Resolution RC/Res. 6, The Crime of Aggression, 11 July 2010.

[238] ICJ, Case concerning Military and Paramilitary Activities in and against Nicaragua (*Nicaragua v. USA*), Judgment, 1986, para. 247.

against the host state under the umbrella of the right of self-defence under contemporary international law.

Ultimately, it should be highlighted that the positions taken by numerous states with regard to the 'unwilling or unable' argument seems to induce a certain reluctance whether toward the intervention in Syria[239] or generally.[240] But of course, as Olivier Corten puts it, 'no one can predict what the future of international law will be and, who knows which future legal instruments could be adopted in the name of the fight against terrorism'.[241]

5. Fighting Contemporary Islamic Jihadism and *Jus in Bello* Limitations

Jus in bello is arguably the branch of public international law that was most affected by the post 9/11 so-called global war on terror. It was a moment when the historical separation between the two phenomena of terrorism and armed conflict faded away. Ever since then, many international lawyers and policy-makers have been debating whether the rules of IHL are adequate to meet the new challenges imposed by the phenomenon of transnational terrorism.[242] As always, the debate starts once the classification of conflicts exercise begins, which determines the applicable law. The recent fight against ISIL in Iraq, Syria, and elsewhere has raised more complex questions in relation to the application of IHL. The transnationality of the military confrontations and the multiplicity of the international actors involved in these conflicts seem to challenge the established dichotomy between international and non-international armed conflicts.

In Chapter 3, I discussed many aspects related to the classification of conflicts that can easily be utilized to answer a number of the legal queries raised in contemporary conflicts.[243] For instance, with regard to the fight against ISIL in Iraq, it is evident that there was a non-international armed conflict between

[239] The positions of Russia, Venezuela, Ecuador, China, Brazil, Chad, Belarus, India, Algeria, and South Africa. See Corten, 'The "Unwilling or Unable" Test' (n 235) 787–91.

[240] Paulina Starski, 'Right of Self-defense, Attribution and the Non-State Actor—Birth of the "Unable or Unwilling" Standard?', *Heidelberg Journal of International Law [ZaöRV]* (2015) 75, 455–501; Olivier Corten, *The Law Against War* (Oxford: Hart Publishing, 2010) 739–53, cited in Corten, 'The "Unwilling or Unable" Test' (n 235) 798.

[241] Ibid., 798.

[242] Many, particularly in the United States, have voiced the concerns that the Geneva Conventions are out of date. See Luigi Condorelli and Yasmin Naqvi, 'The War Against Terrorism and jus in bello: Are the Geneva Conventions Out of Date?' in Bianchi (ed.), *Enforcing International Law Norms Against Terrorism* (n 104) 25–38, 25.

[243] See Chapter 3, Section 1.

the Iraqi governmental forces and ISIL, at least since 2014,[244] once the required threshold of intensity and the organizational criteria were met.[245] It is also clear that the intervention of the US-led coalition alongside the Iraqi government forces does not internationalize the pre-existing non-international armed conflict in Iraq,[246] given that the coalition of states is fighting alongside the Iraqi government against an organized armed group (ISIL). Similarly, the intervention of the Russian government forces alongside the Syrian government forces does not internationalize the pre-existing non-international armed conflict between the Syrian governmental forces and ISIL, among many others. The more challenging question, however, is the classification of the airstrikes conducted by the US-led coalition against ISIL in the Syrian territory, without the consent of the Syrian government (as elaborated in the previous section). Would that create an international armed conflict between the US-led coalition and the Syrian governmental forces, despite of the absence of any military confrontations between them, or would it still be considered as a non-international armed conflict because there is no opposition between two or more states? In answer to this complex question, many scholars argue that the absence of military confrontation between the intervening state(s) and the state on whose territory the intervention takes place infers that no armed conflict exists between them. Thus, the only conflict which does exist is the non-international armed conflict between the intervening state(s) and the non-state armed group—in this case, between the US-led coalition and ISIL—because, again, one of the warring parties is not a state, therefore the conflict can only be considered as a non-international armed conflict.[247] Other scholars argue that such foreign intervention triggers an international armed conflict between the intervening state(s) and the state on whose territory the hostilities take place.[248] They base

[244] ICRC, Annual Report 2014 (2015), 480.

[245] According to established case law by the ICTY, two criteria are relevant for establishing the existence of a non-international armed conflict: (i) the intensity of the conflict and (ii) the organization of the parties. See ICTY, The *Prosecutor v. Dusko Tadic*, Judgment, IT-94-1-T, 7 May 1997, paras 561–568; ICTY, The *Prosecutor v. Fatmir Limaj*, Judgment, IT-03-66-T, 30 November 2005, para. 84

[246] ICRC, 'International Humanitarian Law and the Challenges of Contemporary Armed Conflicts', Report prepared for the 32nd International Conference of the Red Cross and the Red Crescent, Doc. 32IC/15/11, 31 October 2015, 15. Available at: <http://www.icrc.org/en/document/international-humanitarian-law-and-challenges-contemporary-armed-conflicts> (last accessed 25 May 2019); ICC, *Prosecutor v. Bemba*, ICC-01/05-01/08, 15 June 2009, para. 246.

[247] Tamas Hoffmann, 'Squaring the Circle? International Humanitarian Law and Transnational Armed Conflicts', in Michael J. Matheson and Djamchid Momtaz (eds), *Rules and Institutions of International Humanitarian Law Put to the Test of Recent Armed Conflicts* (Leiden: Martinus Nijhoff Publishers, 2010) 217–74, 217, 253–4; Andreas Paulus and Mindia Vashakmadze, 'Asymmetrical War and the Notion of Armed Conflict: A Tentative Conceptualization', *International Review of the Red Cross* (2009) 91(873), 95–125, 111–12, cited in Vaios Koutroulis, 'The Fight Against the Islamic State and Jus in Bello', *Leiden Journal of International Law* (2016) 29, 827–52, 837.

[248] Dapo Akande, 'Classification of Armed Conflicts: Relevant Legal Concepts' in Elizabeth Wilmshurst (ed.), *International Law and the Classification of Conflicts* (2012) 32–79, 73; Marco Sassoli,

their argument on the absence of consent on behalf of the latter state as the principal element in classifying the conflict as an international armed conflict rather than the existence of military confrontations between two states.[249] While it might seem counterintuitive to proclaim that an international armed conflict exists between two states despite the absence of active military confrontation between them, such confrontation has never been decisive for the purposes of classifying a conflict as international.[250] According to the International Committee of the Red Cross (ICRC), an international armed conflict can arise where a state uses unilateral force against another state even if the latter does not or cannot respond with military means.[251] In this regard, the attacking state does not have to direct its attack against the armed forces of another state.[252] It is correct that an international armed conflict is fought between states. In addition to the government and its armed forces, constitutive elements of a state include the territory and civilian population.[253] Therefore, any resort to force against the territory, infrastructure, or persons in the state could trigger the classification of the conflict as an international armed conflict.[254]

Accordingly, one might deduce that the coalition's airstrikes created two distinct conflicts in Syria; namely, an international armed conflict between the coalition and Syria, and a non-international armed conflict between the coalition and ISIL.[255] These two parallel yet interrelated conflicts raise another interesting legal question about the applicable law. As elaborated in Chapter 3, it is evident that the applicable rules in these two conflicts are distinct. The rules that govern non-international armed conflicts are less detailed and less protective than those governing international armed conflicts. In a situation like Syria, however, the complexity stems from the fact that almost all the military operations of the coalition will simultaneously be part of both conflicts. For instance, any targeting by the coalition against ISIL-held roads,

'Transnational Armed Groups and International Humanitarian Law', *Program on Humanitarian Policy and Conflict Research, Harvard University* (2006) 6 Occasional Paper Series 1, 2–50, 5; Koutroulis, 'The Fight Against the Islamic State and Jus in Bello' (n 247) 827–52, 838.

249 Ibid.
250 Koutroulis, 'The Fight Against the Islamic State and Jus in Bello' (n 247) 838.
251 ICRC, 'International Humanitarian Law and the Challenges of Contemporary Armed Conflicts' (n 246).
252 Ibid.
253 Ibid.
254 Ibid.
255 The author of this study is aware that there are many other conventional international and non-international armed conflicts currently taking place in Syria. However, the aim of this study is not to explore all the conflicts that are taking place in Syria but rather to discuss the challenging legal nuances triggered in a very few of them.

buildings, refineries, or bridges is also destroying Syrian infrastructure. In such cases, which law would apply to this particular conduct: international or non-international armed conflict laws? While most IHL rules have acquired customary status and are therefore claimed to apply to both international and non-international armed conflicts equally,[256] the answer to this question might still prove significant when it comes to the application of some rules whose customary status is contested by a coalition state or states.[257] Furthermore, the classification of the conflict may have a direct impact on whether the conduct constitutes a grave breach of Geneva Conventions and the First Additional Protocol or another war crime under international criminal law, and thus may affect the individual criminal responsibility related to any criminal act committed in such contexts. This is because under IHL, grave breaches exist only in international armed conflicts and confer obligations on states to enact domestic penal legislation, search for suspects, and prosecute them or hand them over to another state for trial.[258] Prosecuting violations of the law committed in the context of non-international armed conflict, meanwhile, is left to the discretion of the states parties to the relevant IHL treaties.[259] In addition, under the Rome Statute of the International Criminal Court (ICC), the war crimes applicable in an international armed conflict are more numerous than those applicable in a non-international armed conflict.[260]

Another legal concern of conflict classification is the temporal duration of a non-international armed conflict against an organized armed group that is designated as terrorist group such as ISIL. As previously attested, a non-international armed conflict exists for as long as the armed confrontation remains sufficiently intense and the parties involved in the conflict are sufficiently organized. In this regard, the International Criminal Tribunal for the former Yugoslavia (ICTY) stated that, for the purpose of IHL applicability, a non-international armed conflict ceases when a 'peaceful settlement' is reached.[261]

[256] Jean-Marie Henckaerts and Louise Doswald-Beck (eds), *Customary International Humanitarian Law* (Geneva/Cambridge: ICRC and Cambridge University Press, 2005) Vol. I: Rules. Out of the 161 identified as customary, 142 IHL rules are applicable both to international and non-international armed conflicts.

[257] John B. Bellinger and William J. Haynes, 'A US Government Response to the International Committee of the Red Cross study Customary International Humanitarian Law', *International Review of the Red Cross* (2007) 89, 443–71, 443; Koutroulis, 'The Fight Against the Islamic State and Jus in Bello' (n 247) 842.

[258] Marko Divac Oberg, 'The Absorption of Grave Breaches into War Crimes Law', *International Review of the Red Cross* (2009) 91(873), 163–83, 165.

[259] Ibid.

[260] Rome Statute, Article 8.

[261] ICTY, *The Prosecutor v. Ramush Haradinaj, Idriz Balaj, Lahi Brahimaj*, Case No. T-04-84*bis*-T, Judgment, 29 November 2012, para. 396.

Taking this statement literally would mean that for a non-international armed conflict to end, the government armed forces should reach a peaceful settlement with a group that they consider as terrorist. This scenario is unlikely to take place with a group like ISIL. The ICRC commented on this matter by stating that 'this criterion does not provide sufficient practical guidance, and may even be interpreted as introducing a measure of formalism in a determination that should, first and foremost, be driven by facts on the ground'.[262] It was suggested that the notion 'peaceful settlement' should be interpreted as a situation where a factual and lasting cessation of hostilities has been achieved, which may or may not be marked by a formal ceasefire, peace agreement, or any other modalities recognizing the factual situation on the ground.[263] Despite this practical interpretation, the current tactics and strategies of groups like ISIL will make it extremely difficult to determine whether the hostilities have actually ceased or whether it is only an operational, strategic, or timing choice not to launch an attack. It is submitted that the violence of these groups can be sporadic and low level but can rapidly flare up before falling back again to a lower level of intensity.[264] Therefore, this temporary low level of violence should not automatically be considered as signalling the end of a non-international armed conflict, as this could lead to a premature conclusion with regards to the end of applicability of IHL.[265] Taking this feature of non-international armed conflicts into account, the ICRC added 'the risk of resumption' test to the 'complete cessation of hostilities' criterion, in order to ensure that 'the determination of the end of a non-international armed conflict is based not solely on the cessation of hostilities, which may be short-lived, but on an evaluation that related military operations of a hostile nature have also ended'.[266]

One more legal challenge that manifests itself in the context of the fight against ISIL, a group that does exist and control territories not only in Iraq and Syria but also in different countries across the world,[267] is the question of the geographical scope of application of IHL. To put it more simply, what are the territories on which IHL can be invoked to justify a strike against ISIL?

[262] ICRC, 'International Humanitarian Law and the Challenges of Contemporary Armed Conflicts' (n 246).

[263] Ibid. Ben Saul, 'Terrorism and International Humanitarian Law' in Saul (ed.), *Research Handbook on International Law and Terrorism* (n 51) 208–31, 221.

[264] Ibid.

[265] ICRC, 'International Humanitarian Law and the Challenges of Contemporary Armed Conflicts' (n 246) 10.

[266] Ibid., 11.

[267] For a list of the original names and countries of the organizations that pledged allegiance to ISIL across the globe, see Mohammad-Mahmoud Ould Mohamedou, *A Theory of ISIS* (London: Pluto Press, 2018)115–117.

Needless to say, this challenge arises largely because of the fact that IHL does not have any explicit provision on its scope of territorial applicability. The first question, in this vein, is whether IHL applies to the targeting of ISIL fighters anywhere in Iraq and Syria or is it restricted to the battlefield within their territories? In other words, can the coalition target—under IHL—an ISIL fighter located in Baghdad or Damascus or do they have to be in Mosul or Raqqa or any other zone of active hostilities or combat? The ICTY explicitly answered this question by holding that:

> there is no necessary correlation between the area where the actual fighting takes place and the geographical reach of the laws of war. The laws of war apply in the whole territory of the warring parties, or in the case of internal armed conflicts, the whole territory under the control of a party to the conflict, whether or not actual combat takes place there.[268]

This means that IHL would be applicable to any attack launched against an ISIL fighter anywhere in the territories of Iraq and Syria, and not only in the combat zones. The ICRC, however, made an interesting caveat in this regard. Since IHL does not explicitly regulate the degree of force that is permissible against legitimate targets, the ICRC emphasized that the applicability of IHL to the territories of the parties to a conflict does not entail that there are no legal restraints, apart from those related to the prohibition of specific means and methods of warfare, including on the use of lethal force against persons who may be lawfully targeted under IHL (in this case, ISIL fighters), particularly outside the battlefield.[269] This was actually reflected in the recommendations of the ICRC's 2009 Interpretive Guidance on the Notion of Direct Participation in Hostilities under International Humanitarian Law, which highlights that: 'the kind and degree of force which is permissible against persons not entitled to protection against direct attack must not exceed what is actually necessary to accomplish a legitimate military purpose in the prevailing circumstances'.[270] This recommendation admittedly creates an additional complex assessment that will probably be dependent on a wide range of operational and contextual forces, which often leads to the unpracticality of its implementation on the

[268] ICTY, *The Prosecutor v. Dragoljub Kunarac, Radomir Kovač and Zoran Vuković*, Judgment, Case No. IT-96-23 & IT-96-23/1-A, 12 June 2002, para. 57.

[269] ICRC, 'International Humanitarian Law and the Challenges of Contemporary Armed Conflicts' (n 246).

[270] ICRC, 'Interpretive Guidance on the Notion of Direct Participation in Hostilities under International Humanitarian Law', Recommendation IX, May 2009. Available at: <http://www.icrc.org/eng/assets/files/other/icrc-002-0990.pdf> (last accessed 25 May 2019).

ground.[271] This recommendation has proven controversial, having been contested by many scholars[272] and receiving support from others.[273]

It should also be pointed out that if we use the same legal argument, namely that IHL applies in the whole territory of the warring parties,[274] we should submit to the fact that IHL would also apply to any attack against an ISIL fighter in the territories of any state party to the coalition operating in Iraq and Syria, such as in the territory of the United States or France.[275] In support of this view, the ICRC invoked the 'principle of equality of belligerents' under IHL stating that states, once they become a party to an extraterritorial non-international armed conflict, should not be able to shield themselves from the applicability of IHL on their territories.[276] This means that some attacks by ISIL, which would certainly be criminalized under the domestic law of coalition state in which the attack took place, may be considered lawful under IHL, providing that the attacks are directed at military objectives. This, however, does not provide much benefit to ISIL fighters as their conducts will be criminalized under domestic law, given that IHL rules applicable in non-international armed conflicts do not give non-state actors the right to participate in hostilities.[277] On the other hand, it liberates the coalition state(s) from being bound solely by the rules regulating the use of force under the International Human Rights Law (IHRL) paradigm by suggesting more of a hybrid paradigm of IHL and IHRL, as set out in the aforementioned ICRC recommendation.[278] State

[271] ICRC, 'International Humanitarian Law and the Challenges of Contemporary Armed Conflicts' (n 246).

[272] Michael N. Schmitt, 'The Interpretive Guidance on the Notion of Direct Participation in Hostilities: A Critical Analysis', *Harvard National Security Journal* (2010) 1(5), 5–44; Dapo Akande, 'Clearing the Fog of War? The ICRC's Interpretive Guidance on Direct Participation in Hostilities', *International & Comparative Law Quarterly* (2010) 59(108), 180–91, 191; Gabriela Blum, 'The Dispensable Lives of Soldiers', *Journal of Legal Analysis* (2010) 2(69), 9–52; William H. Boothby, 'Direct Participation in Hostilities—A Discussion of the ICRC Interpretive Guidance', *Journal of International Humanitarian Legal Studies* (2010) 1(143), 143–68, 163–4; Ryan Goodman, 'The Power to Kill or Capture Enemy Combatants', *European Journal of International Law* (2013) 24(819), 819–53, 820.

[273] Annyssa Bellal and Louise Doswald-Beck, 'Evaluating the Use of Force During the Arab Spring', *Yearbook of International Humanitarian Law* (2011) 14(3), 3–35, 31; Ryan Goodman, 'The Power to Kill or Capture Enemy Combatants', *European Journal of International Law* (2013) 24(819), 819–53; Koutroulis, 'The Fight Against the Islamic State and Jus in Bello' (n 247) 848.

[274] ICTY, *The Prosecutor v. Dragoljub Kunarac, Radomir Kovač and Zoran Vuković*, Judgment, Case No. IT-96-23 & IT-96-23/1-A, 12 June 2002, para. 57.

[275] For supporters of IHL applicability to the territory of states involved in extraterritorial non-international armed conflicts, see Louiese Arimatsu, 'Territory, Boundaries and the Law of Armed Conflict', *Yearbook of International Humanitarian Law* (2009) 12(157), 157–92, 178; Jann Kleffner, 'Scope of Application of International Humanitarian Law' in Dieter Fleck (ed.). *The Handbook of International Humanitarian Law*, 3rd edn (Oxford: Oxford University Press, 2013) 43–78, 56–7.

[276] ICRC, 'International Humanitarian Law and the Challenges of Contemporary Armed Conflicts' (n 246).

[277] Koutroulis, 'The Fight Against the Islamic State and Jus in Bello' (n 247) 849.

[278] ICRC, 'Interpretive Guidance on the Notion of Direct Participation in Hostilities under International Humanitarian Law' (n 246).

practice up to now indicates that states have not applied IHL to attacks against ISIL inside their territories but rather IHRL,[279] which may be reflective of a political choice rather than a legal conviction that IHL is not applicable.[280] One recent example is the reaction of France to attacks by ISIL fighters in Paris (13 November 2015). It was evident that because it considers ISIL to be a terrorist criminal group, France opted for a law enforcement operation against the group under IHRL rather than the IHL regime.[281]

The last conundrum related to the geographical scope of the application of IHL is whether IHL applies to an attack directed by a coalition state(s) against an ISIL fighter in the territory of a non-belligerent state, such as in the territory of a state like Tunisia or Mauritania. If IHL were to apply to such an attack, it would technically mean that the fighter automatically carries with him or her the non-international armed conflict wherever they go. In this vein, since the very early days of the 'global war on terror', the United States has adopted this approach in their targeting policy against *Al-Qaeda* members,[282] and in their fight against ISIL later on.[283] Under this approach, the decisive factor in determining the geographical application of IHL 'is not where the hostile acts occur but whether, because of their nexus to the conflict, they actually represent 'acts of war'.'[284] Regardless of any other *jus ad bellum* arguments that might challenge this approach, the ICRC has explicitly rejected it by emphasizing that 'this reading would lead to an acceptance of the legal concept of a "global battlefield"'. This, however, does not appear to be supported by the essentially territorial focus of IHL, which on the face of it seems to limit IHL's applicability to the territories of the states involved in an armed conflict. A territorially unbounded approach would imply that a member of an armed group or an individual civilian directly participating in hostilities would be deemed to automatically 'carry' the 'original' non-international armed conflict wherever they go when moving around the world. Thus, based on IHL, they would remain targetable within a potentially geographically unlimited space. With

279 Koutroulis, 'The Fight Against the Islamic State and Jus in Bello' (n 247) 849.

280 Ibid.

281 Ibid.

282 US Department of Justice, 'Lawfulness of a Lethal Operation Directed Against a US Citizen Who Is a Senior Operational Leader of *Al-Qaeda* or an Associated Force', White Paper, 2011. Available at: <https://www.globalsecurity.org/security/library/policy/national/doj-wp-imminent-threat.htm> (last accessed 25 May 2019).

283 US Department of Defense, Statement from Pentagon Press Secretary Peter Cook on US strike in Libya, 14 February 2015. Available at: <http://www.defense.gov/News/News-Releases/News-ReleaseView/Article/628954/statement-from-pentagon-press-secretary-peter-cook-on-us-strike-in-libya> (last accessed 25 May 2019).

284 ICRC, 'International Humanitarian Law and the Challenges of Contemporary Armed Conflicts' (n 246).

very few exceptions, state practice and *opinio iuris* do not seem to have accepted this legal approach and the great majority of states do not appear to have endorsed the notion of a 'global battlefield.. In addition, in practical terms, it is disturbing to envisage the potential ramifications of the territorially unlimited applicability of IHL if all states involved in a non-international armed conflict around the world were to rely on the concept of a 'global battlefield'.[285]

Another legal challenge is related to the applicability of IHL in non-international armed conflicts in which an organized armed group party to the conflict is categorized as a terrorist organization. In recent years, international and national courts, as well as international organizations, have identified groups that are designated as terrorists by the UN and the state against which it is fighting as parties to armed conflicts.[286] Accordingly, IHL applies equally to all the parties to the conflict, be they states or non-state armed groups designated as terrorist. It is worth mentioning, however, that the applicability of IHL does not confer legitimacy to the non-state armed groups by any means.[287] Nonetheless, as previously mentioned, some of the non-state armed groups' attacks against states' military objectives and individuals, which are considered as 'terrorist acts' under counterterrorism national and international laws, would be permitted or at least not prohibited under IHL. This means that members of terrorist groups will most probably face national prosecutions (and often harsh penalties) for using violence against the state regardless of the lawfulness of their actions under IHL. This intrinsic inconsistency between the two legal frameworks is part of the reason why non-state armed groups often disregard IHL norms,[288] as members of the terrorist groups have no legal incentive to abide by IHL when they can be equally sanctioned if captured by the state irrespective of whether they fought according to IHL or not. The Second Additional Protocol, in an attempt to remedy the imbalance between the belligerents in a non-international armed conflict, encourages states at the end of hostilities to 'grant the broadest possible amnesty to persons who have participated in the armed conflict, or those deprived of their liberty for reasons related

[285] Ibid., 15.

[286] ICTY, *Boskoski case*, Judgment (ICTY-04-82-T), 10 July 2008, para. 291; ICTY, *Boskoski case*, Appeal Judgment (ICTY-04-82-A), 19 May 2010, paras 31 and 23; US Supreme Court, *Hamdan, Salim Ahmed v Rumsfeld, Donald H, Secretary of Defense et al.*, Judgment (126 Sct 2749), 2006; United Nations, Report of the Commission of Inquiry on Lebanon (UN Doc. A/HRC/3/2), paras 8, 9, and 57, cited in Andrea Bianchi and Yasmin Naqvi (eds), *International Humanitarian Law and Terrorism* (Oxford: Hart Publishing, 2011) 27; ICRC, Annual Report 2014, 2015, 480.

[287] Common Article 3 to the Geneva Conventions.

[288] Jelena Pejic, 'Armed Conflict and Terrorism: There is a (Big) Difference' in Ana Maria Salinas De Frias, Katja Samuel, and Nigel White (eds), *Counter-Terrorism: International Law and Practice* (Oxford: Oxford University Press, 2012) 171–204, 182.

to the armed conflict, whether they are interned or detained'.[289] The implementation of this provision has been supported by number of states, the UNSC, the UNGA, and other UN and regional bodies.[290] This provision, however, does not apply to any international crimes that might have been committed by the terrorist groups during the conflict, including war crimes, crimes against humanity, and genocide.[291] It is also submitted that adding an additional layer of incrimination (to the already existing domestic law incrimination), which designated acts that are not prohibited under IHL as terrorist acts, makes the proposition of amnesties extremely difficult whether on the legal level or the political level.[292]

One final IHL limitation that has proved quite challenging in recent conflicts is the internment of 'terrorists' during non-international armed conflicts. Internment, which is the deprivation of liberty of a person without criminal charge as a preventative security measure, commonly takes place during armed conflicts. Thus, understanding the rules that safeguard the internment of 'protected persons' is particularly significant to ensure that the process is conducted according to the applicable law. In international armed conflicts, IHL is very clear on this matter. It provides that combatants captured by the enemy, prisoners of war (POWs), are protected by the dictates of the 1949 Third Geneva Convention that allows the detaining states to 'subject prisoners of war to internment',[293] and obliges detaining states to release them without delay after the cessation of active hostilities.[294] It further provides grounds for a possible internment of a civilian 'if the security of the Detaining Power makes it absolutely necessary', or for 'imperative reasons of security'.[295] While they should be released 'as soon as the reasons which necessitated his internment no longer exist',[296] or 'after the close of hostilities' if they remained interned until the end of the conflict.[297] It also obliges states to subject the detention to regular procedures and periodic independent review at least every six months as well as to satisfy minimum conditions of humane treatment.[298] In non-international

[289] Article 6(5), AP II.

[290] ICRC Customary IHL Study, Rule 159. Available at: <https://ihl-databases.icrc.org/customary-ihl/eng/docs/v1_rul_rule159> (last accessed 25 May 2019).

[291] Pejic, 'Armed Conflict and Terrorism' (n 288) 184.

[292] Ibid., 185.

[293] Article 21, GC III. In this case, it is generally uncontroversial that the detaining state is not obliged to provide review, judicial or other, of the lawfulness of POW internment as long as active hostilities are ongoing, because the combatant status signifies that a person is *ipso facto* a security threat.

[294] Ibid. Article 118 (1).

[295] Articles 42 and 78, GC IV.

[296] Ibid., Article 132.

[297] Ibid., Article 133.

[298] Ibid., Articles 27, 43, and 78; Article 75, AP I.

armed conflicts, however, the issue is less clear. Common Article 3 and the Second Additional Protocol provide no specific grounds for internment. Yet the Second Additional Protocol in Articles 5 and 6 contemplates that internment occurs in non-international armed conflicts but provides no guidance regarding procedures either to assess the decision to intern or to terminate captivity.[299] The customary IHL rule that prohibits the arbitrary deprivation of liberty in non-international armed conflicts equally does not provide any guidance in this regard.[300] Accordingly, it has been argued that IHRL should step in to fill this apparent and dangerous gap,[301] thereby triggering one of the most complicated issues in this area: the relationship between IHRL and IHL. This relationship is often referred to as complementary;[302] however, both disagreement and ambiguity remain as to what this means in practice. In this regard, the Preamble of the Second Additional Protocol establishes a rather undefined link between its provisions and the 'international instruments relating to human rights that offer a basic protection to the human person'.[303] As previously stated, IHL is triggered only by the occurrence of armed conflict, while IHRL is deemed to apply at all times, unless some rights have been derogated '[i]n time of public emergency which threatens the life of the nation'.[304] The ICJ has attempted several times to provide an explanation of the complementarity approach between IHL and IHRL. In its *Nuclear Weapons* Advisory Opinion, the ICJ first opined that in situations of armed conflict, IHL as the *lex specialis* (the special norm) displaces the *lex genaralis* (the general norm) of IHRL.[305] Subsequently, in the *Wall* Advisory Opinion, the Court softened its stance and emphasized that IHRL may not be entirely displaced and could be applicable in situations of armed conflict, observing three situation wherein this relationship is relevant: 'some rights may be exclusively matters of IHL; others may be exclusively matters of IHRL; yet others may be matters of both these branches

[299] Articles 5 and 6, AP II.

[300] Rule 99, ICRC Customary IHL Study. Available at: <https://ihl-databases.icrc.org/customary-ihl/eng/docs/v1_rul_rule99> (last accessed 25 May 2019).

[301] ICJ, *Legal Consequences of the Construction of a Wall in the Occupied Palestinian Territory*, Advisory Opinion, 9 July 2004, para. 109; Laura M. Olson, 'Practical Challenges of Implementing the Complementarity between International Humanitarian and Human Rights Law—Demonstrated by the Procedural Regulation of Internment in Non-International Armed Conflict', *Case Western Reserve Journal of International Law* (2009) 40(3), 437–61, 437.

[302] UN Human Rights Committee, *General Comment No. 31: Nature of the General Legal Obligation Imposed on States Parties to the Covenant* (UN Doc. CCPR/C/21/Rev.1/Add 13), 29 March, 2004; ICRC, 'International Humanitarian Law and the Challenges of Contemporary Armed Conflicts' (n 246) 14.

[303] Preamble, AP II.

[304] Article 4(1), International Covenant on Civil and Political Rights (ICCPR).

[305] ICJ, *Nuclear Weapons case*, Advisory Opinion, 8 July 1996, ICJ Reports 1996, para. 25.

of international law'.[306] This means that it is not the body of the law that should be the focus but the specific provision and the unique situation in which the provision is applied.[307]

Accordingly, since IHL is silent about internment in non-international armed conflicts, it is IHRL that should automatically apply to fill the gap. This, however, might still face several obstacles. The first obstacle is the legal and practical capacity of the non-state armed group to fulfil IHRL obligations. In non-international armed conflict, as previously stated, it is undisputed that IHL binds each 'party to the conflict',[308] whether the non-state armed group side or the governmental side. However, for IHRL this is much more controversial. On the one hand, a number of human rights scholars advance sound reasons and arguments as to why non-state armed groups should not be considered as addressees of human rights.[309] On the other hand, there is an increasing soft law in the human rights field that includes, *inter alia*, statements of international governmental and non-governmental (NGO) bodies, some judicial decisions, and scholarly writings that claim that non-state actors or specifically armed groups have human rights obligations.[310] Aside from the legal debate, there are also practical considerations that limit the ability of non-state armed groups to apply IHRL, due to the fact that most such groups do not have the capacity to comply with the full range of IHRL obligations because they cannot perform the government-like functions on which the implementation of IHRL rules is premised. For example, it is likely that non-state armed groups will neither be able to provide by law the reasons for internment nor have the capacity to offer periodic judicial review to the internees. There are also several other obstacles related to the controversy of the exterritorial reach of IHRL obligations, especially in the context of non-traditional non-international armed conflicts, such as the cross-border, multinational, and transnational scenarios previously mentioned,[311] in addition to the controversy over the derogability of the right

[306] ICJ, *Legal Consequences of the Construction of a Wall in the Occupied Palestinian Territory*, Advisory Opinion, 9 July 2004, para. 106.

[307] Olson, 'Practical Challenges of Implementing the Complementarity between International Humanitarian and Human Rights Law' (n 301) 449.

[308] Common Article 3 to the Geneva Conventions.

[309] Nigel Rodley, 'Can Armed Opposition Groups Violate Human Rights Standards?' in Kathleen Mahoney and Paul Mahoney (eds), *Human Rights in the Twenty-First Century* (1993) 297–318.

[310] Andrew Clapham, 'Human Rights Obligations of Non-State Actors in Conflict Situations', *International Review of the Red Cross* (2006) 88(863), 491–523, 494–507.

[311] For more about the controversy of the exterritorial reach of IHRL obligations, see generally European Court of Human Rights (ECtHR), *Al-Skeini and Others v. the United Kingdom*, Application no. 55721/07, 2011. The ECHR applies to the UK operations overseas under its effective control; ICJ, *Armed Activities on the Territory of the Congo* (*Democratic Republic of the Congo v. Uganda*), Judgment, 19 December 2005, paras 178–179; Marko Milanovic, *Extraterritorial Application of Human Rights Treaties: Law, Principles, and Policy* (Oxford: Oxford University Press, 2011).

to *habeas corpus* (judicial review) under IHRL. Further discussion of these issues, however, is beyond the scope of this study.[312]

6. Conclusion

This chapter introduced the emerging legal paradigm that the international community has put in place in order to respond to 'Islamic Jihadism', namely the counterterrorism legal framework. It focused on exploring the legal implications of fighting contemporary Islamic Jihadism under the evolving counterterrorism frameworks and the challenges that it might pose to the other pre-existing legal frameworks, such as domestic laws, IHL, and IHRL. This is, however, without undermining the pressing need to regulate the phenomenon of terrorism that clearly disturbs states' public order and often threatens international peace and security. It started by highlighting how the ambiguity of the term 'terrorism'—as reflected by UNGA/UNSC resolutions and the relevant conventions—and the absence of any concrete definition made almost every state interprets the term in light of their political interests.

It, further, questioned the emerging role of the UNSC in dealing with the phenomenon of terrorism, including the legally binding Resolutions and the creation of the '1267 Committee', the 'ISIL and *Al-Qaeda* Sanctions Committee', and the CTC that have arguably acquired a quasi-judicial and legislative character, as discussed. Having said that, nowadays terms such as 'terrorism' and 'terrorists' have frequently been used to stigmatize, delegitimize, and dehumanize those at whom it is directed, including legitimate political opponents, which clearly risks blurring the line between the acts that deserve triggering counterterrorism measures and the other acts that could be regulated by other branches of international law. Thus, this chapter, suggested that the phenomenon of terrorism should be addressed by careful legislation because a clear definition can shape states' understanding of the problem, delimit their responses to it, and help to distinguish lawful from unlawful responses.

[312] For more about the controversy over the derogability of the right to *habeas corpus* (Judicial review) under IHRL, see generally Human Rights Committee, General comment No. 35, CCPR/C/GC/35, 16 December 2014, para. 66 (the right to judicial review is non-derogable); *Hamdi v. Rumsfeld*, 542 US 507 (2004) (the US nationals captured abroad have the right to habeas corpus); *Boumediene v. Bush*, Supreme Court Judgement 553 US 723 (2008) (foreign nationals detained at Guantánamo Bay falling under the US territorial jurisdiction have the rights to challenge the legality of detention before the US courts under the Constitution's habeas corpus provision); *Al Maqaleh et al. v. Gates*, 899 F.Supp.2d 10 (2012) (foreign nationals held by the US forces in Bagram, Afghanistan had no right to *habeas corpus* before the US courts); *Hassan v. the United Kingdom*, Judgment of Grand Chamber, ECtHR (2014) para. 104

This chapter also tackled the approach of the OIC—as it is often claimed to be the collective voice of the Muslim states—*vis-à-vis* the phenomenon of terrorism. It particularly highlighted its position towards the ongoing negotiations on the text of the draft UN Comprehensive Convention on International Terrorism, on which the OIC wished to include an exemption for 'people's struggle against foreign occupation, aggression, colonialism, and hegemony, aimed at liberation and self-determination' that arguably led to the impasse of the Convention. Further, it fleshed out the definition of terrorism adopted under the OIC Convention on Combating International Terrorism that has been ratified by only fourteen Muslim states, which confirms that this convention carries nothing for Muslim states but a symbolic value.

Last but not least, this chapter discussed many aspects related to the challenges posed by the contemporary fight against Islamic Jihadism *vis-à-vis* the applicable *jus ad bellum* and *jus in bello* frameworks. This included, on the *jus ad bellum* side, the usage of the intervention by invitation and the 'unable and unwilling' test to justify the use of force by states against ISIL. On the *jus in bello* side, this involved the complexity of the classification of conflicts, the geographic scope of application of IHL, the applicability of IHL to non-international armed conflicts in which an organized non-state armed group party to the conflict is categorized as a terrorist organization, and the internment of 'terrorists' during non-international armed conflicts.

5

Integrated Approach in Fostering Compliance by Islamic Jihadist Groups

1. Law and Religion: International Law and Islamic Law

At no time have expectations been higher for the role of law and religion in influencing international relations than in the last two decades, especially since the evolution of *Al-Qaeda* and its offshoots into transnational Islamic armed groups. Those groups, unquestionably, threaten international peace and security in general, and jeopardize the political stability of many Muslim states in particular. Today, a significant number of states across the globe, including major military powers, are involved in devastating armed conflicts against one or more Islamic Jihadist groups, whether they reside on their territories or abroad. The narrative of the 'war on terror', which seeks to impose counterterrorism measures to combat such groups, is dominating the political sphere nationally, regionally, and internationally, leaving very limited space for any other narratives to take hold, including those pertaining to International Humanitarian Law (IHL) and International Human Rights Law (IHRL). While many international lawyers, including myself, have devoted significant efforts to achieving legal solutions in order to prove that our disciplines are sufficiently equipped to face the emerging phenomenon of transnational Islamic armed groups, this study is seeking a different legal proposal. The overarching question this chapter poses is whether or not fostering compliance by Islamic Jihadist groups is possible through integrating aspects of international law and Islamic law. In an attempt to answer this question, this chapter is divided into the following sections: Section 1: Law and Religion: International Law and Islamic Law; Section 2: Ambiguous Texts and Diverse Interpretations; Section 3: The Interpretive Methods under Islamic Law; and Section 4: The Way Forward: An Integrated Approach.

It is evident from all the international law textbooks I read, whether in Arabic or English, that the standard approach in dealing with the subject of

Islamic Jihadism and the Laws of War. Omar Mekky, Oxford University Press. © Omar Mekky 2023.
DOI: 10.1093/oso/9780198888369.003.0006

religion in international law is either to mention it briefly in an early chapter on the history and/or sources of international law or to neglect the subject altogether. This might make sense for Western-educated lawyers since religion is often distinguished from law in Western legal and political philosophy. However, it is not the case in the legal cultures of most Muslim states, where religion and law are relatively interlinked and intertwined. However, the extent to which religion (Islam) and law are blended varies from one Muslim state to another. For instance, a state like the Kingdom of Saudi Arabia considers the *Quran* and *Sunnah* (the primary sources of Islamic law) as the Kingdom's only constitution,[1] while many other Muslim states include Islamic law in their constitutions either as the main source of legislation or at least one of the sources.[2] Some Muslim states have gone even further by explicitly imposing limitations on the ratification and/or implementation of treaties or human rights-related conventions that contradict Islamic law.[3] Thus, arguably, Islamic law does play at least some role in shaping the legal systems and behaviours of most of the Muslim states, if not all of them. This role is multiplied when applied to the influence of Islamic law on the behaviours of Islamic Jihadist groups, which openly and exclusively cite self-interpreted Islamic law arguments as the justification for most of their day-to-day actions, including those related to combat. Additionally, most of these groups perceive themselves to be outside the scope of traditional international law.[4] It is not just that they distrust and disagree with international law; they often delegitimize the states that accepted its rules and principles. This fact makes using the international law language alone to pursue any legal communication or dialogue with those groups less relevant or at least less persuasive. In this regard, many frontline humanitarian practitioners affirmed that rooting negotiations with this type of armed groups in

[1] 'The Kingdom of Saudi Arabia is a sovereign Arab Islamic state with Islam as its religion; God's Book and the *Sunnah* of His Prophet, God's prayers and peace be upon him, are its constitution, Arabic is its language and Riyadh is its capital.' Article 1, Constitution of the Kingdom of Saudi Arabia, March 1992.

[2] See, e.g., Article 2, Constitution of Egypt, 2014 ('The principles of Islamic Sharia are the main source of legislation'). For further information about the relationship between Islamic law and constitution, see Nathan J. Brown and Mara Revkin, 'Islamic Law and Constitutions: The Oxford Handbook of Islamic Law', *Oxford Handbook Online* (2015) 778–818. Available at: <https://mararevkin.files.wordpress.com/2015/12/islamic-law-and-constitutions-oxford-handbooks.pdf> (last accessed 25 May 2019).

[3] Article 77, Constitution of the Islamic Republic of Ira, 1979, amended 1989, states that 'international treaties, protocols, contracts, and agreements must be approved by the Islamic Consultative Assembly'. Article 26, Basic Law of Saudi Arabia, 1992, states that '[t]he State shall protect human rights in accordance with the Sharia'.

[4] The reason I used the term 'most' in this sentence is the fact that some Islamic armed groups such as Hamas, *Hezbollah*, and a few other 'conventional' Islamic militias believe that their *modus operandi* should be based entirely on Islamic law while at the same time being part of the traditional International law that their host states are bound to, Palestine and Lebanon.

international law can certainly be counterproductive.[5] In fact, they suggest framing the 'principles of international law in terms of national laws or other normative frameworks [which are] potentially more relevant to local interlocutors'.[6] This confirms what Bianchi once wrote as one of the aims of his recent textbook *International Law Theories*:

> [t]he idea, still entertained by many in the profession, that international law is a *lingua franca* through which we communicate and do things together at the international level is inaccurate and somewhat naïve ... international law is not a truly universal language anymore, if it ever was; rather, it comprises a traditional way of thinking that goes hand in hand with multiple diverse approaches ... hence, in order to be a competent practitioner or a learned scholar, it is important to be familiar with the different dialects and languages in which international law is spoken nowadays.[7]

In line with this view, this research attempts to argue that using the Islamic law language, either alone or hand in hand with international law, might serve as a better strategic tool of communication to influence the behaviours of the members of the Islamic Jihadist groups. This is done without any discredit to the legitimacy and applicability of the traditional rules of international law.

Throughout my research I came across numerous substantial commonalities between international law and Islamic law that prove how rich and useful this relationship could be, as can be observed in Chapters 2 and 3. It would not be an exaggeration to claim that the vast majority of the *jus ad bellum* and *jus in bello* rules under international law and Islamic law surprisingly share the same morale, rationale, and underlying objectives. These similarities, indeed, make the interaction between these two bodies of law appealing and rather promising. There are three main characteristics, however, that I find identical in both legal systems that rather complicate this relationship and challenge its smooth development. First, the fact that both international law and Islamic law are crucial normative social regimes that relate to fundamental social phenomena in

[5] 'Humanitarian Negotiation Series: The Role of Laws and Norms', ATHA, Harvard Humanitarian Initiative. Available at: <http://atha.se/podcasts/humanitarian-negotiation-series-role-laws-and-norms> (last accessed 25 May 2019); Rob Grace and Stephen Wilkinson, 'Preliminary Report on the Role of Laws and Norms in Humanitarian Negotiations', *Advanced Training Program on Humanitarian Action (ATHA), Harvard Humanitarian Initiative* (2016). Available at: <http://www.atha.se/sites/default/files/law_and_negotiation_-_preliminary_report.pdf> (last accessed 25 May 2019).

[6] Ibid.

[7] Andrea Bianchi (ed.), *International Law Theories* (Oxford: Oxford University Press, 2016) 2.

human society,[8] which often stimulate 'passionate disagreement about their proper content and functions'.[9] Second, both systems are susceptible to constant change and adaptation as they are tied to an extremely vibrant social phenomenon. Third, they are often subject to misinterpretation, politicization, and manipulation by elites.[10] While the first and second characteristics are logical results to any ongoing social process, the third is particularly worthy of further contemplation.

2. Ambiguous Texts and Diverse Interpretations

Like many who researched this topic before me, when I started writing this book five years ago I was naively hoping to find some certainty and consistency in the norms of Islamic law and how it has been interpreted and applied throughout history. I was seeking to find the stability and predictability that I did not find in international law. As is commonly known for any reasonable international lawyer, one is doomed to work with relatively ambiguous texts that invite constant interpretations and argumentations. The intellectual struggle that international lawyers undertake to interpret terms such as 'terrorism', 'direct participation in hostilities', 'concrete and direct military advantage anticipated . . .', and 'armed attack occurs . . .', to mention just a few, is painstaking and far from efficient to say the least.[11] Koskenniemi commented on the overwhelming ambiguity and 'open-endedness' of international law terms, by stating that:

> international law remains indeterminate because it is based on contradictory premises and seeks to regulate a future in regard to which even single actors' preferences remain unsettled. To say this is not to say much more than that international law emerges from a political process whose participants have contradictory priorities and rarely know with clarity how such priorities should be turned into directives to deal with an uncertain future.[12]

[8] Mashood A. Baderin, 'Religion and International Law: Friends or Foes?', *SOAS School of Law Legal Studies Research Paper No. 4, European Human Rights Law* (2010) 5, 637–58, 639.

[9] Steven. D. Jamar, 'Religion and International Law', *Journal of Law and Religion* (2001)16, 609–12.

[10] Baderin, 'Religion and International Law: Friends or Foes?' (n 8) 639.

[11] See, e.g., the Overview of the ICRC's Expert Process (2003–2008) that ultimately adopted the Interpretive Guidance on the Notion of Direct Participation in Hostilities. Available at: <https://www.icrc.org/en/doc/assets/files/other/overview-of-the-icrcs-expert-process-icrc.pdf> (last accessed 25 May 2019).

[12] Koskenniemi provides an illustrative example on this matter by saying: 'Even where there is little or no semantic ambiguity about an expression in a rule—say, about "armed attack" in Article 51 of the UN Charter—that expression cannot quite have the normative force we would like it to have. It cannot

For example, Chapter 2 discusses how Article 51 preserves the right to use force in self-defence 'if an armed attack occurs'.[13] Here, the interpretation of the ambiguous term 'armed attack' is a matter of significant disagreement among international lawyers and policy-makers. Unfortunately, the Charter itself offers no guidance on this issue. While it is clear from the language of the provision that self-defence is lawful only when an armed attack occurs and not as a first strike option, it is fairly unclear at which point in time an 'armed attack' begins and whether the use of force in cases when an armed attack is about to occur could also be considered lawful.[14]

Based on a restrictive reading of Article 51, some insist that the right to use force in self-defence is confined only to circumstances in which an actual armed attack has taken place.[15] And yet the contrary position, which is that states have the right to invoke self-defence in order to avert the threat of an *imminent* attack—commonly referred to as 'anticipatory self-defence'—is widely accepted in the contemporary international law literature.[16] As for the proponents of this position, the right to self-defence is a customary right that includes the anticipatory self-defence to avert imminent attacks.[17] However, the problem remains in the ambiguity of the term 'imminent'. As Svarc stated:

because it is also threatening—what about an imminent attack? The same reason that justifies the rule about self-defence also justifies setting aside its wording if this is needed by the very rationale of the rule—the need to protect the State. And because no rule is more important than the reason for which it is enacted, even the most unambiguous rule is infected by the disagreements that concern how that reason should be understood and how it ranks with competing ones: what is it, in fact, that is necessary to "protect the State" and how does that reason link with competing ones such as those of "peaceful settlement"?' See Martti Koskenniemi, *From Apology to Utopia: The Structure of International Legal Argument* (Cambridge: Cambridge University Press, 2005) 590–1.

[13] See Chapter 2, Section 1.

[14] Dominika Svarc, 'Redefining Imminence: The Use of Force Against Threats and Armed Attacks in the Twentieth Century', *ILSA Journal of International & Comparative Law* (2007) 13(1), 171–91, 178.

[15] ICJ, *Case concerning Military and Paramilitary Activities in and against Nicaragua (Nicaragua v USA)*, 1986 ICJ Rep. 14, para. 194; ICJ, *Case Concerning Oil Platforms (Islamic Republic of Iran v. United States of America*, 2003, ICJ Rep. paras 61–64 and 72.

[16] Richard J. Erickson, *Legitimate Use of Military Force Against State Sponsored International Terrorism* (Alabama: Air University Press, 1989) 138 (listing the members of the expansive school of thought who interpret Article 51 as permitting anticipatory self-defence in response to imminent armed attack). Available at: http://www.au.af.mil/au/awc/awcgate/au/erickson.pdf> (last accessed 25 May 2019).

[17] Claud H. M. Waldock, 'The Regulation of the Use of Force by Individual States in International Law' in *Collected Courses*, Vol. 81 (The Hague: Academy of International Law, 1952) 455–517451, 496, and 497; Derek W. Bowett, *Self Defense in International Law* (Manchester: Manchester University Press, 1958) 188–92, cited in Leo Van Den Hole, 'Anticipatory Self-Defence Under International Law', *American University International Law Review* (2003) 19(1), 69–106, 77. In this regard, Judge Schwebel in his dissenting opinion said: 'I wish ... to make clear that, for my part, I do not agree with a construction of the United Nations Charter which would read Article 51 as if it were worded: "Nothing in the present Charter shall impair the inherent right of individual of collective self-defense if, and only if, an armed attack occurs...." I do not agree that the terms or intent of Article 51 eliminate the right of self-defense under customary international law, or confine its entire scope to the express terms of Article 51.') ICJ Military and Paramilitary Activities Case (*Nicar. v. US*), Judgment, 27 June 1986, 347.

> the concept of imminence is the most problematic variable of anticipatory self-defense and one that has no precise definition in international law. It is currently rather unclear when an attack is sufficiently 'imminent' to justify military action in self-defense and it may indeed be very difficult to ever express the imminence of a particular threat 'in a legally robust fashion'.[18]

The *Caroline* standard of 'imminence', in this regard, seems to have centred its interpretation on the temporal dimension of the notion. It considers the threat to be imminent when the attack is just about to occur or when an 'attack is in evidence',[19] which means that a state that is a potential victim of an attack may only use force based on clear and convincing evidence that the enemy is preparing to attack. Accordingly, the defence must be carried out within a reasonable time from the attack in order to fit the characterization of the lawful self-defence.

This latter restrictive/narrow interpretation of the standard of 'imminence' is currently been challenged by governments such as the United States under the claim that such a standard 'could hardly ever be satisfied in the context of asymmetric warfare launched by terrorists or hostile governments'.[20] Based on the fact that '[a]pplying the narrow standard of temporal imminence in an age in which technology allows great devastation to be wrought in a very short period of time would disable a State from effectively repelling the attack and protecting its population from potentially great harm'.[21] Accordingly, the United States, in light of the contemporary compelling needs of the new security environment, proposes a broader interpretation of this standard—beyond the latter traditional 'narrow standard of imminence'—in order to enable states to launch preventive military actions against more remote threats before they have fully materialized.[22] This proposition is particularly valid with respect to contemporary terrorism characterized by clandestine preparations and surprise attacks: 'the evidence of a specific attack coming will usually be only the attack itself'.[23] And yet adopting such broad interpretation to accommodate contemporary security concerns might still invite more counterproductive uncertainties to already ambiguous standard of international law. The margin of

[18] Svarc, 'Redefining Imminence' (n 14) 182.

[19] Mary Ellen O'Connell, 'The Myth of Preemptive Self-Defense', *ASIL Task Force Papers*, *The American Society of International Law* (2002) 1–21, 9. Available at: <https://www.nyccriminallawyer.com/wp-content/uploads/2014/07/oconnell.pdf> (last accessed 25 May 2019).

[20] Svarc, 'Redefining Imminence' (n 14) 183.

[21] Ibid.

[22] Ibid., 172.

[23] Christopher Greenwood, 'International Law and the Pre-emptive Use of Force: Afghanistan, *Al-Qaeda*, and Iraq', *San Diego International Law Journal* (2003) 4, 7–38, 16

error and the potential for abuse by using such interpretation will most likely be multiplied. The recourse to force against some 'unspecified hypothetical threats' that might occur at some point in the future would not be anticipatory military action anymore but rather preventive, which falls under states' 'offensive strategic response to a long-term threat, not a defensive tactical response to an impending attack', as the underlying rationale of lawful anticipatory self-defence.[24] Hence, in light of the existing legal framework on self-defence under international law, one could comfortably say that it is evident that such broad interpretation lacks any clarity or objective criteria for its implementation under any well-defined legal scrutiny, which is likely to lead to the unrestricted use of military action that threaten the well-established prohibition on the use of force under international law.

Similarly, Islamic law offers no exception in terms of the ambiguity of the dictates of some of its rules. Like any legal text, some of the *Quran*'s legal sentiments are clear-cut and straightforward (definitive) while others are ambiguous and indeterminate (tentative).[25] This ambiguity and/or indeterminacy has led to a diversification of legal interpretations and practices throughout Islamic history and will presumably continue to do so.

I highlighted in Chapter 2 the overall commonalities between Islamic law and international law with regard to the prohibition of the use of force and the boundaries of invoking the right to self-defence. I indicated that these two bodies of law, generally speaking, agree on the principle of the maintenance of peace and the prohibition of the use of force or military Jihad in international relations between states—and within a state under Islamic law.[26] They further share the same exception on the use of force in self-defence—if an armed attack has taken place or to avert an imminent attack—and they adopt similar criteria for the permissive exercise of this right; namely, immediacy, necessity, and proportionality.[27] However, ambiguity or indeterminacy of a single term within either text could go so far as to jeopardize the seemingly harmonized relationship between the two laws. As mentioned earlier, in the Quranic verse that reads: 'And fight them until there is no *fitnah* and [until] the religion, all of it, is for Allah. And if they cease—then indeed, Allah is seeing of what they do', Muslim jurists disagree on the interpretation of the meaning of the Arabic word *fitnah*.[28] Many of them claim that the word *fitnah* in this verse

[24] Svarc, 'Redefining Imminence' (n 14) 187.
[25] Mohamed H. Kamali, *Sharia Law: An Introduction* (London: Oneworld Publications, 2008) 23.
[26] See Chapter 2, Section 1.
[27] See Chapter 2, Section 2.
[28] *Quran* (8:39).

means polytheism or disbelief, which is the plain and ordinary meaning of the word.[29] According to the proponents of this interpretation, Muslims are permitted to fight the polytheists until polytheism is eradicated from Mecca and even from the rest of the world, if possible.[30] However, this interpretation is in total contradiction with all the other Islamic *jus ad bellum* rules that promote peaceful coexistence with other states and religions and permit military Jihad only in its defensive form. It also overrides the Islamic *jus in bello* system of rules, as it makes being a believer or not the only determinant factor to be targeted or spared by Muslim fighters. On the other hand, other Muslim jurists interpret *fitnah* in a more contextual manner, as they define it as the act of persecution or oppression.[31] According to their interpretation that is allegedly in line with the context in which the verse had been revealed, the text is permitting Muslims to fight the *Qurayshite* polytheists in Mecca, who have been persecuting Muhammad and his followers only because they were practising Islam.[32] In other words, the verse allows Muslims to fight their persecutors until they gain the freedom to practise their religion by repelling the enemy.[33] Thus, from reading these two different interpretations, a reasonable observer could comfortably tell that the discrepancies between Muslim Jurists over the interpretation of the meaning of one single term, *fitnah*, led to the theorization of two different forms of Jihad.[34] One that advocates for a 'holy war', like offensive Jihad, in which Muslims should fight until their enemies believe in Islam or are killed for being polytheist, and the other, which aligns with the notion of defensive Jihad or perhaps the principle of humanitarian intervention in Islam, depending on the circumstances.[35]

[29] See *Tafsir* (the interpretation) of *Al-Saadi*, *Al-Qortoby*, and *Baghawy*. Available (in Arabic) at: <http://quran.ksu.edu.sa/tafseer/tabary/sura8-aya39.html#tabary> (last accessed 25 May 2019).

[30] Muhammad ibn 'Umar al-Rāzī, *Al-Tafsīr al-Kabīr aw Mafātīh al-Ghayb* (Beirut: Dār al-Kutub al-'Ilmiyyah, 2000/1421), Vol. 15, 131; Yūsuf Al-Qaradawi, *Fiqh al-Jihād: Dirāsah Muqāranah li-Ahkāmih wa Falsafatih fī Daw' al-Qur'ān wa al-Sunnah* (Cairo: Maktabah Wahbah, 2009) Vol. 1, 257, 259–63.

[31] Muhammad ibn Jarīr Al-Tabarī, *Jāmi' al-Bayān 'an Ta'wīl Āy al-Qur'ān*, 30 Vols (Beirut: Dār al-Fikr, 1984–1985/1405) Vol. 9, 248–50; Muhammad ibn 'Alī ibn Muhammad Al-Shawkānī, *Fath al-Qadīr: Al-Jāmi' bayn Fannay al-Riwāyah wa al-Dirāyah min 'Ilm al-Tafsīr*, 5 Vols (Beirut: Dār al-Fikr, n.d.) Vol. 2, 308; Ahmad Mustafā Al-Marāghī, *Tafsīr al-Marāghī*, 30 Vols (Cairo: Mustafā al-Bābī al-Halabī, 1946/1365) Vol. 9, 207.

[32] 'This passage was revealed at the battle of Badr (624 AD). This battle took place as a consequence of the continued persecution the Muslims faced by the Quraish. It was the Quraish who came to Madinah for war, not the other way around.' See 'Fight With Them Until There Is No More Fitna [Disbelief] . . .?' *Quran* 8:39, Discover the Truth. Available at: <https://discover-the-truth.com/2016/04/09/fight-with-them-until-there-is-no-more-fitna-disbelief-quran-839/> (last accessed 25 May 2019).

[33] Al-Tabarī, *Jāmi' al-Bayān 'an Ta'wīl Āy al-Qur'ān* (n 31), Vol. 9, 248–50; Al-Shawkānī, *Fath al-Qadīr* (n 31) Vol. 2, 308; Al-Marāghī, *Tafsīr al-Marāghī* (n 31) Vol. 9, 207.

[34] Ahmed Al-Dawoody, *The Islamic Law of War: Justifications and Regulations* (New York, NY: Palgrave Macmillan, 2011). 63.

[35] Ibid.

A third form of Jihad, however, has been theorized by Qutb (one of the most prominent Islamic ideologues of the Jihadists' movements) who took the second interpretation too far, by arguing that *fitnah* could take place through an armed attack by the enemy or by simply creating the condition to corrupt the Islamic society. For instance, in his opinion, Muslims should fight whoever stands as an obstacle in the path of Allah or those who restrict Muslims' freedom of belief.[36] He added in his very influential writings, by way of example: 'such as a communist regime that prohibit the teaching of religion and promote atheism, legislate laws that allows adultery and alcohol', which he considers as a type of regime worth fighting.[37] As previously argued,[38] Qutb's and a few other like-minded Islamic scholars' broad interpretation of the meaning of the term *fitnah* in the *Quran* has led to the increasing use of the notion of Jihad by many contemporary Islamic Jihadist groups in order to justify the use of force against what would later be referred to as 'far enemies' and 'near enemies' of Islam.[39] As Bassiouni rightly put it:

> In contemporary times, the proponents of this view believe that the duty to establish Islam on earth extends to: stopping the decline of Islam within the Muslim *Ummah* (whose meaning includes smaller communities of Muslims); opposing corrupt or deviant Muslim leaders and regimes; confronting the imperialistic/hegemonistic anti-Muslim forces; reconstituting the ideal Muslim *Ummah* and restoring it to its earlier greatness; and separating Muslim values, governance, and economic system from Western values and systems.[40]

In Chapter 3, I explored a few other examples that raise similar intellectual controversies, where Muslim jurists came to a completely contradicting conclusions with regard to the interpretations of the meaning of one verse, *hadith* or another. Take for instance the fact that in the opinion of some Muslim jurists, absolute power is given to political authorities in Muslim state(s) to decide about the fate of the prisoners of war (POWs), which might permit their

[36] Sayyid Qutb, *Fi Zilal al-Quran*, Vol. 6, 11th edn (Cairo: Dar al-Shuruq, 1985).
[37] Ibid.
[38] See Chapter 2, Section 4.
[39] The 'far enemies', from the perspective of most of the Jihadist movements today, are particularly the United States and its Western allies, while the 'near enemies' are most of the governments in the Islamic world, and particularly in the Arab world, who are perceived by Jihadists as merely puppets at the hands of the Western powers.
[40] M. Cherif Bassiouni, 'Evolving Approaches to Jihad: From Self Defense to Revolutionary and Regime Change—Change Political Violence', *Chicago Journal of International Law* (2007) 8, 119–46, 134. Available at: http://chicagounbound.uchicago.edu/cjil/vol8/iss1/8> (last accessed 25 May 2019).

execution or enslavement.[41] Another example is related to the jurists' opinions with regard to the permissibility of using some of the means and methods of warfare. In most of these cases, the jurists tended to favour the principle(s) of military necessity and/or reciprocity as opposed to favouring humanitarian considerations and restrictions embodied in the text.[42]

Here, in all such cases of multiplicity and complexity of the Islamic text interpretations, which often derive various contradicting juristic opinions, in addition to the absence of any authoritative doctrinal body of interpretation on the subject, Muslims find themselves in a perplexing position, not knowing who to believe, which legal argument to follow, and on what basis. On the one hand, they watch dozens of videos created by *Al-Qaeda* and Islamic State of Iraq and the Levant (ISIS) where they see members of these groups citing passionately, by way of example, the *fitnah* verse before they start executing their heinous activities against their victims, both civilian and combatant. On the other hand, they watch plenty of daily TV shows and videos showing Muslim jurists interpreting the same verse, persistently and strictly, in its permissible defensive form of Jihad.[43] Who is right and who is wrong? What is legal and what is not? What is *halal* and what is *haram*? In this research, I am not sure I would be able to deliver any definite answers to these 1,400-year-old questions. At the end of the day, who am I to attempt to do so? The most I can offer to satisfy the curiosity of the reader, however, is to highlight a few elements that might help explain how different interpretations of a text emerged and by what process they become eligible for consideration as the correct interpretation of a text.

3. The Interpretive Methods under Islamic Law

Similar to any other law, the purpose of interpretation in Islamic law is to identify the intention of the lawgiver (God) with regard to what has been left

[41] See Chapter 3, Section 2.ii.

[42] See Chapter 3, Section 3.

[43] As you might be aware, the ISIS videos are often blocked a few minutes after being uploaded by the media arm of ISIS. Nonetheless, I came across a YouTube video in which a Muslim jurist supports the interpretation of the meaning of '*fitnah*' to justify fighting the polytheists. See Sheikh Dr. Abd Allah bin Mohamad Al-Amin, YouTube Video. Available (in Arabic) at: <https://www.youtube.com/watch?v=zV1Bt0x0GDc> (last accessed 25 May 2019). As for the videos supporting the defensive Jihad interpretation of the verse, see Sheikh Dr. Hakem Al-Motiery, YouTube video. Available (in Arabic) at: <https://www.youtube.com/watch?v=_wpDiu7GCTg> (last accessed 25 May 2019). Sheikh Dr. Ahmed Abdul Rahman Al-Nakib, YouTube video. Available (in Arabic) at: <https://www.youtube.com/watch?v=llUV-1EXkw4> and <https://www.youtube.com/watch?v=tNIa8I4pTHs> (last accessed 25 May 2019).

unexpressed or ambiguous, as a matter of necessary inference from the surrounding circumstances.[44] However, the interpretation process of Islamic law has very particular characteristics and possibly extremely critical consequences. Its particularity derives from the complexity of the interpretive methods of Islamic law, while its consequential criticality stems from the significance of the legal and moral knowledge and values (in the neutral sense of the term) that this process supposes to produce, namely the law that informs Muslims of the conduct acceptable to God. This process, under Islamic law, is referred to as *Ijtihad*, which is scientifically defined as the intellectual activity of discovering the rules of Islamic law and extracting its jurisprudence from detailed Islamic sources.[45] These sources—mainly the *Quran* and *Sunnah*—do not specify the law in the way it is traditionally codified in specialized law manuals, such as domestic criminal laws. Rather, they contain some rulings (*ahkam*) and other indications (*dalalat*) that lead to the legal reasons of these rulings.[46] Based on these givens, a *Mujtihad* (a jurist who is entitled to interpret the law) may attempt to interpret an Islamic law text. This jurist (*Mujtihad*) should possess, broadly speaking, *Ijazah* (equivalent to a Doctorate of Laws)[47] and a profound understanding of the *Quran*, *Sunnah*, the principles of inference, analogical reasoning, the verification of the transmission and transmitters of *hadith*, customs, and most importantly the Arabic language.[48]

Be that as it may, the *Mujtihad*'s—juristic—interpretation, even if one acquires the required authority, only gains its legitimacy from the persuasive force it possesses within the Islamic community, provided that one follows the Islamic interpretive methods.[49] The two main interpretive methods of interest to this research are *Usul al-Fiqh* (which literally means the Science of Jurisprudence) and *Maqasid Al-Sharia* (which literally means the purpose of the law).[50] *Usul al-Fiqh* offers a step-by-step process for producing an interpretation of Islamic law.[51] According to this process, if the jurist failed to find

[44] Mohamed H. Kamali, *Principles of Islamic Jurisprudence*, 3rd edn (Cambridge: Islamic Text Society, 2005) 84.
[45] See Chapter 1, Section 1.ii.
[46] Wael B. Hallaq, 'Was the Gate of Ijtihad Closed?', *International Journal of Middle East Studies* (1984) 16, 3–41, 4.
[47] *Ijazah* is a 'degree certificate attesting that one was authorized by a higher authority to transmit a certain subject or text of Islamic knowledge'. This 'higher authority' was often a group of other renowned competent Muslim jurists. See Ibid., 6–7; Hamid Khan, *Practitioner's Guide: Islamic Law* (International Network to Promote the Rule of Law, 2013).
[48] Hallaq, 'Was the Gate of Ijitihad Closed?' (n 46) 6; Khan, *Practitioner's Guide: Islamic Law* (n 47) 24.
[49] Mamoud Munes Tomeh, 'Persuasion and Authority in Islamic Law', *Berkeley Journal Middle East & Islamic Law* (2010) 3, 141–71, 143.
[50] Khan, *Practitioner's Guide: Islamic Law* (n 47) 21.
[51] Ibid., 23.

a precedent interpretation that enjoys the consensus of the renowned Muslim jurists' (referred to in Islamic law as *Ijma*) on a given topic, then the following steps must be observed. Firstly, one should look into the *Quran, Sunnah*, and *Ijma* for a legal reasoning given on a similar topic which can lend itself to the new topic.[52] Secondly, the Jurist should apply *Qiyas* or analogical reasoning to reach to the needed 'correct' interpretation.[53] Needless to say, the interpretation produced by such process should not contradict by any means the dictates of Islamic law as stated in the *Quran, Sunnah*, and *Ijma*.

Usul al-Fiqh, since its inception, proved to be a very useful, precise, and highly technical interpretive method, yet its strict adherence to the language and textual interpretation of the primary Islamic sources led to its failure to take into account broader philosophical and contextual considerations, which are often not explicitly spelled out by the dictates of the text.[54] In response to this flagrant deficiency, *Maqasid Al-Sharia* as an interpretive method was evolved to fill in the gap or, more precisely, to complement the already widely accepted *Usul Al-Fiqh*.[55] *Maqasid Al-Sharia* is best understood as an interpretative method used to ensure that the juristic interpretations remain consistent to the overarching objectives of Islamic law.[56] According to this method, jurists are required, while looking into the legal reasoning of any given text, to consider the object and purpose of the text, in addition to the causes and circumstances surrounding its revelation.[57] The rationale behind developing such interpretive methods, as cogently put by Khan, 'was that the sources, while divine in origin, were intrinsically responsive to the plight of the people for whom the knowledge was revealed; inspection of the circumstances surrounding the revelation—and not just of the text itself—would help reveal the intent of the Divine Author'.[58]

Al-Dawoody, in line with these two interpretive methods, argued that the Quranic verses related to the notion of Jihad 'must be read in their sociopolitical

[52] Hallaq, 'Was the Gate of Ijitihad Closed?' (n 46) 4.

[53] Ibid. p.5 (To apply *Qiyas*, four elements should exist: an original subject *'asl'*; a new subject *'far'*; a common cause in both *'illa'* and a rule derived from *Qiyas 'hukm'*). See Chapter 1, Section 1.ii.

[54] Khan, *Practitioner's Guide: Islamic Law* (n 47) 38–9.

[55] Ibid.

[56] 'Early *maqasid* proponents argued that, based on a close inspection of the sources, Islamic law had five general goals: the protection of faith, intellect, lineage, property, and, perhaps most fundamental, the protection of life. Later, a sixth would be added: the protection of honor ... By the early twentieth century, *maqasid* proponents argued that the sources reflected a broad array of goals, including fulfilling contracts, sincerity, moral trustworthiness, social welfare support, human dignity, freedom, fundamental rights, economic development, and research and development in science and technology.' Ibid.

[57] Ibid.

[58] Ibid.

and linguistic context'.[59] Further, he explained that this requires Muslim jurists to define the meaning of the words and the identity of the rule addressees (i.e. the warring parties). Additionally, it is vital to reconstruct the situation in which the parties involved instigated war, including the justifications for the initiation of a particular act.[60] Having said that, it must be noted that the argument that calls for combining these two interpretive methods—the textual and the contextual—as the most appropriate approach for interpreting any given text is equally valid and compelling under Islamic law and international law. Many international law lawyers argue along the same lines. Bianchi, for instance, affirmed that the plain meaning of the text cannot be ruled out as a text might have clear meaning that goes without saying.[61] Yet he further highlighted that such 'plain meaning is not the product of linguistic analysis but rather of context, broadly understood'.[62] This context, in his view, includes not only a set of circumstances that are external to the interpreter but also the interpreter's internal context, namely their past experience, the knowledge one has of the domain, and his/her presuppositions.[63] He argues that this internal context creates 'a communicational structure which allows the interpreter to dispel the ambiguities surrounding the text—or, even, not to notice them at all'.[64]

When examining the authenticity of controversial interpretations of Islamic law in light of the aforementioned interpretive method(s), this approach might help the reader to understand the circumstances surrounding the emergence of such interpretations. Also, it elucidates the interpreters' motivational strategies and intentions, and ultimately the eligibility for such interpretation to be considered 'correct'. This approach encourages and engages the readers or the recipients of the interpretation to undertake a critical reading and analytical exercise. It invites them to ask as many questions as they possibly can, not only regarding 'what' and 'how' but also regarding 'who', 'when', and 'where'. To put it simply, historical texts—sacred or not, and characters and events—holy as they

[59] See Chapter 2, Section 4.

[60] Ibid.

[61] Andrea Bianchi, 'Textual Interpretation and (International) Law Reading: The Myth of (in) Determinacy and the Genealogy of Meaning' in P. Bekker (ed.), *Making Transnational Law Work in the Global Economy—Essays in Honour of Detlev Vagts* (Cambridge: Cambridge University Press, 2010) 34–56; P. Bekker P. Bekker (ed.), *Making Transnational Law Work in the Global Economy—Essays in Honour of Detlev Vagts* (Cambridge: Cambridge University Press, 2010) 41. Available at: SSRN: https://ssrn.com/abstract=1732001 (last accessed 25 May 2019).

[62] Bianchi, 'Textual Interpretation and (International) Law Reading' (n 61).

[63] Ibid.

[64] Ibid.

may be, should be questioned and examined in their context and 'in light of the social and linguistic structure in place at the time'.[65]

For the sake of elaboration, if we take the example of Qutb's interpretation of the meaning of the term *fitnah*, since it was picked up by several Islamic Jihadist groups, one must attempt to ask a number of questions before reaching any conclusion with regard to the authenticity of such interpretations. Some of these questions are: is this interpretation in line with the overall objective and purpose of Islamic law? Does it contradict any other Islamic law injunctions? What was the reaction of the renowned Muslim jurists at the time? Did he follow the sanctioned interpretive methods of Islamic law interpretation? Is he a qualified jurist or a *Mujtihad*? Who is Qutb? What is his educational background? Where did he study? What was his experience in his scholarly mission in the United States in 1948? Why are some people so influenced by his writings? What posts did he occupy in Egypt? What was his relationship with the Free-Officers and President Gamal Abd-Al-Nasser before and after 1952? When did he join the Muslim Brotherhood? What was the *modus operandi* of this group at the time? Why was he arrested in 1954? What was his experience in his first ten years in jail? What did he write while in jail? Why was he re-arrested, prosecuted, and hanged one year after his release? How did his writings affect many Jihadists across the Muslim world? Who are they? Is there any common denominator between them? These as well as many other questions come to mind.

There are dozens of research studies conducted in the East and West on the biography and ideology of Qutb which might help whoever is interested in arriving at particular answers to these questions.[66] Yet this was never the purpose of this research. If there is one thing that I am sure of it is the fact that I am not interested, at least for now, in arguing for or against one interpretation or

[65] Bianchi, *International Law Theories* (n 7) 180.

[66] See, e.g., Adnan A. Musallam, *From Secularism to Jihad: Sayyid Qutb and the Foundations of Radical Islamism* (Westport, CT: Praeger, 2005); James Toth, *Sayyid Qutb: The Life and Legacy of a Radical Islamic Intellectual* (Oxford: Oxford University Press, 2013); Charles Tripp, 'Sayyid Qutb: The Political Vision' in Ali Rahnema (ed.), *Pioneers of Islamic Revival* (London: Zed Books, 1994) 154–83; Ahmad S. Mousalli, *Radical Islamic Fundamentalism: The Ideological and Political Discourse of Sayyid Qutb* (Beirut: American University of Beirut, 1992); Sayed Khatab, *The Power of Sovereignty: The Political and Ideological Philosophy of Sayyid Qutb* (New York, NY: Routledge, 2006); Sayed Khatab, *The Political Thought of Sayyid Qutb: The Theory of Jahiliyyah* (London: Routledge, 2006); John Calvert, *Sayyid Qutb and the Origins of Radical Islamism* (New York, NY: Columbia University Press, 2010); Muhammad Hafiz Diyab, *Sayyid Quṭb: Al-Khitāb wa al-Aydiyūlūjiyāh* (Sayyid Qutb: Discourse and Ideology) (Cairo: Dar al-Thaqafa al-Jadida, 1987); ʿAdil Hamuda, *Sayyid Quṭb: Min al-Qarya ila al-Misnaqa; Tahqīq wathāʿiqī* (Sayyid Qutb: From the Village to the Gallows; A Documentary Study) (Cairo: Sina li-l-Nashr, 1987); Salah ʿAbd al-Fattah al-Khalidi, *Sayyid Quṭb, Al-Shahīd al-Ḥayy* (Amman: Maktabat Al-Aqsa, 1981); Salah ʿAbd al-Fattah al-Khalidi, *Sayyid Quṭb: Min al-Mīlād ila al-istishhād* (Sayyid Qutb: From birth to martyrdom) (n.p., 1991).

another. That being said, the reason I wrote these lines is merely to point out that there is a problem within Islamic law interpretations and that this problem is costing us innocent lives day after day. This is mainly due to the fact that some of the rules of Jihad under Islamic law lack coherency and consistency, and that the Islamic religious establishment has historically failed and is still failing to solve this problem. Bassiouni, in the same vein, writes:

> [T]he contemporary politicization of Jihad is due in part to the absence of a coherent and authoritative doctrinal body of interpretation on the subject. Credible secular Muslim scholars have also failed to counterbalance the views of politically and economically motivated clerics with reform notions of Jihad. As result, Jihad as political violence has become nothing more than a revolutionary doctrine to justify those who engage in it by appealing to the legitimacy of their self-proclaimed ends.[67]

4. The Way Forward: An Integrated Approach

Having said that, what is an international lawyer, who wishes to promote compliance with international law, to make of Islamic law? Is there any benefit to a partnership between international law and Islamic law? Would it be of any use to armed conflicts where Islamic Jihadist groups are involved? Is it worth it? Is it not too risky to open the door to Islamic law to legitimize its rules—at least morally—and possibly allow its 'dark' side to invade the international legal system in the future? Is it not safer to distance our discipline from any further complexities brought in by Islamic law? Is it not a double-edged sword?[68] One must admit that yes, there are hundreds of reasonable concerns and valid reasons for international lawyers to hesitate to walk down this road, yet this does not refute the fact that Islamic Jihadist groups exist and are evidently dominant parties in many armed conflicts that are taking place in the world today. This will also not refute our deliberate incapacity to respond to such growing phenomena with the limited traditional legal tools we are trained to use. The Islamic Jihadist groups, exclusively, use and misuse Islamic law as they deem necessary and convenient to justify their military operations and political goals, on a daily basis. They openly negate any authority of international

[67] Bassiouni, 'Evolving Approaches to Jihad' (n 40) 121.

[68] Carolyn Evans, 'The Double-Edged Sword: Religious Influences on International Humanitarian Law', *Melbourne Journal of International Law* (2005) 6, 1–32.

law rules and principles over their combat actions. We must admit that international law has very little to offer in this regard. Despite the canons of the UNSC Resolutions and counterterrorism domestic legislation, it is evident that the one-way security/military response of states to Islamic Jihadism has not been—at least sufficiently—efficient and it is unlikely to be in the future. After the US-led campaign against *Al-Qaeda* in the context of the so-called global war on terror, many expected—or rather wished—that Islamic Jihadist groups would disappear, only to watch them growing stronger and more organized twelve years later, not to speak of the many IHL and IHRL rules that had to be compromised under the dust of the process. My concern here is that amidst all these ideological battles, there are many victims, mainly civilians, who pay the highest price for our reluctance to engage with other more well-equipped disciplines. The question that we should ask ourselves sooner than later is, shall we take any pragmatic steps to reach the very objective of the laws of war or shall we stand still to protect the legitimacy of our discipline while its apparent shortcomings in this particular context are brought to light? The damage that is done in the name of the religion of Islam can only be countered by a pragmatic partnership between people of good will working together from both Islamic law and international law perspectives.[69] In this research, I argued that there is much common ground and many areas in which a partnership—even a cautious, limited one—could prove beneficial to both.[70] A partnership that emphasize those areas where both laws share common humanistic values, while working faithfully together on adjusting our areas of differences, without downplaying any of them. If we walk along this road and we do not find any fruits on the other side, we can proudly say that we tried.

In the coming pages, I will envisage with the reader the main pillars of the proposed partnership, or what I will call from now on the integrated approach. The rationale behind adopting this approach is to attempt to create a pragmatic humanistic legal formula, inspired by the common values of international law and Islamic law, which could be used by international lawyers, international organizations, and states' lawyers and policy-makers to bolster the compliance and commitment of Islamic Jihadists groups to the laws of war.

While researchers who seek a partnership between the two disciplines are often warned and advised neither to let one discipline swallow the other nor to trade on its prestige and vocabularies,[71] that is exactly what I am willing to do.

[69] Ibid.
[70] Ibid.
[71] Bianchi, *International Law Theories* (n 7) 11.

I want international law, as the dominant *lingua franca* of states, to accommodate and digest the rules and language of Islamic law within its legal system in order to reach our pursued objective. It is, mainly, an integration process. Now, the question is: how can this possibly be done without crossing any redlines in either discipline? In this research, I argue that the success of this integrated approach is based on four main pillars: (i) approaching the Islamic Jihadist groups by engaging them in a legal discussion (Islamic law and international law) through one of the three provided forms of consent ('special agreements', unilateral declarations, or internal codes of conducts); (ii) negotiating with states with regard to granting any concessions related to the criminal punishments (amnesty, combatant like privilege, or punishment reductions); (iii) finding an appropriate intermediary (the International Committee of the Red Cross (ICRC) or any other impartial body) that is capable of coordinating the political, logistical and technical aspects of the process; and (iv) mobilizing third states that have influence on Islamic Jihadists groups to encourage them to comply with the law. It should be noted that while these pillars are not mutually exclusive, it is important to stress the fact that they are not mutually inclusive either. As such, it is possible for one or the other to find success regardless of the progress made on the other fronts.

(i) The Consent of the Islamic Jihadist Groups

The first thing to be realized, at the outset of this integration process, is the fact that any sort of integration that is processed without the involvement of the concerned state(s) and the Islamic Jihadist group(s) is doomed to fail. This means that any theoretical efforts conducted between 'irrelevant' international lawyers and 'moderate' Muslim jurists, who do not belong to the group(s) or at least share their ideology, will only be useful as a first step,[72] yet it is not what we are looking for in this process. As any basic negotiation manual would dictate, the most efficient method to secure commitment to implementation of an agreed outcome is 'to ensure that all parties feel a sense of ownership of the final agreement'.[73] In other words, to get the 'buy-in' of all stakeholders,

[72] It might be an important step to explore the scope of interaction between international law and Islamic law, yet neither the state nor the Islamic Jihadists groups will feel any sense of ownership with such initiatives and thus it is very unlikely that they will bound themselves to any of its outcomes.

[73] UN Office for the Coordination of Humanitarian Affairs, Gerard McHug, and Manuel Bessier, 'Humanitarian Negotiations with Armed Groups, A Manual for Practitioners' (New York, 2006). Available at: <https://www.unocha.org/sites/unocha/files/HumanitarianNegotiationswArmedGroupsManual.pdf> (last accessed 25 May 2019).

including those that may not be represented directly at the negotiating table, is of extreme significance to the success of the process.[74]

Having said that, it is often reiterated that international law is based on the notion of state consent.[75] As a result, states' international legal obligations are overwhelmingly based on their consent to be bound by its rules.[76] This is not the case, however, with respect to non-state armed groups, which are often, if not always, the enemy of the state that holds the upper hand when it comes to the making and development of national and international laws.[77] They are mainly perceived by states as individuals over whom the state seeks to maintain iron control by imposing its domestic laws and international law, if relevant, on the territory on which these individuals operate.[78] International law, as it is today, does not give non-state armed groups any say with regard to the making or applicability of the rules to which they are bound. For example, if an Islamic Jihadist group is a party to a non-international armed conflict, the group is legally bound to comply with the relevant IHL rules, regardless of their consent.[79] However, this lack of consent is one of the main reasons why many armed groups, as argued elsewhere, reject the fact that they are bound by international law obligations. For them, these rules have been drafted and ratified by states with which they had significant disagreements, to say the least. Thus, one of the main motives behind this integration process is to delicately try to grant the Islamic Jihadist groups an opportunity to express their consent to be bound by international law, something that, once again, is not provided for in existing treaty law. The hope is that undertaking this initiative will increase the possibility of compliance and dissemination of international law rules by the Islamic Jihadist groups, and offer a unique opportunity of engagements with these group(s) on issues related to the protection of victims of armed conflicts under their control.

In this respect, this research argues that the consent of the Islamic Jihadist groups to be bound by international law rules could take one of three forms: (i) signing a 'special agreement' between the group(s) and the state(s); (ii) providing a unilateral declaration by the groups of their commitment to comply

[74] Ibid.

[75] Andrew Guzman, 'The Consent Problem in International Law', *Working Paper Series, Berkeley Program in Law and Economics* (2011) 1–63. Available at: <https://escholarship.org/content/qt04x8x174/qt04x8x174.pdf> (last accessed 25 May 2019).

[76] Ibid.

[77] Zakaria Dabone, 'International Law: Armed Groups in a State-centric System', *International Review of the Red Cross* (2011) 93(882), 395–424, 397.

[78] Ibid.

[79] Common Article 3 to the Geneva Convention; Article 1, AP II. For details about the criteria of the non-state armed groups subject to the application of these Articles, see Chapter 3.

with international law rules; or (iii) adopting an internal code of conduct incorporating international law rules.[80] These forms of consent, however, are to be considered in light of the dictates of the last paragraph of Common Article 3, which provides that the application of the Convention in cases of non-international armed conflict (which is mainly the context in which these groups operate) 'shall not affect the legal status' of the non-state armed groups by any means.[81] In other words, it confirms that while IHL provides for equal rights and obligations of the parties to the conflict with regard to the treatment of people in their power, this does not confer any specific recognition or legitimacy by the *de jure* government on the Islamic Jihadist groups that are parties to a conflict.[82] Accordingly, any consent expressed by the Islamic Jihadist groups to be bound by any IHL norm is to be considered merely for humanitarian reasons and does not add to the legitimacy or the legal authority of the groups in any way. It is also worth mentioning, in this regard, that IHL applies if and when the conditions for its applicability are met,[83] regardless of the qualification of the members of the Islamic Jihadist groups as 'terrorists' or its actions as 'terrorist'.[84] Thus, seeking the groups' consent in order to enhance their compliance with IHL rules should not be affected by the fact that they are labelled as 'terrorist' either. To put it simply for states' lawyers, who are often concerned about these two particular elements, engaging with terrorist groups to induce compliance with international law rules, in the context of armed conflicts, will neither give them legitimacy nor would it strip them from their label as 'terrorists' under national and international law rules.

The first form of consent by Islamic Jihadist groups could be acquired by entering into a 'special agreement' with the state, provided for in Common Article 3.[85] Through such agreements the parties to a non-international armed conflict may make an explicit commitment to comply with a broader range of IHL rules, beyond the obligations embodied in Common Article 3 and in other rules applicable in non-international armed conflicts. The purpose of such agreements is to agree on a more comprehensive set of norms

[80] ICRC, 'Improving Compliance with International Humanitarian Law', ICRC Expert Seminars, October 2003, 21.

[81] Common Article 3 (2) to the Geneva Conventions: 'The application of the preceding provisions shall not affect the legal status of the Parties to the conflict'.

[82] ICRC, Commentaries of Common Article 3, paras 863–865.Available at: <https://ihl-databases.icrc.org/applic/ihl/ihl.nsf/Comment.xsp?action=openDocument&documentId=59F6CDFA490736C1C1257F7D004BA0EC#_Toc465169955> (last accessed 25 May 2019).

[83] For more information about the criteria of classification of armed conflicts, see Chapter 3.

[84] Ibid., para. 867.

[85] 'The Parties to the conflict should further endeavor to bring into force, by means of special agreements, all or part of the other provisions of the present Convention'. See Common Article 3.

that protect the victims of armed conflicts. This may include IHL rules applicable to international armed conflicts, weapons' conventions, customary IHL, and IHRL rules.[86] I would also argue here that there is no rule or reasonable reason under international law that would dictate that Islamic law rules, which do not contradict the international law applicable rules, should not be included in such 'special agreements'. For example, the rules related to the dead body management in armed conflicts, which are known to be more comprehensive and context-specific under Islamic law, could be considered for this purpose.[87]

One of the benefits of such agreements is the fact that the achieved mutual consent by the two parties would add an automatic incentive to the Islamic Jihadist groups to comply with the agreement. As such, agreements reassure the groups—and the states—that they are equal before the law. Additional benefits of these special agreements go beyond the content of the agreements themselves. For instance, the idea of bringing the two parties to the conflict to the negotiation table to discuss an IHL-related agreement might open the door to parallel agreements, such as ceasefire or peace agreements or any similar initiatives to conclude the hostilities altogether.[88] Here, I find it worth highlighting that despite the states' overwhelming hesitancy to enter into such agreements with non-state armed groups, either because they refuse to acknowledge armed groups as party to the conflict or because they refuse to classify the conflict as a non-international armed conflict, many 'special agreements' have been concluded in this regard, whether between a non-state armed group and the state against which it is engaged in hostilities or between two non-state armed groups fighting one another.[89]

Where a 'special agreement' cannot be reached, the second form of consent by Islamic Jihadist groups could be acquired by a unilateral declaration in

[86] ICRC, Commentaries of Common Article 3, para. 846.

[87] For detailed information about the subject of the management of the dead from Islamic law perspective, see Ahmed Al-Dawoody, 'Management of the Dead from the Islamic Law and International Humanitarian Law Perspectives: Considerations for Humanitarian Forensics', *International Review of the Red Cross* (2017) 99, 759–84.

[88] These parallel agreements, whether 'a peace agreement, ceasefire or other accord may also constitute a special agreement for the purposes of common Article 3, or a means to implement common Article 3, if it contains clauses that bring into existence further obligations drawn from the Geneva Conventions and/or their Additional Protocols'. See ICRC, Commentaries of Common Article 3, para. 850.

[89] Examples include the agreements concluded between the Parties to the armed conflicts in the former Yugoslavia in the 1990s to bring many provisions of the Geneva Conventions and some provisions of the Additional Protocols into force; he Humanitarian Exchange Accord between the *Fuerzas Armadas Revolucionarias de Colombia* (FARC) and the government of Colombia, concluded in 2001; the Humanitarian Cease Fire Agreement on the Conflict in Darfur, concluded in 2004; the Ceasefire Code of Conduct between the Government of Nepal and CPN (Maoist), concluded in 2006; and the Comprehensive Agreement on Respect for Human Rights and IHL in the Philippines, concluded in 1998. See ICRC, Commentaries of Common Article 3, para. 849.

which a group declares its commitment to comply with international law rules. The purpose of such declarations is to provide a self-disciplining mechanism for the group, in particular where the group is concerned about its public image and reputation.[90] Although there might be a risk that unilateral declarations might be made only as a political gesture by the group, they could still serve a 'positive function as an additional tool of leverage to encourage compliance' with international law rules.[91] Some international organization have successfully pursued such declarations with non-state armed groups.[92] Geneva Call (a non-governmental organization) took this matter to a completely different level.[93] Geneva Call developed a mechanism known as a 'Deed of Commitment' that allows non-state armed groups to pledge respect to specific international law norms and be held publicly accountable for their commitments.[94] At the time of writing, three Deeds of Commitment have been developed, namely a Deed of Commitment for Adherence to a Total Ban on Anti-Personnel Mines and for Cooperation in Mine Action (2000); a Deed of Commitment for the Protection of Children from the Effects of Armed Conflict (2010); and a Deed of Commitment for the Prohibition of Sexual Violence in Situations of Armed Conflict and towards the Elimination of Gender Discrimination (2012).[95] The three Deeds are drafted in line with international law standards. The Deeds of Commitment are often signed by the leadership of the non-state armed group and countersigned by Geneva Call and the Government of the Republic and Canton of Geneva.[96] The signed documents are deposited with the Canton of Geneva, which serves as custodian of the Deeds of Commitment.[97] Today, many non-state armed groups have signed these instruments.[98] In this regard,

[90] ICRC, 'Improving Compliance with International Humanitarian Law' (Background Paper prepared for Informal High-Level Expert Meeting on Current Challenges to International Humanitarian Law), *Humanitarian Policy and Conflict Research*, 25–27 June 2004, 7. Available at:<https://www.icrc.org/en/doc/assets/files/other/improving_compliance_with_international_humanitarian_law.pdf> (last accessed 25 May 2019).

[91] Ibid.

[92] For example, a faction of the Sudan Liberation Army signed an 'action plan' with UNICEF in which it 'pledged to end recruitment and release all children under the age of 18'. The UN Office of the Special Representative of the Secretary-General for Children and Armed Conflict has signed such 'action plans' with a number of other non-state armed groups and states to prevent and/or halt the use or recruitment of children in armed conflicts.

[93] 'Geneva Call is a neutral and impartial non-governmental organization dedicated to promoting respect by armed non-State actors (ANSAs) for international humanitarian norms in armed conflict and other situations of violence, in particular those related to the protection of civilians'. See Geneva Call website: <https://genevacall.org/who-we-are/> (last accessed 25 May 2019).

[94] Geneva Call, 'Deed of Commitment'. Available at: <https://genevacall.org/how-we-work/deed-of-commitment/> (last accessed 25 May 2019).

[95] Ibid.

[96] Ibid.

[97] Ibid.

[98] To date, fifty-two groups have signed the Deed of Commitment banning AP mines, twenty-six have signed the Deed of Commitment protecting children in armed conflict, and twenty-four have

as well, I would not see any valid reason that would prevent us from considering to integrate compatible Islamic law language while negotiating and drafting these instruments.

If neither a 'special agreement' nor a unilateral declaration is attainable, the third form of consent by Islamic Jihadist groups could be acquired by adopting an internal code of conduct incorporating international law rules. The term 'code of conduct' is commonly defined as documents that, 'albeit different in length and form, contain at their core lists of rules and responsibilities that armed groups' hierarchies set out for their members. These rules aim to regulate both the members' internal behavior and their relations outside the group.'[99] Despite the fact that this form of consent is less formal than the two previous ones, the impact of such a form might be greater in terms of the implementation of international law norms by the armed group, and thus more directly impact their training and dissemination.[100] These codes of conduct often refer to normative IHL or IHRL rules or other social and ethical principles.[101] These rules mainly have the advantage of being short and simple texts.[102] They also 'provide an important glimpse into the ideological and organizational structure of an armed group, its chain of command, and the rights and obligations that the hierarchy of the armed group chooses to bestow on its members'.[103] The willingness of an armed group to include international law provisions in a code of conduct could also be made public in order to encourage the group to comply with the content of their commitment.[104] In many instances, the perceived deterrent value of punishment for violations of rules stipulated by the group itself may be more effective than the threat of any other external prosecution imposed by the state or international mechanisms.[105]

signed the Deed of Commitment prohibiting sexual violence and gender discrimination. Ibid. For the list of non-state armed groups that are engaged by Geneva Call, see Geneva Call, 'Armed Non-State Actors'. Available at: <https://genevacall.org/how-we-work/armed-non-state-actors/> (last accessed 25 May 2019).

[99] ICRC, 'A Collection of Codes of Conduct Issued by Armed Groups' (2011) 93(882), 484, Available at: <https://international-review.icrc.org/sites/default/files/irrc-882-codes-conduct.pdf> (last accessed 25 May 2019).

[100] ICRC, 'Improving Compliance with International Humanitarian Law' (n 90) 7.

[101] ICRC, 'A Collection of Codes of Conduct Issued by Armed Groups' (n 99).

[102] Ibid., 485.

[103] ICRC, 'Improving Compliance with International Humanitarian Law' (n 90) 483.

[104] Ibid.

[105] Ibid., 486.

(ii) The Domestic Criminal Punishments: States' Concessions

While the consent of states is essential to conclude a 'special agreement' with an armed group, it is not necessary for neither the group's unilateral declaration nor its adoption of a code of conduct. In this regard, however, it is recommended that states are kept informed about any initiatives undertaken by armed groups that operate on their territories, as states can play a key role in incentivizing the armed groups to comply with the law. Unquestionably, states hold the most significant card on the negotiation table, namely: criminal punishment. As previously discussed, armed groups often lack sufficient incentive to abide by IHL, as they are aware that they will be equally punished if captured by the state whether they fought according to IHL or not.[106] Since states' domestic laws, anyway, criminalize taking up of arms against the government, regardless of the respect of IHL by the arms' carrier. Changing this reality, however, or at least mitigating it, might have a great impact on the compliance of armed groups with international law rules. This is an area in which serious negotiations have to be undertaken in order for governments to cooperate. This cooperation would be also in line with Article 6(5) of the Second Additional Protocol, encouraging states to grant amnesties to former fighters for direct participation in the hostilities. One must admit, however, that the fact that this amnesty comes only at the end of hostilities does not help with the armed groups' compliance to the law during the hostilities as much as it helps and facilitates the peace-building process.

Having said that, what could be more effective is to link a state's proposed grant of amnesty to an express commitment by the armed group to comply with IHL.[107] This can be negotiated either directly between the two parties to the conflict during the 'special agreement' conclusion process or indirectly within the processes of enacting unilateral declarations or internal codes of conduct. To put it simply, during the negotiation processes, states can make a grant of amnesty contingent upon the armed group's commitment to and subsequent compliance with IHL. Through this, the members of the armed groups are given the necessary guarantees, according to which they might be more willing to commit themselves to abide by IHL rules. At the end of the day, it is a states' civilian population, wounded soldiers, infrastructure, and so on that will be spared if such groups respect the laws of war. States, in case of 'special agreements', could possibly put this proposal on the negotiation table themselves,

[106] See Chapter 4, Section 5.
[107] ICRC, 'Improving Compliance with International Humanitarian Law' (n 90) 6.

while in the other two forms of armed groups' consent, they can pass it through intermediaries, such as Geneva Call with regard to the unilateral declaration mechanisms, or the ICRC, or any other organization involved in these sort of processes, including the drafting of internal codes of conduct.

While granting amnesty is the most appealing proposal for armed groups, it is not the only option. States could also consider the possibility of granting members of armed groups some sort of 'combatant-like' status if they fulfil certain conditions.[108] For example, such conditions could be borrowed from the IHL rules applicable in international armed conflict, such as carrying arms openly, having a fixed distinctive sign recognizable at a distance, respecting IHL, and so forth.[109] With such status, members of armed groups will not be prosecuted for their mere participation in hostilities or for acts that are conducted in line with the rules of IHL applicable in non-international armed conflict. In other words, the acts that are not prohibited under international law would also not be prohibited under domestic law. Last but not least, states might also consider a reduction of punishment in cases of compliance with IHL during the conflict.[110] Accordingly, during the prosecution process of the armed groups' members, the court could take the respect levels of IHL rules into consideration when deciding upon the appropriate sanctions or sentences.[111] Yet again, for these proposals to be effective in impacting IHL compliance by armed groups, the states' willingness to link amnesties with compliance to IHL is vital. In other words, granting the members of the groups 'combatant-like' status or a reduction in punishment, and compliance by the armed groups to IHL should be announced during, or prior to the end of the conflict.

(iii) An Appropriate Intermediary: The Dialogue of Integration

Now that we have tackled the procedural aspects related to the consent of the Islamic Jihadist groups to comply with the law, in addition to the concessions that states could propose in this regard, I find it significant to highlight how the substantial aspects of the integration process would be undertaken. It is submitted that the extremely heated and polarized political climate that surrounds the conflicts that involve Islamic Jihadist groups makes it very unlikely

[108] Ibid., 5.
[109] Ibid.
[110] Ibid.
[111] Ibid.

that states or armed groups would initiate any such contact. Even if this were to happen for one reason or another, their political disagreement is most likely to strike down the process before it starts. Therefore, in my view, the success of the pursued integration process stands, *inter alia*, on a main cardinal pillar; namely, having a neutral intermediary that safeguards the entire process. This neutral intermediary must be accepted by the armed group as well as the state in which the group operates. It should also be able to initiate contacts with the parties to the conflict to explore their interests; identify clear objectives of the process and the margin the drafters have for negotiations; ensure the parties' inclusiveness throughout the drafting process; and guarantee that the drafted instrument is in line with international law rules.

To this end, Common Article 3 suggests that an impartial humanitarian body, such as the ICRC, may offer its services to facilitate the application of the provided protections.[112] Among these protection services are ones that require parties to the conflict to cease or prevent the occurrence (or recurrence) of any violations of the norms applicable to them,[113] which includes assisting the parties to the conflict in the conclusion and implementation of 'special agreements'.[114] It is worth mentioning here that this offer of service may not be regarded as 'an unfriendly act nor as an unlawful interference in a State's domestic affairs in general or in the conflict in particular'.[115]

Having said that, despite the fact that the ICRC was mentioned in Common Article 3 by way of example only, I believe that the ICRC is among a very few existing humanitarian organizations—if not the only one—that has the legal, political, and technical capacities to play such a delicate intermediary role. The specific legal status, privileges, and immunities that are granted to the ICRC by states in order to enable the organization to carry out its mandate in armed conflicts, places it, operationally, in an advantageous position compared with other equally impartial humanitarian bodies.[116] The ICRC, today, is effectively

[112] Common Article 3, GC IV.
[113] ICRC, Commentaries of Common Article 3, para. 816.
[114] Ibid., para. 859.
[115] Ibid., para. 804.
[116] 'Adequate legal capacity and privileges and immunities allow the ICRC to protect and assist victims of armed conflict and other situations of violence in a timely and efficient manner, tailored to their immediate needs. They enable the ICRC to fully live up to its Fundamental Principles of neutrality, independence and impartiality and its commitment to a confidential bilateral dialogue with those concerned. As such, they contribute significantly to the ICRC's capacity to ensure better respect for international humanitarian law and to act as a neutral intermediary between parties to armed conflicts, as well as to the ICRC's access and proximity to victims and to the security of its staff on the ground.' For more details about the ICRC legal status, privileges, and immunities, see Els Debuf, 'Tools to Do the Job: The ICRC's Legal Status, Privileges and Immunities', *International Review of the Red Cross* (2016) 97(897/898), 319–44.

delivering humanitarian assistance in most of the conflict zones where Islamic Jihadist groups operate. As commonly known, the ICRC seeks dialogue with all the parties in a given situation of armed conflict, including non-state armed groups, as well as with the people suffering the consequences, in order to gain their acceptance and respect.[117] This approach generally gives the ICRC the widest possible access both to the victims and to the parties involved in the conflict.[118] Moreover, the ICRC's exceptional expertise on IHL and long-standing experience on treaties and 'special agreements' negotiations[119] is another reason for favouring it to take up this intermediary role. Last but not least, the ICRC, in the last two decades, developed robust collaborations with prominent Islamic institutions and scholars in the Muslim world.[120] The purpose of such collaboration is to explore the common humanitarian grounds between Islamic law and international law, with the purpose of making use of the Islamic precepts in generating greater respect for the essential humanitarian rules in war.[121] While it is too early to measure the level of success of the ICRC's approach in this regard, one can observe that it has significantly contributed in overcoming misperceptions on both sides and creating a constructive dialogue with various warring parties across the world.[122]

Accordingly, the ICRC stands in a unique position to play such a critical role in armed conflicts taking place in the world today, particularly where Islamic Jihadist groups are involved. This position, however, is not intended to rule out the fact that any other impartial body might be capable of playing the same role if supported by the international community and the relevant state and armed group, for example the UN Assistance Mission in Afghanistan or Geneva Call.[123] As previously elaborated, the pursued integration process

[117] Pierre Kraehenbuehl, 'The neutral intermediary role of the ICRC: at the heart of humanitarian action', *Interview*, 7 July 2008. Available at: <https://www.icrc.org/en/doc/resources/documents/interview/neutral-intermediary-interview-070708.htm> (last accessed 25 May 2019).

[118] Ibid.

[119] Bosnia and Herzegovina, Agreement No. 1 (1992 Agreement), 22 May 1992, *reproduced in*: M. Sassòli, A. Bouvier and A. Quintin, 'How Does Law Protect in War'.

[120] ICRC, 'Faith-based Organizations and Religious Leaders: Essential Partners in Humanitarian Action'. Available at: <https://www.icrc.org/en/document/faith-based-organizations-and-religious-leaders-essential-partners-humanitarian-action> (last accessed 25 May 2019); ICRC, 'First Global Expert Workshop on IHL and Islamic Law in Contemporary Armed Conflicts'. Available at: <https://www.icrc.org/en/document/first-global-expert-workshop-ihl-and-islamic-law-contemporary-armed-conflicts> (last accessed 25 May 2019).

[121] Omar Mekky, 'An Unwarranted Human Sacrifice in the Middle East', *Humanitarian Law and Policy* ICRC blog, 26 September 2016. Available at: <https://blogs.icrc.org/law-and-policy/2016/09/26/human-sacrifice-middle-east/> (last accessed 25 May 2019)

[122] Ibid.

[123] 'UNAMA is a political mission that provides political good offices in Afghanistan; works with and supports the government; supports the process of peace and reconciliation; monitors and promotes human rights and the protection of civilians in armed conflict; promotes good governance; and

is not about creating a new legal paradigm to govern these conflicts. On the contrary, it is about enhancing the existing applicable international law by integrating a new language to it that is more familiar to its recipient. No matter what the negotiated form of consent might be or the level of concessions agreed upon, once it is realized that there might be an interest by one concerned party or the other, the integration process should be initiated. A good start for this process is to unpack some of the most agreed upon international law rules in a simplified Islamic law language. It is an exercise similar to writing the commentaries of the Geneva Conventions and the Additional Protocols, yet this time in a context specific nature that is formulated in the language of Islamic law. The main aim of this exercise is to give people, the Jihadists in particular, an understanding of the law as it is interpreted in Islamic law, which should not contradict international law rules. For example, this unpacking process could be conducted by a joint committee of the ICRC legal advisers and Islamic law experts nominated by the armed group, in addition to other neutral competent Muslim jurists who can advise with regard to complex issues related to Islamic jurisprudence. States' representatives can also be present should there be a prior arrangement that the substance of this process might be translated into 'special agreement'.

An appropriate place to start would be the commentary on Common Article 3, which represents the minimum required standards that should be respected by the warring parties during non-international armed conflicts. As discussed in Chapter 3, most of the rights and obligations embodied in this article fall within the common area of intersection between Islamic law and international law.[124] However, the only part in this article that might invite different interpretations and disagreements is the notion of 'active' participation in hostilities, which is key to determine when a civilian becomes a lawful target under IHL. For instance, in one of the interviews of the late senior member of *Al-Qaeda* in the Arabian Peninsula, Anwar Al-Awlaki, while admitting that Muslims should distinguish between civilians and combatants, commented on the notion of active participation in hostilities, by saying that 'all American citizens are not to be considered civilians, as they predominantly voted for the current president who waged the war against us

encourages regional cooperation.' See United Nations Mission in Afghanistan, UNAMA Mandate. Available at: <https://unama.unmissions.org/mandate> (last accessed 25 May 2019).

124 For more details about the level of compatibility between IHL and Islamic law, particularly with regard to the protection of people and object, see Chapter 3.

[*Al-Qaeda*], despite the fact that they had other candidates who would have been more peaceful'.[125]

Here, in the same way that the ICRC enters into dialogue with states in the case of radical disagreement that might jeopardize the premises of the laws of war through the misinterpretation of any IHL concept by states, the ICRC should seek a dialogue with the Islamic Jihadist group to guide it to what international law says. In this dialogue, ICRC can cooperate with Muslim jurists who have credibility among the armed groups in order to convince them with an interpretation that is more in line with international law. At the end of the day, one must not forget that we are engaging in a pragmatic negotiation process with the ultimate goal of enhancing compliance of the Islamic Jihadist groups with the law. Thus, an 80 per cent outcome is better than a 50 per cent one, and both are better than nothing. This dialogue may further enable the ICRC, or any other institution that the international community would support to do the job, to discuss and perhaps integrate some rules and principles that have not been listed *per se* in Common Article 3, such as the principle of distinction and proportionality. It can also tackle issues related to means and methods of warfare, such as suicide bombings and the use of human shields. It can additionally be a solid base for an agreement with respect to humanitarian access to the frontlines and detention visits in the territories under the control of the armed group.

Once the unpacking process is done and the disagreements are settled to the greatest possible extent, the armed group can extract the rules and principles from the outcome instrument (the commentary-like document) in a way that is communicable to their fighters. This, in my opinion, is the most significant part in the process; to communicate the law to the rank and files of the Islamic Jihadist groups in a language that is comprehendible to them. It is for this reason that this study suggests that internal codes of conducts are more influential on the behaviours of combatants and armed groups' compliance with IHL than any other formal form of consent, such as unilateral declarations or 'special agreements', yet, of course, the best-case scenario would be to have them both. These codes of conduct can be as simple as verses from *Quran* or a prophetic *hadith* that reflect the following dos and don'ts: fight only combatants; attack only military targets; spare civilian persons and objects; respect the signs of the Red Cross and the Red Crescent; collect and care

[125] Fadel Soliman Response to Sheikh Anwar Al-Awlaki (which includes parts of Al-Awlaki's interview, YouTube Video, 5 June 2019. Available at: <https://www.youtube.com/watch?v=EgDotWRV Mhk> (last accessed 25 May 2019).

for the wounded enemy; hand them over to your superior or to the nearest medical personnel; respect medical personnel and facilities; treat the captured detainees humanely; respect civilians and treat them humanely; protect them against ill-treatment; vengeance and the taking of hostages are forbidden; and respect the civilian's property, do not damage or steal it.[126] Again, any disagreement on any of these basic humanitarian rules and principles, no matter how radical it might be, should not be a deal breaker. Our criteria in measuring the success or failure of this process should be tied to our objective. Every dos and don'ts included in these codes means more lives saved and properties spared.

(iv) The Role of Influential Third States

The last vector that might be of help for the success of this integrated approach is the role that could be played by the third states that have some sort of influence over the Islamic Jihadist groups. It is commonly known that 'no-one fights alone' today. Coalitions of states in various forms join their resources against common enemies in a number of battlefields, whether in Iraq, Syria, Libya, Yemen, or elsewhere.[127] States do not only support each other but they also support non-state armed groups, sometimes referred to as proxies, irregulars, or auxiliaries.[128] Such support takes place in variety of ways including financing, equipping, training, instructing, providing weapons and transport facilities, sharing intelligence and logistics, and evacuating and treating the armed groups' casualties.[129]

In this respect, aside from the international legal responsibility that states might bear on the basis of attribution for the conduct of non-state armed groups,[130] Common Article 1 of the Geneva Conventions provides that state parties 'undertake to respect and to ensure respect for the present Convention in all circumstances'.[131] This Article also applies with respect to the obligations

[126] ICRC, 'Improving Compliance with International Humanitarian Law' (n 90) 487–501.
[127] Cordula Droege and David Tuck, 'Fighting Together: Obligations and Opportunities in Partnered Warfare', *Humanitarian Law and Policy* ICRC blog, 27 March 2017. Available at: <https://medium.com/law-and-policy/fighting-together-obligations-and-opportunities-in-partnered-warfare-362c9dfb741a> (last accessed 25 May 2019).
[128] Ibid.; Belgin San-Akca, 'Dangerous Companions: Cooperation Between States and Non-State Armed Groups (NAGs)', *Koç University, Istanbul* (2015), 1–46. Available at: <https://www.armedgroups.net/publish/codebook-2015.pdf>.
[129] Ibid.
[130] 'The conduct of a person or group of persons shall be considered an act of a State under international law if the person or group of persons is in fact acting on the instructions of, or under the direction or control of, that State in carrying out the conduct.' See Article 8, DASR; Articles 5–11, DASR.
[131] Common Article 1 to the Geneva Conventions.

provided for in Common Article 3 in the context of non-international armed conflicts.[132]

Common Article 1 is generally interpreted to impose a responsibility on third States not to become involved in an armed conflict and to ensure respect for IHL by the parties to an armed conflict in two significant ways: first, by conferring a negative legal obligation on states to neither encourage a party to an armed conflict to violate IHL nor to take action that would assist in such violations; and second, by imposing a positive legal obligation on them to take appropriate steps, whether unilateral or collective, against parties to a conflict who are violating IHL, and in particular to intervene with states or armed groups over which they might have some influence to stop the violations.[133] This positive obligation, however, 'is one of due diligence, in order to avoid breaching it, states must make every lawful effort in their power, regardless of whether they attain the desired result or not'.[134] For that purpose, states can select among the different means at their disposal, with the exception of military intervention, which would only be lawful if undertaken in accordance with the UN Charter.[135] Among these means, those states that have any sort of influence on Islamic Jihadist groups can engage in 'confidential or discreet negotiations' with those groups to encourage them to respect IHL.[136] This could also include encouraging the groups to enter into agreements or dialogue with the intermediary in order to reach a common understanding on the applicable laws of war, under both Islamic and international law.[137]

Along the same lines, senior ICRC legal experts suggest a few concrete, non-exhaustive steps to be followed by supporting states in order to ensure

[132] In the same vein, the ICJ held, in the *Nicaragua* case, that the United States was 'under an obligation not to encourage persons or groups engaged in the conflict in Nicaragua to act in violation of the provisions of Article 3 common to the four 1949 Geneva Conventions'. See *Military and Paramilitary Activities in and against Nicaragua* (*Nicaragua v. United States of America*), ICJ Reports 1986, 14, para. 115; Similarly, according to DASR, 'a State which aids or assists another State in the commission of an internationally wrongful act by the latter is internationally responsible for doing so'; ILC, Draft Articles on Responsibility of States, Article 16.

[133] ICRC, 'Improving Compliance with International Humanitarian Law' (n 90) 2.

[134] Knut Dörmann and Jose Serralvo, 'Common Article 1 to the Geneva Conventions and the obligation to prevent international humanitarian law violations', *International Review of the Red Cross* (2014) 96(895–896), 707–36, 735.

[135] Ibid.

[136] ICRC, 'Improving Compliance with International Humanitarian Law' (n 90) 3.

[137] It is submitted that the international legal obligations embodied in Common Article 1 serve as the basis for Rule 144 identified in the ICRC CIHL study, which applies equally in international and non-international armed conflicts, that reads: 'States may not encourage violations of international humanitarian law by parties to an armed conflict. They must exert their influence, to the degree possible, to stop violations of international humanitarian law.' See Rule 144, 'ICRC CIHL Study'. Available at: <https://ihl-databases.icrc.org/customary-ihl/eng/docs/v1_rul_rule144#Fn_B1EF7BDE_00015> (last accessed 25 May 2019).

that non-state armed groups, as well as partnering states, respect IHL. These steps include: training and instructing the parties to armed conflict on IHL and other relevant laws and standards; monitoring their partners' conduct, including through joint, after-action reviews, and assisting them to develop and implement robust processes for accountability in case of serious violations of IHL; sharing and developing best practices and learning, as necessary, from one another's mistakes; and encouraging the parties to engage with neutral, impartial humanitarian organizations.[138] At this very moment, these suggestions are being developed by the ICRC as a fully fledged strategy, in the form of concrete recommendations, to be used in the operational dialogue with supporting states with the aim of reducing the humanitarian consequences of armed conflicts.

5. Conclusion

This chapter posed the main question of the research, namely whether or not fostering compliance by Islamic Jihadist groups to the laws of war is possible through integrating aspects of international law and Islamic law. In its humble attempt to respond to this question, the chapter examined the relevance and challenges of such a process of integration. It began by arguing that Islamic law plays a significant role in shaping the legal systems and behaviours of most of the Muslim states, if not all. It further affirmed that this role is multiplied when applied to the influence of Islamic law on the behaviours of Islamic Jihadist groups, which—as discussed—openly reject the applicability of the traditional rules of international law and exclusively cite instead self-interpreted Islamic law arguments to justify most of their daily combat-related actions. Therefore, this chapter suggested to benefit from the fact that the vast majority of the *jus ad bellum* and *jus in bello* rules under international law and Islamic law share the same morale, rationale, and underlying objectives, in order to build an integrated and pragmatic humanitarian formula which could be used by international lawyers and policy-makers to bolster the compliance by Islamic Jihadist groups to the laws of war.

This chapter also argued that the most challenging factor to the adoption of such an integrated approach between these two bodies of law is the complexity of their texts' interpretation processes. In particular, many of the Islamic law rules—similar to the international law ones—are ambiguous and

[138] Droege and Tuck, 'Fighting Together' (n 127).

indeterminate, which often lead to a diversification of legal interpretations and practices throughout Islamic history and will presumably continue to do so. This fact is exacerbated by the absence of any authoritative doctrinal body of interpretation on the subject in the Muslim world. Therefore, the most recognized interpretive methods, under Islamic law, that are frequently used by Muslim jurists to interpret any Islamic text—namely *Usul al-Fiqh* and *Maqasid Al-Sharia*—were extensively tackled in order to elaborate how rules are regularly extracted from detailed primary Islamic sources.

Finally, this chapter put forward the four main pillars of this integrated approach in order to build the pursued partnership between international law and Islamic law, as practical guidelines for those interested to apply it in relevant contemporary warfare.

Concluding Remarks

In today's world, the discussion on any topic related to 'Islamic Jihadism' is predominantly stuck in a dynamic whereby positions and assumptions confine most international lawyers and political analysts to 'Manichean logic of bipolarity, attack and defense, rise and fall, emergence and disappearance, us and them'.[1] States' rhetoric to dehumanize and demonize the members of Islamic Jihadist groups is as prevalent as ever.[2] Aside from very minimal work on countering violent extremism, the international community seems not to be very interested in exerting any effort to explore and/or engage with the ideological roots of such groups, in spite of the fact that the Islamic ideology, arguably, has the solution as it also, allegedly, has the problem.

Chapter 1 discussed the concept and sources of Islamic law, revealing that it is mostly a product of rational intellectual thinking that has been developed in different cultural environments throughout hundreds of years. It highlighted the historical and contextual evolution of the notion of Jihad from the 'Medinan ideal' state of Muhammad to the now collapsed 'state' of Abu Bakr Al Baghdadi and attempted to prove how every Islamic state or group used or misused the notion of Jihad throughout Islamic history based on various socio-political considerations. It is evident that the evolution of the notion of Jihad has always been a reaction to a new socio-political reality that has been either attempted by or imposed on the Islamic community, which pushed the Islamic state or a group to seek one form of Jihad or another. At the early stages of Islam, while Muhammad's Jihad seemed to be predominantly defensive in nature, the Rightly Guided Caliphs undertook different forms of Jihad that were mainly expansionist to further the national interest of the then growing Islamic empire. Towards the end of the Rightly Guided Caliphs period, however, the intra-Islamic conflicts that erupted during Ali's era led to the crystallization of the Islamic law of non-international armed conflicts. It also created two distinct Islamic sects—Sunni and Shiites—that would continue to influence the

[1] Mohammad-Mahmoud Ould Mohamedou, *A Theory of ISIS* (London: Pluto Press, 2018) 185.

[2] *New York Times*, 'Red Cross Warns of 'Dehumanizing' Rhetoric in ISIS Fight', 26 October 2017. Available at: <https://www.nytimes.com/2017/10/26/world/middleeast/red-cross-islamic-state.html> (last accessed 25 May 2019).

Islamic Jihadism and the Laws of War. Omar Mekky, Oxford University Press. © Omar Mekky 2023.
DOI: 10.1093/oso/9780198888369.003.0007

conflicts and politics of the Islamic community to this day. Later on, the rapid decline of the Islamic empires in the early eighteenth century would inspire theologians like Muhammad ibn Abd al-Wahab, who endorsed a strict traditionalist approach of Islamic law with the aim of reviving the old powerful Islamic state, to reintroduce the concept of *takfir*. According to this concept, a Muslim who is not pious enough for the taste of one particular group is to be declared apostate or disbeliever and thus targeting him or her is to be considered legitimate. Then, in the early twentieth century, the decay of the last Islamic Caliphate and the colonization of many Islamic countries by Western powers led to the creation of two mainstream Islamic organizations—namely: the Muslim Brotherhood in Egypt and *Jamat e-Islami* in India—the members of which used Jihad with the purpose of ending colonization in Islamic countries and creating a unified Islamic nation. In 1979, however, the Soviet Union's invasion of Afghanistan took the Jihadist Movement to a completely different level, where Muslims from around the world rallied to the call for anti-Soviet Jihad. It also led to the formation of *Al-Qaeda*, which later became the most prominent transnational Jihadist group across the globe. Following the events of September 11, the 'global war on terror' intensified military confrontations between many Western states and allied governments in the Islamic world, on the one hand, and *Al-Qaeda* and its offshoots, including Islamic State of Iraq and the Levant (ISIS), on the other. During this period, these latter groups would use Jihad to legitimize their armed force against their perceived enemies both domestically and internationally.

Chapters 2and 3 tackled the laws of war (*jus ad bellum* and *jus in bello*) from international law and Islamic law perspectives. The main purpose of these two chapters was to shed the light on the commonalities and differences between these two existing legal paradigms as they are, mainly, the norms regulating the wars of and against 'Islamic Jihadism' in our contemporary world. With regard to *jus ad bellum*, the two bodies of law (international and Islamic laws), generally speaking, agree on the principles of the maintenance of peace and the prohibition of the use of force or military Jihad in international relations between states—and within one state according to Islamic law. They further share the same exception on the use of force in self-defence—if an actual armed attack has taken place or to avert a threat of imminent attacks—and they adopt similar criteria for a permissive exercise of this right, namely immediacy, necessity, and proportionality. It is also apparent that the principle of humanitarian intervention for the protection of nationals/Muslims abroad is equally accepted under Islamic law and international law, whilst protection of foreign nationals/non-Muslims abroad is uncertain and underdeveloped in the jurisprudence of both laws. Finally, the research thoroughly evaluated the positions and debates of Muslim jurists *vis-à-vis* the notion of offensive Jihad, highlighting the risk of adopting any interpretation that supports such a theory. As to *jus in bello*, international law and Islamic law define it in the same way with the aim of protecting those who do not or no longer directly participate in hostilities and by restricting the rights of parties to the conflict to use particular means and methods of warfare. It fleshed out the fact that the two bodies of law apply only in armed conflicts with distinctive sets of rules that are devoted to international and non-international armed conflicts. However, their classification methodologies and underlying motivations vary a great deal. On the one hand, international law draws on sovereignty and territorial-based interests (statehood) to justify its classification of conflicts, while on the other hand, Islamic law conflict classification is determined by community-based interests (Muslimhood). Accordingly, each of them has its own criteria to determine the typology of the armed conflicts. Nonetheless, the substantial rules related to the protection of the victims of armed conflict are quite similar, including the protection of civilians, civilian objects, wounded, sick, medical personnel, the prohibition of mutilation, and the treatment of prisoners of war (POWs) and detainees. However, there is significant disagreement between Muslim jurists on the rules related to the termination of captivity. The research further highlighted that the principles of distinction, proportionality, and precaution are equally enshrined under Islamic law and international law. Yet, with regard to the means and methods of warfare, despite a relatively comprehensive legal framework provided by international law to regulate the warring parties' rights to use particular means and methods of warfare during armed conflicts, it is evident that the Islamic *jus in bello* paid little attention to this subject, mostly due to the basic types of weapons used in the early stages of Islamic wars. However, some context-related means and methods of warfare have been debated among Muslim jurists, such as the legality of using suicide attacks, human shields, weapons of mass destruction (WMDs), and so forth.

Chapter 4 discusses the relatively 'new' legal paradigm that the international community is developing in order to respond to 'Islamic Jihadism', namely the counterterrorism legal framework. This chapter focused on the challenges that the implementation of this newly developed framework poses to the other pre-existing legal frameworks, such as domestic laws, International Humanitarian Law (IHL), and International Human Rights Law (IHRL). The research highlighted how the ambiguity of the term 'terrorism'—as introduced by United Nations General Assembly (UNGA) and Security Council (UNSC) Resolutions—and the absence of any concrete definition, made every state interpret the term in light of their political interests. Accordingly, the term has frequently been used to stigmatize, delegitimize, and dehumanize those at whom it is directed, including legitimate political opponents, which risks blurring the line between the acts that deserve triggering counterterrorism measures and the other acts that could be regulated by other branches of international law. This is, however, without undermining the pressing need to regulate the phenomenon of terrorism that clearly disturbs states' public order and often threatens international peace and security. This chapter further questioned the emerging role of the UNSC in dealing with the phenomenon of terrorism, including the legally-binding Resolutions and the creation of the '1267 Committee', the 'ISIL and *Al-Qaeda* Sanctions Committee', and the Counterterrorism Committee (CTC) that have arguably acquired a quasi-judicial and legislative character (SC Res. 1267/2253/1390/1373). This research also tackled the approach of the Organization of Islamic Cooperation (OIC)—as it is often claimed to be the collective voice of the Muslim states—towards the phenomenon of terrorism. The OIC highlighted its position *vis-à-vis* the ongoing negotiations on the text of the draft UN Comprehensive Convention on International Terrorism and insisted to include an exemption for people's struggle against foreign occupation, aggression, colonialism, and hegemony, aimed at liberation and self-determination, which arguably led to the impasse of the Convention. While also tackling the definition of terrorism adopted under the OIC Convention on Combating International Terrorism that has only been ratified by fourteen Muslim states. Last but not least, this chapter discussed the *jus ad bellum* and *jus in bello* challenges that are posed by the contemporary fight against Islamic Jihadism. This included, on the *jus ad bellum* side, the usage of the intervention by invitation and the 'unable and unwilling' test to justify the use of force by states against ISIL. On the *jus in bello* side, this involved the complexity of the classification of conflicts, the geographic scope of application of IHL, the applicability of IHL to non-international armed conflicts in which an organized non-state armed group party to the conflict is categorized as a terrorist organization, and the internment of 'terrorists' during non-international armed conflicts.

Finally, Chapter 5 discussed how the interaction between Islamic law and international law could be useful in fostering compliance by Islamic Jihadist groups. It attempted to explain some of the challenges of such interaction while proposing how an integrated approach could be useful to reach the desired end. This research argued that due to the distrust and rejection of the Islamic Jihadist groups to the norms of the traditional international law and the significant role that Islamic law plays in influencing the behaviours of the Islamic Jihadist groups, which openly and exclusively cite self-interpreted Islamic law arguments as the justification for most of their combat related actions, a partnership between international law and Islamic law should be pursued. The rationale behind such a partnership is to create a pragmatic humanitarian legal formula, inspired by the common values of international law and Islamic law, which could be used by international lawyers and policy makers to bolster the compliance and commitment of Islamic Jihadist groups to the laws of war. The research also highlighted how the ambiguity and indeterminacy of one term in the Islamic text could go so far as to jeopardize any build up to the pursued partnership. This fact is aggravated by the complexity of the Islamic text interpretation processes, which often drives various contradicting juristic opinions, in addition to the absence of any authoritative doctrinal body of interpretation on the subject. Thus, this research has tackled the most recognized interpretive methods (*Usul al-Fiqh* and *Maqasid Al-Sharia*) under Islamic law that Muslim jurists use to interpret any Islamic text and to extract the rule and jurisprudence from detailed Islamic sources. Finally, in order to respond effectively to Islamic Jihadism, the research suggested an integrated approach that is based on four main pillars: (i) approaching the Islamic Jihadist groups by engaging them in a legal discussion (Islamic law and international law) through one of the three provided forms of consent ('special agreements', unilateral declarations, or internal codes of conducts); (ii) negotiating with states with regard to granting any concessions related to the criminal punishments (amnesty, combatant-like privilege, or punishment reductions); (iii) finding an appropriate intermediary (the ICRC or other impartial body) that is capable of coordinating the political, logistical and technical aspects of the process; and (iv) mobilizing third states that have influence on Islamic Jihadists groups to encourage them to comply with the law.

Thus, the ambition of this research is that, by examining the notion of Islamic Jihadism through a comparative and interdisciplinary approach between international law and Islamic law, international lawyers and policy-makers will become more reflexive, open-minded, humble, and ready to engage with other legal cultures other than the one that they are used to, in order to ultimately reach to their pursued objectives. In the same vein, the research attempts to give the reader an opportunity to see the world through the eyes of others to help him or her realize that things are regulated differently somewhere at some time. It is submitted that we might not always admire what the other has to say or share, and we might view their values as a threat to ours; yet failing to listen and engage with others is dangerous in its own right and may lead to stronger backlash and deeper polarization in the longer-term.[3]

Wisdom says 'the cave you fear to enter holds the treasure you seek'.[4] We, international lawyers in particular are obliged to seek partnership with other more equipped disciplines, such as Islamic law, in order to solve the flagrant incapacity of the traditional international law rules in responding to 'Islamic Jihadism'. We should not be intimidated by the *horror vacui* arguments that raise the alleged risk inherent in abandoning our current comfortable intellectual frames for explaining reality, which thrive on our endemic fear of disorder and uncertainty and seeks to maintain the *status quo*.[5] Instead, we should see international law and its normative problem-solving as a 'practice of attempting to reach the most acceptable solution in the particular circumstances of the case. It is not the application of a ready-made, general rules or principles but a conversation about what to do here and now'.[6] In the end, international law is nothing more than 'what international lawyers do and how they think about what they are doing'.[7] In this spirit, I believe that we can certainly contribute in resolving the quest of responding to Islamic Jihadism if we manage to engage in a constructive dialogue between international law and Islamic law, including all its diverse interpretations, a dialogue that uniforms the similarities between the two laws and embraces their differences, while bearing in mind that it is very unlikely that this dialogue or said partnership would create any utopian results. And yet one would still hope that this humble attempt serves as a brick for other more capable scholars to build bridges between two distant communities and cultures through civil and respectful dialogues. May this research place me among those people about whom God says: 'and if anyone saved a life, it would be as if he saved the life of all mankind'.[8]

[3] Anthea Roberts, *Is International Law International?* (Oxford: Oxford Scholarship Online, 2017) 321–6, Conclusion.

[4] Attributed to Joseph Campbell, but no-one knows where it was mentioned.

[5] Andrea Bianchi (ed.). *International Law Theories* (Oxford: Oxford University Press, 2016) 39.

[6] Marti Koskenniemi, *From Apology to Utopia: The Structure of International Legal Argument* (Cambridge: Cambridge University Press, 2005) 486, cited in ibid 150.

[7] Bianchi (ed.), *International Law Theories* (n 5).

[8] *Quran* (5:32).

Bibliography

1. International and Regional Treaties and Other Legal Documents

Declaration Renouncing the Use, in Time of War, of Explosive Projectiles Under 400 Grammes Weight (Saint Petersburg, 29 November–11 December 1868)

Hague Declaration (IV, 2) concerning Asphyxiating Gases (The Hague, 29 July 1899)

Convention (IV) respecting the Laws and Customs of War on Land and its annex: Regulations concerning the Laws and Customs of War on Land (The Hague, 18 October 1907)

Geneva Protocol for the Prohibition of the Use of Asphyxiating, Poisonous or Other Gases, and of Bacteriological Methods of Warfare (Geneva, 17 June 1925)

Charter of the United Nations (San Francisco, 1945)

Convention (I) for the Amelioration of the Condition of the Wounded and Sick in Armed Forces in the Field (Geneva, 12 August 1949)

Convention (II) for the Amelioration of the Condition of Wounded, Sick and Shipwrecked Members of Armed Forces at Sea (Geneva, 12 August 1949)

Convention (III) relative to the Treatment of Prisoners of War (Geneva, 12 August 1949)

Convention (IV) relative to the Protection of Civilian Persons in Time of War (Geneva, 12 August 1949)

Treaty Banning Nuclear Weapon Tests in the Atmosphere, in Outer Space, and Under Water (Moscow, 5 August 1963)

Convention on Offences and Certain Other Acts Committed on Board Aircraft (Tokyo, 14 September 1963)

International Covenant on Civil and Political Rights (New York, 16 December 1966)

Treaty on Principles Governing the Activities of States in the Exploration and Use of Outer Space, including the Moon and Other Celestial Bodies (Outer Space Treaty) (London, Moscow, and Washington, 27 January 1967)

Treaty for the Prohibition of Nuclear Weapons in Latin America (Treaty of Tlatelolco) (Mexico City, 14 February 1967)

Treaty on the Non-Proliferation of Nuclear Weapons (London, Moscow, and Washington, 1 July 1968)

Vienna Convention on the Law of Treaties (Vienna, 23 May 1969)

Charter of the Organization of Islamic Cooperation (Cairo, 25 September 1969)

Convention for the Suppression of Unlawful Seizure of Aircraft (The Hague, 16 December 1970)

Treaty on the Prohibition of the Emplacement of Nuclear Weapons and Other Weapons of Mass Destruction on the Seabed and the Ocean Floor and the Subsoil Thereof (Seabed Treaty) (London, Moscow, and Washington, 11 February 1971)

Convention on the Prohibition of the Development, Production and Stockpiling of Bacteriological (Biological) and Toxin Weapons and on their Destruction (London, Moscow, and Washington, 10 April 1972)

Convention on the Prevention and Punishment of Crimes against Internationally Protected Persons, including Diplomatic Agents (New York, 14 December 1973)

Protocol Additional to the Geneva Conventions of 12 August 1949, and relating to the Protection of Victims of International Armed Conflicts (Protocol I) (8 June 1977)

Protocol Additional to the Geneva Conventions of 12 August 1949, and relating to the Protection of Victims of Non-International Armed Conflicts (Protocol II) (8 June 1977)

Convention on Prohibitions or Restrictions of the Use of Certain Conventional Weapons Which May Be Deemed to be Excessively Injurious or to Have Indiscriminate Effects (Geneva, 10 October 1980, as amended in Geneva, 21 December 2001)
Protocol on Non-Detectable Fragments (Protocol I) (Geneva, 10 October 1980)
Protocol on Prohibitions or Restrictions on the Use of Mines, Booby-Traps and Other Devices (Protocol II) (Geneva, 10 October 1980, amended in 1996)
Protocol on Prohibitions or Restrictions on the Use of Incendiary Weapons (Protocol III) (Geneva, 10 October 1980)
South Pacific Nuclear Free Zone Treaty (Rarotonga, 6 August 1985)
Treaty on the Elimination of American and Soviet Intermediate-Range and Shorter-Range Missiles (Moscow and Washington, 8 December 1987)
Convention on the Marking of Plastic Explosives for the Purpose of Detection (Montreal, 1 March 1991)
Convention on the Prohibition of the Development, Production, Stockpiling and Use of Chemical Weapons and on their Destruction (Paris, 13 January 1993)
Protocol on Blinding Laser Weapons (Protocol IV) (Geneva, 13 October 1995)
Treaty on the Southeast Asia Nuclear Weapon-Free Zone (Bangkok, 15 December 1995)
African Nuclear Weapon-Free Zone Treaty (Treaty of Pelindaba) (Cairo, 11 April 1996)
Comprehensive Nuclear Test-Ban Treaty (New York, 10 September 1996)
International Convention for the Suppression of Terrorist Bombings (New York, 15 December 1997)
Arab Convention on the Suppression of Terrorism (Cairo, April 1998)
Convention of the Organization of the Islamic Cooperation on Combating International Terrorism (Burkina Faso, 1 July 1999)
International Convention for the Suppression of the Financing of Terrorism (New York, 9 December 1999)
International Convention for the Suppression of Acts of Nuclear Terrorism (New York, 13 April 2005)
Treaty on a Nuclear Weapon-Free Zone in Central Asia (Semipalatinsk, 8 September 2006)
Convention on Cluster Munitions (Dublin, 19–30 May 2008)
Amendments on the Crime of Aggression to the Rome Statute of the International Criminal Court, Resolution RC/Res.6 of the Review Conference of the Rome Statute, 11 June 2010
Treaty on the Prohibition of Nuclear Weapons (New York, 7 July 2017)

2. International and Regional Jurisprudence

International Court of Justice (ICJ)

Case Concerning United States Diplomatic and Consular Staff in Tehran (United States of America v. Iran), Judgment, 24 May 1980
Case Concerning Military and Paramilitary Activity in and against Nicaragua Case, Judgment, 27 June 1986
Legality of the Threat or Use of Nuclear Weapons, Advisory Opinion, 8 July 1996
Case Concerning Oil Platforms (Islamic Republic of Iran v. United States of America), Judgment, 6 November 2003
Legal Consequences of the Construction of a Wall in the Occupied Palestinian Territory, Advisory Opinion, 9 July 2004
Armed Activities on the Territory of the Congo (Democratic Republic of the Congo v. Uganda), Judgment, 19 December 2005

International Criminal Tribunal for the former Yugoslavia (ICTY)

The Prosecutor v. Duško Tadić, Appeals Chamber, Decision on the Defence Motion for Interlocutory Appeal on Jurisdiction, Case No. IT-94-1-AR72, 2 October 1995

The Prosecutor v. Duško Tadić, Trial Chamber, Judgment, Case No. IT-94-1-T, 7 May 1997

The Prosecutor v. Fatmir Limaj, Trial Chamber, Judgment, Case No. IT-03-66-T, 30 November 2005

The Prosecutor v. Ramush Haradinaj, Idriz Balaj and Lahi Brahimaj (Haradinaj et al.), Trial Chamber, Judgment, Case No. IT-04-84-T, 3 April 2008

The Prosecutor v. Ljube Boškoski and Johan Tarčulovski, Trial Chamber, Judgment, Case No. IT-04-82-T, 10 July 2008

The Prosecutor v. Ljube Boškoski and Johan Tarčulovski, Appeal Chamber, Judgment, Case No. ICTY-04-82-A, 19 May 2010

Special Tribunal for Lebanon (STL)

Interlocutory Decision on the Applicable Law: Terrorism, Conspiracy, Homicide, Perpetration, Cumulative Charging, STL-11-01/I/AC/R176bis, 16 February 2011

European Court of Human Rights (ECtHR)

Al-Skeini and Others v. The United Kingdom, Judgement, Application No. 55721/07, 7 July 2011

Hassan v. The United Kingdom, Judgment, Application No. 29750/09, 16 September 2014

3. United Nations (UN) Documents

General Assembly

Resolution 2625 (XXV), 'Declaration on Principles of International Law concerning Friendly Relations and Co-operation among States in accordance with the Charter of the United Nations', A/RES/2625, 24 October 1970

Resolution 3034 (XXVII), 'Measures to Prevent International Terrorism', A/RES/3034, 18 December 1972

Resolution 3314 (XXIX), 'Definition of Aggression', 14 December 1974

Resolution 49/75 'Request for an advisory opinion from the International Court of Justice on the legality of the threat or use of nuclear weapons', A/RES/49/75, 15 December 1994

Resolution 49/60, 'Measures to Eliminate International Terrorism', A/RES/49/60, 17 February 1995

Resolution 51/210, 'Measures to Eliminate International Terrorism', 17 December 1996

Security Council

Resolution 262 (1968), S/RES/262, 31 December 1968

Resolution 286 (1970), S/RES/286, 9 September 1970

Resolution 457 (1979), S/RES/457, 4 December 1979

Resolution 461 (1979), S/RES/461, 31 December 1979

Statement by the President of Security Council, S/17554, 2618th meeting, 9 October 1985

Resolution 579 (1985), S/RES/579, 18 December 1985

Resolution 635 (1989), S/RES/635 14 June 1989

Resolution 731 (1992), S/RES/731, 21 January 1992

Resolution 748 (1992), S/RES/748, 31 March 1992

Resolution 883 (1993), S/RES/883, 11 November 1993

Resolution 1160 (1998), S/RES/1160, 31 March 1998

Resolution 1189 (1998), S/RES/1189, 13 August 1998
Resolution 1192 (1998), S/RES/1192, 27 August 1998
Resolution 1193 (1998), S/RES/1193, 28 August 1998
Resolution 1199 (1998), S/RES/1199, 23 September 1998
Resolution 1203 (1998), S/RES/1203, 24 October 1998
Resolution 1214 (1998), S/RES/1214, 8 December 1998
Resolution 1244 (1999), S/RES/1244, 10 June 1999
Resolution 1257 (1999), S/RES/1257, 3 August 1999
Resolution 1267 (1999), S/RES/1267, 15 October 1999
Resolution 1333 (2000), S/RES/1333, 19 December 2000
Resolution 1368 (2001), S/RES/1368, 12 September 2001
Resolution 1371 (2001), S/RES/1371, 26 September 2001
Resolution 1506 (2003), S/RES/1506, 12 September 2003
Resolution 1566 (2004), S/RES/1566, 8 October 2004
Resolution 1757 (2007), S/RES/1757, 30 May 2007
Resolution 1989 (2011), S/RES/1989, 17 June 2011
Resolution 2170 (2014), S/RES/2170, 15 August 2014
Resolution 2178 (2014), S/RES/2178, 24 September 2014
Resolution 2195 (2014), S/RES/2195, 19 December 2014
Resolution 2199 (2015), S/RES/2199, 12 February 2015
7387th Meeting, 'The Situation in Libya', S/PV.7387, 18 February 2015
Resolution 2249 (2015), S/RES/2249, 20 November 2015
Resolution 2253 (2015), S/RES/2253, 17 December 2015
Consolidated List (generated on 19 May 2018). Available at: <https://scsanctions.un.org/fop/fop?xml=htdocs/resources/xml/en/consolidated.xml&xslt=htdocs/resources/xsl/en/consolidated.xsl> (last accessed 25 May 2019)

Security Council Counter-Terrorism Committee

Chairman of the Counter-Terrorism Committee (Ambassador Jeremy Greenstock), 'Combating International Terrorism: The Contribution of the United Nations', Presentation to Symposium (Vienna, 3–4 June 2002)
'Comprehensive international framework to counter terrorist narratives', *Annex*, Letter dated 26 April 2017 from the Chair of the Security Council Committee established pursuant to resolution 1373 (2001) concerning counterterrorism addressed to the President of the Security Council, S/2017/375, 28 August 2017
Letter dated 17 January 2018 from the Chair of the Security Council Committee pursuant to resolutions 1267 (1999), 1989 (2011), and 2253 (2015) concerning Islamic State in Iraq and the Levant (Da'esh), Al-Qaeda and associated individuals, groups, undertakings and entities addressed to the President of the Security Council, S/2018/14/Rev.1, 27 February 2018
Security Council Counter-Terrorism Committee, 'Foreign Terrorist Fighters'. Available at: <https://www.un.org/sc/ctc/focus-areas/foreign-terrorist-fighters/> (last accessed 25 May 2019)

United Nations Human Rights Committee

General Comment No. 21, HRI/GEN1/Rev. 9, 6 April 1992
General Comment No. 31, CCPR/C/21/Rev.1/Add.13, 29 March 2004
General Comment No. 35, CCPR/C/GC/35, 15 December 2014

Other

Grace, Rob, and Wilkinson, Stephen. 'Preliminary Report on the Role of Laws and Norms in Humanitarian Negotiations', *Advanced Training Program on Humanitarian Action (ATHA), Harvard Humanitarian Initiative* (2016). Available at: <https://hhi.harvard.edu/publications/preliminary-report-role-laws-and-norms-humanitarian-negotiations>

International Law Commission, *Draft Articles on Responsibility of States for Internationally Wrongful Acts*, Supplement No. 10 (A/56/10), November 2001

UN Office for the Coordination of Humanitarian Affairs, Gerard McHug, and Manuel Bessier, 'Humanitarian Negotiations with Armed Groups, A Manual for Practitioners' (New York, 2006). Available at: <https://www.unocha.org/sites/unocha/files/HumanitarianNegotiationswArmedGroupsManual.pdf> (last accessed 25 May 2019)

UN Press Release, 'Importance of Preventing Conflict Through Development, Democracy, Stressed: As Security Council Unanimously Adopts Resolution 1674 (2006)', SC/8710, 28 April 2006. Available at: <http://www.un.org/press/en/2006/sc8710.doc.htm> (last accessed 25 May 2019)

UN Press Release, 'Security Council Authorizes Establishment of Special Tribunal to Try Suspects in Assassination of Rafiq Hariri', SC/9029, 30 May 2007. Available at: <https://www.un.org/press/en/2007/sc9029.doc.htm> (last accessed 25 May 2019)

Report of the Special Rapporteur on extrajudicial, summary or arbitrary executions, Addendum, 'Study on targeted killings', written by Philip Alston, A/HRC/14/24/Add.6, 28 May 2010

UN Office on Drugs and Crime, *Combating Trafficking in Persons in Accordance with the Principles of Islamic Law* (New York: UNODC, 2010)

UN News, 'New UN report lays bare widespread ISIL 'atrocities' committed against Yazidis in Iraq', 18 August 2016. Available at: <https://news.un.org/en/story/2016/08/536922-new-un-report-lays-bare-widespread-isil-atrocities-committed-against-yazidis> (last accessed 25 May 2019)

UN Assistance Mission in Afghanistan (UNAMA), Mandate. Available at: <https://unama.unmissions.org/mandate> (last accessed 25 May 2019)

4. International Committee of the Red Cross (ICRC) Documents

ICRC, 'The Geneva Conventions and their Commentaries'. Available at: <https://www.icrc.org/en/war-and-law/treaties-customary-law/geneva-conventions>

ICRC, 'Overview of the ICRC's Expert Process (2003–2008)'. Available at: <https://www.icrc.org/en/doc/assets/files/other/overview-of-the-icrcs-expert-process-icrc.pdf> (last accessed 25 May 2019)

ICRC, 'The neutral intermediary role of the ICRC: at the heart of humanitarian action', *Interview*, 7 July 2008. Available at: <https://www.icrc.org/en/doc/resources/documents/interview/neutral-intermediary-interview-070708.htm> (last accessed 25 May 2019)

Melzer, Nils, *Interpretive Guidance on the Notion of Direct Participation in Hostilities under International Humanitarian Law* (Geneva: ICRC, 2009)

ICRC, 'Violence and the Use of Force', 2011. Available at: <http://www.use-of-force.info/images/un/additional-reading/General/ICRC%20Violence%20and%20the%20use%20of%20force%202014.pdf> (last accessed 25 May 2019)

ICRC, *Annual Report 2014* (ICRC, May 2015)

ICRC, 'International humanitarian law and the challenges of contemporary armed conflicts', *Report*, 31 October 2015

ICRC News release, 'Historic agreement banning nuclear weapons a "victory for our shared humanity", ICRC says', 7 July 2017. Available at: <https://www.icrc.org/en/document/historic-agreement-banning-nuclear-weapons-victory-our-shared-humanity-icrc-says> (last accessed 25 May 2019)

ICRC, 'Customary IHL', *IHL Database*. Available at: <https://ihl-databases.icrc.org/customary-ihl/eng/docs/home> (last accessed 25 May 2019)

ICRC, 'What Is International Humanitarian Law?' Available at: <https://www.icrc.org/eng/assets/files/other/what_is_ihl.pdf> (last accessed 25 May 2019)

5. Organization of Islamic Cooperation (OIC) Documents

Fifth Islamic Summit Conference, Resolution No. 2/5-P(IS), 'The City of Al-Quds Al-Sharif' (Kuwait, 26–29 January 1987). Available at: <http://ww1.oic-oci.org/english/conf/is/5/5th-is-sum(political).htm> (last accessed 25 May 2019)

Islamic Conference of Foreign Ministers, Final Communiqué of the Ninth Extraordinary Session (Doha, 10 October 2001). Available at: <http://articles.islamweb.net/media/index.php?id=76925&lang=A&page=article> (last accessed 25 May 2019)

Council of Foreign Ministers (CFM), 'Resolutions on the Cause of Palestine, Al-Quds Al-Sharif, and the Arab–Israeli Conflict', *OIC/CFM-45/2018/PAL/RES/FINAL* (Dhaka, 5–6 May 2018). Available at: <https://www.oic-oci.org/docdown/?docID=1867&refID=1078> (last accessed 25 May 2019)

OIC, 'History'. Available at: <https://www.oic-oci.org/page/?p_id=52&p_ref=26&lan=en>

6. National Legislation

Egypt

Constitution (2014)

Islamic Republic of Iran

Constitution (1979, amended 1989)

Kingdom of Saudi Arabia

Constitution (1992)

United States

Instructions for the Government of Armies of the United States in the Field. General Order No. 100 (Lieber Code) (24 April 1863)

7. National Case Law

United States

Supreme Court, *Hamdi et al. v. Rumsfeld, Secretary of Defense, et al.*, 542 U.S. 507 (2004)

Supreme Court, *Hamdan et al. v. Rumsfeld, Secretary of Defense, et al.*, 126Sct 2749 (2006)

Supreme Court, *Lakhdar Boumediene, et al. v. George W. Bush, et al.*, 553 U. S. 723 (2008)

District Court, District of Columbia, *Al Maqaleh et al. v. Gates*, 899 F.Supp.2d 10 (2012)

8. Other National Practice

Iraq

Letter dated 25 June 2014 from the Permanent Representative of Iraq to the United Nations addressed to the Secretary-General, S/2014/440, 25 June 2014

Letter dated 20 September 2014 from Permanent Representative of Iraq to the United Nations addressed to President of the Security Council, S/2014/691, 22 September 2014

Letter dated 11 December from Permanent Representative of Iraq to the United Nations addressed to the President of the Security Council, S/2015/963, 14 December 2015

Russian Federation

Letter dated 15 October 2015 from the Permanent Representative of the Russian Federation to the United Nations addressed to the President of the Security Council, S/2015/792, 15 October 2015

Turkey

Ministry of Foreign Affairs, 'Press Release Regarding the Bashiqa/Zelikan Training Camp', *No. 313*, 19 December 2015. Available at: <http://www.mfa.gov.tr/no_-313_-19-december-2015_-press-release-regarding-the-bashiqa_zelikan-training-camp.en.mfa> (last accessed 25 May 2019)

United Kingdom

Office of the Prime Minister, 'Responsibility for the Terrorist Atrocities in the United States', *Press Release*, 11 September 2001, updated 14 November 2001

United States

US Working Paper on Draft Convention for the Prevention and Punishment of Certain Acts of International Terrorism, UN Doc A/C.6/L.850, 25 September 1972

US President, Address before the US Congress, Joint Session 'War on Terrorism', 20 September 2001

White House, 'Humane Treatment of Taliban and al Qaeda Detainees', *Memorandum*, 7 February 2002. Available at: <http://www.pegc.us/archive/White_House/bush_memo_20020207_ed.pdf> (last accessed 25 May 2019)

National Commission on Terrorist Attacks Upon the United States, 'The 9/11 Commission Report', July 2004. Available at: <http://govinfo.library.unt.edu/911/report/911Report.pdf> (last accessed 25 May 2019)

UN Counter-Terrorism Committee Executive Directorate, 'The United Nations in the Fight Against Terrorism: Five Years After 9/11'. Available at: <https://www.un.org/sc/ctc/wp-content/uploads/2017/01/2006_01_26_cted_lecture.pdf> (last accessed 25 May 2019)

US Department of State. 'Address to the Annual Meeting of the American Society of International Law: The Obama Administration and International Law' (25 March 2010). Available at: <http://www.state.gov/s/l/releases/remarks/139119.htm> (last accessed 25 May 2019)

US Department of Justice, 'Lawfulness of a Lethal Operation Directed Against a US Citizen Who Is a Senior Operational Leader of *Al-Qaeda* or an Associated Force', *White Paper*, October 2011. Available at: <https://www.globalsecurity.org/security/library/policy/national/doj-wp-imminent-threat.htm> (last accessed 25 May 2019)

White House, 'Statement by the President on ISIL', 10 September 2014. Available at: <http://www.whitehouse.gov/the-press-office/2014/09/10/statement-president-isil-1> (last accessed 25 May 2019)

Letter dated 23 September 2014 from the Permanent Representative of the United States of America to the United Nations addressed to the Secretary-General, S/2014/695, 23 September 2014

US Department of Defense, 'Statement from Pentagon Press Secretary Peter Cook on U.S. strike in Libya', 14 November 2015. Available at: <www.defense.gov/News/News-Releases/News-ReleaseView/Article/628954/statement-from-pentagon-press-secretary-peter-cook-on-us-strike-in-libya> (last accessed 25 May 2019)

US Department of Defense, 'Operation Inherent Resolve: Targeted Operations Against ISIL Terrorists'. Available at: <http://www.defense.gov/News/Special-Reports/0814_Inherent-Resolve (last accessed 25 May 2019)

9. Monographs and Collective Books

Abou Al-Fadl, Khaled. *Rebellion and Violence in Islamic Law* (Cambridge: Cambridge University Press, 2001)

Abou Al-Fadl, Khaled. *Speaking in God's Name: Islamic Law, Authority and Women* (London: Oneworld Publications, 2001)

Abou El-Wafa, Ahmed. *Islam and the West: Coexistence or Clash?* (Cairo: Dar Al-Nahda, 2006)

Al-Dawoody, Ahmed. *The Islamic Law of War: Justifications and Regulations* (New York, NY: Palgrave Macmillan, 2011)

Al-Sergani, Rgheb. *Islamic History Encyclopedia* (Cairo: Iqraa Foundation, 2013)

Armstrong, Karen. *Islam: A Short History* (New York, NY: Random House Inc., 2002)

Aslan, Reza, *No God But God: The Origins, Evolution and Future of Islam* (New York, NY: Random House Trade, 2011)

Baderin, Mashood A. (ed.). *International Law and Islamic Law* (London: Ashgate, 2008)

Bar, Shmuel. *Warrant for Terror: Fatwās of Radical Islam and the Duty of Jihād* (Lanham, MD: Rowman & Littlefield, 2006)

Bassiouni, M. Cherif (ed.). *International Terrorism and Political Crimes* (Springfield, IL: Charles C Thomas, 1975)

Bassiouni, M. Cherif (ed.). *Legal Responses to International Terrorism* (Dordrecht: Martinus Nijhoff, 1988)

Bassiouni, M. Cherif. *Manual on International Humanitarian Law and Arms Control Agreements* (New York, NY: Transnational Publishers, 2000). Available at: <https://www.researchgate.net/publication/331605693_A_Manual_on_International_Humanitarian_Law_and_Arms_Control_Agreements_International_and_Comparative_Criminal_Law_v1_Edited_by_M_Cherif_Bassiouni_Ardsley_NY_Transnational_Publishers_Inc_2000_Pp_xix_84> (last accessed 25 May 2019)

Bassiouni, M. Cherif. *The Sharia, Islamic Law, and Contemporary Post-Conflict and Transitional Justice* (Cambridge: Cambridge University Press, 2013)

Bassiouni, M. Cherif, and Guellali, Amna (eds). *Jihad—Challenges to International and Domestic Law—Hague Colloquium on Fundamental Principles of Law Series* (The Hague: Hague Academic Press, 2010)

Ben-Naftali, Orna (ed.). *International Humanitarian Law and International Human Rights Law* (Oxford: Oxford University Press, 2011)

Bhala, Raj. *Understanding Islamic Law* (New York: LexisNexis, 2011)
Bianchi, Andrea (ed.). *International Law Theories* (Oxford: Oxford University Press, 2016)
Bianchi, Andrea, and Keller, Alexis. *Counterterrorism: Democracy's Challenge* (Oregon, OR: Hart Publishing 2008)
Bianchi, Andrea, and Naqvi, Yasmin (eds), *International Humanitarian Law and Terrorism* (Oxford: Hart Publishing, 2011)
Bonner, Michel. *Jihad in Islamic History: Doctrine and Practices* (Princeton, NJ: Princeton University Press, 2006)
Bonney, Richard. *Jihad from Quran to Bin Laden* (New York, NY: Palgrave Macmillan, 2004)
Boothby, William H. *Weapons and the Law of Armed Conflict* (Oxford: Oxford University Press, 2009)
Bowett, Derek W. *Self Defense in International Law* (Manchester: Manchester University Press, 1958)
Calvert, John. *Sayyid Qutb and the Origins of Radical Islamism* (New York, NY: Columbia University Press, 2010)
Cheng, Bin. *General Principles of International Law as Applied by International Courts and Tribunals* (Cambridge: Cambridge University Press, 2006)
Clapham, Andrew, and Gaeta, Paola (eds). *The Oxford Handbook of International Law in Armed Conflicts* (Oxford: Oxford University Press, 2014)
Corten, Olivier. *The Law Against War* (Oxford: Hart Publishing, 2010)
Coulson, Noel J. *The History of Islamic Law* (Edinburgh: Edinburgh University Press, 1964)
David, Rene, and Brierly, John E. C. *Major Legal Systems in the World Today* (New York, NY: Macmillan, 1978)
Dinstein, Yoram. *War, Aggression And Self-Defense*, 4th edn (Cambridge: Cambridge University Press, 2005)
Erickson, Richard J. *Legitimate Use of Military Force Against State Sponsored International Terrorism* (Alabama: Air University Press, 1989)
Esposito, John (ed.). *Oxford Encyclopedia of the Islamic World* (Oxford: Oxford University Press, 1995)
Esposito, John. *Islam the Straight Path* (Oxford: Oxford University Press, 2005)
Farrall, Jeremy Matam. *United Nations Sanctions and the Rule of Law* (Cambridge: Cambridge University Press, 2007)
Firestone, Reuven. '*Jihād: The Origin of Holy War in Islam*' (Oxford: Oxford University Press, 1999)
Fleck, Dieter (ed.). *The Handbook of International Humanitarian Law*, 3rd edn (Oxford: Oxford University Press, 2013)
Franck, Thomas M. *Recourse to Force: State Action Against Threats and Armed Attacks* (Cambridge: Cambridge University Press, 2002)
Gray, Christine. *International Law and the Use of Force*, 2nd edn (Oxford: Oxford University Press, 2004)
Green, Leslie, *The Contemporary Law of Armed Conflict*, 3rd edn (Manchester: Manchester University Press, 2008)
Guillaume, Alfred (trans.). *The Life of Mohamed: A Translation of Ibn Ishaq: Sirat Rasul Allah* (Oxford: Oxford University Press, 2002)
Hallaq, Wael B. *A History of Islamic Legal Theories: An Introduction to Sunni Usul al-fiqh* (Cambridge: Cambridge University Press, 1999)
Halliday, Fred. *Islam and the Myth of Confrontation: Religion and Politics in the Middle East* (London: I.B. Tauris, 2003)

Hammidullah, Mohamed. *The Battlefield of the Prophet Muhammad, with Maps, Illustration and Sketches: A Continuation in Muslim Military History* (New Delhi: Kitab Bhavan, 2003)

Hashmi, Sohail H. (ed.). *Islamic Political Ethics: Civil Society, Pluralism, and Conflict* (Princeton, NJ: Princeton University Press, 2002)

Henckaerts, Jean-Marie, and Doswald-Beck, Louise. *Customary International Humanitarian Law*, 2 Vols (Geneva/Cambridge: ICRC and Cambridge University Press, 2005)

Herik, Larissa J., and Schrijver, Nico (eds). *Counterterrorism Strategies in a Fragmented International Legal Order: Meeting the Challenges* (Cambridge: Cambridge University Press, 2013)

Hook, Steven W. *US Foreign Policy: The Paradox of World Power* (Washington, DC: CQ Press, 2008)

Ibn Rushd, Abul Walid Muhammad. *The Distinguished Jurist's Primer*. Trans. Imran Nyazee (Reading: Garnet Publishing Ltd, 1994)

Iqbal, Afzal. *Diplomacy in Early Islam* (Pakistan: Institute of Islamic Culture, 1988)

Johnson, James Turner. *The Holy War Idea in Western and Islamic Traditions* (Philadelphia, PA: Pennsylvania State University Press, 1997)

Kamali, Mohamed H., *Principles of Islamic Jurisprudence*, 3rd edn (Cambridge: Islamic Text Society, 2005)

Kamali, Mohamed H. *Sharia Law: An Introduction* (London: Oneworld Publications, 2008)

Kelsay, John and Johnson, James Turner (eds). *Just War and Jihad: Historical and Theoretical Perspectives on War and Peace in Western and Islamic Traditions* (New York, NY: Greenwood Press, 1991)

Kennedy, Hugh. *The Prophet and the Age of the Caliphates: The Islamic Near East from the Sixth to the Eleventh Century* (London: Longman, 1986)

Khadduri, Majid. *War and Peace in the Law of Islam* (Baltimore, MD: The Johns Hopkins Press, 1940)

Khadduri, Majid. *The Law of War and Peace in Islam: A Study in Muslim International Law* (London: Luzac & Co., 1946)

Khadduri, Majid. *The Islamic Law of Nations: Shaybani's Siyar* (Baltimore, MD: The Johns Hopkins Press, 1966)

Khan, Hamid. *Practitioner's Guide: Islamic Law* (International Network to Promote the Rule of Law, 2013)

Khatab, Sayed. *The Political Thought of Sayyid Qutb: The Theory of Jahiliyyah* (London: Routledge, 2006)

Khatab, Sayed. *The Power of Sovereignty: The Political and Ideological Philosophy of Sayyid Qutb* (New York, NY: Routledge, 2006)

Koskenniemi, Martti. *From Apology to Utopia: The Structure of International Legal Argument* (Cambridge: Cambridge University Press, 2005)

Lambton, Anna K. S. *State and Government in Medieval Islam* (Oxford: Oxford University Press, 1981)

Lang Jr, Anthony F. (ed.). *Just Intervention* (Washington, DC: Georgetown University Press, 2003)

Laqueur, Walter. *The New Terrorism: Fanaticism and the Arms of Mass Destruction* (Oxford: Oxford University Press, 2001)

Lawrence, Bruce (ed.), *Messages to the World: The Statements of Osama Bin Laden* (London: Verso, 2005)

Lewis, Bernard. *The Middle East: A Brief History of the Last 2,000 Years* (New York, NY: Scribner, 1995)

Lewis, Bernard. *What Went Wrong? The Clash Between Islam and Modernity in the Middle East* (New York, NY: Harper Perennial, 2002)
Lewis, Bernard. *The Crisis of Islam: Holy War and Unholy Terror* (New York, NY: Random House Trade, 2004)
Malanczuk, Peter, and Akehurst, Michae. *Akehurst's Modern Introduction to International Law*, 7th edn (London: Routledge, 1997)
Matheson, Michael, and Momtaz, Djamchid (eds). *Rules and Institutions of International Humanitarian Law Put to the Test of Recent Armed Conflicts* (Leiden: Martinus Nijhoff Publishers, 2010)
Milanovic, Marko. *Extraterritorial Application of Human Rights Treaties: Law, Principles, and Policy* (Oxford: Oxford University Press, 2011)
Mohamedou, Mohammad-Mahmoud Ould. *A Theory of ISIS* (London: Pluto Press, 2018)
Moinuddin, Hasan. *The Charter of the Islamic Conference and Legal Framework of Economic Cooperation Among its Member States: A Study of the Charter, the General Agreement for Economic, Technical and Commercial Co-operation and the Agreement for Promotion, Protection and Guarantee of Investments Among Member States of the OIC* (Oxford: Clarendon Press, 1987)
Mousalli, Ahmad S. *Radical Islamic Fundamentalism: The Ideological and Political Discourse of Sayyid Qutb* (Beirut: American University of Beirut, 1992)
Murphy, Sean D. *Humanitarian Intervention: The United Nations in an Evolving World Order* (Philadelphia, PA: University of Pennsylvania Press, 1996)
Musallam, Adnan A. *From Secularism to Jihad: Sayyid Qutb and the Foundations of Radical Islamism* (Westport, CT: Praeger, 2005)
Nasr, Vali. *The Shia Revival: How Conflicts Within Islam Will Shape the Future* (New York, NY: W.W. Norton & Company Inc., 2007)
Olusanya, Olaoluwa. *Identifying the Aggressor Under International Law: A Principle Approach* (Oxford: Peter Lang Verlag, 2006)
Orakhelashvili, Alexander. *Akehurst's Modern Introduction to International Law*, 8th edn (London: Routledge, 2018)
Pictet, Jean (ed.), *Commentary on the Fourth Geneva Convention relative to the Protection of Civilian Persons in Time of War* (Geneva: ICRC, 1958)
Pruthi, Raj K. (ed.). *Encyclopedia of Jihad* (New Delhi: Anmol Publications, 2002)
Rahnema, Ali. *Pioneers of Islamic Revival* (London: Zed Books, 1994)
Reisman, Michael. *Nullity and Revision. The Review and Enforcement of International Judgments and Awards* (New Haven, VT: Yale University Press, 1971)
Roberts, Anthea. *Is International Law International?* (Oxford: Oxford Scholarship Online, 2017)
Rousseau, Jean-Jacques. *The Social Contract or Principles of Political Right*, translated by H. J. Tozer (Hertfordshire: Wordsworth Editions, 1998)
Ruthven, Malise. *Islam in the World* (Oxford: Oxford University Press, 1984)
Ryus, Tom. *Armed Attack and Article 51 of the UN Charter: Evolutions in Customary Law and Practice* (Cambridge: Cambridge University Press, 2010)
Sassòli, Marco, Bouvier, Antoine A., and Quintin, Anne. *How Does Law Protect in War?* (Geneva: ICRC, 2011). Online updated version available at: <https://casebook.icrc.org>
Saul, Ben. *Defining Terrorism in International Law* (Oxford: Oxford University Press, 2006)
Saul, Ben (ed.). *Research Handbook on International Law and Terrorism* (Cheltenham/Northampton: Edward Elgar Publishing, 2014)
Shah, Niaz A. *Islamic Law and the Law of Armed Conflict: The Armed Conflict in Pakistan* (New York, NY: Routledge, 2011)

Simma, Bruno, Khan, Daniel-Erasmus, Nolte, Georg, and Paulus, Andreas. *The Charter of the United Nations: A Commentary*, 3rd edn, Vol. II (Oxford: Oxford University Press, 2012)

Springer, Devin R., Regens, James L., and Edger, David N. *Islamic Radicalism and Global Jihad* (Washington, DC: Georgetown University Press, 2009)

Swisher, Clarice (ed.). *The Spread of Islam* (San Diego, CA: Greenhaven Press, 1999)

Toth, James. *Sayyid Qutb: The Life and Legacy of a Radical Islamic Intellectual* (Oxford: Oxford University Press, 2013)

Vanhullebusch, Matthias. *War and Law in the Islamic World* (Leiden: Brill Nijhoff, 2015)

Wajis, Nik. *The Crime of Ḥirāba in Islamic Law* (PhD Thesis, Glasgow Caledonian University, 1996)

Walter, Christian, Vöneky, Silja. Roeben, Volker., and Schorkopf, Frank (eds). *Terrorism as a Challenge for National and International Law: Security versus Liberty?* (Berlin: Springer-Verlag, 2004)

Weeramantry, Christopher G. *Islamic Jurisprudence: An International Perspective* (London: Palgrave Macmillan, 1988)

Wet, Erika de. *The Chapter VII Powers of the United Nations Security Council* (Oxford: Hart Publishing, 2004)

Wilson, Harold Albert. *International Law and the Use of Force by National Liberation Movements* (Oxford: Clarendon Press, 1988)

Yemin, Edward. *Legislative Powers in the United Nations and Specialized Agencies* (Leiden: Sijyhof, 1969)

10. Chapters of Edited Books

Abi-Saab, George. 'Wars of National Liberation in the Geneva Conventions and Protocols' in *Collected Course*, Vol. 169 (The Hague: Academy of International Law, 1981) 353–445

Akande, Dapo. 'Classification of Armed Conflicts: Relevant Legal Concepts' in Elizabeth Wilmshurst (ed.), *International Law and the Classification of Conflicts* (Oxford: Oxford University Press, 2012) 32–79

Bassiouni, M. Cherif. 'A Policy-Oriented Inquiry into the Different Forms and Manifestations of "International Terrorism"' in M. Cherif Bassiouni (ed.), *Legal Responses to International Terrorism* (Dordrecht: Martinus Nijhoff, 1988) i–liii

Bianchi, Andrea. 'Enforcing International Law Norms Against Terrorism: Achievements and Prospects' in Andrea Bianchi (ed.), *Enforcing International Law Norms Against Terrorism* (Oxford: Hart Publishing, 2004) 491–534

Bianchi, Andrea. 'International Law, Counterterrorism and the Quest for Checks and Balances: Why the Calling Sirens of Constitutionalism Should be Resisted' in Andrea Bianchi and Alexis Keller (eds), *Counterterrorism: Democracy's Challenge* (Oxford: Hart Publishing 2008) 395–424

Bianchi, Andrea. 'Textual Interpretation and (International) Law Reading: The Myth of (in) Determinacy and the Genealogy of Meaning' in P. Bekker (ed.), *Making Transnational Law Work in the Global Economy—Essays in Honour of Detlev Vagts* (Cambridge: Cambridge University Press, 2010) 34–56

Boulden, Jane. 'The United Nations General Assembly and Terrorism' in Ben Saul (ed.), *Research Handbook on International Law and Terrorism* (Cheltenham/Northampton: Edward Elgar Publishing, 2014) 555–72

Brichambaut, Marc Perrin de. 'The Role of the United Nations Security Council in the International Legal System' in Michael Byers (ed.), *The Role of International Law in International Politics* (2001), 269–76

Condorelli, Luigi, and Naqvi, Yasmin. 'The War Against Terrorism and jus in bello: Are the Geneva Conventions Out of Date?' in Andrea Bianchi (ed.), *Enforcing International Law Norms Against Terrorism* (Oxford: Hart Publishing, 2004) 25–38

Ginsborg, Lisa. 'The United Nations Security Council's Counter-Terrorism Al-Qaida Sanctions Regime: Resolution 1267 and the 1267 Committee' in Ben Saul (ed.), *Research Handbook on International Law and Terrorism* (Cheltenham/Northampton: Edward Elgar Publishing, 2014) 608–26

Higgins, Rosalyn. 'The General International Law of Terrorism' in Rosalyn Higgins and Maurice Flory (eds), *International Law and Terrorism* (London: Routledge, 1997) 13–29

Hoffmann, Tamas. 'Squaring the Circle? International Humanitarian Law and Transnational Armed Conflicts', in Michael J. Matheson and Djamchid Momtaz (eds), *Rules and Institutions of International Humanitarian Law Put to the Test of Recent Armed Conflicts* (Leiden: Martinus Nijhoff Publishers, 2010) 217–74

Kleffner, Jann. 'Scope of Application of International Humanitarian Law' in Dieter Fleck (ed.). *The Handbook of International Humanitarian Law*, 3rd edn (Oxford: Oxford University Press, 2013) 43–78

Kräehenmann, Sandra. 'Protection of Prisoners in Armed Conflict' in Dieter Fleck (ed.), *The Handbook of International Humanitarian Law*, 3rd edn (Oxford: Oxford University Press, 2013) 359–412

Mahmassani, Sobhi. 'The Principle of International Law in Light of Islamic Doctrine' in *Collected Courses*, Vol. 117 (The Hague: Academy of International Law, 1966) 201–328

Mettraux, Guenael. 'The United Nations Special Tribunal for Lebanon: Prosecuting Terrorism' in Ben Saul (ed.), *Research Handbook on International Law and Terrorism* (Cheltenham/Northampton: Edward Elgar Publishing, 2014) 651–66

Murphy, John. 'United Nations Proposals on the Control and Repression of Terrorism' in M. Cherif Bassiouni (ed.), *International Terrorism and Political Crimes* (Springfield, IL: Charles C Thomas, 1975) 493–506

Pejic, Jelena. 'Armed Conflict and Terrorism: There is a (Big) Difference' in Ana Maria Salinas De Frias, Katja Samuel, and Nigel White (ed.), *Counter-Terrorism: International Law and Practice* (Oxford: Oxford University Press, 2012) 171–204

Roberts, Adam. 'Countering Terrorism: A Historical Perspective' in Andrea Bianchi and Alexis Keller (eds), *Counterterrorism: Democracy's Challenge* (Oregon, OR: Hart Publishing 2008) 3–43

Rodley, Nigel. 'Can Armed Opposition Groups Violate Human Rights Standards?' in Kathleen Mahoney and Paul Mahoney (eds), *Human Rights in the Twenty-First Century* (Dordrecht; London: Martinus Nijhoff Publishers, 1993) 297–318

Samour, Nahed. 'Modernized Islamic International Law Concepts as a Third World Approach to International Law' in Rüdiger Wolfrum (ed.), *Max Planck Encyclopedia of Public International Law* (Oxford: Oxford University Press, 2010) 543–77

Sassoli, Marco. 'The Role of Human Rights and International Humanitarian Law in New Types of Armed Conflicts' in Orna Ben-Naftali (ed.), *International Humanitarian Law and International Human Rights Law* (Oxford: Oxford University Press, 2011) 34–94

Saul, Ben. 'Terrorism and International Humanitarian Law' in Ben Saul (ed.), *Research Handbook on International Law and Terrorism* (Cheltenham/Northampton: Edward Elgar Publishing, 2014) 208–31

Tripp, Charles. 'Sayyid Qutb: The Political Vision' in Ali Rahnema (ed.), *Pioneers of Islamic Revival* (London: Zed Books, 1994) 154–83

Waldock, Claud H. M. 'The Regulation of the Use of Force by Individual States in International Law' in *Collected Courses*, Vol. 81 (The Hague: Academy of International Law, 1952) 455–517

Walter, Christian. 'Defining Terrorism in National and International Law' in Christian Walter, Silja Vöneky, Volker Roeben, and Frank Schorkopf (eds), *Terrorism as a Challenge for National and International Law: Security versus Liberty?* (Berlin: Springer-Verlag, 2004) 23–45

Wood, Michael. 'The Role of the UN Security Council in Relation to the Use of Force Against Terrorists' in Larissa van den Herik and Nico Schrijver (eds), *Counterterrorism Strategies in a Fragmented International Legal Order: Meeting the Challenges* (Cambridge: Cambridge University Press, 2013) 317–33

Zlataric, Bogdan. 'History of International Terrorism and its Legal Control' in M. Cherif Bassiouni (ed.), *International Terrorism and Political Crimes* (Springfield, IL: Charles C Thomas, 1975) 474–84

11. Journal Articles

Abu-Nimer, Muhammed. 'A Framework for Nonviolence and Peace Building in Islam', *Journal of Law and Religion* (2000–2001) 15(1/2), 217–65

Akande, Dapo. 'Clearing the Fog of War? The ICRC's Interpretive Guidance on Direct Participation in Hostilities', *International & Comparative Law Quarterly* (2010) 59, 180–91

Al-Dawoody, Ahmed. 'Management of the Dead from the Islamic Law and International Humanitarian Law Perspectives: Considerations for Humanitarian Forensics', *International Review of the Red Cross* (2017) 99, 759–84

Al-Fadl, Khaled Abou. 'Political Crime in Islamic Jurisprudence and Western Legal History', *U.C. David Journal of International Law and Policy* (1998) 4, 1–26

Al-Ubaydi, Muhammad, Lahoud, Nelly, Milton, Daniel, and Price, Bryan. 'The Group That Calls Itself a State: Understanding the Evolution and Challenges of the Islamic State', *The Combating Terrorism Center at West Point* (2014) 1–102

Al-Zuhili, Wahba. 'Islam and International Law', *International Review of the Red Cross* (2005) 87(858), 269–83

Ambos, Kai. 'Judicial Creativity at the Special Tribunal for Lebanon: Is There a Crime of Terrorism under International Law', *Leiden Journal of International Law* (2011) 24(3), 655–75

Amjad-Ali, Charles W. 'Jihad and Just War Theory: Dissonance and Truth', *Dialog* (2009) 48(3), 239–47

Arimatsu, Louise. 'Territory, Boundaries and the Law of Armed Conflict', *Yearbook of International Humanitarian Law* (2009) 12(157), 157–92

Badar, Mohamed E. 'Ius in Bello under Islamic International Law', *International Criminal Law Review* (2013) 13, 593–625

Badawi, Nesrine. 'Islamic Jurisprudence and The Regulation of Armed Conflict', *Humanitarian Policy and Conflict Research at Harvard University* (2009) 1–13

Baderin, Mashood A. 'Religion and International Law: Friends or Foes?', *SOAS School of Law Legal Studies Research Paper No. 4, European Human Rights Law* (2010) 5, 637–58

Banniler-Chirstakis, Karine 'Military Interventions against ISIL in Iraq, Syria and Libya, and the Legal Basis of Consent', *Leiden Journal of International Law* (2016) 29, 743–75

Bassiouni, M. Cherif. 'Evolving Approaches to Jihad: From Self Defense to Revolutionary and Regime Change—Change Political Violence', *Chicago Journal of International Law* (2007) 8(1), 119–46

Bassiouni, M. Cherif, and Badr, Gamal M. 'The Shari'a: Sources, Interpretation, and Rule Making', *UCLA Journal of Islamic and Near Eastern Law* (2002) 135, 135–78

Bellal, Annyssa, and Doswald-Beck, Louise. 'Evaluating the Use of Force During the Arab Spring', *Yearbook of International Humanitarian Law* (2011) 14(3), 3–35

Bellinger, John B., and Haynes, William J. 'A US Government Response to the International Committee of the Red Cross study Customary International Humanitarian Law', *International Review of the Red Cross* (2007) 89, 443–71

Bennet, Andrew M. 'Islamic History & *Al-Qaeda*: A Primer to Understanding the Rise of Islamist Movements in the Modern World', *Pace International Law Review Online Companion* (2013) 3, 316–70

Bennoune, Karima. 'As-Salamu Alaykum? Humanitarian Law in Islamic Jurisprudence', *Michigan Journal of International Law* (1994) 15, 605–43

Bianchi, Andrea. 'Assessing the Effectiveness of the UN Security Council's Anti-Terrorism Measures: The Quest for Legitimacy and Cohesion', *European Journal of International Law* (2006) 17, 881–919

Bianchi, Andrea. 'The International Regulation of the Use of Force: The Politics of Interpretive Method', *Leiden Journal of International Law* (2009) 22(4), 651–76

Blum, Gabriella, 'The Dispensable Lives of Soldiers', *Journal of Legal Analysis* (2010) 2(69), 9–52

Boon, Kristen E. 'Are Control Tests Fit for the Future? The Slippage Problem in Attribution Doctrines', *Melbourne Journal of International Law* 1 (2014) 15(1), 1–48

Boothby, William H. 'Direct Participation in Hostilities—A Discussion of the ICRC Interpretive Guidance', *Journal of International Humanitarian Legal Studies* (2010) 1(143), 143–68

Brown, Nathan J., and Revkin, Mara. 'Islamic Law and Constitutions: The Oxford Handbook of Islamic Law', *Oxford Handbook Online* (2015) 778–818. Available at: <https://mararevkin.files.wordpress.com/2015/12/islamic-law-and-constitutions-oxford-handbooks.pdf> (last accessed 25 May 2019)

Bunzel, Cole. 'From Paper State to Caliphate: The Ideology of the Islamic State', *Analysis Paper No. 19*, Brookings Project, Center for Middle East Policy (2015) 1–45

Byers, Michel. 'Terrorism, the Use of Force and International Law After 11 September', *International and Comparative Law Quarterly* (April 2002) 51, 401–14

Byrne, Max. 'Consent and the Use of Force: An Examination of "Intervention by Invitation" as a Basis for US Drone Strikes in Pakistan, Somalia and Yemen', *Journal on the Use of Force and International Law* (2016) 3, 97–125

Cassese, Antonio. '*Ex Inuiria Ius Oritur*: Are We Moving towards International Legitimation of Forcible Humanitarian Countermeasures in the World Community?', *European Journal of International Law* (1999) 10, 23–30

Charney, Jonathan. 'The Use of Force Against Terrorism and International Law', *American Journal of International Law* (2001) 95, 835–9

Cheema, Sujata Ashwarya. 'Sayyid Qutb's Concept of Jahilyya as a Metaphor for Modern Society', *Islam and Muslim Societies* (2006) 2(2), 1–32

Clapham, Andrew. 'Human Rights Obligations of Non-State Actors in Conflict Situations', *International Review of the Red Cross* (2006) 88(863), 491–523

Clark, Anthony. 'International Law and the Preemptive Use of Military Force', *The Washington Quarterly* (2003) 26(2), 89–103

Corten, Olivier. 'The "Unwilling or Unable" Test: Has it Been, and Could it be, Accepted?', *Leiden Journal of International Law* (2016) 29, 777–99

Dabone, Zakaria. 'International Law: Armed Groups in a State-centric System', *International Review of the Red Cross* (2011) 93(882), 395–424

Debuf, Els. 'Tools to Do the Job: The ICRC's Legal Status, Privileges and Immunities', *International Review of the Red Cross* (2016) 97(897/898), 319–44

Deeks, Ashley. 'Unwilling or Unable: Toward a Normative Framework for Extraterritorial Self-Defense', *Virginia Journal of International Law* (2012) 52, 483–550

Dörmann, Knut, and Serralvo, Jose. 'Common Article 1 to the Geneva Conventions and the Obligation to Prevent International Humanitarian Law Violations', *International Review of the Red Cross* (2014) 96(895–896), 707–36

Doswald-Beck, Louise. 'The Legal Validity of Military Intervention by Invitation of the Government', *British Yearbook of International Law* (1985) 56(1), 189–252

Evans, Carolyn, 'The Double-Edged Sword: Religious Influences on International Humanitarian Law', *Melbourne Journal of International Law* (2005) 6, 1–32

Franck, Thomas M. 'When, if Ever, May States Deploy Military Force Without Prior Security Council Authorization?', *Singapore Journal of International Law* (2000) 4, 362–76

Franck, Thomas M. 'Terrorism and the Right of Self-Defense', *American Journal of International Law* (2001) 95, 839–43

Freamon, Bernard K. 'Martyrdom, Suicide, and the Islamic Law of War: A Short Legal History', *Fordham International Law Journal* (2003) 27(299), 299–369

Goodman, Ryan. 'The Power to Kill or Capture Enemy Combatants', *European Journal of International Law* (2013) 24(819), 819–53

Greenwood, Christopher. 'International Law and the Pre-emptive Use of Force: Afghanistan, *Al-Qaeda*, and Iraq', *San Diego International Law Journal* (2003) 4, 7–38

Grossman, Patricia. 'Afghanistan in the Balance', *Middle East Report* (2001) 221, 8–15

Guzman, Andrew. 'The Consent Problem in International Law', *Working Paper Series, Berkeley Program in Law and Economics* (2011) 1–63. Available at: <https://escholarship.org/content/qt04x8x174/qt04x8x174.pdf> (last accessed 25 May 2019)

Hakimi, Monica. 'Defensive Force against Non-State Actors: The State of Play', *International Law Studies* (2015) 91(1), 1–32

Hallaq, Wael B. 'Was the Gate of Ijtihad Closed?', *International Journal of Middle East Studies* (1984) 16, 3–41

Hassan, Farooq A. 'The Sources of Islamic Law', *American Society in International Law Proceedings* (1982) 76, 65–75

Heck, Paul. 'Jihad Revisited', *The Journal of Religious Ethics* (2004) 32(1), 95–128

Henzel, Christopher. 'The Origins of *Al-Qaeda*'s Ideology: Implications for US Strategy', *Parameters: The US Army War College Quarterly* (2005) 35(1), 69–80

Hurd, Ian. 'Is Humanitarian Intervention Legal? The Rule of Law in an Incoherent World', *Ethics & International Affairs* (2011) 25(3), 293–313

Jackson, Sherman. 'Domestic Terrorism in the Islamic Legal Tradition', *Muslim World* (2001) 91(3-4), 293–310

Jamar, Steven. D. 'Religion and International Law', *Journal of Law and Religion* (2001) 16, 609–12

Kamali, Mohamed H. 'Freedom of Religion in Islamic Law', *Capital University Law Review* (1992) 21, 63–81

Khadduri, Majid. 'The Maslaha (Public Interest) and Ilta (cause) in Islamic Law', *New York University Journal of International Law & Policy* (1979) 12, 213–17

Khan, Khizr M. 'Juristic Classification of Islamic Law', *Houston Journal of International Law* (1983) 6, 23–35

Kirsch, Stefan, and Oehmichen, Anna. 'Judges Gone Astray: The Fabrication of Terrorism as an International Crime by the Special Tribunal for Lebanon', *Durham Law Review Online* (2011) 1, 1–20

Koutroulis, Vaios. 'The Fight Against the Islamic State and jus in bello', *Leiden Journal of International Law* (2016) 29, 827–52

Lewis, Bernard. 'The Roots of Muslim Rage', *The Atlantic Monthly* (1990) 266, 47–60

Lippman, Mathew. 'Islamic Criminal Law and Procedures: Religious Fundamentalism v. Modern Law', *Boston College International and Comparative Law Review* (1989) 12(1), 347–80

Mani, Venkateshwara Subramaniam. 'International Terrorism: Is a Definition Possible?', *Indian Journal of International Law* (1978) 18, 206–11

Marsoof, Saleem. 'Islam and International Humanitarian Law', *Sri Lanka Journal of International Law* (2003) 15, 23–8

Milojevic, Momir. 'Prohibition of the Use of Force and Threats in International Relations, Law and Politics', *Facta Universitatis Series: Law and Politics* (2001) 1(5), 581–604

Moore, John Norton. 'Towards Legal Restraints on International Terrorism', *American Society of International Law Proceedings* (1973) 67(88), 87–94

Morris, Virginia, and Christiane Bourloyannis-Vrailas, M. 'The Work of the Sixth Committee at the Fifty Ninth Session of the UN General Assembly', *American Journal of International Law* (1995) 89, 542–54

Munir, Muhammad. 'Suicide Attacks and Islamic Law', *International Review of the Red Cross* (2008) 90(869), 71–89

Munir, Muhammad. 'The Layha for the Mujahideen: An Analysis of the Code of Conduct for the Taliban Fighters Under Islamic Law', *International Review of the Red Cross* (2011) 93(881), 81–102

Munir, Muhammad. 'Islamic International Law (Siyar): An Introduction', *Hamdard Islamicus No. 4, International Islamic University Islamabad* (2012), 37–60. Available at: <http://works.bepress.com/cgi/viewcontent.cgi?article=1041&context=muhammad_munir> (last accessed 25 May 2019)

Oberg, Marko Divac. 'The Absorption of Grave Breaches into War Crimes Law', *International Review of the Red Cross* (2009) 91(873) 163–83

O'Connell, Mary Ellen. 'The Myth of Preemptive Self-Defense', *ASIL Task Force Papers, The American Society of International Law* (2002) 1–21. Available at: <https://www.nyccriminallawyer.com/wp-content/uploads/2014/07/oconnell.pdf> (last accessed 25 May 2019)

Okon, Etim O. 'Islam, War and International Humanitarian Law', *European Scientific Journal* (2014) 16(14), 100–15

Olson, Laura M. 'Practical Challenges of Implementing the Complementarity between International Humanitarian and Human Rights Law—Demonstrated by the Procedural Regulation of Internment in Non-International Armed Conflict', *Case Western Reserve Journal of International Law* (2009) 40(3) 437–61

Paulus, Andreas, and Vashakmadze, Mindia. 'Asymmetrical War and the Notion of Armed Conflict: A Tentative Conceptualization', *Internaticonal Review of the Red Cross* (2009) 91(873), 95–125

Paust, Jordan J. 'Use of Armed Force Against Terrorists in Afghanistan, Iraq, and Beyond', *Cornell International Law Journal* (2002) 35, 533–56

Peters, Anne. 'Humanity as the A and Ω of Sovereignty', *European Journal of International Law* (2009) 20(3), 513–44

Pettygrove, Margaret. 'Conceptions of War in Islamic Legal Theory and Practice', *Macalester Islam Journal* (2007) 2(3), 34–42

Reisman, Michael, and Armstrong, Andrea, 'The Past and Future of the Claim of Preemptive Self-Defense', *American Journal of International Law* (2006) 100, 525–50

Robinson, Edward H. 'The Distinction between State and Government', *7/8 Geography Compass* (2013) 556, 556–66

San-Akca, Belgin. 'Dangerous Companions: Cooperation Between States and Non-State Armed Groups (NAGs)', *Koç University, Istanbul* (2015), 1–46. Available at: <https://www.armedgroups.net/publish/codebook-2015.pdf>

Sassòli, Marco. 'Legitimate Targets of Attacks Under International Humanitarian Law', *Background Paper, International Humanitarian Law Research Initiative*, Humanitarian Policy and Conflict Research at Harvard University (2004) 1–10

Sassòli, Marco. 'Transnational Armed Groups and International Humanitarian Law', *Program on Humanitarian Policy and Conflict Research, Harvard University* (2006) 6 Occasional Paper Series 1, 2–50

Sassòli, Marco. 'Taking Armed Groups Seriously: Ways to Improve their Compliance with International Humanitarian Law', *Journal of International Humanitarian Legal Studies* (2010) 1(1) 5–51

Saul, Ben. 'Definition of Terrorism in the UN Security Council: 1985–2004', *Chinese Journal of International Law* (2005) 4(141), 141–66

Saul, Ben. 'Legislating from a Radical Hague: The United Nations Special Tribunal for Lebanon Invents an International Crime of Transnational Terrorism', *Leiden Journal of International Law* (2011) 24(3) 677–700

Schmitt, Michael N. 'Human Shields in International Humanitarian Law', *Columbia Journal of Transitional Law* (2009), 47, 292–383

Schmitt, Michael N. 'The Interpretive Guidance on the Notion of Direct Participation in Hostilities: A Critical Analysis', *Harvard National Security Journal* (2010) 1(5), 5–44

Shah, Niaz A. 'The Use of Force Under Islamic Law', *The European Journal of International Law* (2013) 24(1), 343–65

Simma, Bruno. 'NATO, the UN and the Use of Force; Legal Aspects', *European Journal of International Law* (1999) 10, 1–22

Sinanovic, Ermin. 'Humanitarian Intervention in International and Islamic Law', *The American Journal of Islamic Social Sciences* (2003) 20(1), 88–106

Smith, Michael J. 'Humanitarian Intervention: An Overview of the Ethical Issues', *Ethics & International Affairs* (1998) 12, 63–79

Smith, Michael J. 'The Interpretive Guidance on the Notion of Direct Participation in Hostilities: A Critical Analysis', *Harvard National Security Journal* (2010) 1(5), 5–44

Ssenyonjo, Manisuli. 'Jihad Re-Examined: Islamic Law and International Law', *Santa Clara Journal of International Law* (2012) 10(1), 1–33

Starski, Paulina. 'Right of Self-defense, Attribution and the Non-State Actor—Birth of the "Unable or Unwilling" Standard?', Heidelberg Journal of International Law [ZaöRV] (2015) 75, 455–501

Svarc, Dominika. 'Redefining Imminence: The Use of Force Against Threats and Armed Attacks in the Twentieth Century', *ILSA Journal of International & Comparative Law* (2007) 13(1), 171–91

Szasz, Paul. 'The Security Council Starts Legislating', *American Journal of International Law* (2002) 96, 901–5

Tabassum, Sadia. 'Combatants, Not Bandits: The Status of Rebels in Islamic Law', *International Review of the Red Cross* (2011) 93(881) 121–39

Tomeh, Mamoud Munes. 'Persuasion and Authority in Islamic Law', *Berkeley Journal Middle East & Islamic Law* (2010) 3, 141–71

Tsagourias, Nicholas. 'Self-Defence against Non-state Actors: The Interaction between Self-Defence as a Primary Rule and Self-Defence as a Secondary Rule', *Leiden Journal of International Law* (2016) 29, 801–25

Van Den Hole, Leo. 'Anticipatory Self-Defence Under International Law', *American University International Law Review* (2003) 19(1), 69–106

Ventura, Manuel. 'Terrorism According to the STL's Interlocutory Decision on the Applicable Law: A Defining Moment or a Moment of Defining?', *Journal of International Criminal Justice* (2011) 9(5), 1021–42

Wilmshurst, Elizabeth. 'The Chatham House Principles of International Law on the Use of Force in Self-Defense', *International & Comparative Law Quarterly* (2006) 55, 963–72

Wippman, David. 'Military Intervention, Regional Organizations, and Host-State Consent', *Duke Journal of Comparative & International Law* (1996) 7, 209–39

Young, Reuven. 'Defining Terrorism: The Evolution of Terrorism as a Legal Concept in International Law and Its Influence on Definitions in Domestic Legislation', *Boston College International and Comparative Law Review* (2006) 29(23) 23–105

Zedalis, Rex. 'Protection of Nationals Abroad: Is Consent the Basis of Legal Obligation', *Texas International Law Journal* (1990), 25, 209–70

12. Blogs

Droege, Cordula, and Tuck, David. 'Fighting Together: Obligations and Opportunities in Partnered Warfare', *Humanitarian Law and Policy* ICRC blog, 27 March 2017. Available at: <https://medium.com/law-and-policy/fighting-together-obligations-and-opportunities-in-partnered-warfare-362c9dfb741a> (last accessed 25 May 2019)

Mekky, Omar. 'An Unwarranted Human Sacrifice in the Middle East', *Humanitarian Law and Policy* ICRC blog, 26 September 2016. Available at: <https://blogs.icrc.org/law-and-policy/2016/09/26/human-sacrifice-middle-east/> (last accessed 25 May 2019)

Scobbie, Iain. 'Strange Angel: Reflections on War', *EJIL Talk!*, 14 December 2015. Available at: <https://www.ejiltalk.org/strange-angel-some-reflections-on-war/> (last accessed 25 May 2019)

13. Publications in Arabic Language

Abd Al-rahman, Ahmed. *Al-Islam w-al-qital* (Cairo: Dar al-Sharq Al-Awsat Lel-Nashr, 1990)

Abd Al-rahman, Ahmed. *Al-Islam w-al-qital* (Dar al-Sharq Al-Awsat Lel-Nashr, n.d.)

Abu al-Abas Ahmad b. Jabir al Baladhuri. '*Kitab Futuh al-Buldan*'. Trans. Philip Khuri Hitti, Vol. 1 (New York, NY: Columbia University, 1916)

Abū al-Ṭayyib, Sadīq ibn Ḥasan ibn ʿAli al-Ḥusseini al-Qannūji al-Bukhārī. *Al-Rawḍah al-Nadiyyah Sharaḥ al-Durar al-Munīryyah* (Cairo, Idārah al-Ṭibāʿah al-Munīrīyah, n.d.)

Abū Dāwūd, Sulaymān ibn al-Ashʿath. *Sunan Abī Dāwūd*. Ed. Muhammad Muhyī al-Dīn *ʿAbd al-Hamīd*, 4 Vols (n.p.: Dār al-Fikr, n.d.)

Abū Zahrah, Muhammad. *Al-ʿAlāqāt al-Dawliyyah fī al-Islām* (Cairo: Al-Dār al- Qawmiyyah lil-Tbāʿah wa al-Nashr, 1964/1384)

Abū Zahrah, Muhammad. *Al-Jarīmah wa al-'Uqūbah fī al-Fiqh al-Islāmī: al-Jarīmah* (Cairo: Dār al-Fikr al-'Arabī, 1998)

Abū Zahrah, Muhammad. *Introduction to Sharh Siyar al-Kabir* (Cairo: M'atb'at Cairo University, n.d.)

Abū Zahrah, Muhammad. *Tanzīm al-Islām lil-Mujtama'* (Cairo: Dār al-Fikr al-'Arabī, n.d.)

Al-'Abdarī, Muhammad ibn Yūsuf ibn Abī al-Qāsim. *Al-Tāj wa al-Iklīl: Sharh Mukhtasar Khalīl*, 2nd edn (Beirut: Dār al-Fikr, 1977–8/1398)

Al-'Asqalānī, Ibn Hajar. *Fath al-Bārī Sharh Sahīh al-Bukhārī*. Ed. Muhib al-Dīn al-Khatīb (Beirut: Dār al-Ma'rifah, n.d.)

Al-Anṣārī, Abū al-'Abbās Šihāb-ad-Dīn al-Bakīr. *Asnā al-maṭālib šarḥ rawḍ aṭ-ṭālib* (Cairo: Dār al-Fikr, 2008)

Al-Bouti, Mohamed. *Al-Jihad fi-al-Islam* (Beirut: Dar al-fekr, 1993)

Al-Buhūtī, Mansur Ibn Yunus Ibn Salah Al-Din. *Al-rawd al-murbi' sharh zad al-mustaqni'* (Riyadh: Maktabah al-Riyadh al-Hadīthah, 1970–1/1390)

Al-Buhūtī, Mansur Ibn Yunus Ibn Salah Al-Din. *Kashshāf al-Qinā' 'an Matn al-Iqnā'*. Ed. Hilāl Misīlhī Mustafā Hilāl (Beirut: Dār al-Fikr, 1981–1982/1402)

Al-Buhūtī, Mansur Ibn Yunus Ibn Salah Al-Din. *Sharh Muntahā al-Irādāt al-Musammā Daqā'iq 'Ulī al-Nuhā Li-Sharh al-Muntahā*, 2 edn (Beirut: 'Ālam al-Kutub, 1996)

Al-Bukhārī, Muhammad ibn Ismā'īl. *Al-Jāmi' al-Sahīh al-Mukhtasar*. Ed. Mustafā Dīb al-Baghā, 3rd edn (Beirut: Dār ibn Kathīr, 1987/1407),

Al-Bukhārī, Muḥammad ibn Ismā'īl. *Mukhtaṣar Ṣaḥīḥ al-Imām al-Bukhārī*. Ed. Muḥammad Nāsr al-Albānī (Riyadh: Maktabah al-Ma'arif, 2002)

Al-Dahhāk, Ibn Abī 'Āṣīm. *Al-Āhād wa al-Mathānī* (Riyadh: Dar Alrayah, 1991)

Al-Firjānī, Umar Ahmad. *Usūl al-'Alāqāt al-Dawliyyah fī al-Islām*, 2nd edn (Tripoli: Dār Iqra', 1988/1397)

Al-Ghazālī, Muhammad. *Al-Wajīz fī Fiqh al-Imām al-Shāfi'ī*. Ed. 'Alī Mu'awwad and 'Ādil 'Abd al-Mawjūd (Beirut: Dār al-Arqam ibn Abī al-Arqam, 1997/1418)

Al-Ghazālī, Muhammad. *Al-Wasīt fī al-Madhhab*. Ed. Ahmad Mahmūd Ibrāhīm and Muhammad Tāmir (Cairo: Dār al-Salām, 1997/1417)

Al-Hindī, Ihsān. *Ahkām al-Harb wa al-Salām fī Dawlah al-Islām* (Damascus: Dār al-Numayr, 1993/1413)

Al-Jawlānī, Abū Muhammad. *al-I 'lān 'an Jabhat al-Nusra* (Minbar al-Tawh: Īd wa'l-Jihād, 2012)

Al-Jawlānī, Abū Muhammad. *Kalima sawtiyya lil-fātih. Abī Muh. Ammad al-Jawlānī* (Mu'assasat al-Manāra al-Bayda, 10 April 2013)

Al-Jundī, Khalīl ibn Ishāq ibn Musā. *Mukhtasar Khalīl fī Fiqh Imām Dār alHijrah*. Ed. Ahmad 'Alī Harakāt (Beirut: Dār al-Fikr, 1994–5/1415)

Al-Kāsānī, 'Alā al-Dīn. *Badā'i' al-Sanā'i' fī Tartīb al-Sharā'i'*, 2nd edn, 7 Vols (Beirut: Dār al-Kitāb al-'Arabī, 1982)

Al-Khalidi, Salah 'Abd al-Fattah, *Sayyid Quṭb, Al-Shahīd al-Ḥayy* (Amman: Maktabat Al-Aqsa, 1981)

Al-Khalidi, Salah 'Abd al-Fattah. *Sayyid Quṭb: Min al-Mīlād ila al-istishhād* (Sayyid Qutb: From birth to martyrdom) (n.p., 1991)

Al-Khayyāt, 'Abd al-'Azīz. 'Al-Islām Dīn al-Salām: Mafhūm al-Harb wa al-Salām fī al-Islām', *Islam and the 21st Century*, Researches and Facts, the Tenth General Conference of the Supreme Council for Islamic Affairs (Cairo: Supreme Council for Islamic Affairs, 1999/1420)

Al-Khiraqī, 'Umar ibn al-Husayn. *Mukhtasar al-Khiraqī min Masā'il al-Imām Ahmad Ibn Hanbal*. Ed. Zuhayr al-Shāwīsh, 3rd edn (Beirut: Al-Maktab al-Islāmī, 1982)

Al-Marāghī, Ahmad Mustafā. *Tafsīr al-Marāghī*, 30 Vols (Cairo: Mustafā al-Bābī al-Halabī, 1946/1365)

Al-Māwardī, Alī ibn Muhammad ibn Habīb. *Nasīhah al-Mulūk*. Ed. Khidr Muhammad Khidr (Al-Safah, Kuwait: Maktabah al-Falāh, 1983/1403)

Al-Mirdāwī, Alī ibn Sulaymān. *Al-Insāf fī Ma'rifah al-Rājih min al-Khilāf 'alā Madhhab al-Imām Ahmad Ibn Hanbal*. Ed. Muhammad Hamid al-Fiqī, 12 Vols (Beirut: Dār Ihyā' al-Turāth al-'Arabī, n.d.)

Al-Mutrrazi, Nasiruddin and Fakhori, Mahmood (eds). *Al-Mugrib fi Tartib al-Mu'rib*, Vol. 1 (Syria-Halab: Maktab Usama ibn Zayd, 1979)

Al-Nawawī, Muhyī al-Dīn ibn Sharaf. *Al-Majmū': Sharh al-Muhadhdhab*. Ed. Mahmūd Matrajī, 22 Vols (Beirut: Dār al-Fikr, 2000)

Al-Qaradāwī, Yūsuf. *Fiqh al-Jihād: Dirāsah Muqāranah li-Ahkāmih wa Falsafatih fī Daw' al-Qur'ān wa al-Sunnah*, 2 Vols (Cairo: Maktabah Wahbah, 2009)

Al-Qushayrī, Muslim ibn al-Hajjāj. *Sahīh Muslim*. Ed. Muhammad Fū'ād 'Abd al-Bāqī (Beirut: Dār Ihyā' al-Turāth al-'Arabī, n.d.)

Al-Rahaybānī, Mustafā al-Suyūtī. *Matālib Ulī al-Nuhā fī Sharh Ghāyah al-Muntahā*, 6 Vols (Damascus: Al-Maktab al-Islāmī, 1961)

Al-Ramlī, Muhammad ibn Abī al-'Abbās Ahmad ibn Hamzah. *Nihāyah al-Muhtāj ilā Sharh al-Minhāj*, 8 Vols (Beirut: Dār al-Fikr, 1984/1404)Al-Rāzī, Muhammad ibn 'Umar. *Al-Tafsīr al-Kabīr aw Mafātīhal-Ghayb*, 32 Vols (Beirut: Dār al-Kutub al-'Ilmiyyah, 2000/1421)

Al-Sā'atī, Aḥmad 'Abd al-Raḥmān al-Bannā, *Badā'i' al-Manan fi Jami' wa Tartīb Musannad al-Shafi'i wa al-Sanan: Mudhayla bi-al-Qawl al-Ḥasan Sharaḥ Badā'i' al-Manan*, 2nd edn (Cairo: Maktabah al-Furqān, 1983)

Al-Sālihī, Muhammad ibn Yūsuf. *Subul al-Hudā wa al-Rashād fī Sīrah Khayr al-'Ibād*. Ed. 'Ādil Ahmad 'Abd al-Mawjūd and 'Alī Muhammad Mu'awwad (Beirut: Dār al-Kutub al-'Ilmiyyah, 1993–4/1414)

Al-Sana'ānī, 'Abd al-Rāziq ibn Hammām. *Al-Musannaf*. Ed. Habīb al-Rahman al-A'zamī, 2nd edn, 11 Vols (Beirut: Al-Maktab al-Islāmī, 1982–3/1403)

Al-Sarakhasi, Muhammad Ibn Ahmad, *Kitab al-Mabsut*, Vol. 10 (Beirut: Dar Ehia al-Tourath al-'Arabi, 2002)

Al-Sarakhsī, Muhammad ibn Ahmad ibn Abī Sahl. *Kitāb al-Mabsūt*, 30 Vols (Beirut: Dār al-Ma'rifah, n.d.)

Al-Shāfi'ī, Muhammad ibn Idrīs. *Al-Umm*, 2nd edn, 8 Vols (Beirut: Dār al-Ma'rifah, 1973/1393)

Al-Shawkānī, Muhammad ibn 'Alī ibn Muhammad. *Nayl al-Awtār: Min Ahādīth Sayyid al-Khyār Sharh Muntaqā al-Akhbār*, 9 Vols (Beirut: Dār al-Jīl, 1973)

Al-Shawkānī, Muhammad ibn 'Alī ibn Muhammad. *Al-Sayl al-Jarrār al-Mutadaffiq 'alā Hadā'iq al-Azhār*. Ed. Mah(mūd Ibrāhīm Zāyid, 4 Vols (Beirut: Dār al-Kutub al-'Ilmiyyah, 1984–1985/1405)

Al-Shawkānī, Muhammad ibn 'Alī ibn Muhammad. *Fath al-Qadīr: Al-Jāmi' bayn Fannay al-Riwāyah wa al-Dirāyah min 'Ilm al-Tafsīr*, 5 Vols (Beirut: Dār al-Fikr, n.d.)

Al-Shaybānī, Muhammad ibn al-Hasan. *Al-Siyar al-Kabīr*. Ed. Salāh al-Dīn al-Munjid, 5 Vols (Cairo: Ma'had al-Makhtūtāt, n.d.)

Al-Shaykh, Nizām and a group of Indian scholars. *Al-Fatāwā al-Hindiyyah: Fī Madhhab al-Imām al-A'zam Abī Hanīfah al-Nu'mān*, 6 Vols (n.p.: Dār al-Fikr, 1991/1411)

Al-Shihābī, Ibrāhīm Yahyā. *Mafhūm al-Harb wa al-Salām fī al-Islām: Sirā'āt wa Hurūb amm Tafā'ul wa Salām?* (n.p.: Manshūrāt Mu'assasah Maī, 1990/1399)

Al-Shirāzī, Ibrāhīm ibn 'Alī ibn Yūsuf. *Al-Muhadhdhab: Fī Fiqh al-Imām al-Shāfi'ī*. Ed. Zakariyyā 'Imīrat, 3 Vols (Beirut: Dār al-Kutub al-'Ilmiyyah, 1995/1416)

Al-Shirbīnī, Muhammad al-Khatīb. *Al-Iqnā' fī Hall al-Fāz Abī Shujā'*. Ed. Maktab al-Buhūth wa al-Dirasāt, 2 Vols (Beirut: Dār al-Fikr, 1994–5/1415)

Al-Shirbīnī, Muhammad al-Khatīb. *Mughnī al-Muhtāj ilā Ma'rifah Ma'ānī Alfāz al-Minhāj*, 4 Vols (Beirut: Dār al-Fikr, n.d.)

Al-Tabarī, Muhammad ibn Jarīr. *Jāmi' al-Bayān 'an Ta'wīl Āy al-Qur'ān*, 30 Vols (Beirut: Dār al-Fikr, 1984–1985/1405)

Al-Tabarī, Muhammad ibn Jarīr. *Tārīkh al-Tabarī: Tārīkh al-Umam wa al-Mulūk*, 6 Vols (Bierut: Dār al-Kutub al-'Ilmiyyah, 2001/1422)

Al-Tirmidhī, Muhammad ibn 'Isā. *Al-Jāmi' al-Sahīh Sunan al-Tirmidhī*. Ed. Ahmad Muhammad Shākir et al., 5 Vols (Beirut: Dār Ihyā' al-Turāth al-'Arabī, n.d.)

Al-Zayd, Zayd ibn 'Abd al-Karīm. *Muqaddimah fī al-Qānūn al-Dawlī al-Insānī fī al-Islām* (Cairo: ICRC, 2004)

Al-Zuhaylī, Wahbah. *Āthār al-Harb fī al-Islām: Dīrāsah Muqāranah*, 3rd edn (Damascus: Dār al-Fikr, 1998/1419)

Arafah, Muhammad. 'AlKhatar al-Nawawī fī Mirāh 'Ālim 'Āzharī', supplement to *Majalah al-Azhar* (June 2004/Rabī' al-Ākhir 1425)

Awdah, 'Abd al-Qādir. *Al-Tashrī' al-Jinā'ī al-Islāmī: Muqāranā bi-al-Qānūn al-Wad'ī*, 2 Vols (Beirut: Dār al-Kitāb al-'Arabī, n.d.)

Awdah, 'Abd al-Qādir. *Criminal Law of Islam*. Trans. Zakir Aijaz, Vol. I (New Delhi: Kitab Bhavan, reprint, 2005)

Diyab, Muhammad Hafiz. *Sayyid Quṭb: Al-Khitāb wa al-Aydiyūlūjiyāh* (Sayyid Qutb: Discourse and Ideology) (Cairo: Dar al-Thaqafa al-Jadida, 1987)

Dumairia, Uthman. *Manhj Al-Islam fi al-Harb wa al-Salam* (Kuwait: *Mktabat Dar al-Arqam*, 1982)

Ghunaym, Ahmad. *Al-Jihād al-Islāmī: Dirāsah 'Ilmiyyah fī Nusūs al-Qur'ān wa Sihāh al-Hadīth wa Wathā'iq al-Tārīkh* (Cairo: Dār al-Hammamī, 1975/1394)

Hamuda, ʿAdil. *Sayyid Quṭb: Min al-Qarya ila al-Misnaqa; Tahqīq wathāʾiqī* (Sayyid Qutb: From the Village to the Gallows; A Documentary Study) (Cairo: Sina li-l-Nashr, 1987)

Hāshim, Ahmad 'Umar. 'Ma'sāh al-Ghazw al-'Irāqī wa Wājib al-'Arab wa al-Muslimīn', *The Islamic Fiqh Council Journal* (1991/1411) 5, 101–18

Hassān, Husayn Hāmid. 'Hukm al-Sharī'ah fī Ghazw al-Irāq lil-Kuwayt', *The Islamic Fiqh Council Journal* (1991/1411) 5, 189–94

Ibn 'Abd al-Barr, Yūsuf. *Al-Kāfī fī Fiqh Ahl al-Madīnah* (Beirut: Dār al-Kutub al-'Ilmiyyah, 1986–7/1407)

Ibn 'Ābidīn, Muhammad Amīn ibn 'Umar. *Hāshiyah Radd al-Muhtār 'alā al-Durr al-ukhtār: Sharh Tanwīr al-Absār Fiqh Abū Hanīfah*, 8 Vols (Beirut: Dār al-Fikr, 2000/1421)

Ibn Hazm, 'Alī ibn Ahmad ibn Sa'īd. *Al-Muhallā*, 11 Vols (Beirut: Dār al-Āfāq al-Jadīdah, n.d.)

Ibn Husām al-Dīn, Alā al-Dīn. *Kanz al-'Ummāl fī Sunan al-Aqwāl wa alAf'āl*. Ed. Mahmūd 'Umar al-Dumyātī (Beirut: Dār al-Kutub al-'Ilmiyyah, 1998/1419)

Ibn Ishāq, Muhammad. *Al-Sīrah al-Nabawiyyah*. Ed. 'Abd al-Malik ibn Hishām, annotated by Fu'ād ibn 'Alī Hāfiz (Beirut: Dār al-Kutub al-'Ilmiyyah, 2000)

Ibn Kathīr, Ismā'īl ibn 'Umar. *Al-Sīrah al-Nabawiyyah* (Beirut: Dār al-Kitāb al-'Arabī, 1997)

Ibn Mājah, Muhammad ibn Yazīd. *Sunan Ibn Mājah*. Ed. Muhammad Fū'ād 'Abd al-Bāqī, 2 Vols (Beirut: Dār al-Fikr, n.d.)

Ibn Mālik, Anas. *Muwatta' al-Imām Mālik*. Ed. Muhammad Fū'ād 'Abd al-Bāqī, 2 Vols (Cairo: Dār Ihyā' al-Turāth al-'Arabī, n.d.)

Ibn Mawdūd, ʿAbd Allah ibn Mahmūd. *Al-Ikhtiyār li-Taʿlīl al-Mukhtār*. Ed. ʿAbd al-Latīf Muhammad ʿAbd al-Rahman, 3rd edn, 5 Vols (Beirut: Dār al-Kutub al-ʿIlmiyyah, 2005/1426)

Ibn Muflih, Muhammad. *Al-Furūʿ*. Ed. Abī al-Zahrāʾ Hāzim al-Qādī, Vol. 6 (Beirut: Dār al-Kutub al-ʿIlmiyyah, 1997/1418)

Ibn Najīm, Zayd al-Dīn. *Al-Bahr al-Rāʾiq Sharh Kanz al-Daqāʾiq*, 2nd edn, 8 Vols (Beirut: Dār al-Maʿrifah, n.d.)

Ibn Qayyim al-Jawziyyah, Muhammad ibn Abī Bakr. *Zad al-maʿad*, Vol. 3 (Cairo: University Library, n.d.)

Ibn Qudāmah, Muwaffaq al-Dīn ʿAbd Allah ibn Ahmad. *ʿUmdah al-Fiqh*. Ed. ʿAbd Allah Safar al-ʿAbdalī and Muhammad Dughaylib al-ʿUtaybī (Taif: Maktabah al-Tarafayn, n.d.)

Ibn Qudāmah, Muwaffaq al-Dīn ʿAbd Allah ibn Ahmad. *Al-Mughnī: fī Fiqh al-Imām Ahmad Ibn Hanbal al-Shaybānī*, 10 Vols (Beirut: Dār al-Fikr, 1984–1985/1405)

Ibn Rushd, Muhammad ibn Ahmad ibn Muhammad. *Bidāyah al-Mujtahid wa Nihāyah al-Muqtasid*, 2 Vols (Beirut: Dār al-Fikr, n.d.)

Ibn Taymiyyah, Ahmad ibn ʿAbd al-Halīm. *Majmūʿ Fatāwā Shaykh al-Islām Ahmad Ibn Taymiyyah*. Compiled by ʿAbd al-Rahman ibn Muhammad ibn Qāsim al-ʿĀsimī, Vol. 28 (Cairo: Maktabah ibn Taymiyyah, n.d.)

Ibn Uthaymeen, Muhammed. *Fataawa Manaar al-Islam* (Riyadh: Dar Al-Watan, 1995/1415)

Khallaf, Abd al-Wahhab. *Al-Siyasa al-Shariyya* (Cairo: Dar Al Ansar, 1931/1350)

Mahmassani, Sobhi. *Al-Qānūn wa al-ʿAlāqāt al-Dawliyyah fī al-Islām* (Beirut: Dār al-ʿIlm lil-Malāyīn, 1972/1392)

Nagi, Abu Bakr. *Edaret Al-tawahoush* (Syria: Dar al-tamroud, n.d.)

Qutb, Sayyid. *al-Adala al-Ijtimaiyya* (Cairo: Dar Al-Shorouk, 1954)

Qutb, Sayyid. *Maʿalem Ala al-tariq* (Milestones) (Cairo: Dar Al-Shrouk, 1973)

Qutb, Sayyid. *Fī Zilāl al-Qurʾān* (Beirut: Dar Al-Shorouk, 1982)

Qutb, Sayyid. *Fī Zilāl al-Qurʾān*, Vol. 6, 11th edn (Cairo: Dar Al-Shorouk, 1985)

Ridā, Muhammad Rashīd. *Tafsīr al-Qurʾān al-Hakīm: Al-Shahīr bi-Tafsīr al-Manār*, 12 Vols (Cairo: Dār al-Manār, 2002)

Sābiq, al-Sayyid. *Fiqh alSunnah* (Cairo: Al-Fath lil-Iʿlām al-ʿArabī, n.d.)

Saqr, ʿAbd al-ʿAzīz. *ʿAl-ʿAlāqāt al-Dawliyyah fī al-Islām Waqt al-Harb: Dirāsah lil- Qawāʿid al-Munazzimah li-Sayr al-Qitāl*, Mashrūʿ al-ʿAlāqāt al-Dawliyyah fī al-Islām 6 (Cairo: Al-Maʿhad al-ʿĀlamī lil-Fikr al-Islāmī, 1996)

Tantāwī, Muhammad Sayyid. ʻAl-Hukm al-Sharʿī fī Ahdāth al-Khalījʼ, *The Islamic Fiqh Council Journal* (1991/1411) 5, 49–100

The Mecca Declaration of the Third Islamic Summit Conference (Mecca: the Kingdom of Saudi Arabia, 26–28 January 1981)

14. Other Documents

Abu Aaliyah Surkheel, ʻKhawarij Ideology, ISIS Savagery: Part Oneʼ, 2015. Available at: <http://muslimmatters.org/2015/08/24/khawarij-ideology-isis-savagery-part-one/> (last accessed 25 May 2019)

al-Adnānī, Abu Muhammad. ʻHādha waʿd Allāhʼ, 2014. Available (in Arabic) at: <https://archive.org/details/Waad_201408> (last accessed 25 May 2019)

Al-Baghdādī, Abū Bakr. ʻBāqiya fī ʼl-ʻIrāq waʼ-l-Shāmʼ, *Muʾassasat al-Furqān*, 15 June 2013

Al-Mubarak, Malik Abdulazeez. ʻWarfare in Early Islamʼ (PhD thesis, University of Glasgow, 1997)

Alsumah, Abdulrahman M. ʻThe Sunni Concept of Jihad in Classical Fiqh and Modern Islamic Thoughtʼ (PhD Thesis, University of Newcastle, 1998)

Ayman al-Zawāhirī, 'Letter to Abū Bakr al-Baghdādī and Abū Muhammad al-Jawlānī', 23 May 2013. Available at: <http://www.aljazeera.com/news/middleeast/2013/06/2013699425657882.html> (last accessed 25 May 2019)

Azzam, Abdulla. 'Defense of Muslim Lands', 1 February 2002. Available at: <http://www.religioscope.com/info/doc/jihad/azzam_defence_3_chap1.htm> (last accessed 25 May 2019)

Azzam, Abdulla. 'Join the Caravan'. Available at: <https://archive.org/stream/JoinTheCaravan/JoinTheCaravan_djvu.txt> (last accessed 25 May 2019)

'Bayān bi-sha'n 'alāqat Jamā'at Qā'idat al-Jihād bi-Jamā'at 'al-Dawla al-Islāmiyya fī 'l-'Irāq wa'l-Shām'. Available (in Arabic) at: <http://www.arrahmah.com/arabic/tnzym-qadt-al-jhad-al-qyadt-al-amt-byan-bshan-alaqt-jmat-qadt-al-jhad-bjmat-ad-dwlt-al-islamyt.html> (last accessed 25 May 2019)

'Beyond *Al-Qaeda*: The Global Jihadist Movement', RAND Project Air Force Report (2006), 17. Available at: <http://www.rand.org/content/dam/rand/pubs/monographs/2006/RAND_MG429.pdf> (last accessed 25 May 2019)

Bin Laden, Usama. 'Fatwa: Background and Declaration of War Against the Americans Occupying the two Holy Places', 1996. Available at: <http://www.mideastweb.org/osamabinladen1.htm> (last accessed 25 May 2019)

Bin Laden, Usama. 'Declaration of the World Islamic Front for Jihad against the Jews and the Crusaders', 1998. Available at: <http://www.mideastweb.org/osamabinladen2.htm> (last accessed 25 May 2019)

Cordesman, Anthony H. 'Losing on All Fronts: The Mattis Resignation and Trump's Failed Strategies for America's Wars', Center for Strategic and International Studies (CSIS) (September 2018). Available at: <https://www.csis.org/analysis/losing-all-fronts-mattis-resignation-and-trumps-failed-strategies-americas-wars?fbclid=IwAR1d1N7K6v8xCyUqaEfQrF3cIizOTQUtknVlydad2gFgvreWs73ceVYkcJU> (last accessed 25 May 2019)

Eisenstadt, Michael, and Khalaj, Mehdi. 'Nuclear Fatwa: Religion and Politics in Iran's Proliferation Strategy', *Policy Focus 115*, The Washington Institute for Near East Policy, September 2011. Available at: <https://www.washingtoninstitute.org/uploads/Documents/pubs/PolicyFocus115.pdf> (last accessed 5 May 2019)

Geneva Call. 'Armed Non-State Actors'. Available at: <https://genevacall.org/how-we-work/armed-non-state-actors/> (last accessed 25 May 2019)

Geneva Call. 'Who Are We'. Available at: <https://genevacall.org/who-we-are/> (last accessed 5 May 2019)

Hassaballah, Hesham A. 'The Real Name for ISIS Should Be KIL: The Kharijites of Iraq and the Levant'. Available at: <https://www.beliefnet.com/columnists/commonwordcommonlord/the-real-name-for-isis-should-be-kil-the-kharijites-of-iraq-and-the-levant/> (last accessed 25 May 2019)

Human Rights Watch. 'No to Terrorism, Yes to Human Rights: Letter to Tunisians', 28 April 2016. Available at: <https://www.hrw.org/news/2016/04/28/no-terrorism-yes-human-rights> (last accessed 25 May 2019)

'Humanitarian Negotiation Series: The Role of Laws and Norms', ATHA, Harvard Humanitarian Initiative. Available at: <http://atha.se/podcasts/humanitarian-negotiation-series-role-laws-and-norms> (last accessed 25 May 2019)

International Institute of Humanitarian Law. 'The Distinction Between International and Non-International Armed Conflicts: Challenges For IHL?', *38th Sanremo Round Table* (Sanremo, 3–5 September 2015). Available at: <http://www.iihl.org/wp-content/uploads/2015/12/Pedrazzi.pdf> (last accessed 25 May 2019)

International Law Association, Committee on the Use of Force. 'Report on Aggression and the Use of Force', Washington Conference, 2014. Available at: <http://www.ila-hq.org/download.cfm/docid/DA12E88E-5E44-4151-9540DC83D4A0EA78> (last accessed 25 May 2019)

McElroy, Damien. 'Rome will be conquered next, says leader of "Islamic State"', *The Telegraph*, 1 July 2014. Available at: <http://www.telegraph.co.uk/news/worldnews/middleeast/syria/10939235/Rome-will-be-conquered-next-says-leader-of-Islamic-State.html> (last accessed 25 May 2019)

Muhammed, Sheikh, and Al-Munajjid, Salih. 'Greater and Lesser Jihad', *Fatwa 10455* (2001). Available at: <https://islamqa.info/en/answers/10455/greater-and-lesser-jihaad> (last accessed 25 May 2019)

Sanger, David E. 'A Nation Challenged: The Evidence; White House Approved Data Blair Released', *The New York Times*, 6 October 2001. Available at: <https://www.nytimes.com/2001/10/06/world/a-nation-challenged-the-evidence-white-house-approved-data-blair-released.html> (last accessed 25 May 2019)

Sputnik International. 'Turkey Not Part of US-Led Coalition in Iraq—Coalition Spokesman', 2 February 2016. Available at: <https://sputniknews.com/middleeast/201602021034091107-turkey-us-led-coalition-iraq/#ixzz3zUitAmx1> (last accessed 25 May 2019)

The New York Times. 'Red Cross Warns of 'Dehumanizing' Rhetoric in ISIS Fight', 26 October 2017. Available at: <https://www.nytimes.com/2017/10/26/world/middleeast/red-cross-islamic-state.html> (last accessed 25 May 2019)

The Religion of Peace. 'Terror Attacks—About the List of Attacks, 2001–2008'. Available at: <http://www.thereligionofpeace.com> (last accessed 25 May 2019)

'Towards Understanding the Quran'. Available at: <http://www.islamicstudies.info/tafheem.php?sura=59&verse=1&to=5> (last accessed 25 May 2019)

Wilson, Sean P. 'The Evolution of *Al-Qaeda*' (unpublished MA thesis, American Military University, 2007)

Index

For the benefit of digital users, indexed terms that span two pages (e.g., 52–53) may, on occasion, appear on only one of those pages.

Introductory Note

References such as '178–79' indicate (not necessarily continuous) discussion of a topic across a range of pages. Wherever possible in the case of topics with many references, these have either been divided into sub-topics or only the most significant discussions of the topic are listed. Because the entire work is about 'Jihadism', the use of this term (and certain others which occur constantly throughout the book) as an entry point has been restricted. Information will be found under the corresponding detailed topics.